D1598536

FORGOTTEN**TRIBES**

FORGOTTEN**TRIBES**

Unrecognized Indians and the
Federal Acknowledgment Process

Mark Edwin Miller

University of Nebraska Press | Lincoln and London

A portion of Sherman Alexie's poem "Recognition
of Distance," previously published in the *Journal of
Ethnic Studies* 16, no. 2 (1988): 49, is reprinted with his
kind permission.

Library of Congress Cataloging-in-Publication Data
Miller, Mark Edwin, 1966–
Forgotten tribes: unrecognized Indians and the federal
acknowledgment process / Mark Edwin Miller.
p. cm.
Includes bibliographical references and index.
ISBN 0-8032-3226-8 (hardcover: alk. paper)
1. Indians of North America—Tribal citizenship.
2. Indians of North America—Legal status, laws, etc.
3. Indians of North America—Government policy.
I. Title.
E93.M5818 2004
323.1197'073—dc22
2003026574

Contents

ACKNOWLEDGMENTS

Many people and organizations have guided this project to its ultimate completion. Both in professional and personal terms, I could not have finished this work without the support of numerous individuals who lent much needed aid at key moments. First, I must thank Karen Anderson for her unwavering support, intellectual guidance, and periodic "pep talks." In her company are three other individuals who graciously agreed to help with this undertaking: Katherine Morrissey, who offered critical insights and suggestions to improve my prose and ideas; Roger Nichols, who continued to aid my writing and focus; and David Wilkins, who offered enthusiastic support while bringing his expertise on acknowledgment issues to this project. I also extend a warm round of thanks to the Indian people who opened their voices to me and to non-Indian policymakers and scholars who graciously told me stories they had gleaned over the years. In particular, I am indebted to members of the Pascua Yaqui Tribe, Ysleta del Sur Pueblo, and United Houma Nation, who shared insights into their experiences with the acknowledgment process. I would also like to thank the outside reviewers for the University of Nebraska Press, who offered kind and valuable insights into ways to improve the work. Finally, Leonard Dinnerstein and Maureen Fitzgerald always will hold a special place in my heart, having taken an interest in me and my welfare since my first days at the University of Arizona.

I also benefited from help given to me by numerous archivists, librarians, and philanthropic institutions. In Arizona, I must thank the librarians at the Special Collections at the University of Arizona Main Library, the Arizona Historical Society, the Arizona State Museum, Northern Arizona University, and the Hayden Library of Arizona State University. In California, the Death Valley National Park office allowed me access to its files. In Texas, Tom Diamond happily let me roam over his large collection, while the staffs at the University of Texas at El Paso, the LBJ Presidential Library, the Texas State Archives, and the Institute of Texan Cultures all helped me mine sources. The archivists at Louisiana State University, the Louisiana State Library, and Northwest State University proved highly helpful as well. Access to the vast holdings at the National Archives was also invaluable. I would also like to thank the Bureau of Indian Affairs' Branch of Acknowledgment and Research and Steve Austin, in particular, for allowing me access to their records. They proved patient and helpful at all stages of this work. Finally, I benefited from the kind financial support of many institutions, including the American Historical Association's Littleton-Griswold fund, the Charles Redd Center for Western Studies at Brigham Young University, the Arizona Archaeological and Historical Society, the East Texas Historical Society, and the Udall fund from the University of Arizona Library. At the University of Arizona, my home department, the Social and Behavioral Sciences Research Institute, and the Graduate College all provided additional funds to support this project in its early stages.

Where would this project have been, however, without the help of family and friends through the years? To my wife, Gia, goes the ultimate thanks for sustaining me on a daily basis and listening to my complaints and ideas when her life was often much more difficult than mine. And we are both thankful for our new baby daughter, Delaney Elizabeth, who has brightened the final stages of this project. Thanks also go to my mother, Penny Castle, for believing in my career choice and having constant enthusiasm about my work; and to my father, Charlie Miller, and his wife, Laurie, for their support through more years than any parent should see a child in school. In Tucson, Gia's parents, Dee and Bette DeGiovanni, were always a positive presence in our lives. I must also thank Alan and Stacy Cotton for opening their home in Maryland to us longer than any friend should see a visitor stay. And to my newfound colleagues and friends at Ouachita, especially Tom Auffenberg, Hal Bass, Eric Benson, Trey Berry, Wayne Bowen, and Chris Ward, goes another round of thanks. All told, to my family and these kind souls goes the last, and final, word of gratitude.

ABBREVIATIONS

AIM - American Indian Movement
AIPRC - American Indian Policy Review Commission
ANA - Administration for Native Americans
BAR - Branch of Acknowledgment and Research
BCCM - Biloxi, Chitimacha Confederation of Muskogees
BIA - Bureau of Indian Affairs
BLM - Bureau of Land Management
CAP - Community Action Programs
CCC - Civilian Conservation Corps
CENA - Coalition of Eastern Native Americans
CETA - Comprehensive Employment and Training Act
CILS - California Indian Legal Services
DVTS - Death Valley Timbisha Shoshone
EDA - Economic Development Administration
FAP - Federal Acknowledgment Process
HEW - Health, Education and Welfare
HUD - Housing and Urban Development
IBIA - Interior Board of Indian Appeals
IGRA - Indian Gaming Regulatory Act of 1988
IHS - Indian Health Service
IRA - Indian Reorganization Act of 1934
LLE - Louisiana Land and Exploration Company
MAYO - Mexican-Americans, Yaquis, and Others
NARF - Native American Rights Fund
NCAI - National Congress of American Indians
NIYC - National Indian Youth Council
NPS - National Park Service
NTCA - National Tribal Chairmen's Association
NWCWB - Northwest Cherokee Wolf Band
OEO - Office of Economic Opportunity
ONAP - Office of Native American Programs
PACIT - Point aux Chien Indian Tribe
PYA - Pascua Yaqui Association
RCIIB - Red Clay Inter-tribal Council Indian Band
SECC - Southeastern Cherokee Confederacy
STOWW - Small Tribes Organization of Western Washington
UHN - United Houma Nation
USET - United Southeastern Tribes
VISTA - Volunteers In Service To America
YIC - Yaqui Improvement Committee

FORGOTTEN**TRIBES**

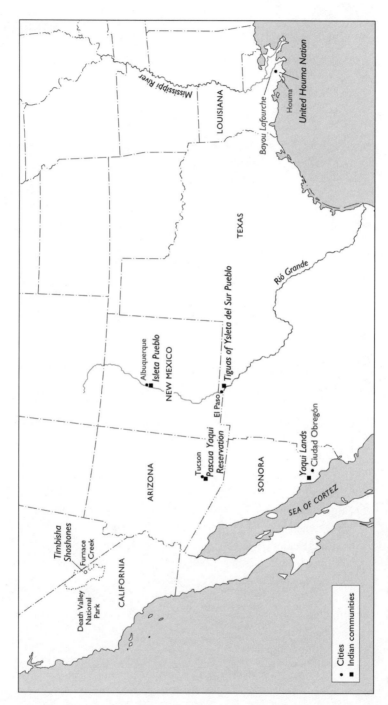

Indian communities featured in this study

INTRODUCTION

It was in the early 1990s that the small Mashantucket Pequot Tribe of Connecticut burst upon the national scene, indelibly marking popular perceptions of once unacknowledged Indian tribes in the public conscious. After struggling for centuries without federal tribal status, the Pequots under Richard "Skip" Hayward dashed with aplomb into the twenty-first century, leading the march toward self-sufficiency and self-government through their phenomenally successful Foxwoods Casino complex situated midway between New York City and Boston. Making one billion dollars annually by the end of the decade, Foxwoods was the most lucrative gambling Mecca in the United States, drawing widespread attention up and down the East Coast. A decade earlier when the tribe had secured federal acknowledgment through an act of Congress in 1983, the development had raised few eyebrows, however, causing more relief than alarm because it settled a lengthy and bitter land dispute between the Pequots and neighboring property owners. Some observers undoubtedly felt that the obscure tribe, once widely believed to be extinct, had finally gotten its revenge for past injustices. Other locals simply were happy to have a place to gamble so close to their homes, cheering the Pequots for making this possible and perhaps being a little amused by the whole unlikely scenario. Questions soon arose, however, when the group possessing Indian, European, and African ancestry grew increasingly rich and powerful, with its gambling enterprise shattering the once bucolic Connecticut countryside with crowds, traffic jams, and high-rise development. Angered by their suddenly powerful neighbor, many locals began to ask: Who were these people that variously appeared white, Indian, black, or something in-between? If they looked and lived much like their well-to-do neighbors, was the group really an Indian tribe at all? Clearly, tribal acknowledgment had given the Pequots all the benefits of tribal status and sovereignty. But it had not allowed them to exist in obscurity as before. Every year during the 1990s tensions and recriminations grew. When a book emerged claiming that the Pequots may have tricked the federal government into believing they were an Indian tribe, local leaders clamored to have their status overturned. By 2000 the continuing deluge of press coverage ensured that the Mashantucket Pequots became the dominant face of recently acknowledged Indian tribes in the United States.[1]

At the same time, in stark contrast to the glitz and wealth of the Pequots stood a struggling band of Shoshones in California. A world away from Connecticut in the desert sands of Death Valley National Park, the Timbisha Shoshone Indians also existed without federal acknowledgment until the early 1980s. The Shoshones were unlike the Pequots at first glance, however, and few non-Indians doubted that the tiny Timbisha group was Indian. In the late 1970s the Shoshones were struggling against the National Park Service's efforts to evict them from their ancestral homeland, clinging to their crumbling adobe casitas and modest trailers that shifting sand dunes threatened to swallow at any moment. Decades earlier the Park Service had corralled them into a single village to make room for its luxury hotels, golf course, and RV resort to cater to tourists hoping to escape the northern winters or recapture the "Wild West" for a weekend. Like the Pequots, the Timbisha Shoshones also secured acknowledgment in 1983, but this new status provided few of the fringe benefits afforded the Connecticut tribe. In 2000 the band still lacked a federal reservation and lived in poor housing much like it had before recognition. The Timbisha Shoshones presented another face of once unacknowledged Indian peoples in the modern United States. The experience of the over two hundred other unacknowledged groups likely lies somewhere in between.

ISSUES

This work is about the process of acknowledging Indian tribes, whether accomplished through the administrative channels of the Bureau of Indian Affairs (BIA) or through Congress.[2] At its core it is about modern Indian identity: how the state identifies and legitimizes tribes and how recognized tribes, non-Indian scholars, and the American public perceive Indians. Along the way it provides a rare glimpse into Indian and non-Indian representations of "Indianness" and tribalism. These pages also present the histories of four unacknowledged tribal groups viewed through the prism of their efforts to gain federal recognition. Federal tribal acknowledgment or recognition is one of the most significant developments in Indian policy in the post–World War II era, yet is also one of the most acrimonious methods of sorting out and defining Indianness in the United States.[3] As the list of over two hundred groups seeking to secure federal tribal status grows each year, federal acknowledgment policy has become increasingly controversial and contested terrain for determining Indian authenticity.[4]

Tribal recognition is contentious precisely because it involves definitions of what constitutes an Indian tribe, who can lay claim to being an Indian, and what factors should be paramount in the process of identifying Indian tribes. Akin to the recognition of foreign governments, federal tribal acknowledgment is highly valued because it establishes a "government-to-government" relationship between the federal government and an Indian group. Federal status thus allows a newly recognized federal tribe the power to exercise sovereignty and participate in federal Indian programs emanating from the BIA and the Indian Health Service. It also affects issues as diverse as Indian self-government, health care, Native American cultural repatriation, Indian gaming, and public lands held by the National Park Service and other federal agencies. Beyond these facts the acknowledgment process can determine the life or death of struggling groups while providing unacknowledged tribes outside validation of their racial and cultural identity as Indians.

Selecting among approximately 250 petitioners, I am throwing into relief four once unrecognized Indian groups and their struggles to gain federal status through the BIA's Federal Acknowledgment Process (FAP) or via legislation. The following pages detail the experiences of the Pascua Yaquis, the Timbisha Shoshones, the Tiguas, and the United Houma Nation. As I flesh out their stories, the history of these Native peoples reveals the clear relationship between Indian ethnic identity and state bureaucracy, while highlighting Indian participation in the political process. Ultimately these communities' struggles to gain recognition expose the complex legal issues involved in federal acknowledgment while revealing the extreme burdens that groups face in proving their identity using non-indigenous historical and anthropological evidence.

Tribal acknowledgment burst upon the national scene as an issue during the civil rights struggles of the 1970s. At that time the rising number of unrecognized Indians and the complex issues of tribal acknowledgment were enveloped within the larger context of increased demands by indigenous peoples for rights and resources. Especially after the 1960s, once obscure unacknowledged Indians joined the growing legal and social activism prompted by similarly situated urban, terminated, and other nonreservation Indian peoples. Together, these neglected Indians increasingly demanded an end to their second-class status and pressed for their full rights to self-determination and cultural survival in modern America. Ultimately their demands forced the BIA to create its acknowledgment process in 1978.

By affirming the right of unacknowledged Indian tribes to gain recognition, the federal government clearly rejected previous termination and assimilation agendas for indigenous peoples. Yet although the 1978 BIA program allowed for significant variations in tribal organization and blood quantum, my work reveals that the FAP largely continued federal policy precedents witnessed in the Dawes Severalty Act and the Indian Reorganization Act of seeking to apply a single model to all groups, despite their differences. Since 1978 the BIA's approach has resulted in inequities.

Because of the complexities of tribal acknowledgment, it is little surprise that the process has become highly politicized. It elicits strong reactions from reservation tribes, social scientists, federal bureaucrats, and the general public because of the benefits and special legal status that acknowledgment confers upon petitioning groups. It is often an ugly process, pitting Indians against Indians, state and local governments against petitioning groups, and local residents against the federal government. The process of divining Indian tribalism only promises to become more complex and controversial, however, as precontact racial and cultural aspects of Indianness recede or evolve over time through the effects of mass culture and globalization. As the issues surrounding tribal acknowledgment represent a simmering cauldron of cultural, racial, and financial concerns, the history of unrecognized Indian peoples represents a cross section of some of the most salient issues facing Native America today.

AN AMBIGUOUS ENDEAVOR

Since the late 1970s the majority of unacknowledged groups have had to prove their tribal identity to a group of scholars within the Bureau of Indian Affairs. In 1978 the BIA created new regulations for acknowledging tribes, standards that were to make tribal acknowledgment more expeditious and more objective than in the past. That year the bureau established the Federal Acknowledgment Project, later renamed the Branch of Acknowledgment and Research (BAR), to deal with the complex recognition issues that had arisen in the previous decade. After 1978, although Congress and the federal courts maintained the power to confer acknowledgment, the BIA method essentially superceded these routes. In order for groups to gain federal status, the regulations require that petitioners locate records documenting their existence since historical contact, prove descent and identity from a historical tribe, demonstrate political structures and influence over their members, and prove they maintained strong community and social ties. Despite initial high hopes for the BIA program, it soon became apparent that defining and measuring these slippery concepts would not be an easy task.

Almost from its inception the BIA acknowledgment project came under attack from petitioning groups angry over its glacial bureaucratic procedures and the rigorous documentation required to prove tribal identity. By the mid-1980s recognized tribes and non-acknowledged Indians, lawyers, anthropologists, and politicians became entrenched in an acid-tinged debate over federal acknowledgment.[5] The debates are still raging. At the close of the 1990s the BIA process clearly had not lived up to expectations; its slow pace had finalized the acknowledgment of only fourteen groups and denied acknowledgment of thirteen others, while several other groups were enmeshed in appeals following initial denials by the BAR. As of 1999 the bureau had also acknowledged three tribes by internal means outside the FAP, and Congress recognized seven others, including the Mashantucket Pequots. In 2002 the political fallout generated by several proposed positive findings left several groups with affirmative determinations up in the air. As problems mounted into the new century, many parties clamored for an end to the bureaucratic program, hoping to replace it with an independent commission.[6]

The following pages reveal that the federal acknowledgment process is an inherently ambiguous endeavor because the foundational concepts used in determinations are extremely contested terrain. Together, the hazy concepts involved have ensured that the BIA process, in particular, has remained controversial and debated. With the defining characteristics of Indian tribes so open to debate, the whole undertaking is emblematic of the uncertainties of the postmodern age. Yet my work makes clear that when judged against its stated aims of providing a fair, objective, and expeditious review of unacknowledged groups, the BIA process has failed to live up to its promise. Although it does not appear that these shortcomings stem from the malicious intent of the BAR scholars, my writings demonstrate the bureau has a clear conflict of interest in deciding the issue, while the process has grown to be more time-consuming and costly than is reasonable.

In tackling the thorny issue, federal officials have come face-to-face with the difficulties inherent in divining Indian tribalism. Put simply, the majority of acknowledgment determinations are cloaked in shades of gray. In any government forum, determining whether a group really is an Indian "tribe" is a patently ambiguous pursuit because it involves concepts as slippery as ethnicity, community, culture, political allegiance, and psychological motive all rolled into one seemingly all-encompassing "package" of tribe—itself a contested term that arguably obscures more than it illuminates. In this light, it is not surprising that the recognition process is a recipe for controversy.[7] Over time each decision inevitably has spawned either joyous celebrations or stinging debates, especially within the circle of unacknowledged communities that are most affected by the federal policy.

Whether in court, Congress, or the BIA acknowledgment process, outside evaluators are forced to undertake two interrelated yet subjective endeavors when acknowledging an Indian tribe: they must recognize the existence of a sovereign, state-like community with leaders and political structures often referred to as a "tribe," and they must identify a racially defined ethnic group sharing common Indian ancestry, personal and group identity, and history. In essence, a petitioning group must be an ethnic group—specifically, a people sharing at least some traits that may include language, religion, community, symbols and systems of meaning, and common descent. But it is not enough that a petitioner is a generic, "Indian" group in the pan-Indian sense. It must also be a government-like entity exercising many of the attributes of sovereignty such as having a core community or territory, leaders, political structures, and community sanctions or laws. As my writings demonstrate, however, defining these concepts is fraught with difficulty.

EVERYMAN'S INDIAN

Growing up, I would spend summers working in and around several Inuit and Athabaskan communities in Alaska. Living in the "bush," I often would hear complaints from non-Indians about indigenous peoples' special hunting and fishing rights. It seemed the locals expected Alaska Natives to still use seal-skin kayaks and bows and arrows if they were to continue to remain "Indian enough" to exercise their treaty rights under United States law. While enlightening to me, these experiences were merely brief encounters with what Robert Berkhofer noted decades ago about Indianness in the United States: Euro-Americans expect Indians to remain in a primordial state if they are to remain authentically "Indian." Native Americans, and especially nonrecognized groups, are a rare ethnicity that must maintain premodern attributes to be accepted as authentic.[8] I came to see that these preconceived beliefs, while untenable in reality, intrude on the recognition debates. As I studied the process, it became clear that groups who assimilated significant aspects of the dominant culture had a difficult time gaining acceptance. The political realities of federal acknowledgment often have forced groups to project stereotypically Indian traits to gain recognition, especially to overcome popular misperceptions that most groups petitioning for recognition are assimilated pretenders with tenuous claims to Indianness.

Popular ideas about "tribes" also affect the process. Most people in Europe and the Americas have particular views of Indians as "tribal" peoples that often have little to do with living Indian communities yet certainly influence whether groups ultimately secure recognition. Imprinted by the popular media, most non-Indians conjure up images of primitive, dark-skinned individuals living in self-contained, egalitarian villages when they think of Indian tribes. Inevitably, non-Indians also envision Indian tribes living in the American West on barren reservations where the modern image of Indian tribes comes to an end. While patently stereotyped, each of these constructs affects how non-Indians and even many recognized tribes view hopeful groups and how each interprets recognition policy. Regrettably, however, my work reveals that these images often leave little room for groups whose histories do not match the media-inspired model.

Despite their visibility in American life, there simply is no accepted definition of Indians in current use, a fact that confuses the recognition debates. Even so, non-Indians generally search in vain for a singular, fixed conception of what it means to be Indian in modern America. Reflecting the ambiguity and confusion, the Bureau of Indian Affairs alone had thirty-nine separate definitions of Indians for its various programs in the late 1970s. Why are there so many separate definitions? Overall, the confusion stems from the general fact that American Indians often are part of several identifiable groups simultaneously. They are part of a larger ethnic group as Native Americans, members of smaller tribal communities with political status and sovereignty, and members of a racially defined group (as descendents of the first or indigenous peoples). In terms of tribal acknowledgment and constitutional law, however, their status as members of an indigenous polity is paramount because tribal sovereignty flows from this membership.[9] Even so, when deciphering tribal existence and its distinctive character, federal evaluators often look to each of the three components to decide whether the community in question is truly indigenous, ethnically distinct, and worthy of a government-to-government relationship.

The acknowledgment process is only the latest manifestation of the non-Indian search for an acceptable way to delineate and define Indian peoples in the United States. Because of the stakes involved, however, it is also an arena where non-Indians and recognized tribes will not accept hopeful groups' self-proclaimed tribal status even though many studies rightly assume that a combination of self-identification and community acceptance is the best method for defining ethnic groups. In fact, the United States Bureau of the Census has concluded that it is patently less contentious to let individuals decide their own race and ethnicity.[10] Yet most concerned individuals scoff at the prospect of allowing all groups claiming to be tribes to gain recognition. Instead, interested parties have looked to timeworn categories, written documentation, and observable indigenous traits to determine whether hopeful tribes are in fact authentic entities. In this postmodern age, however, the search for certainties and clear boundaries has often raised more questions than answers while sparking combustible debates that have become the hallmarks of the recognition process.

The general process of acknowledging tribes has always been based in part on legal fictions and cultural stereotypes about Native Americans. Because it relies on judgments of fallible individuals, subjectivity is at the bedrock of the process. To the present day, successful groups seeking to establish a tribal identity have generally had stereotypically "Indian" motives for petitioning the government. Successful petitioners generally have fought for decades to rise from poverty, to secure sacred lands, or to zealously maintain their Indian culture. In the eyes of most evaluators, those with financial or other material motives somehow have looked less "Indian." Although no forum for acknowledging Indians has required them to live in teepees or hunt for a living, successful tribes generally have clung to a core of visibly "Indian" traits, practices, and political leadership. Less contentious groups have also maintained a central Indian tribal identity above all others because overlapping identities are confusing and contentious.

Much of the controversy surrounding the acknowledgment process centers upon the fact that there is simply no agreement on what a "tribe" is, and therefore there is little consensus on how to recognize one. Anthropologists have long argued that the term is ambiguous, untenable, and of dubious value.[11] Despite this fact, in 1978 a nominal consensus developed over the criteria to be used in acknowledging tribalism for federal purposes. Yet as the process has played out, an agreement on the contours of an "Indian tribe" has failed to materialize. This resulted from the fact that the federal government developed the regulations at a time when the fields of anthropology, ethnohistory, and other disciplines were embracing postmodernism and poststructuralism while rejecting timeworn categories such as race, ethnicity, sex, and tribe as useful tools of analysis to describe their subjects. The new scholarly emphasis pitted cutting-edge academics and theoreticians against bureaucrats and lawyers searching for ways to define their subjects. As the 1980s progressed, noted authorities Vine Deloria Jr., William Sturtevant, and others have chided the BIA for clinging to discredited notions of objectivity and scientific methodology and attempting to assign widely varying peoples into the package of a "tribe." At the same time federal lawyers and bureaucrats replied that they simply were applying time-tested scientific methodologies to legally mandated concepts.

The debate over defining tribes, however, is not new to the federal acknowledgment process. Decades before the FAP the Indian Claims Commission cases of the late 1940s and 1950s spawned scholarly questioning of the concept of tribes. During these proceedings A. L. Kroeber of the University of California and Nancy O. Lurie of Harvard were called to testify as expert witnesses as to tribal territories and like matters for peoples who lived hundreds of years before. In pondering these issues, Lurie and Kroeber began to doubt the usefulness of the term "tribe." They pointed out that most Indian groups saw themselves more as nations or peoples than organized political entities Europeans called tribes. "It was White contact, pressure, edicts, or administration that converted most American Indian nations or nationalities into 'tribes.' It was we Caucasians who again and again rolled a number of related obscure bands or minute villages into the larger package of a 'tribe,' which we then putatively endowed with sovereign power and territorial ownership," wrote Kroeber at the time. [12] Later in the 1970s Columbia University's Morton Fried continued this questioning, noting that "tribes," far from being indigenous forms, were more often created as a result of colonialism, either for the convenience of European officials or by indigenous peoples seeking to unite in defense of their homelands. In most indigenous societies, the family or band was the basic unit of social organization, not a larger tribal body endowed with Western-style political powers. [13] Even so, Indian law and the BIA generally have insisted upon defining tribes along the larger political model rather than accepting tribes as smaller family units.

By the mid-1980s, just as the FAP was in full swing, cutting-edge scholars generally had rejected the usefulness of the concept of Indian "tribes" on which the process rested. At that time scholars went so far as to say that tribes were ethnographic fictions that existed only in the minds of anthropologists. In this light, ironically, BAR team members were judging groups to see if they were an entity that many parties believed did not exist in actual practice without outside intervention. The BAR thus has faced a perplexing dilemma. As noted anthropologist Julian Steward had often argued, the category of "tribe" awakened in the scholar's mind notions of self-contained, organized political bodies that often never existed, yet it is unclear whether BAR scholars, members of Congress, and other outsiders have put aside preconceived notions when judging cases.[14]

Despite serious conceptual problems over the concept of "tribes," my writings show that most reservation communities understandably have resisted traveling down a path that questions the validity of tribes, for such questions could undermine their sovereignty and open anti-tribal floodgates. Clearly, American Indian law is predicated on European notions of retained sovereignty in the unit of the Indian tribe. To reservation leaders and many other officials, it seems dangerous to expose Indian peoples to attacks based on the idea that they lacked retained, aboriginal sovereignty. Although some modern tribes do not have the continuous historical existence now required of all hopeful nonrecognized groups, other recognized tribes clearly have retained unbroken tribal sovereignty on aboriginal lands.[15] Therefore, because of legal precedent, acknowledgment dictates have forced unacknowledged groups to mold their histories to this reality, despite the fact that their experiences often do not match the legal template.

In spite of the hopelessly muddled issues involved, most scholarly definitions of the concept of an Indian tribe do include common elements. There is a loose agreement on the criteria the BIA uses to recognize tribes as well—if not a consensus on exactly how to measure and quantify them. Most concerned parties believe that groups claiming to be "tribes" must have some qualities that distinguish them from others and that they use to distinguish themselves from outsiders. In other words, there has to be a "thing" in being, in order to acknowledge it. Scholars of ethnicity generally hold that tribes are groups with a territory, community, and political organization; many definitions also include common culture, language, genealogy, and identity. In general, many in the anthropological profession believe the term connoted an ethnic group in contrast to the central state that had some loosely defined political structure and group norms that controlled and integrated group behavior. Therefore, despite problems with the acknowledgment process, ethnologists, historians, and lawyers generally continue to find the term "tribe" useful and are loath to throw it out, while American Indians are giving it new life and meaning. Because of its utility and widespread usage, it seems doubtful that the term "tribe" will be banished from the lexicon of English in the near future.[16]

By utilizing the non-indigenous concept of tribe, however, the recognition process has continued the historic bias favoring Indian communities with formal relationships with Euro-American governments. The bias exists because it is these very non-Indian relationships and the structures they generate that allow many modern groups to be historically, genetically, and politically visible as "tribes." As Anne McCulloch and David Wilkins have noted, acknowledgment criteria are patterned upon, and judged against, existing reservation tribes. To gain status, petitioners are forced to exhibit at least some characteristics of recognized tribes or nations such as having some manner of formal or informal territories, laws and sanctions, and structures of government—attributes that many nonreservation peoples simply could not maintain in light of the United States' longtime goal of obliterating these very attributes.[17]

INDIANS IN THE BLOOD

Beyond troubles with the overarching tribal template, another problem with the acknowledgment process has to do with race. Because the BAR, in particular, requires a genealogical link to a historic tribe, its regulations are race-based criteria for defining Indian tribalism.[18] Although most parties agree that Indian tribes must possess some Native American ancestry, social scientists widely reject bloodlines and race as reliable indicators of social phenomena.[19] Clearly, a brief purview of non-acknowledged groups reveals that the terms used to fit people into neat categories such as "Indian," "white," "Hispanic," or "black" do not fit well here. Phrases such as "mixed bloods" also fail to satisfy, as they conjure up false images of pure blood strains that largely do not exist. Even so, C. Mathew Snipp notes that Indians consistently are defined as members of a group descended by blood from the first Americans, a racial discourse continued in acknowledgment criteria.[20] Although groups securing acknowledgment can have only minute traces of Indian ancestry—blood quantum is not required for tribal recognition—petitioners must demonstrate at least some genetic thread to a historic tribe. Because of this requirement, Indian ancestry, and the distasteful racial discourse it evokes, is another controversial component of deciphering Indian identity within the acknowledgment process.[21]

More troubling in the recognition process, however, is the government's effort to authenticate or judge Indian ethnicity, a concept as shrouded in ambiguity as tribe and race.[22] A group hoping to secure recognition must demonstrate that it has visible attributes of a viable ethnic community. In the most basic sense, as Fredrik Barth, Joane Nagel, and others have noted, an ethnic group consists of a body of people who see themselves as descending from common ancestors and who outsiders also view as comprising a community distinct from others. In this vein modern tribal petitioners must demonstrate that they are ethnic groups that maintain a sense of difference vis-à-vis outsiders by maintaining social boundaries (or distinctions) between themselves and the surrounding plural society. Although variable, these distinctions can include norms and rules of behavior, distinctive group traditions, and deep psychological feelings of belonging. Measuring and providing proof of these distinctions, however, has not been a simple task. In the past what was an "ethnic group" seemed rather simple because most people viewed ethnic groups as rather static entities bounded by fairly clear racial, cultural, or religious structures.[23] As the following pages show, however, in the modern acknowledgment process these boundaries often are not entirely clear and certainly not biologically determined.

In judging continuing tribal existence, federal evaluators have asked whether petitioners have continued to maintain distinctive institutions and traits. Contention has inevitably arisen, however, in deciding what these ethnic and social distinctions are and whether they are significant enough to qualify a petitioner as an Indian tribe. On the surface the issue is seemingly simple. In most cases members of ethnic groups and nonmembers generally acknowledge certain defining characteristics (or symbols of difference) that separate them; ethnic identity is thus defined both from within ethnic groups and ascribed from without. Yet, as my writing reveals, federal officials have faced challenges trying to delineate social boundaries and senses of identity within the context of acknowledgment decisions, especially once indigenous cultures and languages have declined or disappeared.

Much of the problem with judging Indian ethnicity and tribalism has come down to the fact that there are two levels of ethnicity: one observable and "objective," the other subjective and psychological.[24] Clearly, the observable symbols of certain ethnic groups such as distinctive dress, foods, housing forms, and colorful ceremonies are the easiest to delineate. Yet as Edward Spicer and Fredrik Barth have observed, the ideological, intangible components of ethnicity are often the most lasting and important. Scholars widely agree that viable ethnic groups survive without territories or unique cultural traits as long as they maintain a sense of history, identity, and descent. [25] However, these subjective feelings and beliefs are rarely accorded much weight as proof in legal forums and are difficult to quantify. Not surprisingly, controversies have arisen when federal evaluators, usually far removed from the environment of local interactions, have attempted to pinpoint subjective identities and distinctive social codes of a tribe in question.

VISIBLE TRIBES AND INVENTED INDIANS

Because of the difficulties of judging subjective identities and feelings, most Americans have traditionally looked to visible cultural traits for answers in deciphering Indianness: Does the claimed tribe still have an Indian language? Do its members practice an indigenous-influenced religion? Does the group maintain distinctive dress or foods? This emphasis on cultural survival stems from the fact that it was once widely believed that cultures were handed down, largely unchanged, by societies from the primordial past. In this vein groups that still possessed indigenous traits were logically still Indian tribes. While this belief is often correct, in the early 1980s Eric Hobsbawn made it widely known that culture is constantly changing and evolving. It is seldom passed down pristinely from the hallowed past. [26] The admission that culture is often "invented" and constructed as groups constantly innovate, revive, renew, import, and discard cultural traits and symbols has added yet another layer to the complexities of the recognition process. [27] The following chapters reveal that although Congress has tended to accept uncritically cultural traits projected by petitioning groups, the BAR has sought to deconstruct the claimed culture and history of groups—neither proving entirely satisfactory or equitable.

Although the search for archaic traditional traits often has proven illusive or illusory, the perceived need for demonstrated proof of ethnic distinctiveness has created a major quandary for judges attempting to decide whether petitioners descend from indigenous populations and maintain tribal and ethnic traits. Overall, despite conceptual difficulties involving culture, groups possessing visible and distinctive cultural traits have had an easier time convincing outsiders that they are Indian tribes. And most observers continue to view surviving Indian culture as highly persuasive of continuing tribal existence.

It is perhaps axiomatic, but the greater the perceived costs of acknowledging a self-defined group, the lesser the chance that such a group will be affirmed by the dominant society, especially if it lacks clearly "indigenous" traits. In the eyes of a skeptical public, if a group's visible racial and cultural traits appear white, black, or otherwise "non-Indian," it faces a long road to acknowledgment and questions about its motives, regardless of the correctness of these perceptions. In essence, as Berkhofer so poignantly noted, the more "they" look like "us," the less they appear to be Indian, no matter how erroneous this line of thought can be at its core. Even so, my work reveals that the current processes offer few brightly lit ethnic, racial, or cultural poles of orbit to look to when evaluating most cases, only vague cultural systems from which groups are borrowing and against which they are adapting.

Despite the lack of clear boundaries and markers, BAR scholars have been willing to acknowledge widely evolved and changed groups. For acknowledgment evaluators, however, the recognition that ethnic traits and history are not always inherited or immutable, ironically, has exposed all unacknowledged groups to scrutiny and doubt about their motivations. Clearly there is a need for caution: many petitioning groups have evolved or assimilated to such a degree that most parties no longer consider them Indian tribes in any sense. In this light, motives matter: the more a group's Indian identity is viewed as a conscious choice rather than ascribed by outsiders, the more the claimant can expect to be scoffed at and questioned. The more a group is viewed as having more than one questionable component of Indian tribalism, the more its history will be challenged. In essence, a petitioner can expect a bumpy road to acknowledgment if its "race" is not readily apparent, its culture is not noticeably "Native," its Indianness appears borrowed or invented, and its core settlement is not small, cohesive, and relatively self-contained. Although past federal policies and racism clearly discouraged Indian identity and tribalism, the government makes no allowance for its past culpability in dispersing or suppressing Indian tribes. All groups are thus on their own to prove they are who they say they are.

Attempting to sidestep the inherent difficulties in deciphering race, ethnicity, and culture, the Bureau of Indian Affairs has insisted that it focuses exclusively upon the existence of a tribal, political unit. Yet this emphasis has spawned issues of its own. At the crux of the problem for most unacknowledged groups is the fact that the state-like unit with political power and retained aboriginal sovereignty is clearly the easiest to see, yet the hardest to maintain. The intangible component of a people or "nation," on the other hand, is most enduring and simplest to maintain, yet also the hardest to see and quantify. [28] Overall, the ephemeral nature of groups and identities has served to confuse and confound attempts at measuring them. As many meaningful aspects of collective identity and culture are hidden within clandestine social spaces and moments, problems arise when evaluators insist upon written documentation to prove "tribal" political functioning. [29] Certainly groups are not visible all the time. They may materialize at ceremonies or meetings, only to have their component parts melt back into the larger society. Yet federal evaluators look for an unbroken visible community existence nonetheless.

STATE HEGEMONY

In addition to the process's anomalies, federal tribal recognition has angered many parties because it is an arena where the state bestows legitimacy upon Indian groups in a forum with inherently unequal power relationships. Unlike in earlier eras, the notion that recognition is a negotiation between equal sovereigns is clearly absent here. The state decides who can lay claim to being a tribe. Tribal acknowledgment is thus an area where the state exercises great power in defining Indian racial, ethnic, and political identity. As Joane Nagel has noted, many non-Indians view the effort to secure tribal recognition and its subsequent ethnic validation as a strategic choice and strategy, and the federal government rigorously regulates this valuable status. [30] With the component parts of the package "tribe" so contested, the state has played a pervasive role in scrutinizing all claimants, jealously maintaining its power to determine which groups qualify for the federal seal. Reflecting almost complete state hegemony, the current acknowledgment process thus has set the parameters and categories of discussion, forcing unacknowledged groups to cast their histories to fit the mold set for them. [31] With such power relationships, unacknowledged groups have come to deeply resent the process as a glaring symbol of the state's power to dictate the terms and forum for asserting long unacknowledged sovereignty.

The details on the following pages reveal that the BIA's effort to fit all groups into seven categories to be recognized as tribes means that some viable groups will be excluded. The structural emphasis, however, often rings untrue in the modern world. [32] Despite this fact, the system's rigidity and rule of law approach appeases skeptical Americans, conservative tribal leaders, budget-conscious bureaucrats, and concerned local citizens. Because the current BIA process clearly has worked to screen out dubious "wannabe" groups, most parties applaud this fact, despite the contradictions. The BIA acknowledgment program reigns supreme precisely because it represents the interests of recognized tribes and the general public by performing its understated function of limiting the number of groups that qualify for federal status. The BIA's Federal Acknowledgment Process is thus an area where Indian self-determination has succeeded, although in a perverse way for many unacknowledged groups. My analysis shows that when the BIA created the stringent process, the interests of recognized tribes and the bureau converged to produce difficult requirements that all groups must meet to secure federal status, demanding rules that severely restrict the number of federal tribes. The program's rigorous, glacial, and document-driven labyrinth reflects the wishes of groups already recognized by the federal government. Although containing many contradictions, federal acknowledgment policy thus has largely continued the historical precedent of restricting membership in the favored group of recognized tribes, a policy goal that has long resulted in some inequitable outcomes.

Even with reservation tribes' influence on the process, however, their dependence on federal funding has dictated they will not make the final acknowledgment decisions. The BIA has a pervasive stake in the outcome of recognition cases and has demanded the final word in determining its service population. Because it would be naive to think that federal officials or the tribes they represent would simply accept the word of groups who hire experts to make their cases, the federal government clearly faces a real dilemma in making binding decision with multiple consequences. A lingering problem, not easily explained or satisfactorily solved by theory or abstractions, is deciding at what point a group no longer exists as a distinct people capable of exercising sovereign powers, administering tribal lands, and controlling its community. In light of these realities, some scholars support the BIA process as the best available in an imperfect world.

My work demonstrates that the FAP has gained preeminence precisely because recognized tribes support it and because the BIA process appears to be more scholarly and equitable than either the judicial or congressional routes. Legislative acknowledgment and federal court decisions generally had favored groups that retained some anachronistic survivals of aboriginal culture and visible racial features; in essence, groups that "looked" Indian. Unacknowledged organizations that secured powerful advocates and that manipulated the political system by projecting stereotypically Indian images of their group or "played Indian" in public discourse succeeded particularly well in Congress. As designed, the FAP changed this emphasis. But in shifting the focus from stereotypes and appearances, it has produced a new set of standards that some legitimate Indian groups cannot meet. Although the BIA process has made numerous valid determinations, by requiring reams of written documentation of political functioning and genealogy and expensive legal experts, the FAP has not made the recognition system inherently more equitable than the processes it has replaced. It is my contention that the concepts rolled up into the process are so ambiguous and contested that the success of groups is often reliant upon their ability to hire experts and secure political allies, or their ability to find scraps of paper or documents pointing to continuous historical existence—records that are often the result of good fortune or the accidents of history.[33]

METHODOLOGY: A COMPARATIVE AND CROSS-CULTURAL APPROACH

Following the encouragement of historians and anthropologists, my work takes a comparative and cultural approach to studying Indian policy.[34] It situates a federal Indian policy squarely within Indian or Indian-identifying communities in various regions of the United States. Although traditional policy studies have indisputable value, this work takes a community-centered approach to incorporate Indians into the story, individuals whom policy studies centered in Washington sometimes omit. This approach places a human face on a federal policy by showing individual agency, accommodation, and resistance while highlighting the survival of several communities that lacked federal sanction. In order to gain a firm grasp of the acknowledgment regimen, I conducted extensive research over several years, a pursuit that resulted in dozens of oral interviews of Indian and non-Indian participants in the process and a dozen boxes of written data culled and copied from archival sources stretching from California to Washington DC. Although some individuals were reluctant to respond, most parties proved receptive to opening their collections and voices to me, a graciousness that ultimately afforded a well-rounded, multidimensional picture of this clouded yet vital indigenous program.

Despite the importance of tribal acknowledgment, at the time of this writing there are no book-length studies of the process and its effects on impoverished, non-acknowledged communities. In light of its newness as an issue, most of the discourse available was produced by parties actively engaged in the government policy, either as scholars for petitioning groups or as former

BIA researchers. From their vantage these scholars bring valuable firsthand insights into the process. Yet these studies generally are invested in some way with the program itself. In this light my work lays bare the Federal Acknowledgment Process by revealing its inherent problems and complexities—an approach new in published discourse. In the end the details embedded within the following pages should provide unacknowledged Indians, scholars, and bureaucrats with a fresh approach to volatile recognition policies.

In the early stages of research it became apparent that modern acknowledgment policy and the community responses to its dictates could not be understood without a historical and ethnological understanding of the complexities of each group's history, culture, and identity. Thus I am throwing into relief the decades-long struggles of several groups that were once unacknowledged. By centering upon the communities, my writings reveal how unrecognized Indian people dealt with the sometimes disastrous effects of the lack of reservations and federal protections of their lands and political forms. These stories also expose the fact that Indian tribalism and identity often evolve independently of federal dictates and programs. Left without federal status, many unacknowledged peoples clearly possessed a dogged persistence, ingenuity, and genuine valuation of Indian religions, identity, ceremonies, and familial ties nonetheless.

Although independent of federal Indian policy for long periods, none of these groups escaped the influence of outside political pressures or economic forces. Researching these peoples' histories made it clear that Indians and their benefactors entered the political and bureaucratic processes as actors, often manipulating the system in modern ways to gain their ultimate desires. Federal prerogatives, however, often demanded that groups construct images of themselves derived from recast histories or Indian stereotypes, while forcing them to parade their culture and ethnicity to gain federal status. Boxed into these confining structures, my account reveals that some groups are better equipped than others to play the federal game.

There are over two hundred petitioners with varying experiences with tribal acknowledgment policy that are worthy of exposing. Yet in examining this issue, I became aware that trying to touch upon each group was patently impossible. There were no "model" communities whose experiences encompassed the myriad problems all groups face in different regions of the United States. I chose to focus my work on four communities in several regions of the United States. In their struggles each of these groups of Native peoples encountered the major dilemmas unrecognized groups face in different parts of the nation.

Although it is axiomatic that all groups are by their nature unique, the contours of acknowledgment policy lay in similar outlines upon groups in different regions; therefore the history of peoples such as the Yaquis demonstrates how federal recognition policies and programs played out at the local level in similar ways. As with the over two hundred other unrecognized groups, however, the acknowledgment efforts, issues, and motivations of these four Indian communities varied considerably.

The simple fact that there are several hundred groups petitioning for federal tribal acknowledgment underscores the magnitude of the issue. There are unrecognized Indians in virtually every region of the United States. In the late 1970s there were approximately 133 unrecognized enclaves, with a population of over 111,000, seeking to secure acknowledgment; by 1999 the number stood at over 200. Undoubtedly there are dozens of other entities that have yet to come forward. In comparison, the federal government recognized 332 Indian tribes, bands, or other entities (outside of Alaska) as eligible for services from the Bureau of Indian Affairs. [35] A map of groups presently petitioning the BIA reveals that hopeful groups exist in the majority of states in the Union. The bulk of the groups, however, live in a semi-circle stretching from the Northeast, through the Old South, continuing more sparsely along the border of Mexico, and ending in pointed clusters in California and Washington State. Another major concentration exists in the Great Lakes region. Approximately one quarter of all petitioners hail from California alone, and approximately one half live along the eastern seaboard and the southern states. [36]

There are historical reasons for the prevalence of unrecognized Indian groups in these areas. Indigenous peoples in Michigan, the South, and the eastern United States all experienced early contact with Europeans and the ensuing demographic collapse, political disintegration, forced acculturation, and loss of tribal lands. Indian groups in these regions were buffeted by colonial forces long before the creation of the United States and often remained ignored by federal Indian policies, treaties, and protections. By the time of U.S. independence, federal Indian policy came to focus on the western regions on the nation, with tribes living in the American West generally securing federal lands while eastern Indians found themselves passed by and neglected. Although many unrecognized tribes assimilated into the dominant society, others escaped federal removals by refusing to move to reservations or eking out an existence on state Indian reserves that lacked federal sanction. Other individuals retreated to marginal areas, reverted to the family as their basic unit of social organization, and assumed the outward appearances and customs of European Americans or African Americans. Despite their outward appearances, however, these people still clung to an Indian identity. Most California Indians experienced a similar fate, although they had later contact with Europeans and an often more brutal experience once outside settlement began.[37]

There is no historical or rational reason why some indigenous groups have federal status and others do not. Although maps reveal distinct regional groupings, region has not been the deciding factor where Indian communities exist without federal status. Region also is not conclusive of the ability of groups to succeed in the acknowledgment process, as many groups have achieved acknowledgment from areas that experienced federal neglect and early contact. However, my writing reveals that groups who experienced later contact and who maintained more elements of their aboriginal culture have had less difficulty securing recognition than eastern groups because they present fewer ambiguities to federal officials.

By design, the Native communities on which I focus live in different regions of the United States. From east to west, they include the United Houma Nation near New Orleans, Louisiana, the Tiguas of Ysleta del Sur Pueblo southeast of El Paso, Texas, the Yaquis of Arizona, and the Timbisha Shoshones of Death Valley National Park, California. These groups followed different paths to acknowledgment with varying success. Each thus has a compelling story to tell.

As with all Indian peoples, unacknowledged tribes vary widely in their composition: my study seeks to expose this fact. My work explores the efforts of the Pascua Yaquis, who by-passed the FAP by securing legislative recognition, the labors of the Timbisha Shoshones, who succeeded through the BIA process, the struggles of the United Houma Nation, a southeastern people the BIA currently declines to acknowledge, and the history of the Tiguas of Ysleta del Sur Pueblo, who sought alternatives to BIA dependency only to become enmeshed in the Indian gaming controversies of the 1980s. The unique battles of these indigenous peoples to gain acceptance as American Indian tribes lay at the heart of this work.

The struggles of these communities, however, also illuminate issues common to non-acknowledged groups. Despite their distinctive attributes, each community experienced a similar fate as part of a group of unrecognized Indian tribes. What attributes did these groups share? All were distinct peoples or ethnic enclaves that identified as Indian and that outsiders also labeled as Native American; all faced modern pressures and community stresses stemming from their lack of federal status and reservations; and each group in some way faced doubts whether it was an Indian "tribe." Because all lacked unambiguous recognition, non-Indians forced them to enter the political arena to prove their Indian race, culture, and tribalism, with all the ambiguities and pitfalls this entailed. Hoping to secure federal status, each group surrendered to the task of conforming to definitions and images of tribalism dictated by the dominant society. In the power structures of federal Indian policy, the peoples I write about constructed images of their groups as functioning Indian tribes to match the template created by federal officials. Typical of most acknowledgment cases, however, their efforts to secure status often pitted them against federal officials and, at times, reservation tribes. It is a sad fact that each of the once unacknowledged enclaves I detail found itself on the margins of marginalized people, literally the "other" and the in-between.

Like most unrecognized Indian peoples, the United Houmas, Yaquis, Tiguas, and Timbisha Shoshones also adapted and responded in specific ways to forces against them. Many clung to traditions and relied on outside benefactors to aid them, while others, also maintaining Indian identity, pursued tribal agendas by playing federal officials for their own agendas. Each of the groups I discuss, however, existed and moved within the modern world and power structures; none was static; none was consistently perfect or traditionally "Indian" in stereotypical or mystical manifestations. The Yaquis, United Houma Nation, Timbisha Shoshones, and Tiguas were seeking similar things yet chose different strategies to accomplish their group goals. These stories show that groups such as the United Houmas battled discrimination and poverty while continually negotiating what it meant to be Indian and tribal in the modern United States. Over centuries each of these communities faced the difficult choices of whether to maintain tribalism, to preserve aspects of their culture, or to redefine their ethnicity. In the end these very struggles provide a richer, more complex picture of Native Americans in the late twentieth century than would be possible from a Washington-centered study.

RECOGNIZING THE ULTIMATE "OTHER"

The following pages provide both a detailed history of a federal Indian policy and a series of histories dramatizing its effect on several groups identifying as Indians in different regions of the United States. As of this writing, my work serves as one of the only historical analyses of this highly contentious development in Indian affairs, which has been called one of the most significant developments in postwar Indian policy by both the National Congress of American Indians (NCAI) and Indian policy veteran Senator Daniel Inouye of Hawaii. Beyond policy, it provides a glimpse into the lesser-known histories of several obscure Indian groups and presents evidence that Indian communities continue to exist without federal supports or status. Endeavoring to keep identity alive, people in these communities routinely made choices and took actions that redefined their cultures, their Indian identities—and at times stretched the definitions of Indianness—all the while taking steps that enabled their people to survive as Indians in the modern United States.

In the late 1980s celebrated Spokane/Coeur d'Alene poet Sherman Alexie wrote a piece titled "Recognition of Distance." In it he reflected:

> sisters do not wrap yourself in old
> blankets praying for the white man
> to go back to Europe
>
> there is nothing that changes back
> the forests will remain thin
> so when I see an Indian stranger
>
> staring I stare back in recognition
> we have the same eyes mirrors
> reflecting what we have shared[38]

If only recognition were so readily apparent. As the twenty-first century dawns, acknowledgment of Indians and tribes promises only to become more and more elusive as the traditional symbols of Indianness recede from the naked eye. In many ways, many unacknowledged groups have remained the ultimate "other," fitting neither the dominant society's image of Native Americans nor blending into the larger society. In lacking federal status and validation, most unacknowledged Indian groups are truly the "other" and the in-between.

ONE. ADRIFT WITH THE INDIAN OFFICE

The Historical Development of Tribal
Acknowledgment Policy, 1776–1978

Seven miles off the Massachusetts coast, Jacqueline Kennedy Onassis's se-
cluded four-hundred-acre estate on the resort island of Martha's Vineyard was
surely a welcome retreat from the constant gaze of the gawking public on
the mainland. From her nineteen-room shingled home the former first lady
and American icon could look out in privacy over the windswept dunes to the
moody, swirling Atlantic beyond. Shortly after she purchased the estate in the
late 1970s, however, this scene abruptly changed as Onassis, like hundreds
of other land owners up and down the East Coast, found herself embroiled
in a lawsuit with members of a non–federally recognized Indian group, the
Gay Head Wampanoags. It seemed the small tribe was demanding the return
of lands or monetary compensation for acreage their ancestors lost in the
preceding century. Suddenly the glamorous symbol of the Kennedy dynasty
found herself in the awkward position of opposing members of the struggling
Indian community for control of a one-and-a-half-acre strip of dunes, a small
sliver of land that the Wampanoags coveted for its sacred significance and that
Onassis needed for keeping celebrity seekers at bay. Though troubling to the
former first lady and others, the tiny Gay Head tribe clearly had arrived on the
national scene.[1]

At the time, however, the Martha's Vineyard group was just one of over
two dozen Indian enclaves living on or near state reservations or former
colonial Indian reserves on the East Coast that lacked federal sanction. By
the early 1970s these groups and other unacknowledged Indian communities
across the country began demanding fishing rights, the return of tribal lands,
and ultimately the formal federal recognition that they believed the national
government had denied them for centuries. Fired by a sense of pride in their
Indian heritage, the forgotten enclaves came to demand an end to their second-
class status among Native Americans, yet because they were unacknowledged,

it was unclear what rights, if any, they possessed. Although the Gay Head Wampanoags were awakening the country to their existence, their actions also created a crisis in Indian affairs in the process. Their movement would eventually set the stage for the BIA's Federal Acknowledgment Process or Project, a program designed to end the arbitrary policies of the past and to bring justice to unacknowledged communities by determining which were Indian tribes within the meaning of federal law. As the following pages show, a primary goal of the Bureau of Indian Affairs and its tribal constituency was to create exacting standards that all groups had to meet to join the ranks of acknowledged tribes.[2]

Like other unrecognized Indians, the tiny three-hundred-member Massachusetts group was an unlikely force with which to reckon. The once mighty Wampanoag Federation—the same people who aided the Pilgrims and who were the subject of a popular 1829 play, Metamora; or The Last of the Wampanoags—had in popular consciousness become extinct. Yet the group seemingly was rising from a nineteenth-century grave to upset what one indignant Gay Head vacation homeowner described as the "harmonious atmosphere" of the island. In 1974, with the help of attorney Tom Tureen and the Native American Rights Fund (NARF), the Indians on Martha's Vineyard filed suit for the return of 238 acres of dunes, bluffs, and marshes that were then held as common lands by the town of Gay Head. In the suit the Wampanoags claimed that the state legislature had illegally taken the group's lands in the nineteenth century by violating the obscure 1790 federal Indian Nonintercourse Act that forbade any party but Congress from dealing in Indian lands. Like another case Tureen had filed for the Mashantucket Pequots at the same time, the court proceedings cast a cloud over land titles in the area, prompting locals to hire prominent attorneys to fight the Indians.[3]

From the start local whites questioned whether these groups were indeed tribes and expressed doubts about their Indian identity. To the eastern landowners, most of these groups "looked" variously white, black, Indian, or something in between. They clearly did not fit the image of the horse-riding, buffalo-hunting Indians they had seen in Hollywood westerns. In court the town attorneys proceeded to impugn the cultural and tribal integrity of these people, claiming that the groups had long ago abandoned their tribal organizations and assimilated into American society and culture. Despite the Wampanoags' assertions that the land on Martha's Vineyard was sacred to their people and that they maintained a vibrant tribal organization, town lawyers echoed a popular belief that the Wampanoags—if they were a group at all—

were assimilated individuals hoping to get rich off land claims. Because the rights asserted were group rights, the hopes of the Martha's Vineyard Indians and others ultimately rested on whether they were still an Indian "tribal" entity.[4]

In examining these claims, however, all sides came to realize that federal law and policies gave them little help in deciding the issue. Despite the fact that federal Indian law was premised on tribal sovereignty, at this time officials discovered—incredibly—that there was no congressional or other federal definition of an Indian "tribe" to apply to these vexing cases. Lawyers for the towns and some BIA officials claimed that the lack of recognition, in itself, was reason enough to deny these groups' standing in court. Other officials discovered, however, that the reasons for nonrecognition were not so simple. BIA lawyers eventually admitted that previous acknowledgment policy had been, at best, characterized by consistent arbitrariness. Congress and the federal courts began to take steps to provide some order to the chaotic environment.[5] Fearing an end to its hegemony in recognition cases, the Bureau of Indian Affairs and its tribal base also rushed to devise new acknowledgment regulations. Seizing the initiative in 1978, the BIA finalized rules for acknowledging tribes that were designed to provide an objective and timely process yet at their core were aimed at protecting the sovereignty, funding, and cultural integrity of currently recognized Indians.

When designing the new program, all parties realized that previous tribal acknowledgment policy had followed a twisting, serpentine path. This stemmed from the fact that tribal recognition activity generally mirrored the ebb and flow of federal Indian policies and dominant ideologies about Native peoples and indigenous sovereignty. Once widely recognized because of their power in intercolonial relations, American Indian tribes had faced a long, general assault on their sovereignty in the ensuing years. After several tribes gained recognition during the late 1960s and early 1970s, however, a new era had dawned: one where the national government once again was willing to acknowledge that a government-to-government relationship existed between it and many small, forgotten tribes scattered across the country. In light of the new stance most parties clearly welcomed the BIA acknowledgment process in 1978 because it seemed to represent a decisive rejection of past anti-tribal agendas while promising to restore pride, dignity, and self-government to all Indian peoples. Concerned people of all stripes hoped that the previous arbitrary and ambiguous policies would be a thing of the past.

Prior to the 1970s, however, tribal recognition had not always been such an arbitrary proposition at the complete power and discretion of the federal government. From the American Revolution until 1871 federal officials routinely recognized Indian nations through the treaty-making process. During these years many Indian groups were still formidable military foes on the western borders of the expanding nation, and army negotiators and the Senate actively recognized tribes as sovereign nations, acts that followed existing international laws and procedures. To accomplish its immediate goals of ending frontier warfare and securing land for the growing nation, the federal government signed 372 treaties with Indian nations before ending the practice in 1871. Treaty recognition provided unambiguous confirmations of a tribe's self-government, of its territorial integrity, and later of its status as a beneficiary of a federal trust relationship. By clearly acknowledging the sovereignty of Indian tribes, federal treaties provided the legal basis on which their special, "anomalous" relationship in the federal system rests.[6]

From the first years of the fledgling nation the existence of independent Indian tribes as separate nations within the United States proved contentious. After decades of controversies, John Marshall, chief justice of the Supreme Court, attempted to settle the issue once and for all. In the landmark *Cherokee Cases* of the 1830s, Justice Marshall announced the limits of tribal sovereignty, noting that Indian tribes were "domestic dependent nations" whose relationship with the United States resembled that of a ward to his guardian.[7] American Indian tribes thereafter fell under the plenary or absolute power of Congress yet generally remained free to govern their internal affairs while remaining independent from state laws and regulations. It was this sovereign status vis-à-vis local non-Indian communities that would generate heated controversies in future years.

During the 1970s researchers discovered that Congress had left few clues on how to define or recognize Indian tribes, despite their importance within the federal system. Perhaps because what constituted a "tribe" seemed obvious or taken for granted, the formative documents in American history such as the Articles of Confederation, the Constitution, and the Northwest Ordinance all left a definition of an "Indian tribe" unformulated. In the Commerce Clause of the Constitution and a series of six Indian Trade and Nonintercourse Acts, Congress reserved for itself plenary or absolute power in dealing with Indian tribes or nations. In each of these acts, however, Congress maintained a vague use of the term "tribe," stating simply that these laws applied to "any Indian nation or tribe of Indians."[8] As late as 1921 the sweeping Snyder Act maintained this imprecise usage by identifying its beneficiaries simply as "the Indians throughout the United States."[9] Flowing from this undefined terminology, for certain groups during the treaty-making era tribal recognition was an uncertain, arbitrary proposition. Throughout the nation federal officials often overlooked many viable Indian tribes and peoples, seeing them as simply too weak, dependent, or numerically insignificant to bother with. These forgotten tribes were left outside the federal circle as a result.

With the majority of indigenous groups on reservations by 1871, however, Indians gradually lost the power to dictate terms of negotiation and tribal existence. Acknowledgment eventually became less of an issue to policymakers. The period of active treaty making and acknowledgment thus slowly came to an end during the 1870s and 1880s. Between 1871 and 1934 it is not surprising that few tribes gained recognition of their sovereignty, for non-Indians used all tools at their disposal to destroy Indianness and tribalism. During these years missionaries, local settlers, and federal officials descended upon tribal communities seeking to stamp out their tribal governments and cultures. Although federal courts sometimes were concerned with whether Indian entities could be recognized as being federal "wards" or trust beneficiaries during the late nineteenth century, the entire thrust of congressional policy sought to destroy tribalism and break up Indian lands through mechanisms such as the Dawes Severalty Act, a largely disastrous law for most Indian communities. During these years it was a matter of faith to non-Indians that full acculturation was the best solution to the "Indian problem" in the country; establishing new trust relations would only slow the Indians' eventual assimilation into the mainstream.[10]

As non-Indian views of Native peoples forever change, the federal emphasis swung again during the 1930s. In the midst of an economic and military crisis between 1934 and 1945, a new, gentler policy toward Native Americans emerged. At this time idealistic Indian commissioner John Collier pushed the Indian Reorganization Act of 1934 (IRA), a significant piece of legislation that became the centerpiece of the "Indian New Deal." Through the IRA a new federal agenda was born: one that promoted Indian tribalism and cultures while seeking to reorganize widely varying Indian governments along Euro-American political lines.[11] As a result these years were marked by a strengthening of tribal status and sovereignty overall. By this time, however, tribal recognition was no longer a negotiation between equals, but a process dictated by the federal government and its bureaucrats.

The Indian New Deal ushered in the modern tribal acknowledgment issue. During the 1930s and early 1940s questions regarding tribal acknowledgment arose as Indian Office lawyers had to decide which Indian communities qualified as tribes or bands eligible to hold elections and organize under the Indian Reorganization Act. Specifically, the IRA listed three types of Indians authorized to organize tribal governments: "recognized" tribes, descendents of recognized tribes residing on a reservation in 1934, and other persons of one-half or more Indian blood. Indian officials had to determine which peoples fit these descriptions. [12] Ultimately during this era Harvard-trained lawyer Felix Cohen, who later authored the standard *Handbook of Federal Indian Law*, developed a set of criteria the government used in deciding difficult jurisdictional cases. Until the BIA created the 1978 regulations, the "Cohen Criteria" were the primary templates officials used when determining Interior Department jurisdiction. According to Cohen, the department's criteria were based on the limited case law on the matter and past federal policies. The Supreme Court decision *Montoya v. United States* (1901) was particularly salient.[13]

The *Montoya* case arose under the Indian Depredation Act of 1891 and involved the Mescalero Apache Tribe of New Mexico and local businessmen. In the late 1800s E. Montoya and Sons of Socorro, New Mexico, sued the Mescalero Apache Tribe for damages their company incurred during a raid conducted by Victorio's Band in 1880, an event that would prove to be one of the last of the Indian "wars" in the American West. At issue was whether the Mescalero Apache Tribe was liable for the deeds of Victorio's Band or whether his group had acted as a separate and distinct body or tribe. In deciding that the band had in fact acted independently, the Court handed down a common law definition of "tribe." According to the justices: "by 'tribe' we understand a body of Indians of the same or similar race, united in a community under one leadership or government, and inhabiting a particular though sometimes ill-defined territory."[14] The *Montoya* definition of tribe, although somewhat vague and imprecise, would be the primary common law definition of the concept used by the Interior Department during the 1930s and early 1940s. As revealed here, to white officials a tribe was a political unit living under leaders who controlled and directed the community's behavior.

While relying on the Mescalero case, the "Cohen Criteria" also included both political and ethnological factors in determining tribal status under the IRA. As Cohen noted, his office decided cases of "special difficulty" by looking at several factors: whether the group had treaty relations with the United States, whether the group had been denominated a tribe by an act of Congress or executive order, whether the group had been treated as having collective rights to lands or funds, whether the group was treated as a tribe by other tribes, and whether the group exercised political authority over its members via a tribal council or other government. Interior lawyers also considered whether the federal government had extended special appropriations for the group in question. Additionally, BIA officials examined the Indian group's social solidarity and considered other ethnological and historical considerations that Cohen did not list. The "Cohen Criteria" thus contained a combination of legal precedent and ill-defined historical and anthropological methodology and concepts. Significantly, Interior Department lawyers never made clear the weight afforded to each factor.[15]

In debating existing Indian groups, however, Interior Department lawyers came to realize that the central categories and concepts of "tribes" and "recognition" were not easily demarcated. Felix Cohen noted that the term "tribe" was used in both an ethnological and political sense. Some ethnological tribes such as the Sioux (Lakota) with the same culture and language had been divided into separate political "tribes" for administrative purposes. These ethnological tribes are more properly referred to as nations or peoples sharing a common identity, language, and cultural sense of themselves as a people. In other cases, for administrative convenience federal officials combined separate ethnological tribes or peoples such as the Umatilla, Cayuse, and Walla Walla peoples of Oregon to form a single political "tribe." Units like these were now federally recognized tribes yet had no historical existence as "tribes" previously.[16] Interestingly, in this case an individual could be a member of two "tribes" simultaneously yet be a member of only one federally recognized one.

As revealed in the Umatilla case and numerous others, federal officials had clearly created "tribes" that had not existed before from assortments of ethnic groups or family-centered bands. Despite this fact, during the New Deal the BIA announced a legal principle that has affected current acknowledgment policy. Interior Department lawyers stated that tribes had to have an unbroken existence in order to be recognized as semi-sovereign entities. Federal lawyers thus promoted the legal fiction that all presently exiting tribes had had a continuous existence since time immemorial. To be recognized a tribe not only had to exist in the present but also had to have always existed. As Cohen remarked, "It is not enough to show that any of the foregoing elements existed at some time in the remote past." A group may well "pass out of existence" voluntarily and cease to exist as a recognizable tribal unit.[17] If this occurred, a tribe was gone forever, at least to federal officials.

Many principals announced during this era were fraught with conceptual difficulties. It was never clear how to decide whether a tribe's extinction was voluntary, or how to determine if the band in question was really extinct. And although Cohen had declared that a tribe must be a political unit and not a "mere" voluntary association or society, delineating between these concepts was never simple. The fine distinction between a "voluntary" grouping and a "political" tribal unit has never been satisfactorily worked out. Since the 1930s this vague distinction has been used numerous times, however, to deny the tribal status of groups with Indian heritage.[18]

With these procedures announced, the BIA recognized several Indian groups from 1935 until World War II. Yet the Indian Service often applied the "Cohen Criteria" in an arbitrary and inconsistent manner. This was almost inevitable in light of the vague and subjective distinctions the criteria contained. In reality, how were outsiders to adequately determine whether a group followed a set of leaders or possessed a sense of social solidarity? Determinations thus often hinged on the perceived level of assimilation of the group in question, racial issues, finances, or opinions whether the group needed wardship—not necessarily on the merits of a group's tribal identity or status. In one case the Indian Service declined to allow the Shinnecocks and Poosepatucks of New York to organize as federal tribes on the basis that a researcher determined that the two tribes were too intermarried with blacks, despite the fact that both groups lived on centuries-old state Indian reservations on Long Island. In another instance government anthropologists took skull measurements and determined that twenty-two individuals from several Lumbee families were "half bloods" able to organize under the act, yet some of their direct siblings, incredibly, were not able to do so. John Collier and the Indian Service also denied recognition to many Chippewa and Ottawa bands in Michigan for the simple reason that federal funds were thin during the Great Depression.[19]

Collier's administration, however, did foster a fairly favorable climate toward acknowledging tribes and federal trust responsibilities compared to the preceding decades. On the positive side his office established written criteria for acknowledging tribes, although its application of them continued the inconsistent recognition policies of the past. Studying the record of the 1930s, a BIA official found little consistency in many of these cases beyond reliance on precedents such as the existence of trust lands, treaties, or continuing federal services. Because of their emphasis on precedent, Solicitor's Office lawyers and Congress continued to reject the aspirations of eastern Indians, although they did acknowledge at least twenty-one previously omitted groups who lived mostly in the American West.[20] Significantly, the Indian Office did not widely research whether a group had ceased to exist in earlier decades or test the limits of Cohen's criteria regarding political and social cohesion. Often it seemed enough that a group exhibited characteristics of an Indian tribe and not that it had always existed as a tribal unit since time immemorial. The era of actively acknowledging tribes and federal trust responsibility was brief, however, and died during World War II.[21]

As the political climate swung against tribalism after 1945, federal policy once again worked against recognizing additional Indian tribes. Caught up in the growing Cold War hysteria of the time, many Americans again viewed Indians as aliens and even equated tribalism with communism and anti-Americanism. After World War II both liberal and conservative policymakers thus joined forces ostensibly to "liberate" Indians from the yokes of communal tribal living, hoping to "free" the Indians to compete as equal citizens of the country. As part of this plan, Congress passed a resolution calling for the eventual termination of reservations and the special legal status of Indian tribes. Legislators also took steps to relocate Indians to urban areas. Not surprisingly, until the policy waned in the early 1960s, federal officials refused to acknowledge additional Indian tribes. Congress did investigate the status of many reservation tribes, however, in hopes of terminating them. And between 1945 and 1960 Congress terminated over one hundred Indian tribes and small bands, actions that left them in the same legal status as unacknowledged Indian groups.[22]

As a complimentary program to termination, the federal government also established the Indian Claims Commission, a forum that encouraged several unrecognized groups to mobilize in pursuit of land claims during an otherwise dismal era for Native Americans.[23] Despite its goals, however, the termination program ultimately backfired on its supporters. Instead of ending tribalism, the government's agenda actually served to spawn increased Indian activism and tribal activity. Faced with a concerted threat, Indian leaders demanded a change in federal emphasis, with Red Power activists and pan-Indian organizations such as the National Congress of American Indians (NCAI) and the National Indian Youth Council (NIYC) vocally rejecting the idea that Indian cultures and tribalism were obsolete and dying. As LaDonna Harris, a Comanche leader of the Americans for Indian Opportunity, told Congress, Indians were tired of the government "telling us everyday of our lives that there is no value in our languages, no value in our customs, no value in our culture."[24] In response to Indian demands, the direction of federal Indian policy oscillated once more, this time toward acknowledging federal duties to indigenous peoples. With a new acceptance of cultural pluralism developing, the 1960s would prove an emergent decade for unrecognized Indians.

During the 1960s there was once again considerable public sympathy for the "First Americans" and a pervasive public guilt for crimes committed against indigenous peoples. Along with the blossoming appreciation of Indian culture, a growing number of individuals came out of hiding, expressing newfound pride in their Indian ancestry and heritage. Over the coming decades a greater number of individuals began identifying themselves as Indians in various realms.[25]

Ironically, the detrimental termination policies of the 1950s had a beneficial impact on unrecognized tribes. Suddenly, terminated, relocated, and non-acknowledged Indians all found themselves in the same boat, lacking federal status and access to many federal Indian programs and services provided to Indians on reservations. By the mid-1960s federal bureaucrats began to see these groups in the same light as well, with unrecognized Indians finally becoming a focus of Lyndon Johnson's Great Society anti-poverty programs along with other minorities left out of the "American dream."

Having taken notice, the Johnson administration discovered a fairly bleak picture existed for all off-reservation Indians. In 1966 a presidential task force reported that over 90,000 Indians in the eastern United States, 41 terminated bands in California, and over 200,000 urban Indians struggled without the benefit of federal Indian programs. The task force noted that these Indian peoples often went unnoticed and unidentified as Indians and were worse off than other Native Americans, both economically and psychologically. To alleviate the poverty of these Indians, federal officials instigated a plethora of new programs outside the BIA. New Indian-oriented offices in the Office of Economic Opportunity (OEO) and later within the Office of Indian Education in the Department of Health, Education and Welfare (HEW) had liberal eligibility criteria that encompassed many unacknowledged groups. By strengthening tribal programs, these offices helped neglected tribes such as the Pascua Yaquis and Tiguas while aiding 108 reservation communities as well.[26]

Although assimilation ideologies lingered in Washington, the new federal programs were now encouraging Indian identity and tribalism while admitting the Indians' right to exist in modern America. The promise of self-sufficiency and self-government meant that securing tribal acknowledgment once again was a positive goal, and slowly unrecognized communities mobilized. As the 1970s progressed, a range of new War on Poverty programs had broken the BIA's monopoly on Indian affairs, while rising education levels, community action programs, and federally funded legal rights groups such as NARF had given unacknowledged groups such as the Gay Head Wampanoags the power and insight to demand their rights and equality as Indians.[27]

Beyond federal incentives and programs, unrecognized, urban, and terminated Indians increasingly joined pan-Indian organizations such as the American Indian Movement (AIM) and NIYC to raise public awareness of Indian issues. In dramatic protests from California to Massachusetts, these groups modeled their activities on the black civil rights movement, joining in the Poor People's Campaign and uniting across tribal lines as well as Indian status demarcations. Indian activists electrified the nation by seizing Alcatraz Island, sacking the BIA offices, mounting protests at Mount Rushmore, and laying siege to Wounded Knee in South Dakota. Members of unrecognized Indian groups were involved in dozens of protests. Nonfederal groups such as the Stillaguamish resisted state regulation and pressed for treaty fishing rights in numerous "fish-ins" in the Pacific Northwest, activities that often resulted in violent confrontations and arrests along with national publicity for their cause. On the East Coast, Wampanoag activist Frank James and others joined with AIM leader Russell Means to disrupt Thanksgiving Day celebrations, at one event seizing the *Mayflower* and dumping Pilgrim dummies overboard to remind non-Indians of the settlers' devastating impact on eastern tribes.[28]

Beyond high-profile Red Power protests, many unrecognized Indian groups also organized with the help of scholars and legal aid groups. Many of these collaborations began in 1961 when anthropologist Sol Tax of the University of Chicago and the NCAI sponsored the Chicago Indian Conference. For the first time isolated and powerless eastern groups had a forum to express their concerns while gaining exposure to the larger Indian world. Afterward NCAI leader Vine Deloria Jr. took steps to reach out and help unacknowledged tribes in the South and on the East Coast. By the early 1970s Deloria and the Center for American Indian Law, John Echohawk's Native American Rights Fund, and the Coalition of Eastern Native Americans (CENA), a newly formed organization of non–federally recognized Indians, began actively promoting Louisiana's Tunica-Biloxi Tribe and other neglected Indian communities. CENA, in particular, under the inspiring leadership of Lumbee W. J. Strickland, emerged as the leading voice for nonrecognized eastern Indians by the early 1970s.[29]

The stirring of nonfederal tribes did not please all Native Americans, however. As early as the 1960s a schism emerged between recognized tribes and groups such as CENA, with many acknowledged tribes turning a skeptical eye toward their estranged cousins. Many tribes feared the sheer economic impact of these groups on "Indian only" funds. As the NCAI leadership warned, "CENA's astronomic growth, aided by federal and foundations funding, and their high profile and vocal leadership, [has] caused great concern and opposition among many western tribal leaders."[30] As the eastern nonrecognized tribes rose, anthropologist Hiram Gregory recalled being accused of "hunting" and resurrecting dead Indian tribes, a pursuit many tribal leaders disdained.

By the end of the decade the stage was set for a crisis in Indian Country over the issue of tribal recognition and the rising eastern groups. Alarm mounted as organizations such as the 18,000-member Creek Nation East of the Mississippi began seeking the return of long-lost tribal lands and access to BIA Indian programs. Most disturbing to some conservative reservation tribes was the 40,000-member Lumbee tribe of North Carolina. Although the Lumbees at one point heroically faced down the Ku Klux Klan, their African heritage and apparent lack of major Indian cultural traits engendered a racialized form of resistance from some members of the Indian community. Many reservation tribes and non-Indians simply did not accept them or similar groups as Indian peoples.[31] Of course, the rejection hurt unrecognized people. Tchinouk Karleen McKenzie of Oregon expressed her feelings this way: "Being non-federally recognized has many social problems. In my own life-time being shunned started at an early age; not being chosen to represent or participate was and always will be the hardest hurt. 'What kind of Indian are you?' would be asked, but the answer was never listened to. We were treated as 'joke' people."[32]

Although opposed by some Native Americans, many groups pressed forward anyway, working to secure the federal assistance and status they believed was vital to their continuing survival. Lacking federal protections, all unacknowledged groups were in a precarious position to survive amid myriad changes taking place in modern America. Beyond failing to qualify for BIA programs, unacknowledged groups lacked federally protected trust lands or reservations that were exempt from local taxation. Without reservations, all nonfederal Indians lacked the ability to operate tribal governments independent of local laws and control.

Beyond these material issues, a sense of pride and a feeling of injustice fired most unrecognized Indians. Unacknowledged Indian leaders were incensed over what they saw as their second-class status and sought recognition as a way to affirm their Indianness to both other Native peoples and to the dominant society. Mattaponi leader Curtis Custalow of Virginia phrased his motivation this way: "[we] have been robbed of [our] identity by the federal government. . . . the non-federally recognized Indians want reaffirmation of their identity."[33] Most unacknowledged groups simply felt like second-class Indians facing discrimination and skepticism at all turns. "From colonial times to present," argued Aurelius Piper, Chief Big Eagle of the Golden Hill Paugussett Reservation in Connecticut, "we believe we have the right to be federally recognized and not be discriminated against. We ask only for our identity, services in education, and health."[34]

Taken as a whole, these once obscure tribes' demands sparked increasingly acrimonious debates in Indian Country over the racial composition, Indianness, and sheer size of these groups. Realizing there was no central definition of Indians for federal agencies among several hundred programs serving Indian peoples, federal tribes and policymakers soon realized that something needed to be done to clarify exactly who was an "Indian" for BIA purposes.[35]

Between 1975 and 1977 the crisis over tribal recognition came to a head. By that time several federal court cases and one congressional commission highlighted the need for federal officials to develop a consistent acknowledgment policy. When the federal circuit issued its opinion in the first court case, *United States v. Washington*, in 1974, officials at the Bureau of Indian Affairs clearly were alarmed. According to the judge, Indian tribes who descended from the signatories of several nineteenth-century federal treaties were entitled to half of the commercial fish harvest of the state of Washington. Germane to the acknowledgment issue, the judge also determined that two tribes the BIA considered nonrecognized entities, the Stillaguamish and the Upper Skagits, did have federal treaty rights nonetheless because they had "maintained an organized political structure."[36] Amid an ugly backlash that witnessed demonstrations proclaiming "Shoot the Indians" and a scramble to abrogate Indian treaties, bureau officials had an epiphany: the federal courts would decide issues of tribal existence for them, if only for the limited purpose of treaty fishing rights. In this unstable environment the Stillaguamish and several other groups also were pursuing full administrative acknowledgment within BIA channels, and it was unclear what effect the court ruling would have on the bureau's deliberations. At the same time Interior Department officials soon realized the potential ramifications of similar court rulings on tribal fishing and hunting rights in Minnesota and Michigan where similar battles raged. In essence, despite the BIA's position that some groups were no longer tribes under its administration, the *United States v. Washington* case alerted the bureau that nonreservation Indians did have rights that federal courts would confirm in the coming era.[37]

Also during the early 1970s, on the opposite end of the country a second case winding its way through the federal court system would have an even greater impact on federal acknowledgment policy and the urgency of the situation. In 1972 the Passamaquoddy and Penobscot Indians, two tribes living on forested state reservations in Maine (and not acknowledged by the federal government), quietly brought suit in U.S. District Court. Non-Indians in the state were shocked to find that the two tribes were claiming a territory representing two-thirds of the state, lands worth hundreds of millions of dollars. With the help of NARF and a local attorney, Tom Tureen, the tribes held that most of the state of Maine was illegally transferred by their ancestors to the state in a treaty executed in 1794. In a brilliant insight Tureen litigated under the little remembered Indian Nonintercourse Act of 1790, legislation that prohibited states from purchasing Indian lands without congressional approval. The tribes believed that since Congress was not consulted in 1794, the treaty between Maine and the Indians was thus null and void. In the proceedings the Passamaquoddy and Penobscots also sued the federal government for failing to act on behalf of the tribes. State and federal lawyers countered that the 1790 law did not protect unacknowledged tribes such as the Passamaquoddy and Penobscots. Although at first many observers viewed the case as a long shot, the District Court startled non-Indians by ruling in favor of the tribes. According to the decision, Congress had intended the 1790 law to apply to *all tribes*, regardless of their recognized status at the time of the transaction. Suddenly, as with fishing rights, it was apparent that nonrecognized tribes had land rights under federal law as long as they still existed as viable communities.[38]

To property-conscious Americans, the Passamaquoddy action and subsequent cases were disturbing, eventually causing an uproar as thousands of land owners now feared losing their homes to groups claiming to be Indians, peoples they believed were pretending to be members of long-extinct tribes or, in the alternative, were suddenly grasping and greedy. Reflecting these opinions, a Midwesterner wrote the BIA: "Why do the present-day Indians think they own all the land and water in North America? They are no more entitled to all the benefits the government has given them than the rest of the people."[39] On the Washington coast, fishermen were now crying that Indians were "super citizens" taking advantage of unfortunate sportsmen and working people. Most Americans simply did not comprehend the legal claims of the rising Indian groups. The Interior Department and BIA did, however, and Indian officials were becoming more and more alarmed at the implications of their department's lack of clear policies and standards for recognizing tribes. At the same time forgotten Indian enclaves recognized their moment as well. Within a short time the BIA saw a rapid increase in the number of petitions for acknowledgment coming into its offices. In a few years the number of groups swelled from a handful to over forty.[40]

In the midst of these developments a land case involving the unacknowledged Mashpee Wampanoags of Cape Cod was before the federal court in Massachusetts. It would also affect the number of petitioners seeking recognition via the Bureau of Indian Affairs. Now aware of the seriousness of Indian claims under the Nonintercourse Acts, defense attorneys challenged the Mashpee group on what local property owners saw as their weak point—their tribal status and thus their standing to bring suit. As interpreted by federal courts, only groups that had continuously maintained tribal relations could bring suit for remedies that flowed to a communal or tribal body rather than to individuals. Because a positive determination from the bureau would give them standing in court, the Mashpee desired to stay the proceedings until the BIA made a determination whether they were a federal Indian tribe. Unfortunately for the Mashpee, the court denied their request and went forward, citing the fact that the BIA had not formalized its regulations and that a long delay would cause harm to hundreds of homeowners.

As the Mashpee feared, during the trial the Mashpee Wampanoags' attorneys were unable to prove to skeptical white jurists that their somewhat assimilated group had continuously existed and still comprised a modern Indian tribe.[41] Shortly before the verdict came in, an astute writer for *Akwesasne Notes* declared: "the courts appear to be about to affirm that cultural genocide, successfully pursued, can provide a legal basis for the denial of rights to a people as a Native people."[42] As it played out, the Mashpee case revealed that non-expert juries would have trouble dealing with the complexities of ethnic identity and tribalism. It thus spawned more BIA petitions for acknowledgment because, beyond other benefits, an administrative determination would establish a group's legal standing to bring suit and avoid messy court proceedings like the Mashpee case.

Faced with what it saw as a "deluge" of new petitions, the Department of the Interior issued a moratorium on acknowledging additional tribes at this time. One victim of the freeze was the tiny Stillaguamish Tribe of western Washington. Led by Esther Ross, a seventy-two-year-old veteran of fish-ins and civil rights campaigns, the Stillaguamish were recognized as a tribal body possessing communal fishing rights in the *United States v. Washington* case in 1975. By the middle of 1976, however, the group's petition for full acknowledgment had languished for several years amid the "white tape" of the BIA—despite the recommendations of its BIA area office and the commissioner of Indian affairs that the group should be recognized. Ross's people were caught in a common Catch-22. Federal officials had previously denied acknowledging the band in its quest for status because it lacked a reservation land base, yet when a Stillaguamish elder sought to will his land to the tribe, he was denied because there was no legal entity or tribe to which to deed the land.

Faced with this logic, the tribe sued in federal court in 1976, seeking to prompt the secretary of the interior to rule on its case. Although aided by the NCAI and the Small Tribes Organization of Western Washington (STOWW), the Stillaguamish faced stiff opposition from the neighboring Tulalip Tribes, who questioned the Stillaguamish's legitimacy, although fears over fishing competition lay just below the surface. In September of 1976 the district court ruled that the Interior Department's two-year delay was "arbitrary and capricious" and ordered the secretary to act within thirty days on the Stillaguamish petition. The Indian Office thereafter stepped up plans to establish administrative procedures for recognizing Indian tribes to stave off potentially "endless litigation" over the issue.[43]

At the same time the American Indian Policy Review Commission (AIPRC) was holding hearings of its own to deal with the status and claims of unacknowledged tribes. Prompted by AIM's violent occupation and standoff with the FBI at Wounded Knee in 1973, Congress created the AIPRC, hoping it would provide sweeping mandates for reforming federal Indian policy. Although it fell far short of these lofty goals, the commission did have an impact on recognition policy. Significantly, two of its five Indian commissioners represented nonreservation Indians: one was a member of an urban Indian organization, and one represented nonfederal tribes. Congress actually created an entire task force to deal with terminated and non–federally recognized Indians. With the forceful voices of Lumbee commissioner Adolph Dial within the commission and Passamaquoddy John Stevens, Lumbee Jo Jo Hunt, and attorney Tom Tureen, unacknowledged groups for the first time held significant stature and access to power in federal politics.[44]

Debates surrounding the role of unacknowledged and urban Indians on the commission, however, ultimately strangled its effectiveness and, sadly, presaged controversies that would plague the FAP to the present day. The National Tribal Chairmen's Association (NTCA) went so far as to sue in federal court over the representation on the commission, arguing that the nonreservation commissioners were not "among the mainstream" of Indians in America and that traditional Indians had been largely left out of the process.

Amid bitter recriminations, the NTCA noted that the suit was necessary to "protect the interests of the federally recognized land-based tribes." [45] As it played out, the issue of recognition became one of the principal reasons for tribal opposition to the AIPRC.

The AIPRC task force had positive effects, however, as it held numerous hearings across the nation that helped mobilize unacknowledged Indian groups from Boston to Baton Rouge. Its final volume on terminated and non–federally recognized groups was a stinging chastisement of past policy that helped publicize the plight of nonfederal Indians by highlighting several of the most egregious group histories. Citing "murky precedents, quirky administration, indefensible bureaucratic decisions, and accidents of history," the task force position argued: "Non-recognition is incomprehensible to Indians who have been neglected and forgotten; the BIA has no authority to refuse services to any member of the Indian population." The task force concluded that the Department of the Interior had the "obligation to recognize all tribes." [46] Significantly, the policy commission did not define what a tribe was, however.

Despite controversies, the commission ultimately influenced BIA acknowledgment policy. In 1977 the AIPRC's final recommendation spawned several bills proposed by South Dakota senator James Abourezk that sought to establish congressional procedures for recognizing tribes. Significantly, the proposed legislation was far more inclusive than the ultimate BIA criteria and likely would have resulted in more unrecognized tribes gaining status much more quickly. In essence these proposals established a statutory basis for recognizing tribes and called for Congress to establish an independent office within the Department of the Interior to avoid any conflict of interest with the BIA. In a major concession, the bills largely placed the burden of proof on the Interior Department to show that a petitioning tribe failed to meet a set of criteria. Under Abourezk's legislation the proposed "Office of Acknowledgment" would examine whether a group met only two criteria: that group members had been identified as Indians since 1934 (the date of the Indian Reorganization Act), and that it had evidence of longstanding tribal political influence or authority. If the office determined that the group met these two criteria, the petitioner need only establish one other criterion among five categories. If groups could show they once possessed treaties, legislative acts, or executive orders related to them, this evidence would be prima facie proof of the existence of these groups as tribes. It was then up to the special office to prove that they had not continuously existed as tribal units after these federal acts. The AIPRC proposals also required the special office to pay for petitions and provide technical assistance.[47]

At hearings on these bills, Acting Assistant Secretary of Indian Affairs Rick Lavis and an assortment of recognized tribes strongly opposed the legislation. Put simply, the BIA objected to losing control to an independent commission and to shouldering the burden of acknowledgment cases, a burden that recognized its culpability for failing to protect these tribes in the past. The department similarly rejected the proposed prima facie assumption that groups previously acknowledged had continued to exist unless proven otherwise.[48] Although NARF, Tom Tureen, and many unacknowledged groups such as the Houmas, the Tunica-Biloxis, and several Michigan groups supported Abourezk's bills, the NCAI voted to oppose the legislation. The NCTA also rejected the legislative proposals as too liberal, saying, "we believe that any criteria must be both strict and comprehensive as to specific determinants."[49] With the BIA weighing in that the special office would waste personnel, the opposition carried the day. The bills failed to pass into law. Clearly, the bureau and its constituents did not want to surrender acknowledgment decisions to an independent commission.

Faced with a threat to its hegemony, the bureau seized the reins. The BIA set out to formulate criteria for judging "tribes" eligible for federal acknowledgment, charging attorney Scott Keep and bureau employee John Shapard with taking all the suggestions, court tests, and the myriad political implications into account to produce standardized regulations. When considering criteria, Keep and Shapard were aware of the potential financial impact on the bureau as well as the ramifications of future acknowledgment decisions on Indian land and fishing rights cases and local governments. In 1977 the two developed proposed rules using Felix Cohen's work as a principal guide. According to Shapard, they designed regulations that could "bend" to individual tribal experiences while providing uniform and objective procedures for all. Published 16 June 1977, the original Department of the Interior regulations were significant (along with Abourezk's proposed legislation) because the initial proposals were "entirely" revised upon what one department official described as "intense interest" from the states and recognized tribes. Before objections came in, the proposed rules were more liberal, omitting requirements that petitioners demonstrate a continuous history of political leadership and outside identification of their Indianness.[50]

A major source of objections came from the NCAI and NTCA, which were wary of any inclusive criteria for acknowledging tribes. These organizations demanded a say on the issue. For their part, members of the NCAI rejected what they saw as the American Indian Policy Review Commission's "Open Door Liberalism" that many believed would provide recognition to all groups and to "the more-the-merrier" liberals who maintained that all who claimed to be Indian should be recognized. The NCAI made tribal recognition one of the two major platforms of its 1977 annual convention in Dallas along with the growing anti-Indian backlash sparked in part by the land claims of unacknowledged Indian groups. Not all NCAI members supported the majority view, however, as former executive director Vine Deloria Jr. reportedly tried to paint the NCAI as pawns of the federal establishment, arguing that reservation tribes were simply refusing to share their resources with their less fortunate Indian brothers.[51]

Whether some tribes were greedy or not, tribal acknowledgment struck at the heart of Indian identity, and Native peoples were highly concerned about its implications. A leader of the NTCA summed up the opinion of many reservation tribes: "Since the enactment of Title IV of the Indian Education Act there has been a dangerous broadening of the definition of Indians so that persons of up to 1/124 degree of Indian blood have self-identified as Indian and have received services from the Office of Indian Education—such abuses are unconscionable."[52] As this comment revealed, many conservative tribes accepted blood quantum as a true measure of Indianness. Yakima chairperson Leonard Tomaskin wanted the government to acknowledge only "bona fide" tribes with members having at least one-quarter Indian blood and also having retained their cultures, traditions, and languages. From their vantage point the Yakimas and other western tribes feared diluting the cultural and racial significance of Indian status and identity via any proposed inclusive criteria.[53]

In debates over recognition policy, racial and cultural arguments lay just below the surface. Yet, in public, reservation leaders focused on two concerns: funding and sovereignty. Despite having recently won significant legal victories in areas of fishing and land rights, tribal sovereignty, and self-determination, these gains seemed insecure with the specter of white backlash ever lurking. In 1977 a Washington State congressman introduced a bill called the "Native Americans Equal Opportunity Act" that promised to give Indians the dubious opportunity to "abrogate all treaties entered into by the United States with Indian tribes in order to accomplish the purposes of recognizing that in the United States no individual or group possesses subordinate or special rights."[54] Although it failed to pass, the measure raised concerns about a return to termination ideology. At the same time groups of Native Hawaiians, Latin American Indians, and eastern Indian communities were all hoping to gain federal recognition, developments that worried some tribes. Although not ideologically opposed to the efforts of these peoples, Lakota scholar Sam Deloria urged caution in drafting recognition rules. "There is no doubt that the budgetary impact [will] be tremendous; the recognition of a large number of small tribes would involve a very serious budgetary impact," argued Deloria.[55]

Beyond a loss of funding, tribal leaders also feared a diminution of the significance of their recent hard-won gains in tribal sovereignty if questionable groups became acknowledged. From the reservation perspective, tribes faced an erosion of tribal sovereignty once lawmakers and the general public came to view recently recognized groups as mere social clubs rather than governments with inherent rights. In 1978 outspoken NCAI president Veronica Murdock, a Mohave Indian from Arizona, summed up the feelings of many reservation-based tribes: "we need to secure a process under which those tribes that are valid tribes are recognized by the federal government, however we must make sure that the proper safeguards are incorporated in policy and law to protect the sovereign status of tribes."[56]

Because the proposed BIA rule-making process was such a major issue, the NCAI and the United Southeastern Tribes (USET) called a conference on recognition in Nashville in 1978, inviting BIA officials as well as dozens of unacknowledged Indian communities. The conference was funded by the BIA, and other interested parties included Sam Deloria, the Center for Indian Law, and CENA under Poarch Creek chair Eddie Tullis.[57] Of the 143 tribes in the NCAI, 62 attended the conference along with representatives of unrecognized Indian communities from various regions in the United States. Ultimately the Indian groups reached a consensus and presented their views as twelve principles on tribal recognition to the BIA. Although many unacknowledged groups such as the Narragansetts of Rhode Island attended the NCAI conference, the vast majority of unacknowledged groups lacked voting rights in the organization.[58] At the meeting reservation tribes generally demanded that hopeful tribes provide documentary evidence supplied by white society. As the straight-talking Murdock told the unacknowledged groups present, "I think we cannot get caught up in say the long lost relative concept, because we do not know you, we do not know you so you must let us know who you are. From my reservation we know who we are." Revealing the bent of tribal leaders, Murdock went on to say, "I think we would like explicit information, explicit documentation." Apparently stinging from Vine Deloria's criticism, Murdock joked, "We are not pawns of the federal government. And if we are, then we're very cheaply paid.

We are not greedy [but] we are protective. I think we're protective of what is rightfully ours."[59]

Throughout the recognition debates reservation tribes expressed a strong desire to decide which groups joined their ranks. As one tribal delegate put it, "It is the responsibility and the right of us who have sacrificed much to preserving this Indian way of life who are obliged to determine whether or not our relatives shall be recognized as Indian people. It is not the United States government who is going to grant recognition to these people, it is we."[60] Many Indian leaders clearly feared losing control over defining themselves to either the federal courts or Congress, institutions controlled and dominated by whites. "We don't need Congress to tell us who an Indian is," Yakima leader Leonard Tomaskin said at the time.[61] Other Indians did not want the federal courts involved either. As Mashpee Wampanoag president Russell Peters warned his associates, "[we must] become aware in our own minds . . . what a tribe is in order that we can control that definition."[62] Further complicating the issue, however, many unrecognized communities did not desire the potentially biased recognized tribes to decide acknowledgment cases either.

Realizing their dependence on BIA funding and the opposition to their alleged bias on acknowledgment issues, the reservation tribes of the NCAI opted to support the BIA in its bid to assume hegemony in the recognition arena. At the time members of recognized tribes held considerable power within the Indian Bureau. Due to Indian preference provisions, Indians made up the majority of the BIA employees in the late 1970s, a percentage rising to 80 percent by the 1990s. They increasingly set policy under federal self-determination programs. As defined in various statutes and internal policies, Indian preference applied only to members of recognized tribes or people with at least one-half certified Indian blood. With their power in the BIA, recognized tribes believed that their interests and voice would best be represented if the acknowledgment decisions remained within the bureau.[63]

Believing there was a consensus on the issue in 1978, the NCAI submitted its principles on tribal recognition to the BIA while lobbying against congressional solutions. Significantly, the NCAI principles did not specify what criteria should be used to define tribes, only that they "must be based on ethnological, historical, legal and political evidence."[64] Years later, Eastern Cherokee principal chief Jonathan Taylor and Quinault president Joe De la Cruz testified that all sides agreed to the resulting FAP criteria. Perhaps naiveté, a lack of power, or a faith in the ability of the BIA to apply the criteria liberally in their favor led many nonfederal groups to support the BIA proposals. In any case most were optimistic that the new FAP rules would solve the vexing acknowledgment dilemmas of the past.[65]

Although there were heated differences of opinion on the definition of tribalism, legal scholars and tribes agreed that the federal-tribal relationship was a political one. Most parties believed that the regulations should not acknowledge associations, organizations, corporations, or groups of Indian descendents who had no history as peoples. In general, there was a consensus that federal tribes should possess some degree of Indian descent, maintain some form of political authority, live in an area or community, and have identified themselves consistently as Indians.[66] Although this all sounded good in theory, few realized how difficult it would be to decipher the fine distinctions embedded within these concepts.

Despite an ongoing debate concerning the executive branch's authority to decide recognition cases, the Department of the Interior proceeded to publish final acknowledgement criteria on 1 June 1978.[67] These became effective in fall of that year and provided seven mandatory criteria petitioning groups must meet to be acknowledged. Because Congress had deferred to the interests of reservation tribes and the BIA by not passing legislation, the FAP would be a regulatory, not statutory, process. [68] By the end of 1978 the bureau established its Federal Acknowledgment Project office, later renamed the Branch of Acknowledgment and Research, to decide on the issue.

Rejecting the more inclusive, liberal congressional options, the BIA set strict rules for acknowledging tribes that were based on past precedent, case law, and scholarly and indigenous understandings of tribalism. In doing so it also created a rigorous, document-driven process that is largely used today. With few exceptions, the seven mandatory criteria established what came to be the threshold to Indian tribal status and access to federal Indian services, supplanting congressional and judicial determinations on the issue; significantly, the burden of proof rested with the petitioners. Failure to prove any point would result in the rejection of the group's aspirations for tribal status. Although later modified, the seven criteria in essence required groups to prove by a preponderance of the evidence that (a) the petitioner has been identified historically and continuously until the present as "American Indian"; (b) a substantial portion of the group inhabits a specific region or lives in a community viewed as American Indian, distinct from other populations, and that its members are descendants of an Indian tribe that historically inhabited a particular area; (c) the petitioner has maintained historical and essentially continuous tribal political influence or other authority over its members. The petitioner also had to (d) furnish a copy of the group's present governing document, (e) possess a membership list of individuals who could establish descent from a tribe that existed historically, and prove that (f) the membership of the group is composed principally of persons who are not members of any other Indian tribe; and finally (g) the petitioner is not subject to congressional legislation that has terminated or forbidden the federal relationship.[69]

Having replaced the previously inconsistent and often politically influenced recognition procedures, the BIA contended that its new process would be objective but exacting. As Deputy Commissioner of Indian Affairs Patrick Hayes later argued, "[we are] committed to assuring a fair, thorough, and expeditious review of petitions—at the same time, [our] process must protect the sovereignty of existing recognized tribes."[70] Many tribes were satisfied with the new process and echoed the feelings of Tulalip tribal chairman Stan Jones when he noted, "the acknowledgment regulations [should] be interpreted and applied in a stringent fashion, denying groups that . . . are not by any stretch of the imagination within the common understanding of the meaning of the term 'Indian tribe.' "[71] In 1978 all parties had high hopes for the nascent program.

At the end of the 1970s the controversies of the era combined with the interest of recognized tribes and the BIA to yield the Federal Acknowledgment Process. As the circumstances surrounding their birth indicate, the 1978 criteria represented Indian power and self-determination at work, as the final rules were designed to limit the number of federal tribes while protecting the interests of reservation tribes and the BIA in the realms of culture, federal Indian funding, and treaty rights. The regulations also were geared toward presenting an image of exactness and objectivity to anti-Indian forces seeking to erode Indian sovereignty. In time, however, this stringent process would stress all nonfederal groups.

In 1978, however, the new procedures seemed destined to straighten the road to acknowledgment, a route once laced with switchbacks and dead ends. Before that date federal acknowledgment policy had traveled a serpentine path for over two hundred years, evolving through periods when federal officials negotiated treaties with unambiguous sovereign Indian nations, through decades of active tribal suppression and non-acknowledgment, and finally toward acknowledging long forgotten Indian communities. Tribal acknowledgment had often been political, arbitrary, or subjective prior to 1978. The BIA process thus emerged purporting to be objective, expert, and nonpolitical while representing the interests of its membership: recognized tribes. Federal dependency and hegemony, however, dictated that the bureau would have the final say. Having set these difficult criteria, the BIA could thus stand back and declare its process was scientific, unbiased, and fair.

As the program unfolded, by and large, unacknowledged groups such as the Gay Head Wampanoags grew to resent having the burden of proving their identity, while the economic and political realities consistently demanded that they do so. After a long-fought battle with the BAR, the Gay Head community overcame a negative initial finding in 1987 and gained federal status once and for all. The tribe was overjoyed when a settlement agreement returned over four hundred acres to the community, ending the contentious land dispute that had started the whole process. In time the Wampanoags and Jacqueline Kennedy Onassis also reached a compromise, and the Indians and landowners began to accommodate each other on the small island. Even with their eventual success, however, the experience made many tribal members bitter toward the BIA.[72] In a larger sense, however, the Wampanoag people were part of a greater development. By asserting their identity and pressing their rights as Native peoples, the Gay Head tribe and dozens of other forgotten eastern Indians had forced federal officials to develop procedures for recognizing federal-tribal relationships long neglected by government authorities. In 1987, however, it remained to be seen whether the new process was an improvement over the old system.

TWO. BUILDING AN EDIFICE

The BIA's Federal Acknowledgment Process,
1978–2002

After starting with such high hopes, the BIA's Branch of Acknowledgment and Research was under attack at the close of the century. By 1999 the situation had become so tense that branch anthropologist Steve Austin ushered visitors into the office's secret location within the Department of the Interior Building in downtown Washington, telling stories of bomb threats and mace cans going off in the group's bathroom. A year before, one angry caller warned that branch workers would be "coming home in body bags" if his group received a negative finding. Sadly, unacknowledged groups and the BIA staff had squared off in an adversarial process that did not reflect its nobler origins. Over time the BAR team grew more and more guarded and defensive, while unacknowledged communities found their patience and resources sorely stretched by the whole complex process. Forced to use non-Indian sources to prove their identity, many petitioners were bogged down trying to confirm their tribal functioning every generation since European contact. Having spent an average of over ten years collecting data, paying experts, and waiting for a bureaucratic determination, many hopeful petitioners had grown disgusted by the government regimen. "It is not a process I would wish on anybody," reported Gay Head Wampanoag tribal president Don Widdiss in 1989, and this after gaining acknowledgment through the BIA.[1]

As the twenty-first century began, the ambiguous concepts contained in the acknowledgment criteria and the bureau's interpretation of them had generated continuously whirring controversies. A witness to over a dozen congressional hearings on the acknowledgment process would be hard pressed to come away with a positive impression of the system. The BIA, with its limited budget and concerned tribal base, had a conflict of interest in deciding the issue in an entirely timely and disinterested manner, while the steady rise of Indian gaming during the 1980s did little to help the political environment as well. By the 1990s the process had become far costlier, time-consuming, and injurious to struggling, unrecognized communities than even the most jaundiced observers predicted in 1978. Yet, as revealed here, the vocal opposition masked solid underlying support for the FAP. Although often silent, a significant number of recognized tribes, members of Congress, and concerned local non-Indian groups regularly lined up to support the strict process. To these individuals issues of Indian funding, sovereignty, and culture demanded that unacknowledged groups remain subject to the hegemony of the federal bureaucracy and its criteria for measuring Indian tribalism. "We are just less convinced than certain critics that FAP is as broken as some allege," remarked Poarch Creek leader Eddie Tullis, a successful petitioner in the process. "We do not believe it is a dismal failure."[2]

As the lines were drawn, the acrimonious debates revealed that there was a vague consensus on the criteria used in the process, yet very little real agreement on how to measure, define, and weigh the fuzzy concepts embedded in them. The ambiguity inherent in the concepts of identity, descent, community, and especially political authority meant that few parties would be completely satisfied with any proposed program. As the twenty-first century unfolded, the acknowledgment process thus remained within the bureau, subject to its hegemony over most matters pertaining to Indian affairs. Although not always living up to its stated goals of providing a consistently fair, objective, and expeditious remedy for acknowledgment cases, the FAP survived and reigned supreme over congressional and judicial recognition precisely because it functioned as it was intended: in a burdensome and restrictive manner, thus limiting the number of groups that qualified for federal recognition. While unpopular with academics and unacknowledged groups, the FAP's slow pace matched the dominant society's reluctance to acknowledge Indian tribes and its general skepticism toward nonrecognized Indian entities. As detailed here, reform efforts have proven particularly difficult in light of major federal incentives for securing tribal status. Because of its benefits, most parties continue to insist that access to the favored status remain closely guarded.

In 1978 all these controversies were in the unforeseen future. That fall John "Bud" Shapard, a long-time civil servant and head of the new BIA Federal Acknowledgment Project, gathered together surplus furniture to set up his new office. By early 1979 the FAP was up and running. Having helped create the new rules, Shapard wondered how to apply the fairly innocuous-looking regulations. As he worked them through, for a few short years the FAP enjoyed a honeymoon period when most parties had high regard for the new process.[3]

From its inception the FAP operated with between one and three "teams" consisting of an ethnohistorian, an anthropologist, and a genealogist assigned to evaluate a group's petition for veracity. In its early days the acknowledgment staff faced a real dilemma as its members embarked upon the task of deciding the legal fate of forty-three unacknowledged Indian entities whose number would grow to more than two hundred by the end of the century. Within a few years the FAP was clogged with hopeful groups that had little chance of success. In the late 1970s, for example, the Oklahoma Federation of Indian Women sought recognition as an all woman "tribe," while another group, the Moorish Science Temple, thought that it could qualify as an Indian tribe. Other groups claiming descent from an "Indian Princess" or two also entered the process after 1978. As petitioners kept coming forward, the FAP teams were overwhelmed from the start, a situation that remained constant in the coming decades.[4]

On the BAR team the ethnohistorian evaluated the petitioner's historical documentation to determine whether the group had existed continuously since first contact with whites. The anthropologist worked in conjunction with the historian to verify the group's culture, organization, and present existence while the genealogist plowed over intricate family history charts, straining eyes on faded and obscure deeds, birth records, and other government records that could indicate Indian ancestry. At the branch's inception, Bud Shapard served as project leader, and George Roth, a scholar from Tucson, was hired as anthropologist. These two would become central to the acknowledgment process in future years. Several historians and genealogists came and went in the following decades while Roth remained, and he, anthropologist Holly Reckord, and historian Virginia DeMarce would play a central role in setting the FAP's evolving standards.[5]

Overall, the process required a group to submit a petition with supporting documentation. After an initial review the FAP team would send the group an "obvious deficiency" letter, with the petitioner then submitting additional data. In the process the branch would conduct limited research on the group and then undertake a short one- or two-week field visit. It would then issue a proposed finding followed by a sometimes lengthy "comment period" where interested parties would weigh in on the proposal. Toward the end of the routine, the BIA would write a legal review and produce a final determination. Initially, the bureau estimated that the whole process would take a group two and a half years to complete, yet it generally ran three to four years even in its earliest cases. In addition to conducting limited research the FAP team provided petitioners with "technical assistance" through meetings, advice, and help with locating volunteers and funding sources.[6]

Because of its legal nature and implications, the FAP teams always worked closely with the lawyers of the Interior Department's Solicitor's Office, who conducted legal reviews of the BIA's findings. The Interior Department lawyers determined whether the FAP's proposed reports were "legally sufficient" and advised the assistant secretary of the interior for Indian affairs, the head of the BIA and final authority on the matter, to recommend or reject the FAP team's findings. Although the assistant secretary had nominal final authority, until the end of the 1990s the assistant secretary had never overruled the decisions of the FAP staff, leading many petitioners to question whether midlevel bureaucrats should have this much authority over the lives of unacknowledged Indians. Before leaving office in 2001, however, Assistant Secretary Kevin Gover did overrule the BAR teams' preliminary negative findings on several eastern groups, only to find his office under attack for not following the scholarly advice of the BAR staff.[7]

Because of a financial conflict of interest, the federal government has consistently underfunded the BAR process. Although the program has hobbled along with one to three teams, the small staff and high workload has ensured a slow pace and thus a long wait for new groups hoping to get on the acknowledged list. Overall, the lack of funding has assured that few groups will be acknowledged each year and impact the BIA's limited budget. Deputy Assistant Secretary Hazel Elbert admitted to this fact in 1988: "An upsurge in completed petitions has far outstripped the staff's ability to process them in a timely fashion. However, we have not been willing to make additional resources available to research possible new tribes by reducing programs and services for those tribes we already serve."[8] Originally expected to have four full teams, the FAP struggled with one or two during the 1980s. Under President Bill Clinton, however, the office was reportedly operating at full capacity. Yet a continual stream of new applications generally meant that the BAR had a consistent backlog. Even under Clinton, former BAR anthropologist Steve Austin conceded that their funding was "woefully inadequate." According to Lumbee lawyer Arlinda Locklear, recognition has always been a "low priority" at the bureau.[9] Over time this conflict of interest has hampered the program's effectiveness.

Despite its glacial pace, other BIA employees generally view the Branch of Acknowledgment and Research as one of the bureau's most professional and elite wings. Contrary to a common criticism, potentially biased members of recognized tribes have never been a major part of BAR teams. Yet, although a few of the branch's historians and anthropologists have held Ph.D.s, most have not; many also have lacked specific training in unacknowledged Indian peoples. The BAR therefore gained its internal reputation for academic rigorousness largely because its members have held master's degrees. Valid questions have arisen because many critics and researchers in the process have had higher academic credentials than the BAR staff.[10]

Nevertheless, between 1978 and the early to middle 1980s, the Federal Acknowledgment Project basked in a short-lived honeymoon period. During this time many reservation tribes, unacknowledged Indians, and scholars praised the FAP's professionalism and objectivity, hoping that the new administrative process could solve the vexing dilemmas of the past. Contributing to the good will, several former FAP employees recalled that during these years the FAP was a more fluid, streamlined procedure than it became in the 1990s.[11]

In the first decade of the BAR process, the Indian office disposed of eighteen cases by acknowledging seven tribes and declining eleven. In many ways the tribes that succeeded early in the process—the Grand Traverse Band of Ottawa and Chippewas of Michigan, the Jamestown Clallam (S'klallams) of Washington, the Tunica-Biloxis of Louisiana, the Death Valley Timbisha Shoshones of California, the Narragansetts of Rhode Island, and the Poarch Creeks of Alabama—were fairly unambiguous entities that once had possessed formal relationships with Euro-American governments. According to scholars Hiram Gregory and Vine Deloria Jr., the Tunica-Biloxi Tribe, for example, was a "model" case, possessing a Spanish land grant and having formal leadership structures. In other cases the Indian Service had formerly acknowledged the Timbisha Shoshone and Jamestown S'klallam tribes, even listing the Jamestown band as acknowledged in a 1974 memorandum. Although the fact that the Narragansetts had multiple racial ancestries raised some eyebrows, the tribe possessed a colonial-era state reservation. The other successful early petitioners likewise had previous formal relationships with federal or state governments: the Poarch Creeks had federal treaty relations and Indian allotments; the Grand Traverse Band descended from treaty signatories and had federal annuity rolls; the Jamestown S'klallam had federal treaty relations, received services from the BIA, and possessed federal tribal rolls.[12]

The nature of the tribes acknowledged in the FAP during its first decade also aided the efficiency of the process. Of the successful cases during this time, only the Gay Head Wampanoag Tribe presented major contentious issues to federal officials. All the groups that the BAR acknowledged in its first decade were fairly small, ranging in size from the 199 members of the Timbisha Shoshone Tribe and the 200 members of the Tunica-Biloxi Tribe to the 1,470 members of the Poarch Creeks. Because of their nature, the petitions submitted by successful groups during this period tended to be small and straightforward as well, from eighteen pages produced by the Death Valley Timbisha Shoshones to ninety pages with the Tunica-Biloxis. In its first years, the FAP thus seemed to dispose rather easily of its most simple cases, pleasing most observers in the process.[13]

The groups the BIA declined to recognize in its first decade likewise seemed to arouse little controversy. The BAR rejected eleven groups during its first ten years of operation. It thus appeared to reject more groups than it accepted. These numbers were deceptive, however, as five of these petitioners were related to a large organization, the Southeastern Cherokee Confederacy (SECC), that included three different petitioning organizations in Tennessee, Georgia, and Oregon and two related groups under Chief Malcolm "Thunderbird" Webber, the Kaweah Indian Nation and United Lumbee Nation of California. These groups published newspapers openly soliciting unrelated individuals with unverified Indian ancestry to join. Many parties scoffed at the claims of these groups. The two recognized Cherokee tribes and the Lumbees of North Carolina, in fact, opposed each of these petitioners that claimed to be related to them.[14] Four of the remaining six declined groups were Creek organizations formed with help from Poarch Creek leader Calvin McGhee. The Creek groups varied somewhat and seemed to have stronger tribal claims than the Cherokee groups, yet their rejections also aroused little controversy; the recognized Muskogee (Creek) Nation opposed several of them.[15]

During its first ten years, the new BIA program thus had a fairly even record. Taken together, the groups that were declined during this period do not support a common contention that the BIA sought to reject groups because of their large size or to decline almost every petitioner. In fact, the petitioners the BIA rejected compared in size to the groups it accepted, ranging in size from the 34 members of the Munsee-Thames River Delawares to the 2,696 members of the Creeks East of the Mississippi. As five of the eleven declined petitioners were associated with the SECC and may be considered as one related petitioner, during its first decade the BAR essentially declined seven groups, making the ratio of declined to acknowledged roughly equal. Throughout its early period the branch showed an ability to make common-sense judgments in line with the stated goals of the BIA project.[16]

Despite early optimism and modest results, by the mid-1980s the BAR's output dropped precipitously. During a ten-year period between 1984 and

1994, in fact, the BIA acknowledged only two tribes, prompting petitioning Indian groups to increasingly turn to legislation to circumvent the painfully slow bureaucratic process. In general, members of Congress and reservation tribes were not happy with the rising trend. "I strongly believe that [legislative acknowledgment] is disastrous and can only lead to the recognition of some groups based not on any Indian ancestry but solely on the power and the party affiliation of their sponsor," testified Wyoming congressman Craig Thomas in 1994.[17] In the wake of controversies surrounding the Mashantucket Pequots' 1983 acknowledgment legislation, non-academics more and more supported the BIA method as preferable to congressional or judicial routes. The Bureau of Indian Affairs promoted this view as well, zealously fighting against acknowledgment bills pursued by the Lumbees, Tiguas, and other Indian groups.[18]

As reflected in the rising number of groups turning to Congress, the BAR's honeymoon was clearly over by the late 1980s. Beginning in 1990, the branch handed down negative rulings on the Ramapoughs of New Jersey and the Miamis of Indiana that proved particularly controversial, spawning acrimonious litigation. To many observers the BAR's denial of the petition of the Miamis of Indiana was notably dismaying, especially in light of the group's documented Indian ancestry and past treaty relations with the United States. In the wake of these rejections, however, groups such as the Ramapoughs fought back, securing casino interests and appealing their denials in federal court.[19]

Mirroring American society in general, the Federal Acknowledgment Process grew more and more litigious during the 1980s and 1990s. Declined groups logically appealed the BIA's findings, yet it was not only negative rulings that sparked lawsuits. "We have been sued more for positive findings than negative," remarked BAR anthropologist Holly Reckord in 2000.[20] In fact, in 1997 the Tulalip Tribes appealed the BAR's positive finding on the Snoqualmies, continuing the Snoqualmies' legal problems over fishing issues. In the early 1990s the Navajo Nation likewise mounted a legal challenge to the BIA's positive finding on the San Juan Southern Paiutes, a small tribe living within the Navajo Nation's reservation, while in later years the city of Detroit sued to stop the recognition of a Pottawatomi band over Indian gaming. Unfortunately, by the 1990s lingering issues over fishing rights, race, and culture had combined with new concerns over Indian gaming, with each issue raising the stakes on acknowledgment decisions either way.[21]

In light of these growing controversies it became apparent by the late 1980s that the BAR was literally "raising the bar" on groups in fear of being sued over gaming and other sundry sovereignty issues. While it was not fair, the BIA more and more took a fine comb to its acknowledgment cases. According to BAR employees George Roth and Steve Austin, the rising levels of documentation flowed directly from legal challenges from declined Indian groups themselves, who with the help of NARF were growing in legal sophistication. Not all persons associated with the BAR agreed with this assessment, however. After retiring from the bureau, former branch chief Bud Shapard testified before Congress that he had "created a monster" with the BIA process, especially in light of the increasing levels of proof required by the BIA staff. As he argued in 1992 and 1994: "After 14 years of trying to make the regs which I drafted work, I must conclude that they are fatally flawed and unworkable. The convoluted administrative process cannot be revised, modified, or altered in any way that will make them work."[22]

With multiple explosive issues muddying the waters, between 1994 and 1997 the BAR process moved at a snail's pace, producing approximately one acknowledgment and one denial a year. The slow rate of decisions ensured that a steady din of criticism enveloped the BIA program. By 1999 the number of groups that had entered the process since its inception reached 231 (the majority being only letters of intent), while the number of groups hoping to submit petitions showed no sign of diminishing. At the end of the decade the BAR had acknowledged fourteen tribes, finalized the denial of thirteen others, and had pending one positive finding and six negative determinations. In total, since its inception the FAP had acknowledged fifteen tribes and declined nineteen others. Because of the nature of the early cases, however, the ratio of acknowledgments and denials was roughly equal.[23]

From the cases the FAP processed by the end of the 1990s, a picture of what a federal "tribe" looked like emerged. Successful groups generally were small entities with ties to a centralized locale and with ancestors who had previous and lasting tribal relations with Euro-American officials. To the Bureau of Indian Affairs, a tribe was not a group of Indian descendants who joined together in the twentieth century to secure land or tribal acknowledgment; a tribe was not simply members of one family or a group descended from just one verified Indian ancestor. An Indian tribe, further, was not a group of Indians who descended from several Indian ancestors from different families if the BAR determined these ancestors did not live in "tribal relations" at any point in their history.[24]

Because of its slow pace and methodology, as early as 1988 a bipartisan group in favor of reforming the BIA process gradually coalesced behind

Republican senator John McCain of Arizona and Democratic senator Daniel Inouye of Hawaii. McCain, a former POW in Vietnam, and Inouye, the nation's first Japanese American congressman, routinely chastised the BIA and its acknowledgement problems. Together with Eni Faleomavaega, the congressional delegate to the House of Representatives from American Samoa, Inouye and McCain held numerous hearings on the problems besetting the BIA branch. During the 1980s and 1990s Congress called twelve hearings on the issue—a considerable number for a governmental agency. At these forums the congressmen heard complaints across a broad spectrum. To impassioned individuals such as Alogan Slagle of the Americans for Indian Opportunity, the bureaucratic maze was heartless and unconscionable: killing legitimate Indian peoples for want of caring and compassion. To equally impassioned tribal leaders such as Stan Jones of the Tulalip Reservation in Washington State, the FAP was working fine by denying groups that were not by any stretch of the imagination Indian tribes.

While some charged the Branch of Acknowledgment and Research with racism and malice, the major issues raised at hearings and elsewhere centered on problems inherent in the criteria and the bureau's interpretation of them, rather than the evil intent of the BAR staff. Overall, the BAR clearly was in an unenviable position. Some parties believed that almost every group coming forward was the "real McCoy," while other individuals thought that the majority were charlatans. In this light the BAR was charged with a virtually impossible task of divining the essence of tribalism and ascribing fixity to a form that had historically eluded such efforts. It was also assigned the daunting work of applying the singular label "tribe" to groups that varied widely in their organization, histories, and cultural and racial makeup.

At the heart of the contention was the fact that there was no scholarly consensus on the definition of a tribe, yet it was academic experts, particularly anthropologists, who were charged with providing proof of tribal existence in the FAP. Despite arguments by some members of the American Anthropological Association that the entire pretense of a standardized procedure for recognizing tribes was doomed to fail, the FAP was charged with finding a workable way to demarcate the largely elusive entity. A major quandary was the fact that the federal government was attempting to provide a system of measuring a form whose base concepts of ancestry, ethnic identity, and political community were contested and ambiguous.[25] Added to this problem was the fact the government demanded written proof of these concepts, a requirement that often taxed petitioners to the breaking point.

Prior to contact with Europeans, Indian societies possessed widely varying forms of social organization. The federal criteria for "tribes" enshrined in 1978, however, reflected a non-indigenous model of Indian tribalism that was rooted in legal precedent and past bureaucratic policy. Despite centuries of acculturation and tribal suppression, the BAR was essentially utilizing a tribal template patterned upon reservation tribes existing at the turn of the twentieth century. The issue was complicated, however, by the fact that many reservation tribes supported the white model. After decades of federal intervention and reservation life, recognized leaders looked around them and saw a picture of tribalism in the BIA criteria that seemed to reflect their own existence, however removed it may have been from pre-contact Indian life.[26]

The government's task was made more difficult by the fact that forces of modernization and assimilation were forcing many pre-contact "Indian" traits (such as languages and distinctive material culture) to fade into the past, while the intangible components of Indian ethnicity and social organization were patently difficult to quantify. In measuring how much "tribalism" was retained, scholars for both unacknowledged groups and the federal government were compelled to cite cultural survivals as evidence of continuing ethnic identity and resiliency. After World War II, however, entities without the benefit of isolated reservation homelands clearly were blurring the lines of what it meant to be "Indian" or "tribal." As their members intermarried with other ethnic groups and moved to urban areas, stock images of Indian tribes were breaking down, yet the BIA and Indian law required a group to have some degree of distinctiveness in order to qualify as a federal tribe. Clearly, most would agree that a group of white people who played Indian on the weekends was not an Indian "tribe." But what about a disparate body of largely assimilated families who had some Indian blood, pride in their ancestry, and sense of themselves as "Indian?" The question would remain how much of the past the group retained and what level of proof of tribal survivals was "enough" to allow a group to enter the domain of federal tribes.

A satisfactory solution to defining tribes has proven elusive, however, and as the storm of criticism grew by the early 1990s, many opponents of the Branch of Acknowledgment and Research called for major reforms. Some demanded the BIA throw out the seven criteria enshrined within the FAP or get out of the acknowledgment business altogether. A core group of critics, most notably political scientist Vine Deloria Jr., consultant anthropologists Jack Campisi and Susan Greenbaum, and anthropologists William Sturtevant and Raymond Fogelson, have testified before Congress, offering criticism of four of the seven criteria and the bureau's interpretation of them, which they believe bears little relevance to real tribes, however defined. In 1992 Vine Deloria Jr. summed up the anger and frustration of many when he testified before Congress: "The current FAP shows no sign of intelligence whatsoever; it is certainly unjust to require these Indian nations to perform documentary acrobatics for a slothful bureaucracy." [27] Particularly glaring to lawyers and political scientists was the fact that the current acknowledgment regimen placed little emphasis on past binding treaty relations, instead requiring high levels of proof of community and political functioning. To some critics the fact that a tribe once had treaty relations with federal officials should place the burden on the government to prove that the tribe had ceased to exist thereafter, not the other way around.

Overall, much criticism has centered on a seemingly insurmountable problem with the BAR process: the fact that the program clearly privileges written forms of proof and verification. Although an understandable requirement in light of the status involved, this demand has proven daunting to most groups. To succeed through the process, petitioners must possess written documentation of their existence since historical contact with whites, a span of time often going back to the sixteenth century. Like all legalistic forums, the BAR process discounts oral history as akin to hearsay and rejects the petitioner's own oral traditions concerning its origins and ancestry in favor of government-produced documents or other Euro-American evidence. Not surprisingly this fact has proven troubling for Native societies who traditionally traced ancestry and culture through oral tradition. Taken together, the need for documentation on all seven points has presented a tall order indeed for many groups in proving who they are to the Bureau of Indian Affairs. The emphasis on documentation, however, dismays many Indians. As Colorado senator Ben Nighthorse Campbell put it, "Unfortunately, right now we tend to judge Indianness too much on accumulated documentation that is over in the Bureau somewhere and not enough on the things that have traditionally identified Indian people as Indians, i.e. things like oral tradition and cultural values, the story of creation, their way of believing, historic land bases and things of that nature." [28]

As revealed in the 1970s debates, however, few parties are willing to accept the self-proclaimed identity and oral traditions of groups claiming to be tribes. The bureau regulations have required all groups to present outside verification that their people have been identified over time as Native American. This requirement, however, has disadvantaged many eastern and southern groups whose avoidance strategies and lack of visibility as Indians has often left their descendents with few records confirming that outsiders saw them as Indians in the past. Precisely by following survival strategies and hiding their identity, ancestors of modern groups may have failed to attract attention from observers or scholars that would have made them visible as Indian tribes. [29] Faced with government allotment, removal policies, and antagonistic local non-Indians in earlier eras, eastern groups literally faced death if they were recognized. Because of this, their descendents have found little comfort in proving their historical Indian identity by relying on outside sources.

Beyond proving Indian identity, a more daunting prerequisite of the BIA acknowledgment program has been the requirement that petitioners demonstrate a substantial portion of their membership lives in a community viewed as Indian, and its members have done so since first sustained contact with Europeans. Of the declined groups, all have failed this criterion. Although most sources agree a "tribe" must have some form of community, in light of modern, overlapping webs of social relations, the branch has faced challenges measuring this concept. Over time the BAR has incorporated social science models (not used by past government officials) to measure characteristics of communities such as social cohesion, core group interaction, residency rates, and geographic dispersion to quantify "community." BIA researchers have also looked at marriage rates, church membership, and language retention as markers of community cohesion. [30]

Beyond proving present community existence, all petitioning groups also must produce written evidence that their community has existed continuously from "generation-to-generation" (every twenty to thirty years) since first sustained contact with non-Indians—a time span often going back more than three hundred years. Although the branch has shown flexibility for certain groups on this point, the BIA has suggested that groups provide minutes of meetings and similar documents to demonstrate community functioning— evidence most petitioners whose ancestors lived in loosely organized, pre-literate societies are hard-pressed to produce. Although the BIA has made allowances for lack of records for early periods, the sheer time span has burdened most eastern groups. By the early 1990s former FAP head Bud Shapard came to speak out against this requirement. "To go back to the 1700s—that is ridiculous. I admit to drafting this stuff up; it is just our lack of knowledge at the time and the lack of [knowledge of] the problems," testified Shapard in 1994. [31] In practice this requirement has clearly privileged groups that had some historic relationship with non-indigenous officials, relations that provide records, resources, and acknowledgment that can help modern groups prove "community."

Although once-unacknowledged groups such as the Snohomish agree the requirement for having an Indian community is valid, the BIA's techniques for measuring "social interaction" and "core analysis" of the community have been somewhat variable. In the past the BAR has used both geographical proximity and evidence of actual social interaction as proof of community existence. Because it needs flexibility, the bureau has argued that this variable approach has allowed it to recognize widely diverse communities. Many observers of the process reject this position, however, believing that the variable approaches have allowed the federal government to deny groups at will. In fact, most determinations require a judgment call by the BAR evaluator. As with "tribes," however, there is no consensus on what an "Indian community" is, making agreement on this requirement extremely unlikely. For example, some tribes and anthropologists believe that a group must have a distinct geographic core community to be a real Indian tribe, whereas others believe "community" has more to do with actual social interaction than residency. And although there is little agreement as to what a "community" is, most are reluctant to throw out the concept. Many groups are simply angered at the BAR's manner of defining their organizations. As Snohomish leader Al Cooper testified in 1991, "Lets take a look at defining 'community' as a system of social interactions. It's a good idea, but how do you measure [it] in a fair and objective manner? It should not simply be left to the personal opinion of a government anthropologist."[32] Because of the subjective nature of the process, however, decisions on groups such as the Snohomish often are left to the personal opinions of government researchers with little longstanding knowledge of the entities in question.

Most unacknowledged tribes have come to despise having to prove that their community has always existed. For centuries non-Indian officials did their best to destroy tribal communities, and it now seemed unjust to require groups to prove they existed every twenty years despite the government's best efforts to the contrary. As Michigan Indian leader Carl Frazier told Congress, "my tribe, the Burt Lake Band of Ottawa and Chippewa had its reservation allotted . . . [by the government, yet] we maintained a strong and vibrant Indian community on these lands until the entire community including our homes were burned to the ground to force our eviction after a tax sale."[33] Even so, because in theory a tribe faced with these forces may have "voluntarily" abandoned its community, many non-Indians continue to remain unconcerned with the causes of the tribe's demise. They simply believe the tribe in question became extinct. The bureau has generally followed this position as well, declining modern groups because they had gaps in their records in the belief that they voluntarily disbanded.[34]

Even more controversial conceptually is the FAP's requirement that a group demonstrate it "has maintained tribal political influence" over its members since first contact with non-Indians. As with proving community existence, all declined petitioners have failed to prove this point. In light of the active federal efforts to extinguish tribal governments in the past, many observers believe that this requirement is particularly hypocritical. As Reid Chambers, a former BIA employee who helped formulate the FAP, told Congress in 1989, "I have always had trouble with one of the criteria—that is the requirement that a tribe continuously assert political authority and social cohesion. I thought when I was in the Department that was an unrealistic criterion and I urged against it."[35] Requiring "political" functioning is clearly troublesome. On one hand, the existence of a political body is central to tribal rights and self-government under Indian law. Yet on the other hand, there are Indian groups that possess a longstanding identity as Indians who are organized on the family or kinship level who simply do not have organizations or mechanisms capable of exerting "political authority" over individuals, however defined.

Because of the "messiness" of ethnic identity, BAR members are often forced to look to formal organizations or bureaucratic relationships to make sense of overlapping social webs. As cultural and social historians know, however, this emphasis on political functioning often misses real "on the ground" activity. In light of traditional indigenous social organization patterns, Vine Deloria Jr. and David Wilkins have urged the BIA to recognize more loosely defined, family-centered Indian peoples as tribes, yet the BAR staff has continued to take a more rigid stance. As FAP anthropologist George Roth has often argued, his office is not recognizing an ethnological or ethnic group per se. "It is obvious we are recognizing a political body; that is the basis here because special status rests on the survival of sovereignty [that] must be aboriginal and not extinguished," notes Roth.[36] This emphasis on a political body, however, has disadvantaged groups. Clearly, certain groups lacked any form of formal organization or relations with outside governments that they can point to as evidence of this concept; they now fail to qualify as a tribe.

Despite these issues, the BAR has been somewhat flexible in acknowledging a variety of social and political mechanisms that have evolved in unacknowledged groups. It has recognized groups such as the Gay Head Wampanoags and Matchebenashshewish Band of Pottawatomi in Michigan who maintained a loose, political influence over their members within town governments or

Protestant church organizations. Larger groups, however, with membership spread over wide distances, have faced difficulty proving they exercised political influence over their members.[37]

Beyond problems with proving community and political authority, issues of race and ancestry also plague the BIA regimen. Although there are difficulties involved in proving Indian descent, most parties agree an Indian tribe must have Indian ancestry. Yet, like most matters in acknowledgment process, the issue centers on how to measure it. The BAR rightly eschews the racial appearance or phenotype of petitioners (do these people "look" Indian?) as an unpredictable and potentially racist indicator of ancestry. In some cases people who appear to have Indian ancestry do not actually have Indian blood, whereas other groups that may not "look" Indian actually possess a firm degree of Native American ancestry. Thus to avoid deciding on the appearance of the group as officials sometimes did in the past, the BAR staff has asked groups to provide ancestry charts that are based on evidence derived from birth certificates, marriage licenses, deeds, wills, federal censuses, and tribal rolls. Besides being the records of non-Indians, these documents are often technical, confusing, blurred, faded, or illegible—if they exist at all. They often do not accurately record the race of individuals involved. Together, genealogical documents often leave groups without a tangible written tie to tribes from which they have long believed they descended.[38]

Although some critics charge the BIA with requiring genetic purity, in practice the BAR process requires a level of Indian ancestry that is often very small. There is no blood quantum involved, and groups have gained status whose entire membership measures its "Indian blood" in minute fractions. A more complex issue, however, is the fact that the BIA requires the petitioner to prove genetic links to a known tribe, an endeavor that often proves arduous. Lakota scholar Vine Deloria Jr. objects to the need for genetic proof, saying, "In common sense terms—if a group on first examination is obviously Indian, the Congress should go ahead and recognized them."[39] Many recognized tribes, however, support the genetic standards of the FAP, with some also calling for a blood quantum requirement. Revealing this emphasis, a historian hired by the Poarch Creeks rejected the nearby MOWA Choctaw's claims of Indian ancestry, saying: "Oral history, family tradition, and 'it is said to have been' . . . cannot be considered by any scholar to be the primary source of material."[40]

As issues, race and racial politics are clear, underlying currents in the acknowledgment process at the national level. Despite the fact that there is no existing evidence of racism within the Branch of Acknowledgment and

Research, declined groups such as the Ramapoughs of New Jersey genuinely believe racism was involved in the BAR's decision to decline them. According to the Ramapoughs, the BAR simply perceived them as too black to be Indian. This opinion, however, is difficult to substantiate as other tribes with African ancestry such as the Narragansetts and Gay Head Wampanoags have succeeded through the process. Although former BAR historian William Quinn recalls hearing disparaging remarks from BIA employees (not within the BAR) about groups with African heritage, the effects of this environment on cases is difficult to quantify. Overall, there is no indication, however, the BAR has a racist bias against groups with African heritage.[41]

More convincing arguments concerning bias, however, have come from groups such as the Snohomish in Washington State who have argued the opposite—that evaluators perceived them as simply too white, mainstream, and assimilated to be recognized. Although this claim is exaggerated, Snohomish leader Al Cooper testified in 1991, "In the opinion of the BIA anthropologist—if you eat pizza, drive pick-up trucks, or hold your council meetings under Robert's Rules of Order, you aren't tribal; in [our case] it was held against us that many of our people were employed by the 1920s."[42] On coffee breaks or on local field trips it is not beyond reason that rumors about the racial identity and legitimacy of tribal communities may bleed into the process. Yet it is also just as likely that some petitioners have assimilated to such a degree that they are no longer Indian tribes or peoples by any stretch of the imagination. As in other realms, however, blood requirements have spawned resentment. "The thing that upsets me most is that there are three animals that have to have blood quantum," testified Narragansett Lucile Dawson in 1978. "That is, purebred dogs, thoroughbred horses, and non-federally recognized Indians."[43]

Despite the lack of blood quantum requirements, BAR officials such as Hazel Elbert and Steve Austin maintain they have not declined to acknowledge a single group because of a lack of records on Indian ancestry. Rather, they argue the denied groups actually possessed records that showed non-Indian ancestry for their ancestors for protracted periods. And it is certainly likely there are groups in the FAP that do not have any Indian ancestry whatsoever. Although the BIA rules are race-based requirements and distasteful as such, the racial mores of the dominant society and many Indian tribes continue to dictate that unacknowledged Indians open their family ancestry to the glare of federal researchers to secure acknowledgment.[44]

As it has functioned since 1978, the entire acknowledgment process has raised important questions about the use of scholarship in current concerns and the role of scholars in establishing Indian identity. Since the 1980s, parties have often called the objectivity and academic detachment of the BAR into question, especially since the bureau has an apparent conflict of interest in the matter. Over time BIA employees have consistently denied any impropriety, saying they have never been told how to find on a petition. In the Samish case, however, a federal judge ruled that the bureau met with opposing tribes in contravention to the Samish's interests. While perhaps an isolated incident, many unacknowledged groups believe members of recognized tribes at the BIA work behind the scenes to affect the decisions of the branch scholars. Correct or not, these opinions have nonetheless created an air of suspicion around the entire process, while the fact that more than 80 percent of the BIA is staffed with members of recognized tribes means that there is potential for undue influence.[45] FAP creator Bud Shapard testified to this possibility in 1992: "The fate of unrecognized tribes [is] totally in the hands of a ponderous bureaucracy that is antagonistic to unrecognized tribes and that views newly recognized tribes and restored tribes as an additional unwanted expense."[46]

Many of the allegations of impropriety stem from the fact the BAR essentially presides over a subjective process that allows much leeway in determinations with little quality control. In each acknowledgment case there are countless subjective determinations as to whether groups claiming to be Indian tribes are in fact tribes. On most points in the recognition process both the BAR researchers and the advocates for unacknowledged Indians are forced to take leaps of faith when trying to make sense of weak or non-existent historical documents. Bud Shapard estimated the original rules contained thirty-five words or phrases requiring interpretation, while Assistant Secretary Kevin Gover later admitted the entire endeavor was inherently subjective.[47]

Denying any undue influence and rejecting theoretical criticisms over time, the BAR staff has tenaciously argued they are scientific and objective. George Roth is correct to counter critics that the bureau cannot base its decisions on the unverified claims of hopeful groups. Far from being academic dinosaurs, the BAR teams see themselves as the vanguard of scholarship, following methods pioneered by scholars such as Eric Hobsbawn who deconstructed traditions and in the process showed that ethnic groups routinely invent cultural institutions to serve the needs of the present. In this light the BIA researchers refuse to take any claim of Indian descent or history at face value.[48]

Not surprisingly, however, petitioning groups have not taken kindly to the primarily white scholars deconstructing their founding histories, identities, and core beliefs. For understandable reasons unrecognized groups resent having to prove their identities by revisiting painful racial and social injustices. Linda Hall Navarro summed up these feelings well when she remarked, "It's amazing to us, the fact that we survived what we did, we're here and we're still functioning as a Shasta Nation, and we have to prove to the Bureau of Indian Affairs that we still exist."[49]

Beyond problems with concepts and interpretations, unrecognized communities and outside observers clearly are exasperated by the bureaucratic nature of the FAP. Originally envisioned to be a temporary branch within the BIA, the BAR has become almost self-perpetuating, with an "acknowledgment industry" having developed around the process. Some early tribes such as the Death Valley Timbisha Shoshones and Tunica-Biloxis were in the process for three to four years. Yet the average time taken to hire researchers or find volunteers, locate documents, produce legally sufficient petitions, and wait for the BIA to review and decide on a petition has generally averaged over a decade. Despite the need for caution, knowledgeable sources report that the BAR has single-handedly "raised the bar" on groups. Many BIA critics see this development as especially unfair in light of past acknowledgment cases. Having helped groups secure status prior to the FAP, Vine Deloria Jr. told Congress in 1992, "In no case did these Indian nations have to undergo the prolonged agony and rigorous documentation which has become characteristic of the federal acknowledgment process at the present time."[50]

In early cases such as the Timbisha Shoshones the BIA and related federal agencies aided the group, leading their tribal attorney to remark that the entire affair was surprisingly easy.[51] Few lawyers for current petitioning groups would say likewise. Most now feel the BAR researchers, far from being detached scientists, act like prosecuting attorneys against them. For the mostly impoverished groups, costs involved to produce a petition range from a low of $50,000 to over one million dollars. For many communities the FAP has come to seem like a bureaucratic game they just cannot win. As Miami chair Ray White lamented in 1989, "since 1982, we have spent $241,000 in Administration for Native Americans funds and $128,000 in other funds—but we do not have recognition twelve years after our research began. We believe that what has happened to us is asking too much of any small Indian community."[52]

Because of the costs and legal issues involved, all unacknowledged groups must secure outside funding and expertise to present a convincing case to the BIA. A supreme irony in the entire affair is the fact that poor petitioners often receive federal funds to finance their petitions and then can ultimately find themselves opposed by the federally funded BIA. Since the 1960s, however, advocacy groups such as the American Friends Service Committee, the National Indian Lutheran Board, the Association on American Indian Affairs, the Americans for Indian Opportunity, the California Indian Legal Services, and scholars from numerous universities have unselfishly given their time and energy to help impoverished groups. However, it is doubtful any group currently without lawyers and federal funds could secure acknowledgment through the FAP.[53]

Beyond creating an "industry," the Federal Acknowledgment Process has raised other troubling issues for anthropologists and related scholars. Like the Indian Claims Commission that predated it, the FAP forces academic work to be utilized in pressing life-and-death issues; yet unlike the claims tribunal, BAR scholars also sit in as judge and jury as well. Veteran acknowledgment law expert Russel Lawrence Barsh has chastised the academic community for failing to challenge the inequity of the BAR process, while instead trumpeting the FAP as an employment opportunity. Anthropologist James Clifton has charged acknowledgment scholars with resuscitating long-dead tribes for money or prestige while forsaking all pretensions of objective scholarship when they unabashedly advocate for their chosen groups. Clearly, after working for years with poor groups, many researchers become invested with the cause from heartfelt concern. As volunteer researcher for the MOWA Choctaw, Jacqueline Matte pleaded to Congress in 1992, "I am not related to the Choctaw except through love and through my heart. We know these people have been abused. I think if you will take a look at these wonderful people. You can see obviously that these are Indian people."[54]

Researchers, however, generally do not believe their scholarship is compromised in the process. According to Pete Gregory and James Greenberg of the University of Arizona, they simply present their findings to the groups involved, who then use the data as they wish.[55] Because the BIA discounts or ignores the petitioner's oral history, the BAR process has ensured that primarily white experts determine the question of tribal existence in the federal arena. While raising some ethical issues, overall the acknowledgment process has been both a positive and negative development in the relationship between Indians and scholars. Although the process provides work for academics, the research it has generated has also given many once obscure groups a better sense of their histories.

The lack of an effective appeals process is another undeniable problem with the BIA process that has added credence to calls for reform. For all practical purposes the BAR is essentially the judge and jury of the acknowledgment world. Although declined groups have recourse to appeal to the Interior Board of Indian Appeals (IBIA), the BAR findings are so complex and factual in nature that the IBIA will decide only procedural issues and remand the cases to the bureau for further review. The Miamis of Indiana and the Navajos have failed to overturn BIA decisions in federal court (the last resort) because of the complex factual questions involved. As revealed in the Miamis' appeal, federal judges remain skeptical of the Indianness of modern groups anyway. The BIA appeals process is thus essentially an "in house" affair, prompting knowledgeable commentators such as Senator John McCain to conclude the FAP lacks a "viable appeals" procedure. North Dakota senator Mark Andrews summed up the quandary well in 1983: "if they are pretty well set in their ways, and you go back to the same guy for review—the chances for success are not largely enhanced."[56] Consistently the BAR has rejected the idea that its office lacked a fair appeals process. As sound evidence former BAR anthropologist Steve Austin points out that two tribes, the Gay Head Wampanoags and the Mohegans, overcame initial negative findings. The Miamis of Indiana, however, believe that the BAR is extremely reluctant to reconsider an initial impression or research finding. According to the Miamis, the BIA teams view challenges to their early conclusions as direct attacks on their scholarship and resist new opinions as a result.[57]

Since 1978 the Branch of Acknowledgment and Research has maintained much of its authority because of the complex and technical issues involved in the process. Particularly on questions of ancestry, the BAR keeps the upper hand because of the amount of time needed to analyze the often highly complex genealogical research. Overall, the final reports on declined groups have had a tone of certainty and scholarly rigor, however, that often belies the true ambiguities involved in the cases. In the Golden Hill Paugussetts' case, for example, the BIA reported that there were "little or no records" listing its ancestors as Indian and that the Paugussetts' ancestors were actually part African American rather than Indian. The bureau's initial finding also reported that these ancestors associated primarily with local non-Indians and did not live in an Indian community. Despite these seemingly firm conclusions, an appeals judge determined there were in fact records that referred to the Golden Hill ancestors as "Indian" or "copper" in complexion and there was no basis for the BAR claiming the ancestral Paugussetts associated mainly with non-Indians.[58]

After Indian gaming became interjected into the mix during the 1980s the process grew even more legalistic and complex. By the early 1990s the need for petitions and BIA reports that would stand up to legal scrutiny and appeals had made for an excruciatingly slow process. Part of this resulted from petitions that often came in at over seven hundred pages in length, plus supporting documents that often ran upward of six thousand pages. Having insisted upon detail, BIA researchers had to take time to review these voluminous submissions. A general bureaucratic inertia, however, also hindered the process as materials were checked and double-checked in the BAR, then sent to the Solicitor's Office to be rechecked by attorneys, and then sent back to the BIA to be finalized. As BAR anthropologist Steve Austin noted, appeals and court challenges from declined groups such as the Samish and the Miamis also took BAR teams away from analyzing other cases, further slowing the process.[59]

As layer upon layer was deposited, the bureaucratic process became so lengthy by the late 1980s that once-optimistic parties called for an end to the pain it caused small, struggling groups. At hearings on the FAP the Branch of Acknowledgment and Research became a favorite target of Senator John McCain, who often unleashed his famous temper on the BIA employees. At one of the many hearings on reform bills he sponsored, the senator told the bureau: "The situation is not acceptable; everyone knows that. And it is time or long past time for our being about the business of trying to fix the Federal acknowledgment process for you [Ronal Eden] to be unable to even give me any time as to when we can make these necessary changes. It is, as usual, very frustrating."[60]

By the end of the 1980s critics began pushing to have an outside commission determine acknowledgment cases, a solution that seemed viable in light of the mounting criticism of the process. Petitioners made valid points that the BIA never could tell them how much evidence was enough to satisfy a requirement. Even former BAR chief Bud Shapard turned against the branch, while Vine Deloria Jr., Jack Campisi, and others lobbied Congress, arguing the BAR was increasingly raising its standards. "It's a miracle anyone gets recognized," Campisi testified before the Senate, and "becoming more so—I think they've raised the standards for fear of being sued."[61] Overall, the criticism by both paid and volunteer experts became fairly uniform. Reflecting the view of most critics, anthropologist Raymond Fogelson testified in 1988: "The procedures have proven unwieldy, expensive, and often inappropriate."[62] Countering these attacks, however, the BAR argued that a commission would be too political, and that no process could apply standards the same way in each case. The BAR repeatedly testified that it had to maintain control of the process and retain the elastic criteria to ensure that groups with varying compositions could achieve acknowledgment in a nonpolitical environment.[63]

Aside from issues of objectivity, few could refute that the bureau's slowness caused tangible pain and uncertainty in most unacknowledged communities, many of whom possessed solid claims to Indianness. By the late 1980s this fact alone engendered calls for major reform. After devoting much of their lives to securing acknowledgement, some unrecognized Indians such as United Houma leader Tom Dion died before seeing their goals achieved. From their vantage many unacknowledged peoples came to believe the cards would be stacked against them as long as the process remained in the BIA. As Shasta member Roy Hall testified in 1989, "We do not understand the purpose of the Acknowledgment Committee—[it is] as if they are looking for something about your tribe that you can't possibly give them." [64] In particular, Hall's people were amazed the BIA asked for telephone logs to prove they actually communicated with each other and then, not satisfied, requested that the community fund a full ethnological study.

Even in light of the process's glacial pace, those in power and those with vested interests were loath to lift the process from the bureau, believing it was the best possible forum in an imperfect world. The Tulalip Tribes of Puget Sound in Washington have been perhaps the most vocal and determined opponent of reforming the acknowledgment process. Tribal members have testified at virtually every hearing on the subject in opposition to Indian groups denied fishing rights in the U.S. v. Washington case. The Tulalip Tribes have fought groups such as the Snoqualmie on multiple grounds, arguing these people were the scattered descendents of Indians who historically lacked a tribal organization and who were simply honing in on the Tulalips' fishing resources. Revealing these views, tribal chairman Stan Jones testified before Congress in 1994, "The Tulalip Tribes are the successors of the Snohomish, Snoqualmie and Skykomish Tribes, who honored the Treaty of Point Elliot, and came to the Tulalip Reservation. Members of the historic tribes who refused to move and comply with the terms of the treaty, they forfeited their rights." [65]

Working against reform, many concerned parties also have continued to buy into the "small pie" argument that favors the strict BIA rules. To judge from BIA official comments, financial concerns over the impact of acknowledging new tribes have some merit. As Director of Tribal Services Ronal Eden remarked in 1991, "We have been working that when we do recognize a tribe, that we start moving that on into the budget process so that we are not in the situation where we're continuously taking funds from the rest of the tribes that are there." [66] Although allowances for new groups were made shortly thereafter, fears of lost resources remain. Consistently since the 1970s federal administrators have done little to help quell these concerns. As one BIA official cautioned in the early 1980s: "What's at stake [is] . . . a perpetual expenditure of funds by the Bureau of Indian Affairs and other agencies—Federal Acknowledgment . . . should be cautiously and wisely approved, especially in times of limited budgetary resources."[67] In this light it is no surprise that many reservation communities are reluctant to reform or ease the acknowledgment process.

Exaggerated concerns over the existence of dubious, "wannabe" tribes also has affected efforts to alter the BIA acknowledgment regimen. Ever since the Vietnam era the number of individuals claiming an Indian identity and tribal status has steadily increased, a trend that alarmed many parties and pushed them toward maintaining strict standards for tribal recognition. Beginning in the 1960s thousands of people who may have previously passed as white or entirely identified as Caucasian were continually discovering lost roots and perhaps a "Cherokee Princess" in their family trees. In states such as Alabama, for example, the number of people claiming an Indian identity on the federal census rose 117 percent between 1980 and 1990 alone, an increase not entirely attributable to rising birth rates. While many of these individuals were Indians with strong claims to tribalism, others were not. These people raised real concerns among recognized tribes when they formed large organizations such as the multistate, multitribal Southeastern Cherokee Confederacy, advertised for new members, and ultimately petitioned for tribal status. [68] BAR spokespersons and many reservation tribes have argued the existence of dozens of "wannabe" groups justified maintaining close scrutiny of all groups. Even so, the impact of "wannabe" tribes has been greatly exaggerated. It essentially has served as a "boogeyman" that helps justify the stringent procedures.

With Indian casinos and other (exaggerated) potential benefits in mind, a significant number of non-Indians continue to believe that most groups are simply Indian "pretenders." Coalesced around local governments and right-leaning groups, this segment of the U.S. population has supported the skeptical stance taken by the BAR. Revealing this viewpoint, Congressman Lloyd Meeds of Washington remarked, "Like many of my Indian friends say, there are too many people with a braid and a bead out there posturing, who because of some distant relationship and the desire to find a place in the sun, have become instant Indians—they aren't a real credit to Indians at all."[69] Although recognizing the overemphasis, scholars involved with acknowledgment issues such as Pete Gregory admit that these "wannabes" pose "a devilish problem" that colors the whole process. Precisely because of these dubious groups,

Lakota Eugene Crawford of the National Indian Lutheran Board argued that tribal recognition policy should remain stringent because, as Crawford said, "we do not want any 'want-to-be's' or 'Saturday Night Specials' slipping under the counter."[70]

Concerns over the sheer number of individuals hoping to gain tribal status also have made many reservation tribes reluctant to alter the process. Faced with the economic realities, the BIA has used fears of increased tribal membership to attack reforms of the process. Department of Interior officials such as John Fritz have expressed concern over "the expanding membership problem," noting even small, newly acknowledged tribes often mushroom after securing recognition. This position has some merit, as Indian tribes are free to amend their membership criteria (with Interior Department approval) and generally have liberalized membership requirements, in some cases omitting all blood quantum provisions to ward off eventual tribal extinction. Despite the fact that the Narragansetts of Rhode Island and others see the small pie argument as part of the government's traditional "divide and conquer" strategy, the record shows federal dependence and funding realities have worked against loosening the standards for acknowledgment.[71]

The threat of large groups securing federal status likewise has scared parties into supporting the government process, while making large petitioners feel the BIA will not recognize groups their size. Populous petitioners without major resources or governmental powers are vulnerable to rejection from the BIA based upon a strict reading of both the community and political authority criteria. Although most groups are relatively small with under 2,000 members, larger groups such as the 40,000-member Lumbee Tribe of North Carolina and the 17,000-member United Houma Nation of Louisiana genuinely believe the BIA will not recognize them because of their numbers. BAR anthropologist George Roth adamantly rejects this claim, however, as a "bunch of crap." But at times financial concerns do appear to be at issue. As an example, in 1988 Assistant Secretary Ross Swimmer testified against a Lumbee recognition bill, saying: "a second reason for opposition is the sheer financial impact, which is estimated to be $30 to $100 million per year."[72] Although Swimmer was not against Lumbee acknowledgment per se (he said he wanted them to proceed through the FAP), his comments certainly underscore the brute economic concerns at play when decisions involve large numbers of Indians.

Like the branch researchers, tribal leaders fervently deny that financial concerns lay at the heart of their support for the bureaucratic process. Once a member of an unacknowledged tribe himself, Poarch Creek leader Eddie

Tullis argued in 1994 that "fairness," and a desire "to protect the sanctity of the federal/tribal relationship, are the reasons why tribes feel strongly that an equitable system with uniform criteria is needed, not because of any selfish need to protect what little we now have."[73] The vocal opposition of the recognized Cherokees to dozens of groups claiming to be Cherokee is perhaps the best example of what tribes see as the need to protect the meaning of tribal sovereignty and public perceptions of Indian peoples. Because no less than 269 entities claim to be remnant bands of the Cherokees in states from Florida to Alaska, the recognized Cherokees understandably are concerned with these organizations. In many southern states such as Georgia, the state legislatures have added legitimacy to these organizations' claims by identifying some as state-recognized tribes. Overall, the two recognized Cherokee tribes see the proliferation of these organizations as an affront to their cultural identity and integrity.[74]

The wide-scale use of their tribal name and identity has pushed many of the so-called Five Civilized Tribes of Oklahoma and the Southeast to support the BIA administrative process that has served to screen questionable tribes. In many ways the Cherokees and others see acknowledgment as a personal sovereignty issue. As principal chief of the Eastern Band of Cherokees Jonathan Taylor testified in 1988: " I'll tell this committee that there are only two Cherokee Tribes; one of them is in North Carolina and the other is in Oklahoma." Overall, Taylor and many Cherokees concur with the BIA's position that individuals can be "Indian" in some senses, yet not be eligible to create their own recognized tribe, especially if it is named after the Cherokees. "If I had a dollar for every time I have heard that some stranger's great grandmother was a Cherokee Princess I would be a wealthy man," testified Chief Taylor in 1991. "We have no problem with people taking pride in their ancestry, however in the same way that 500 people of Norwegian descent in Minnesota can not consider themselves to be a second 'country' of Norway, 500 people of Cherokee descent in Tennessee or Arkansas can not consider themselves 'The Cherokee Tribe.' "[75]

Beyond issues of sovereignty many recognized tribes sincerely believe that the bureau's strictness protects their culture and identity as well. In 1995 influential principal chief of the Cherokee Nation of Oklahoma Wilma Mankiller took up the banner to oppose changing the process. "Unlike any other Native American tribe," Chief Mankiller argued, "the Cherokee Nation is experiencing an identity crisis. Who are these individuals who purport to be Cherokee? The Cherokee Nation and other tribes have been embarrassed by groups such as 'The Echota Cherokee Warriors' showing up at the National Congress of American Indians dressed in stereotypical Hollywood garb—a tribe's sovereignty, reputation, and identity are at stake." Faced with these groups, the recognized Cherokee tribes along with the Creek (Muskogee) Nation of Oklahoma and the Mississippi Band of Choctaw have supported the BIA process. According to Chief Mankiller, "A workable process is in place through the Bureau of Indian Affairs, Branch of Acknowledgment and Research."[76]

Ironically some reservation tribes backed the BIA program, not because it is so strict, but because they believe that it is already too lenient. These tribes oppose any indication that Congress will weaken its requirements. In the Southwest, the nation's largest tribe, the Navajo Nation, has spearheaded legal challenges to the San Juan Southern Paiutes, the Canoncito Navajo Band, and Alamo Navajo Band over what it sees as efforts by these groups to use the FAP to break from the main tribal body. Tribes such as the Navajo and Tohono O'odham deeply resent the Branch of Acknowledgment process for interfering with what they see as their internal politics. These large Indian nations fear that any alleged weakening of the criteria would only encourage factions to splinter off and form their own tribes.[77]

Perhaps more than any other development, however, Indian gaming has worked to retard reforming the FAP. Some tribes with gaming interests have opposed unacknowledged groups and have used their gambling profits to fund legal briefs that challenge the Indianness of these groups. Even some recently acknowledged tribes have testified against easing the BAR process in fear that reforms would help newly recognized groups destroy their local gaming monopoly. Overall, strong economic interests in Indian gaming have encouraged tribes to ask Congress to maintain the FAP. "We have some people who are in the process right now of attempting to hold Constitutional Conventions," testified Minnesota Chippewa chairman Darrell Wadena; "they are seeking recognition for the purpose of gaming and that raises some questions and some concerns for us."[78] Overall, Indian gaming clearly has reduced the chances that the process will be eased in significant ways. As Senator John McCain told colleagues in 1995, "Let me . . . rebut the idea that Federal recognition has been invented since the growth of tribal gaming—[it] may have raised the stakes," however.[79]

By the late 1990s issues of tribal acknowledgment caught the attention of the general public, spawning media stories that questioned the motives and Indianness of many groups. Embedded in these still frames were lingering mainstream ideologies that supported tribal assimilation. Proponents of this position generally believed that most groups now seeking status were already too assimilated to qualify as Indian tribes. Alternately, supporters of assimilation argued that putting these groups on reservations would be a step back for them. Others were against Indian sovereignty in general and thus opposed all unrecognized groups on principal. To these individuals the assertions of unacknowledged Indian groups ran counter to their deeply held belief that groups or individuals who had assimilated certain cultural and economic modes of the dominant society had lost their primordial characteristics and ceased to be real Indians. Many non-Indians felt that it was preposterous that these once "invisible Indians" had emerged arguing that they were somehow Indian tribes.[80]

Together, these jaundiced views underscored a pervasive mainstream idea that tribal status and programs were welfare measures rather than the unfulfilled rights that they truly were. During the 1930s when non-Indians viewed acknowledgment as a charity measure, it was more freely given. By the 1980s, however, the mainstream increasingly saw tribal recognition as a maneuver by groups to gain economic windfalls (via tribal casinos) and sovereign immunity from local laws. A skeptical public therefore demanded that recognition become more and more closely guarded and regulated. Not recognizing the deeper federal responsibility it represented, these forces did not see why the government was now creating "new" tribes at all, and they were averse to easing the burdens on groups they did not view as legitimate Indian tribes anyway.

Because of the vagaries of political appointments, high-level government officials also have held these views. In 1988 Assistant Secretary for Indian Affairs Ross Swimmer, a Cherokee, related this opinion: "We know that the Lumbee population are sophisticated, well-educated people; what we're going to do is create another pocket of paternalism with these people by making decisions for them and reviewing their every action; these people are far along in their development and it would be a shame to reverse a history of self-determination that is already being exercised by forcing them into a guardianship/wardship relationship."[81] Swimmer was appointed during the Republican administrations of the 1980s and early 1990s, and his comments reflect assimilation ideology that trickled down from the highest levels of government. In 1988 President Ronald Reagan reportedly argued it was a mistake for the country to have "humored" Native Americans with treaties and special status. A few years earlier his inflammatory interior secretary, James Watt, stated that Indians suffered from a wide range of social problems because they lived under "socialistic government policies" promoted by the federal officials. Together, these remarks reveal the palpable reluctance on the part of some government officials to acknowledge responsibilities to all Indian tribes, much less additional Indian groups. [82]

Apart from ideological issues, conflicts created at the local level after the establishment of new reservations also engendered opposition to reforming the FAP. In areas once devoid of federal reservations, newly acknowledged tribes inevitably clashed with locals as funds from Indian gaming allowed them the power to exercise governmental authority. Non-Indian officials were not pleased as newly established federal tribes created their own police forces and courts while suddenly becoming exempt from all local regulations. As examples emerged of new reservations taking lands from tax bases and expanding, most local agencies circled the wagons against liberalizing the BIA process. In the Pacific Northwest, groups as diverse as the Washington State Sportsman's Council and the National Wildlife Federation have expressed concerns over Indian fishing and new tribes; in eastern states, sheriffs' associations, county governments, and anti-tribal groups have all weighed in opposing the creation of new reservations and Indian casinos that seem to go hand in hand with them. [83]

Even with these forces aligned against reform, proponents of changing the BIA regimen found help during the late 1980s and early 1990s. Between 1989 and 1997 Senator McCain, Senator Inouye, and Congressional Delegate Faleomavaega introduced several bills that sought to establish an independent commission to examine acknowledgment cases. Although some of their bills essentially maintained the BAR criteria, others contained modifications that eased the burden on petitioning groups. One particularly controversial 1989 reform bill set the date for most issues of proof at 1934, the date of the Indian Reorganization Act, and also allowed for oral testimonials as evidence. [84]

The 1989 reform proposal especially alarmed the BIA. Testifying against the bill, bureau spokesperson Hazel Elbert warned that it would provide "blanket recognition" of all groups by greatly reducing the criteria, by lessening the burden of proof involved, and by diminishing the requirements for historical continuity and political relations. To Elbert, the new legislation would recognize "mere social relationships" and create "new tribal governments where no tribal governmental authority exists." Under the proposed legislation, Elbert further cautioned, "we believe that all the current petitioners could be recognized. The estimated membership of all groups who have petitioned is 136,288. Using the figure of $2,066 per year to provide Bureau of Indian Affairs and Indian Health Services to the membership of each of these groups, the estimated cost to implement [the legislation] would be $281,571,008 per year." [85] With these alarming figures in tow, the BIA sent panels to each congressional hearing, arguing that removing the process from the bureau would duplicate jobs and expertise, raise costs, and introduce politics into the equation. Congress understandably was reluctant to act on these reforms. Faced with yearly trips to Capitol Hill, however, bureau officials by 1991 were assuring legislators that reform regulations were in the pike and urged patience. Congress abided their wishes.[86]

In 1991 the BIA began revising its regulations, taking into account recommendations and suggestions from a consulting panel headed by NARF. Finalized in 1994, the revised regulations essentially maintained the original form and content of the 1978 criteria but did contain some significant changes. The new rules required that groups show they had been identified as Indian only since 1900, reducing the burden from the previously stated "from historical times to the present." They also contained provisions that allowed groups to prove their existence since the last clear and unambiguous acknowledgment of their people in treaties or administrative actions rather than since first contact. On the controversial issues of community and political authority, the revised rules set guidelines on measuring these slippery concepts. At a certain point groups would have prima facie evidence of both of these requirements if they could demonstrate at least 50 percent of their membership lived in a core area, intermarried, or maintained distinct cultural practices such as common church membership or Indian language. Because political authority had been so difficult to quantify, the new rules stated that once a petitioner proved its community existed at a certain point, the BIA would assume political authority existed up until that point as well. To speed the process, the revised regulations also allowed the BAR to conduct an "expedited review" on the issue of Indian descent if the BIA researchers believed the group would likely fail this criterion. Although this reform has sped the process, it was of dubious value to groups such as the Golden Hill Paugussetts who were rejected by this procedure, only to appeal and force the bureau to review their full petition anyway.[87]

The BIA's reformed regulations of 1994, coupled with two more active assistant secretaries—Ada Deer, a Menominee, and Clinton appointee Kevin Gover, a Pawnee—have increased the speed of the FAP. The branch recognized six groups between 1994 and 1999 under the revised rules, compared with just eight in the preceding fifteen years. Gover also reaffirmed the status of three tribes outside the FAP at the end of 2000.[88] By the end of the 1990s signs of optimism for a more streamlined procedure had emerged, yet the process remained too slow and frustrating for most unacknowledged Indian groups.[89]

In September of 2000 an emotional Assistant Secretary Gover issued the first high-ranking, formal BIA apology to Indian nations. In the same vein Gover shocked some observers by publicly asking that the acknowledgment process be removed from his bureau, saying, "I have reluctantly reached the conclusion that I will not be successful in reforming this program." [90] The assistant secretary also used his power to acknowledge two Eastern Pequot groups in Connecticut. While on his way out of office Gover rejected the findings of the BAR staff and acknowledged three others, including the small Duwamish Tribe. With these moves, however, the existing tensions over acknowledgment policy exploded in the Northeast. The Connecticut Attorney General's Office and several East Coast congressmen promptly went to the federal auditing agency, the United States General Accounting Office, in protest. Calls went out for a moratorium on all new acknowledgment decisions. At the same time articles appeared claiming Gover was acting out of financial interest by acknowledging these groups. In response, the new assistant secretary, Neal McCaleb, soon challenged the new acknowledgment decisions and their propriety, while actually withdrawing the preliminary recognition of the Duwamish and others. [91] With these developments in 2001 and 2002, any previous signs of optimism faded as powerful forces worked against easing the burdens on petitioning tribes.

In response to the New England groundswell, in the fall of 2001 the General Accounting Office issued a report that was overtly critical of the BIA program. The report concluded the process was not responding to petitions in a timely manner, while also finding the level of evidence was not clearly spelled out and that it varied notably between cases. "A lack of clear and transparent explanations of the decisions reached may cast doubt on the objectivity of decisionmakers," the GAO concluded. In reaction, Assistant Secretary McCaleb agreed to once again revise the procedures. His office promised to create an online precedent bank to give guidance to petitioners and, significantly, proposed reducing the time span under the regulations from "first sustained contact" to the less burdensome from the "creation of the United States." [92] The BIA also had planned to expedite the process by no longer issuing complex reports on groups and by no longer conducting its own research on petitions. These last reforms, although likely to speed the process, only seemed destined to spark further controversies of their own. [93]

With the 1994 revisions in place and promises of further reform, the BAR process has proven highly resilient. Despite its long life, an observer paying attention to the subject would be hard-pressed to leave with a favorable impression of the BIA process. However, the vocal criticism often obscured the significant support for the status quo. According to anthropologist J. Anthony Paredes, opponents largely base their opinions and testimony against the acknowledgment office on hearsay. Former BIA historian William Quinn agrees, believing that a general anti-BIA sentiment and a view of petitioners as "underdogs" are the major reasons for the attacks on the FAP. Overall, vocal support from many reservation tribes, Congress, and the federal courts has served to solidify the position of the process within the BIA. Once an unacknowledged Indian himself, Poarch Creek leader Eddie Tullis summed up the opinion of many recognized tribes when he testified before Congress in 1994: "These criteria have been in place since 1978, and are well accepted by most impartial archaeologists, historians, genealogists, and I might add, very definitely, as well by most tribes, as being reasonable."[94]

As the twenty-first century dawned, many members of Congress and judges within the federal courts appeared to agree that the BIA process was the most objective and expert process available for recognizing Indian tribes. Efforts to ease the contentious criteria have strong validity, yet they have failed because the BIA has consistently raised fears that any relaxation would lead to dire consequences and costs to the BIA and Indian Health Service in excess of $280 million a year. Besides, the other option of creating an independent commission raises the issue of who would staff it.[95]

As a sign of the BAR's reputation, however, more than a hundred unacknowledged groups met in 1995 at a White House conference on recognition and voted 120 to 10 to remove the process from the BIA and take their chances with the politics of a commission. Certain prominent Indian leaders, including NARF director John Echohawk, have also come out against the BIA process. In supporting a Lumbee recognition bill, NCAI executive director Susan Harjo called the FAP "the Bureau of Indian Affairs' game of trying to control all processes dealing with Indian people."[96] Not surprisingly, long-time BIA critic Vine Deloria Jr. offered perhaps the strongest criticism: "It is the mental attitude of the Bureau that makes it inept and the federal recognition process is an example of how long the Bureau can stretch out a reasonably simple process if it really wants to do so."[97] In this light perhaps an independent commission staffed with both Indian and non-Indian members would be an improvement.

Overall, just as there is no consensus on how to define a tribe, there are conflicting ideas on what is wrong with the BIA acknowledgment process and potential remedies that have stalled action on the matter. There is little doubt, however, that the bureau has a conflict of interest in the matter, while the contested concepts embedded in the criteria are a recipe for controversy. Overall the competing and opposing solutions have served only to maintain inertia and keep the acknowledgment process within the Bureau of Indian Affairs. Despite the stalemate, lawyers Arlinda Locklear and Alogan Slagle have perhaps the most persuasive arguments for change. They note that the BAR process requires levels of historical and genealogical evidence that federal officials did not use historically. These attorneys believe it is unfair that the present process discounts federal Indian treaties and other strong legal precedents in favor of subjective, social science criteria. In equity, it seemed odd to them to require groups arbitrarily left out of the federal relationship and subject to cultural suppression to now shoulder the burden of proving their existence.[98]

Despite the BAR's problems, as the new millennium unfolded the branch remained within the Bureau of Indian Affairs precisely because it had vocal support from many recognized tribes that testified before Congress in praise of its professionalism. Although many observers felt the process was far from equitable, others seemed complacent with the burdens it imposed on impoverished petitioners or resigned to the status quo. Perhaps many agreed with BAR researcher Holly Reckord when she said, "fairness is not our 8th criterion."[99] Although fairness was, in fact, an original goal, the nature of the process increasingly meant that a truly equitable and expeditious remedy has eluded many unacknowledged Indian communities. Yet, as of 2003, the BIA process remains in its essential form largely because it serves its understated purpose of operating in a slow and exacting manner to limit the number of Indian tribes entering the federal fold.

THREE. BYPASSING THE BUREAU

The Pascua Yaquis' Quest for
Legislative Tribal Recognition

Just west of the growing Sunbelt city of Tucson, Arizona, in the spring of 1962, a middle-aged Yaqui spiritual leader went wandering in search of wild tea leaves amid the giant saguaro cactus of the Sonoran Desert. In the shadow of the eroded remnant of a long-dead volcano called Black Mountain, Anselmo Valencia had a vision. Perhaps his people, the Yaqui Indians, or Yoemem as they call themselves, could secure this land as a place of refuge for a new community far from the urban environment of their present settlement. Returning home that night to Pascua barrio near downtown Tucson, past the outdoor privies and homemade houses lit by kerosene lamps, Valencia carried the dream. Though he was certainly proud of his heritage, he had to recall, somewhat in shame, bringing visitors to the squalid neighborhood and being embarrassed to be Yaqui. Valencia began thinking. If he and the other Yaquis were to build the dream, the group would need federal aid and funds outside the Yaqui community—but how would they accomplish this?[1]

A major obstacle in the Yaquis' path was the fact that in the early 1960s the Yaquis were an "unrecognized" Indian group. This fact did not make the group unique because at this time the federal government had not formally recognized between one and two hundred such groups in the United States. What did make the Yaquis unique is that in time they would overcome extreme obstacles and succeed in gaining tribal recognition through an act of Congress in 1978—a feat the vast majority of unrecognized Indian groups have failed to achieve.

The Pascua Yaquis were the last group to secure tribal recognition prior to the Federal Acknowledgment Process; they likely would have failed through the BIA process. After the creation of the FAP, various forces have united behind the BIA system, a method of acknowledging tribes that they see as preferable to the more overtly political congressional route. As the following passages reveal, Valencia's people succeeded where others failed largely because they maintained viable and easily identifiable indigenous religious ceremonies, Indian ancestry, and tribal institutions supported, in part, by federal programs. As David E. Wilkins and Anne McCulloch have noted, congressional recognition is highly dependent on social constructions of Indianness. In this light the Pascua Yaquis ultimately gained tribal recognition because they rather unambiguously matched popular and scholarly perceptions of what an Indian "tribe" looked and acted like. The fact that the Yaquis possessed a concentrated village, visible Indian ancestry, and colorful ceremonies helped the Tucson group convince legislators they were an indigenous people as matched against a template modeled upon existing western reservation tribes. Ultimately their enduring racial and cultural traits enabled the Pascua Yaquis to secure powerful congressional and scholarly support, while their astute leaders succeeded brilliantly in projecting an image of their people as a small, united, and impoverished Indian tribe that matched outside expectations. In the end the Pascua Yaquis maneuvered rather easily through a federal Indian identification policy that has forced indigenous peoples to operate within increasingly confined paradigms of Indian authenticity.[2]

The Tucson-area Yaquis originated in the northern Mexican state of Sonora, a rugged country of mountains and deserts bordered by the Sea of Cortez to the west and the state of Arizona to the north. Prior to contact, the Yaquis developed a complex society based on agriculture and on hunting and gathering within the fertile delta region of a rare desert river that came to be called the Río Yaqui or Yaqui River. The people spoke (and continue to speak) Cahitan, a Uto-Aztecan language, and possessed a strong sense of themselves as a people, united in common language, kinship, and culture. In the wake of sustained European contact in the sixteenth century, the Sonoran group successfully integrated Jesuit-based Catholicism and indigenous spirituality to forge an entirely new religious tradition, with a complex set of Lenten ceremonials at its heart.[3]

In the centuries following Spanish contact the Yaquis similarly melded European and indigenous political traditions, combining Yaqui forms with Spanish town government, and ultimately used the new system to resist incursions on their community lands.[4] Fiercely independent, the Yaqui Nation held off Spanish and Mexican colonization until the last half of the nineteenth century, when it faced a concerted assault on its lands and sovereignty. During this era the Mexican government occupied the Yaqui country and targeted the Yaqui towns as some of the last vestiges of powerful tribalism in the region. In the ensuing era of occupation that lasted from 1887 to 1910, the "Yaqui Diaspora" began. Although Yaqui bands conducted an ongoing guerilla war from mountain strongholds, by the early twentieth century the majority of Yaquis had left their country, fleeing to nearby haciendas, mines, and cities. The Mexican government forcibly deported thousands of others to the far reaches of Mexico and distributed Yaqui children to prominent families to be raised as Mexicans. At one point fewer than two thousand Yaquis remained in their country. Fearing for their lives, small groups and haggard individuals fled to Arizona, where they took pains to hide their identity in fear of forced deportation back to Mexico and certain shipment to the Yucatan into virtual slavery. Oddly the outbreak of the Mexican Revolution in 1910 saved the Yaquis from complete dispersal and annihilation at the hands of the central government. Partly as a result of their important fighting during the struggle, the postrevolutionary government established an "indigenous zone" that encompassed part of the Yaqui country in 1937. Afterward the Yaquis continued to strive to reestablish their town and religious organizations within the modern Mexican state.[5]

The Yaquis who fled to the United States similarly attempted to reorganize their community and ceremonial life in Arizona. At first speaking their language only among themselves, the Arizona Yaquis hid their identity from outsiders. At the same time, they congregated together, gradually learning to speak Spanish in the growing Hispanic-Indian barrios of southern Arizona. Always fearful of deportation back to Mexico, Arizona Yaquis for a time ended their public ceremonials. Although they presented themselves as Mexican Americans to outsiders, they still maintained an enduring sense of being a separate people. As they became aware of religious freedoms in America, however, the Yaquis redeveloped various forms of family customs and festivals and reestablished community organization and religious ceremonials. Along with a shared sense of resistance, the religious observances, family networks, and Yaqui language became the basis of Yaqui identity in the United States.[6]

Arizona Yaquis gradually established settlements at Barrio Libre and Pascua near downtown Tucson, at Marana to the northwest of Tucson, at Guadalupe and Scottsdale near Phoenix, and at Somerton in the far western part of the state. By 1940 there were an estimated 2,500 Yaquis in the state. Most worked as migrant farm laborers in the cotton and vegetable fields of the Santa Cruz, Gila, and Salt River valleys and as hands on scattered desert ranches throughout the southern part of the state. Overall, the seasonal work of the fields melded well with the time and labor needs of the Yaqui ceremonial calendar, as the off-season in agriculture corresponded with the Lenten season. In their search for work many Yaquis lived part of the year far from the Yaqui settlements yet returned faithfully for the ceremonial season. Extremely poor, most Yaquis lived as squatters on public lands or settled on plots owned by large agricultural companies, living in homes made of railroad ties, tin, and cardboard from the neighboring city dumps. Few Yaqui homes had running water or plumbing, while most houses had sand and dirt floors well into the twentieth century.[7]

Once in the United States, Yaquis established centralized settlements around Yaqui churches. Here they participated in a unique form of Catholicism that had evolved following contact with Jesuit missionaries. During the seventeenth century the Jesuits had worked desperately to replace Yaqui religion with European Christian belief and practice, yet the resulting collaboration created a wholly new religion, derived from both Indian and Christian tradition, a development common throughout the Americas. Over the years this fused religion would continue to grow and change.[8]

In their effort to reach the Yaquis the Jesuits introduced several religious melodramas to teach key events and concepts of Christian doctrine that the Yaqui refugees carried to Arizona. These fused or syncretic rituals, ironically, became central to the Yaquis' perceived indigenousness and ultimate recognition. The missionaries also established religious societies organized around the melodramas. The most important and enduring pageant among the Arizona Yaquis was the drama of the passion and resurrection of Christ. Every year the Yaqui communities acted out their versions of the passion of Jesus' last days on Earth in ceremonials extending through the forty days of Lent. Most Yaqui parents came to promise their children to one of the ceremonial societies. Having been sponsored by one of the religious organizations, the ceremonial networks and dramas ensured that most Yaquis would participate in the annual ceremonies that came to serve as the heart of Yaqui cultural practice in both the United States and Mexico. Called Waehma in Yaqui, the Lenten ceremonies became a primary vehicle for expressing Yaqui values and bringing together the whole Yaqui community. By fulfilling their ceremonial obligations and labors, Yaquis enhanced group solidarity and identity as well.[9]

During the Easter season the deer dancer (*saila maso*, or little brother deer) became central to the public image of both Sonora and Arizona Yaquis and represented the *huya aniya*, the natural or animal world to the Yaquis. This dance—performed by a bare-chested man who held large red gourd rattles in each hand and who wore a stuffed deer head on his head, accompanied by *masobuikame* (deer singers) singing songs in Yaqui—became perhaps the most visible symbol of Yaquiness to outsiders and eventually appeared on license plates in Sonora and official state statues. At the ceremonies the Yaquis also employed various forms of clowning that involved wearing animal and human masks that became central to the general public's perception of the Yaqui people.[10]

The families that settled at Pascua originally assembled as squatters along the Santa Cruz River on the western fringe of Tucson. Here they were near the Southern Pacific Railroad and the agricultural work they relied upon as well as the city dump, where they obtained materials for housing. Because of their living conditions and revolutionary heritage, however, public officials labeled them a "social and health menace," and immigration officials worried over their refugee status. As a result of these concerns and complaints from the owner of the land that they occupied near the dump, local realtor A. M. Franklin prepared a platted subdivision on the rural fringe of town in 1923 to sell to the group and named it "Pascua" (Easter in Spanish) for their religious ceremonials. Franklin sold the newly named Pascua group individual plots under an installment plan with payments of one dollar per month. At this time twenty families settled at Pascua, yet the majority of Tucson Yaquis refused to join the new community or live under the planned Immigration and Naturalization Service surveillance. The nature of the founding of Pascua provided the basis for a close relationship between the community and local officials, a fact that gave it preeminence among Yaqui settlements. Ironically, however, what came to be perceived as the "traditional" village of Pascua resulted in part from an organized early subdivision effort.[11]

During the 1920s each of the major Arizona settlements began staging the elaborate Waehma ceremonials again, attracting tourists and media attention in the process. Arizona Yaquis also reestablished the *compadrazgo*, or godparent system that served as a fictive kinship network, promoting community cohesion and survival. They did not, however, reestablish their traditional town governments because federal and state agencies already fulfilled these functions in Arizona. From this point until the early 1960s, organized Yaqui community life in Arizona centered on religious societies and church alone. In 1923 the city of Tucson opened a public school at Pascua at the prompting of Thamar Richey, a retired teacher who dedicated the twilight years of her life to the Yaqui children, often forsaking much of her salary to provide medicine and food for the destitute group. On land donated by realtor Franklin, Pascua Yaquis also built a church of railroad ties and scrap at the center of the barrio, christening it San Ignacio de Loyola. Though many Yaquis were concentrated at Pascua near the school and church, the neighborhood also contained non-

Yaquis. Various factions of Yaquis existed within the community as well, and unified activity occurred generally only during ceremonies or within smaller kinship groups.[12]

Despite the neighborhood's early promise, with the onset of the Great Depression many Yaquis simply could not make payments on their lots. Real estate developer Franklin ceased to attempt to make collections at Pascua, yet the Yaquis' hold on the land became precarious. Like many unrecognized Indian communities during the 1930s, the Yaquis at Pascua attempted to organize and obtain federal assistance under the New Deal programs for Indians. Unlike many others, however, issues of nationality ultimately clouded their plans. The initial impetus for contacting the BIA sprang from a concerted effort to deport the alien Indian group. In light of the strains on local relief agencies, federal and state officials began a strident "repatriation" program to deport Mexican nationals. A study conducted in Tucson determined that 80 percent of the Pascua Yaquis were not citizens. As a result some individuals within the local relief community and the Federal Emergency Relief Agency wanted to deport the Yaquis to rid themselves of the welfare burden. The group's uncertain position continued for several years until the State Department determined that their safety could not be guaranteed if they returned to Mexico.[13]

Realizing the Yaquis were here to stay, local charities began looking for ways to aid them. With the Pascuans' acquiescence, Thamar Richey formed a committee that included a wide array of University of Arizona professors and civic-minded business people, including anthropologist John Provinse, Arizona's first congresswoman, Isabella Greenway, and university president H. L. Shantz. The committee envisioned a rehabilitation project that would re-create a "self-sustaining agricultural village" that would ultimately help assimilate the group. The plan dovetailed nicely with the Pascuans' own desire to reestablish the life they had known in Mexico.[14]

Although the Pascua Yaquis desired to re-create agricultural life in Arizona, this effort appears to have been largely spearheaded by local community leaders driven by both paternal and economic concerns. From the perspective of the white community, aiding the Pascuans was a "win-win" situation. Supporting their "colorful" ceremonies would prove a boon to the city's tourist economy while the federally supported Indian village would be an "attractive experiment" in self-government—both for the Yaquis to run and for the university's anthropology department to study. During this time, a mutually beneficial relationship began between the Pascua group and University of Arizona anthropologists such as Province and Edward "Ned" Spicer. In the 1930s Ned and Rosamund Spicer, who would become one of the best-known husband and wife anthropological teams in the Southwest, began studying cultural change and persistence among the residents of Pascua village, later publishing their findings in the influential monograph *Pascua: A Yaqui Village in Arizona* in 1940. In time Pascua would serve as the backbone of Ned Spicer's influential theories of cultural persistence and enduring peoples. In planning for the group, anthropologist Robert Redfield, later well known for his testimony in the landmark school desegregation case *Brown vs. Board of Education*, declared that the village would be a perfect "laboratory of anthropology," and it became just this.[15]

In 1935 the committee submitted a rural resettlement plan to the Indian Office. As would become a prevalent stance, however, the Indian Service originally responded that it had no legal responsibility for the Yaquis because the federal government had never recognized them by treaty, act of Congress, custom, or executive order. Commissioner of Indian Affairs John Collier believed that the Yaquis' situation would have to be met by a special act of Congress, as was done with the Metlakatla Indians, who migrated from British Columbia, Canada, to Alaska at the beginning of the twentieth century. It does not appear, however, that Collier doubted the authenticity of the Yaquis, as he referred to them as "the Yaqui Indians at Tucson" and considered them among the "numerous groups of stranded Indians in various cities of this country who constitute a serious social and health problem for these cities." Demonstrating the paternalistic concerns that made up the thinking of policymakers of the era, Collier made inquiries as to the feasibility of purchasing submarginal lands for the group and "colonizing" them, in hopes the Yaqui Indians would "be properly cared for."[16] In conjunction with the plan Collier sent an Indian education supervisor from Gallup, New Mexico, to visit the Pascua Yaquis and assess the situation. Unlike a similar trip undertaken at the same time by Ruth Underhill to various Louisiana Indian groups, no effort appears to have been made to inquire into the Indian authenticity or blood quantum of the Yaquis at Pascua. As the people appeared to be racially Indian, lived in concentrated communities in the West, and had cultural traits associated with Indians, the agent never questioned the Indian status or racial ancestry of the group and went on to plan the eventual assumption of educational responsibilities by the federal government.[17]

The developments that followed, however, were all too common in the history of unrecognized tribes during the Great Depression and reveal the financial concerns and historical accidents that often resulted in groups remaining unrecognized by the federal government. Upon reviewing their case and the agent's report, Collier suggested the Yaquis could voluntarily relocate to the Colorado River Reservation approximately 250 miles from Tucson. The relocation plan, however, soon became enmeshed in issues of the Yaquis' Mexican nationality and was dropped. Closer to home the Tucson rehabilitation plan also died in light of a congressional bill that prohibited the purchase of Arizona lands for Indians outside of existing Indian reservations.[18] As a result the Pascua Yaquis remained in the unenviable status of unrecognized Indians after the 1930s.

After the demise of the proposed projects the Arizona Yaqui communities continued to exist without federal supports and status. In Pascua, Yaquis maintained their ceremonial life even though it involved great costs and engendered conflicts at the individual level. To keep the group together during the late 1930s and continuing through the 1950s, the Pascua Yaquis attempted to secure title to the lands of the neighborhood. During these years a young Yaqui veteran of World War II, Anselmo Valencia, emerged as the leader of the community. Like many Indian veterans, Valencia returned from war with new eyes. As he recalled, "We served in World War II and when we got back, we became aliens and wetbacks and non-citizens."[19] As leader of the *caballeros* society that functioned during the Easter season, Valencia occupied an important role in the Yaqui ceremonial organization. Considered the Pascua Yaquis' spiritual leader and "chief" to outsiders, Valencia took the initiative in attempting to better the material conditions at Pascua. At this same time University of Arizona anthropology student Muriel Thayer Painter began serving as a social activist for the community, much like teacher Thamar Richey had done previously. Painter had a degree in social work from Wellesley College and began to study the Yaquis, documenting their ceremonials and working tirelessly on their behalf.[20]

During this time period Valencia and others began looking for outside means to support their ceremonial life. In a problem all too common with impoverished, unrecognized groups, the Yaquis were faced with constant tensions trying to maintain their identity and time-consuming ceremonials in the face of social and economic pressures, especially the necessity of maintaining steady employment. After World War II agriculture became increasingly mechanized, cutting off much of the Yaquis' employment that had melded so well with the seasonal needs of their ceremonial life. Because they lacked a reservation homeland that generally serves to enhance tribal organization and power, the Yaquis turned to the local community for assistance. During the 1940s and 1950s Muriel Painter led various efforts by the Chamber of Commerce and the Tucson Festival Society to aid the group by promoting the Lenten events as a tourist attraction for the city of Tucson. With Western films and dude ranches at their zenith, local civic leaders wanted to give visitors to Tucson what they expected to see: colorful, "authentic" Indians. The Yaquis agreed to open their Easter ceremonials to visitors, but they did not maintain them for commercial purposes. Such ceremonies were rooted firmly in the particular world-view and culture of the Yaqui people. In order to maintain the form, however, many Pascua Yaquis willingly promoted at least some aspects of their ceremonies for commercial purposes. [21]

In 1955 the Pascua Yaquis started the San Ignacio Club for the overall betterment of the community. Led by Anselmo Valencia, the club counted virtually the entire adult male population of Pascua by the early 1960s. Through the organization, Pascuans made conscious efforts to make their ceremonies visible by erecting signs to the village, contacting newspapers, and working in partnership with the University of Arizona Anthropology Department in their efforts to study and promote the continuance of the ceremonies. The club also established the Fiesta of San Ignacio, an event that promoted cultural exchange by including Yaqui dancers and musicians from Sonora. Booths set up during events also earned money for the community and ceremonies. As Valencia recalled, "We got together to make plans so that we could help each other out, so that if someone in Pascua has an illness or death in the family we can help pay his debts." [22]

Although academics were intrigued with the Yaqui ceremonials, the Pascuans were not widely encouraged to continue their practices. Since settling in Pascua and elsewhere in Arizona, Yaquis faced constant appeals from Protestant and Mormon missionaries to give up their special blend of Catholicism and indigenous religion. To gain influence within the community, in 1949 a Mormon missionary went so far as to attempt to buy the Pascua lands in arrears for taxes, including the sacred Plaza, for the Mormon Church. Most Yaquis, however, consciously resisted the efforts of missionaries to convert them. Despite this resolve, many Yaqui families were dependent on the churches for various forms of relief and felt pressured to convert. [23]

Lacking a federal reservation, the Pascua group, like most unacknowledged Indian communities, experienced continual difficulties maintaining social cohesion in the face of economic pressures and larger forces of modernization. Most often poor, unacknowledged Indian groups such as the Yaquis faced constant forces pulling individual members away to find employment and stability. In many ways the experience of unrecognized Indian communities paralleled the history of small, rural communities that faced forces of urbanization and industrialization after World War II. Even so, during the 1950s Pascua religious leaders made concerted efforts to secure their ambiguous land base while fending off overtures from missionaries. Overall, the land situation greatly hindered the Yaquis' efforts to improve the community, while the search for employment pulled many from the neighborhood. Geographical distance did not necessarily mean, however, that these people ceased to be Yaqui; many faithfully returned during the ceremonials to their families in the community.[24]

By the mid-1950s the growing city of Tucson had surrounded the once rural neighborhood. One by one, Yaqui families lost title to their lots due to tax foreclosure. A charitable trust called the Marshall Foundation stepped in and purchased Pascua lots in arrears for taxes while encouraging the group to purchase the remaining lots. To help their friends Ned Spicer and Muriel Painter spearheaded a project to assist the group in securing their land base. All the while, the area was becoming more and more industrial, with the Yaquis beset by real estate developers and continual fears of being evicted by the foundation. While most Pascuans expressed the conviction that "we will not be separated" at any cost, many privately worried that if they did not secure deeds to their plots, the land would be sold, and they would "scatter" and not be able to hold ceremonials.[25]

Although vexing at the time, the Pascua Yaquis' continuing efforts to resolve their land and housing problems would prove vital to their subsequent recognition efforts. With Valencia serving as cultural mediator, Spicer and Painter formed the Committee for Pascua Community Housing at the beginning of the 1960s. In many ways Tucson community advocates perceived the housing committee as "a worthwhile civic effort," while the Pascuans saw it as a vehicle to better living conditions and a secure land base. Fortunately just as the Pascua Yaquis were awakening to the political process, many in the larger community were amenable to helping what they called "our Yaquis."[26] Together, the two segments of the Tucson community united for political action.

By the early 1960s the material conditions surrounding Pascua had deteriorated badly. Fearing further loss of land and the crime encircling his neighborhood, in 1962 Valencia began dreaming that his people could move outside Tucson somewhere within the expanse of federal lands that surrounded the city. The Yaqui leader believed time was short, however, because the area surrounding the community was becoming increasingly industrial and socially unstable, crowded with warehouses and shops catering to the poverty-stricken barrio, seedy hotels, nightclubs, and houses of prostitution.[27]

By the standards of the dominant society the living conditions within the community also were deplorable. The majority of the houses appeared much as they had in the 1920s, thrown together with railroad ties, tin, and other scraps from the nearby city dump. Outdoor privies were widely evident, and schoolchildren could be found studying by kerosene lamps at night. For those able to afford electricity and water, their outlets and faucets sprouted an odd-assortment of splitter lines to nearby homes, with their neighbors contributing to the common cost when they could. There were several Yaqui families living in most houses, and leaky roofs and dirt floors were the norm. Because of the surrounding slum environment, elders worried about the rising drug and alcohol use within the village. Overcrowding was a severe problem, as the Yaquis owned only ten acres of the forty in Pascua, and the population of the village had doubled during the previous thirty years to approximately 360 residents.[28]

In early 1962 Valencia decided he needed to move quickly. The Marshall Foundation, previously so paternalistic, began tax foreclosure proceedings on several lots and notified the Yaquis that it would sell them no additional land. In response Valencia approached congressional hopeful Morris K. Udall about his dream. Udall, a former student of Ned Spicer from northern Arizona who was of Mormon heritage, agreed to help, provided he won the seat vacated by his brother, Stewart Udall, who had recently resigned to serve as John F. Kennedy's secretary of the interior. Overall, Udall viewed helping the Pascuans as both a humanitarian gesture and a chance to gain some positive publicity for his congressional campaign in a predominantly Democratic district. Ultimately this encounter would prove fortuitous for Valencia's people: Udall won the election and went on to a noteworthy career in Congress, becoming well known for his support of liberal causes.[29]

In his efforts to develop what became known as the "relocation plan," Valencia also approached his lifelong friends Muriel Painter, Ned Spicer, and anthropologist Edward Dozier, a Pueblo Indian, for help. Together, they developed the Pascua Yaqui Land Development Project as a consciously Yaqui-directed committee. Pascuans Felipa Suarez, Gloria Suarez, Joaquina Garcia, and Raul Silvas served on the committee, and Geronimo Estrella, Ignacio Alvarez, and Eusebia Salvador faithfully attended meetings. Being a highly self-directed and independent individual, Valencia expressed concerns from the start that the non-Yaquis on the project would interfere with other aspects of Yaqui life. Though he had no formal contact with organized Indian activists, Valencia's activities exemplified the rising Indian assertiveness of the early 1960s. In light of his resolve Valencia and Painter worked to self-consciously project the image that Valencia was in charge at all times and to seek wide participation from within Pascua.[30]

The timing for this effort was much better than it had been for the 1930s relocation plan. In the 1960s there was a growing "liberal consensus" and belief that the government should help the poor and minorities. Sympathetic non-Indians felt that injustices to minorities needed to be righted, especially the long litany of abuses against Indians, who were generally left out of the 1950s civil rights movement. Reflecting this sentiment, one constituent asked Udall what he had done for Indians, "a minority that does not have a NAACP or Anti-Defamation League to protect them," while another interested citizen remarked, "these people have been suffering long before the Blacks, the Mexicans, the Jews, or any other person who is not white," and pleaded for Udall to do something about the "shameful, disgusting treatment of these people." [31] The Udall brothers needed little persuading, however. As Mo remarked, "I agree that the American Indians have not been treated fairly by the United States government; I have been trying everything I can to see to it that our Red brothers and sisters are repaid what we took from them." [32]

Because the idea of a "New Pascua" was largely Valencia's from the start, he attempted to persuade all his people that the timing was right to accept the vision. The Pascuans, however, were far from a united community acting with one voice and interest. The neighborhood itself was not an insular Indian village either: approximately 50 percent of residents were Mexican American, ceremonially disassociated from the Yaquis yet having a stake in the community. Factions also existed among the Yaquis who did not cooperate outside the Easter ceremonies. Although Valencia envisioned including other Yaqui settlements in New Pascua, the relocation plan was largely centered on Pascua village, and it was the Pascuans who debated the form the new settlement would take. Ultimately most agreed the village would be patterned on the traditional Yaqui pueblos of Sonora, with a central plaza for community life centered on the church and ceremonial ramada. As the Pascuans planned for the potential new village, the idea of reviving Yaqui traditions and village structure imbued them with a new sense of excitement.[33]

In its outlines, however, neither the Pascuans nor Udall's office viewed this effort as an attempt to gain tribal recognition. Although the termination policy was waning, and Udall was against the ideology in general, the Yaquis themselves did not want to become recognized at this time. Many expressed fears of being forced onto a reservation and becoming dependent on the BIA. When asked the Yaquis' motivation, Valencia argued that the Pascuans wanted only to stay together "because of our religion and because we are poor and we need to help each other."[34] He made it clear that they did not desire government services, and neither Ned Spicer nor Muriel Painter believed it would benefit the independent people to be under the jurisdiction of the bureau. Throughout this time the committee worked hard to avoid having the project appear to have any attribute of an Indian reservation.

The discourse surrounding the potential land transfer to the Yaquis, however, demonstrated a clear waning of termination sentiments and a renewed interest in preserving Indian cultures. Udall's assistants Theodore Heyl and Richard Olson encouraged the group to appeal to liberal concerns for minorities and cultural diversity by using the "vanishing Red Man" trope, warning that their culture would soon die out if federal lands were not secured for them, a prospect previously welcomed by many non-Indians. Heyl also urged Valencia to bring other Yaquis to meetings with Udall to demonstrate unity among his people, and Painter orchestrated a media campaign to get publicity. A skilled mediator, Valencia convinced the Pima County Planning Commission that a new village, developed to resemble a traditional Yaqui pueblo, would be "a valuable asset" to the community as a tourist destination.[35]

In 1962 the Pascuans took steps to formalize their community organization. With help from volunteer attorney Leonard Scheff, they ultimately created the Pascua Yaqui Association (PYA) as a nonprofit corporation so that the federal government would have an entity with which to deal, because like most unrecognized Indian groups, the Yaquis had no organization to work for them politically. In early 1963 the Pascuans held several *juntas*, or meetings, to discuss issues important in the formation of the new political body. Valencia was plowing new ground, as this was the first attempt by an Arizona Yaqui community to formalize its political organization since the aborted attempts of the 1920s and 1930s.[36]

While forming the corporation the Pascuans faced the thorny issue of establishing membership criteria. Traditionally inclusion in the community was informal and fluid. Having a defined membership, however, was of prime importance to policymakers who desired to limit and delineate the service population. According to Painter, creating formal procedures, bylaws, and membership criteria was a trying experience for both Valencia and Geronimo Estrella, who were spearheading the project. In the end, however, the group defined membership in part on Yaqui terms and in part by using the blood quantum requirements of the federal bureaucracy. Working closely with Edward Dozier, the Pascuans drew up formal membership rules. The articles of incorporation of the PYA stated that members would be either one-quarter Yaqui blood or persons who maintained ceremonial association and lived among the Yaquis in Pascua. Revealing a common sentiment among Indians, however, Valencia expressed dismay at the inclusion of an amount of "Yaqui blood." As he remarked, "any Yaqui knows who is a Yaqui."[37]

The committee thus established the association as a formal body for the express purposes of accepting and administering a future federal land grant. To reflect its legal structure as opposed to the previous informal Pascua organization, Scheff drew up articles of incorporation clearly spelling out the functions and duties of the organization. By the spring of 1963 the Pascuans met at the small adobe church of San Ignacio de Loyola in Pascua to accept the document and elect members of the association, which was to have an all-Yaqui board of directors elected to annual terms. Not surprisingly the Yaquis highly involved with the relocation plan were elected members, including Valencia, Estrella, Ygnacio Alvarez, Felipa Suarez, Eusebia Salvador, Raul Silvas, Antonio Valencia, Juan Alvarez, and Virginia Valenzuela. The PYA's stated goal was to maintain and enhance Yaqui culture and provide aid to its members in Arizona. The association was clearly delegated the authority to employ persons, construct improvements on association lands, operate businesses, solicit and accept funds, and grant land for public schools. The board of directors had the power to promulgate formal rules and bylaws, and the charter gave the chairman power over the entire organization. The incorporation document also provided for the continuance of the advisory committee.[38]

With the establishment of a formal organization to deal with the federal bureaucracy, the Pascua Yaquis next turned to constructing a document to convey an image of themselves as impoverished Indians entitled to a land grant from the federal government. As countless other unrecognized Indian groups would later do, the group and its experts composed a "petition" to Congress for a land grant in which the association painted a picture of a long neglected and forgotten Indian group to appeal to the growing awareness of injustice to minorities. When Muriel Painter needed pictures to demonstrate the poor housing at Pascua, however, she recalled that Valencia "looked stricken" at the thought of asking his people to put forward their homes as examples of the "horrible housing" at the village. Eventually other Yaquis stepped in, and full-color pictures of their dilapidated houses were included in the petition.

Overall, the Yaquis needed only to demonstrate that they were poor Indians with a surviving culture, not that they were genetically Native Americans. Their documents stressed that the Yaquis were freedom-loving refugees from Mexico who were "grateful for the asylum offered us," and who also possessed a well-documented and "colorful" culture worthy of preservation. Covering up divisions within Pascua and among Arizona Yaqui settlements, the petition stressed that Pascua was the center of Yaqui life in Arizona. While accenting the Yaquis' poverty, the petition also implied the Yaquis needed federal land to enable them to free themselves from welfare. As Valencia argued, "as we are poor, it is our desire to live as a community in order to help each other in time of need."[39]

To portray their "Indianness" to the BIA and members of Congress, the Yaquis also included Painter's glossy brochure *Faith, Flowers, and Fiestas*, which vividly showed the group's distinctive ceremonies and briefly explained the Lenten activities. With this document the Pascuans clearly fit the image of Native Americans held by policymakers and the dominant society. To present themselves to outsiders the Pascuans had allowed individuals to photograph their sacred ceremonies, a fact that caused dismay at other Yaqui communities. Framed by mountains, the color photos showed Yaquis dancing their deer dances and wearing colorful costumes and masks; their racial heritage appeared to be unambiguous. To fit political definitions of Indian tribes the document also stressed the strong "community feeling" and organization of the Pascuans while noting their "tribal activities."[40] Referring to himself as "chief," Anselmo Valencia astutely used this term, although the Yaquis traditionally did not possess this title. After viewing the completed document, Painter recalled that Valencia "laughed when I said I knew that the Yaquis were not all that *angelic.*"[41]

For successful legislation, however, the Pascuans also needed to show strong non-Indian support for the relocation plan. Udall commented that it was vital that "senators be bombarded" with telegrams and letters. To this end the petition contained letters extolling the Yaquis' culture, their potential tourist value, and their benefit to the University of Arizona from the mayor of Tucson, the Chamber of Commerce, and virtually every branch of city and county government. The Pascuans also provided a petition with 107 signatures, demonstrating unity behind the effort.[42]

Though all Arizona Yaquis theoretically could join in the land project if they associated with the PYA, the plan was largely organized and carried out by Pascua Yaquis alone, and many in the community were actually opposed to the move. Many of Valencia's cohorts did not want to deal with government red tape and began circulating rumors against Valencia's leadership and his dream. As Josefina Cocio put it, many Pascuans were "not all very pleased about it," seeing that Valencia "sprung it" on them.[43] In essence the new plan simply plugged into existing factionalism at Pascua that centered upon community patrons. In the Arizona Yaqui communities, a patron-client network generally existed that fostered divisions and dependency, and both Ned Spicer and his student William Willard reported that the relocation plan only exacerbated ongoing tensions between factions tied to outside agencies.[44] Immediately upon hearing about the relocation plan, social patrons and some Yaquis began mobilizing opposition to the plan. Property-owning Yaquis were the first to raise doubts, expressing fears that the people would fail to assimilate if isolated on the proposed desert tract. In time, however, two factions coalesced in Pascua: one behind Valencia and the Pascua Yaqui Association and the other centered on charity organizations that bitterly opposed the move.

Perhaps the most strident objections came from whites with vested interests in having the Yaquis remain at Pascua. The rhetoric they employed contained strains of racism and self-interest while ultimately arguing in favor of assimilation of the group. Though the Yaquis retained substantial degrees of their culture, as unrecognized Indians they were subjected to attacks impugning their ethnicity and heritage. As A. Turney Smith, a lawyer who owned a ranch adjoining the proposed new site, warned Udall, "These so-called Indians are not Indians in the proper sense of the word. They are a mixture of several breeds—they are filthy and do not care for sanitation, cleanliness or anything high or ideal. It would mean the downfall of this area which is one of the most beautiful locations in Arizona." After informing the congressman that they were not real Indians, however, Smith went on to warn that no one "would consider living out there with a tribe of Yaqui Indians roving around and possibly stealing and raising Hell. To place the Yaqui Indians out there would be even worse than having a leprosy colony there. When Yaquis get hold of liquor they get wild and will do most anything—even killing."[45] Seconding some of these opinions, local realtor Vivian Arnold wrote saying that the publicity regarding relocating the Yaqui had "killed all present and future sales for that section."[46] Another protested that the Indians would "merely create a new slum" and threatened a lawsuit.[47]

Some interested parties protested that the plan was a modern-day Indian removal that would prove a detriment to the Yaqui people. These individuals cautioned it would be a step back for the Yaquis to isolate the group further from "civilization" and close to the influence of other Indians on the Papago (Tohono O'odham) Reservation. As African American community leader and principal of the Pascuans' junior high school Morgan Maxwell Sr. put it, "to relocate these people into greater isolation would only result in further deprivation and a continuation of a paternalistic role" by outsiders.[48]

Local missionary patron John Swank levied perhaps the strongest and most consistent attacks on the land acquisition plan. He and other Protestant missionaries had been working in Pascua for many years to convert the nominally Catholic group. Swank's group opposed any effort to preserve the Yaquis' traditional religious observances because they believed such practices kept the Indians in poverty. According to Swank, "the men who take part in [the ceremonies] are drunkards and in many cases, heroine addicts. A ceremonial fiesta becomes an occasion for drunkenness, debauchery and immorality of the worst kind—our people who come to our missions and who try to live decent lives are plagued by these fiestas and their damnable results."[49] Swank also accused the non-Yaquis involved with the plan of exploiting the Pascuans' ignorance and attempting to create a "tourist attraction" by "making merchandise of these Yaqui people." Beyond other motivations, the reverend was spurred by Valencia's hostility toward his mission. In fact, in planning for New Pascua Valencia flatly told Reverend Swank that the PYA would never allow Protestant missions at the new site. In response Swank and others shot off letters to Washington charging that the New Pascua plan violated the separation of church and state and discriminated against a fair segment of Yaquis who were Protestant.[50]

After making assurances that all faiths would have equal access to build missions at the new site, Udall proceeded to draw up legislation to convey federal land to the group. A common criticism of legislative recognition is that it favors groups that secure powerful advocates. In their early efforts to secure land via legislation the Yaquis certainly had a strong supporter in Udall and the highest possible connections in the Department of the Interior. In addition to Mo Udall, Valencia's group had the aid of Secretary of the Interior Stewart Udall and anthropologist James Officer, the associate commissioner of Indian affairs and a close friend of Ned Spicer. Being from the West and representing a district with one of the nation's largest Indian populations, Udall was assigned to the House Committee on Interior and Insular Affairs, where Indian legislation originates. In light of these personal connections and the political alignment in favor of civil rights, the Pascua Yaquis' chances appeared good.[51]

In May of 1963 Udall introduced a bill to provide for the conveyance of federal lands to the PYA for the purpose of preserving and enhancing Yaqui culture. The bill called for the federal government to deed approximately two hundred acres of Bureau of Land Management (BLM) land to the association free of charge, subject to restrictions found within the association's articles of incorporation. To ensure the land would not be alienated (sold) or used for private gain, the secretary of the interior had the power to impose conditions as the department saw fit—thus creating a form of paternal federal relationship. Specifically the bill had a clause that provided the land would revert back to the federal government if the association broke its founding provisions.[52]

Though the chances for success looked good, there remained many forces against Indian tribalism in the early 1960s. Udall's office noted the BIA still had the objective of "getting out of the Indian business," and there were many voices raised against providing public lands and aid to Indians—lingering sentiments from the concerted efforts to terminate tribes in the late 1940s and 1950s. Because of this Udall's office assured listeners that the Yaquis were not seeking recognition or "wardship." At home Anselmo Valencia likewise told a Yaqui audience: "[this] won't be . . . a reservation!"[53] Even so, as this was a political measure, it became important to find a precedent for a federal land transfer to an Indian group from a foreign country. Working with the Udall brothers and Spicer, James Officer and others within the BIA found the precedents they were looking for in the Rocky Boys Band of Montana and the Metlakatla Indians of Alaska. Both tribes had aboriginal land bases in Canada, yet Congress granted them land after they immigrated to the United States in the late nineteenth and early twentieth centuries. Closer to the Yaquis, in the early twentieth century Congress had also established a reservation in western Arizona for the Cocopah, a small tribe originally living in the Colorado delta of Mexico. With these precedents located, the PYA and Udall worked with the BLM to get the go-ahead for the site.[54] Udall also persuaded Arizona Senator Carl Hayden, the powerful, senior-ranking member of the Senate, to sponsor a companion bill for the Yaqui people. In 1963 the two began ushering their respective bills through the labyrinth of Congress. Despite all the promise, the bill languished and died that year in session. At this time Udall estimated that the House Interior Committee alone processed some four thousand bills during the course of a session of Congress. According to Udall, his major job was to find some time when the committee could take up the legislation. In 1963 the Interior Committee did not find the time.[55]

Because Congress does not operate in a vacuum, its members tend to rely heavily on the opinion of the Department of the Interior and the BIA (and their own research) before voting on Indian-related bills presented in committee. Following the advice of the BIA, Congress has routinely quashed recognition bills since the 1970s, deferring to the bureau's expertise in Indian matters. As Udall's assistant, Theodore Heyl told Valencia at the time, "Unless a favorable report is secured unanimously from all groups this type of legislation has little chance of getting out of committee, much less getting passed into law."[56] In 1963 and early 1964 the small but vocal opposition in Tucson and termination-minded officials in Washington severely threatened the Pascua bill's chances.

To allay opposition within the government, Udall stressed that the legislation would not cost the government anything because it would take lands from the public domain. Upon deliberation, Stewart Udall's department decided it would not object to the passage of the legislation. Emphasizing, however, that the Interior Department considered the Yaquis to be descendants of Indian refugees from Mexico who had no special status as Indians, the BIA made sure that if the land were conveyed, it would not be Indian land within federal law.[57] In keeping with this intent the Senate added a section to the Yaqui bill that unequivocally prohibited a federal-tribal relationship, apparently borrowed word-for-word from a bill recognizing the Lumbee Indians of North Carolina for limited purposes in 1956. The Senate committee inserted Section 4 to the bill stating: "Nothing in this Act shall make such Yaqui Indians eligible for any services performed by the United States for Indians because of their status as Indians, and none of the statutes of the United States which affect Indians because of their status as Indians shall be applicable to the Yaqui Indians."[58] Much like the Lumbee act, the language of the bill effectively recognized the Pascuans as "Indians" yet terminated any relationship with the federal government at the same time.

With support from the Department of the Interior and the persuasive "petition" in hand, Udall steered his bill through the House Committee on Interior and Insular Affairs in 1964 with little opposition. It appeared that no one in Congress doubted either the racial or cultural authenticity of the Pascua Yaquis. As Udall told a priest helping the group, "There is no question in my mind that the Yaquis are a group of people and a culture worthy of protecting."[59] Many individuals involved with the Pascuan land grant seemed to have thoughts of equity rather than legal rationale in mind in their case. According to one interested observer, "Each of us, I am sure, can think of dozens of rational reasons why the Yaquis are not entitled to the [federal aid] . . . at this point I am more interested in the humaneness of the situation and trying to find what can be done to help this destitute and forgotten group."[60] There was, however, considerable ambiguity as to the commitment created by the bill and the status of the Yaquis as Indians. Both the bills and the BIA referred to the Yaquis as "Indians," while Democratic senator Wayne Morse of Oregon, one of only two congressmen who opposed the Gulf of Tonkin Resolution that same year, believed that the land grant was part of the "special trust obligations" of the United States for the "Indians of our country." Likewise, Udall considered a proposed school for New Pascua to be an Indian school that would serve the Pascua Yaquis and perhaps the nearby Tohono O'odham. With a disclaimer that the act should not serve as a precedent for other groups, the Senate committee passed the bill in the fall of 1964. [61] The bill now needed President Lyndon Johnson's signature.

The Pascua Yaquis and their supporters were truly elated when President Johnson signed Private Law 88–350 on October 8, 1964. The Pascuans now had a secure land base. On Halloween 1964 Yaquis held a ceremony commemorating the transfer of the land. Valencia made grand speeches in both Yaqui and Spanish while Udall turned over the deed to the two hundred acres to the PYA.[62] New Pascua now existed as land and Yaqui vision. It was up to the Pascua group to build Valencia's dream on the cactus-studded flats beneath Black Mountain.

Once the euphoria of their success in gaining the federal land wore off, however, the Pascua Yaquis realized they faced an uphill battle in realizing Valencia's dream of a new Yaqui town in the desert west of Tucson. Like all unrecognized Indian groups, the Yaquis were ineligible to receive funding for housing and other services from the BIA, Indian Health Service (IHS), or other government agencies providing services for Indians because of their status as Indians. After such momentous success in obtaining the land, the group now faced a crisis on how to secure funding to build houses at New Pascua. A major hindrance was the fact the PYA held the land of New Pascua in common, with restrictions ruling out mortgaging the land to "protect" it against ever being taken or sold from the group. With these obstacles as a backdrop, the association began looking for ways to finance construction of houses at the desert site.

At the time Ned Spicer informed the group about a new federal program, the Office of Economic Opportunity (OEO), then being started under President Johnson's War on Poverty, that could possibly help the Yaquis. The OEO was created by Johnson's Economic Opportunity Act of 1964 and had several functions, among them administering Community Action Programs (CAPS), Job Corps, and Volunteers In Service To America (VISTA). Realizing its potential, the Pascuans designed a program under the fledgling office. During the course of the 1960s the Pascuans in many ways would be at the forefront of the War on Poverty. Under the auspices of the OEO Valencia and New Pascua would gain leadership training, federal monies to run tribal programs, and, ultimately, preeminence among the various Arizona Yaqui communities in federal circles—all of which were crucial to their later acknowledgment efforts.[63]

From its beginnings, Spicer helped lead the OEO project at New Pascua. In the mid-1960s Spicer was a key part of a group of scholars later called "action anthropologists" in reference to a group of Kennedy advisers known as the "action intellectuals." These individuals, many of them in the field of applied anthropology such as Muriel Painter, believed their scholarship and activities should be geared toward the betterment of the Indian communities they studied. In some ways they were responding to increasing attacks by Indian activists who viewed anthropologists as just another parasitic force of colonialism who earned a living from the Indians and gave nothing in return. The Spicers, Dozier, and Painter, among others, were keenly aware of this criticism and their place and role within Indian communities such as Pascua. Roz Spicer summed up their feelings: "hopelessness, anger, frustration—there is a lot of that . . . [however] being idealistic, or perhaps purely selfish in the picture we want to create of America—we want to do something about it."[64]

In 1965 Spicer developed a grant proposal to start a Community Action Program under the OEO, which was headed by Kennedy family member R. Sargent Shriver. The legal mandate for the office required "maximum feasible participation," and the Yaqui association hoped to gain federal funding to accomplish this at Pascua. In 1966 Valencia's group secured the grant, yet the Pascuans realized the potential pitfalls of participating in bureaucratic programs such as this. Having started a new tribal organization to receive the federal land grant, the Yaquis were embarking on a new form of formalized, governing structure unknown in other Arizona Yaqui communities. Under the OEO and later the Office of Native American Programs (ONAP), paid employees entered the rubric of Yaqui community organization, while more formalized bureaucratic forms entered the community as well. Yaquis and the anthropologists worried the group would become miserably dependent on the bureaucracy and lose control of their community to outsiders. The leaders of the PYA, however, had long been conversant with outside funding and patron-client relations and hoped the effects would not be as drastic as some feared.[65]

The theory of the project was that the religious organization and kinship networks had failed to adapt effectively to dealing with the non-Yaqui world, although they had clearly served well to maintain Yaqui group solidarity. To overcome problems of low formal education, language, unemployment, and isolation from the surrounding community, the PYA's Development Project set out to solidify a new community by developing cohesion and indigenous leadership that would be able to work within the growing bureaucracy. A major goal of the project was to "neutralize" the "patrons of the poor" by creating a new post of "indigenous community development worker" who would organize, plan, and administer the programs of the OEO and ultimately develop skills that would lead to independence from both the welfare patrons and the bureaucracy. For the community workers the Development Project chose individuals intricately linked to the kinship, ritual, and ceremonial systems operating within the community. During the 1960s Anselmo Valencia, Joaquina Garcia, Raul Silvas, Pete Castillo, Virginia Baltazar, and others served as leaders at New Pascua. Despite central funding from the OEO, the New Pascua Development Project was organized through the association, and an all-Yaqui board of directors headed the project with advice from the non-Yaqui advisory committee, while voluntary labor lay at its core.[66]

Within its first years the New Pascua project was providing tangible benefits to Yaquis under the tribal organization, solidifying ethnic ties to the new community at the same time. Through the Pascua Yaqui Association the community development workers utilized the federal funds to provide numerous new services to the Pascua Yaquis, while charitable organizations continued to provide their traditional services as well. In the first four years of the OEO program the Pascua Yaquis received over $433,000 in federal funds, which they used to develop adult education classes, a community center, vocational programs under CETA, welfare assistance, and summer youth programs. Future Yaqui leaders Virginia Baltazar, Mary Jane Martinez, and Mario Flores, among others, were highly involved in these efforts. The association also developed a housing construction demonstration project that built dozens of homes, the first of which was completed for widow Felipa Suarez and her children. In light of its success the project later served as a model for other Indian projects on several reservations.[67]

Beyond the vocational and community programs, the PYA set out to consciously foster and create a sense of Yaqui tradition and history at the new community to combat forces of assimilation. To reinforce their collective history Valencia named streets in New Pascua after Yaqui towns and geographic features in their homeland in Mexico. The association soon established adobe making, a traditional Yaqui trade, as the basis of the construction project. Over the course of the OEO plan, arts and crafts programs were instituted to revive traditional arts. Valencia hoped to produce for sale such Yaqui crafts as wood-hide chairs and floor tiles, pascola ritual masks, Yaqui rosary beads, and gourd rattles yet also felt uneasy that children would grow up believing the purpose of the ceremonial regalia was to produce a profit. At the same time, the PYA developed the Easter ceremonies as a tourist attraction from which the Yaquis themselves could reap a profit. To establish Yaqui ceremonial life in the new village the community built a simple Yaqui church as one of the first buildings and quickly reestablished their ceremonial societies. [68]

Although the federal programs and new community organization under the OEO contributed greatly to New Pascua in its first few years, most Yaquis still struggled with poverty at "Old Pascua," as the older barrio was now known. A 1965 census of Old Pascua revealed that 370 Yaquis lived there. Of the 328 lots in the neighborhood, Yaquis owned only 55, and many of these Yaquis expressed no interest in giving up their homes and moving to the isolated desert site. Certain Yaquis grew suspicious of the new community development workers and became resentful of the material benefits accruing to some Pascuans under the federal programs. Early in the project, community members attacked Valencia, going so far as to accuse him of witchcraft and using adobes made for the church in building his own home. In many ways the Office of Economic Opportunity program entered the matrix of traditional patron-client factionalism that had always existed within the community. Yet the new PYA organization and the programs it administered contributed to new tensions within the community. For a period Old and New Pascua severed their relations. [69]

At various times Basilio Olivas and a Mexican American Pascua resident, Ramon Jaurigue, led a faction within the community that virulently opposed the association under Valencia's leadership. This body originally organized itself as the Yaqui Improvement Committee (YIC) and was supported by the outside patronage of a Protestant missionary organization. The YIC was composed of Protestant Yaquis, non-Yaquis, and Yaquis generally opposed to moving to the isolated desert site. These individuals tended to represent the more assimilationist-minded community members. Many owned their homes in Old Pascua or found it daunting to move so far from the center of Tucson. According to the improvement committee, the Yaquis were "threatened with being driven backward in time to where their ancient culture could be preserved and studied, to the west of Black Mountain to become an added tourist attraction."[70] Despite this group's vocal criticisms, however, a census taken in 1965 revealed that

321 of the 370 Yaquis supported New Pascua, as did Yaquis in Adelanto, South Tucson, and Marana. Even so, the opponents took their case to the press, where they affected public opinion. As African American principal Morgan Maxwell stated in one article, "The planned move is discrimination of the worst kind . . . . ironically financed by the federal government which at the same time is putting forth every effort to end segregation."[71]

Besides the organized opposition, at various times family-based groups with personal antagonism toward the association and Valencia also attacked the new plan. Some Yaquis interpreted every job and service provided by the PYA as favoring one faction over the other. Although community development workers served all the Yaqui barrios in Tucson, including Barrio Libre, Old Pascua, and its neighboring subdivision, Adelanto, some Yaquis perceived that the OEO program was only for New Pascua and the supporters of Valencia. Overall, the influx of new resources clearly led to new problems, jealousies, and competition within the Tucson Yaqui communities. Early in the project vandals went so far as to go to New Pascua and burn down the ceremonial ramada while destroying many partially built houses. In return a group of New Pascua men went to Old Pascua, ransacking and destroying the village church of San Ignacio de Loyola, smashing it until it "looked as if a bomb had exploded within the church."[72] Even so, as Spicer recalled, the organized opposition essentially came and went because they had nothing to consistently offer the Yaquis compared to the legal, medical, educational, and vocational help provided by the OEO.

Despite the divisions, Valencia and the association worked to foster loyalty to their new community. As Spicer clearly detailed in his scholarly work, the Yaquis had a genius for organization and uniting the entire community for the Easter ceremonials, yet the organization of Pascuan society largely stopped there and did not extend to political or economic realms. In Arizona, Yaqui communities were divided into small kin groups that tended to view other kin groups as competitors, especially in economic realms. These groups cooperated in ceremonial matters, but total community cooperation in other realms was not a part of daily life at Pascua, nor was this fact considered abnormal. The internal competition in Pascua contradicted the picture Painter and the PYA presented, however, at fundraisers where the association stressed that "the whole [Yaqui] community concerns itself with [any Yaquis'] plight."[73] At New Pascua the leaders of the PYA hoped to create a Yaqui community where everyone did in fact pull together for the entire community beyond the religious ceremonials, although the leadership roster largely evolved from the religious societies.[74]

Though there were divisions in the Tucson Yaqui communities centered on specific places, the Yaquis had never defined their community by residency or geographical factors. They continued to base membership on ceremonial participation, and thus Yaquis from South Tucson, Barrio Libre, Adelanto, Marana, and to a certain extent Guadalupe near Phoenix maintained cultural and participatory exchanges with the Pascua Yaquis. Some Yaquis from all Arizona settlements eventually came to settle in New Pascua. Yet other Yaqui political organizations functioned apart from New Pascua and the PYA during this time. Although the Marana Yaquis associated with the Pascuans in their ceremonies, they continued to exist as the Marana Area Yaqui Association, electing a pueblo governor and operating their own community improvement projects. By most accounts the state's largest Yaqui community, Guadalupe, near Phoenix, organized itself as the Guadalupe Yaqui Tribal Council as well.[75]

From the start of the New Pascua project Valencia's people engaged in a continual series of funding drives and grant writing. The OEO grants secured by the Pascua Yaqui Association required matching funds, and over time the PYA succeeded in gaining funding from the Ford Foundation, the Raskob Foundation, and the Episcopal Church to carry out their programs under the OEO. The Pascua Yaquis also secured aid in running their tribal government from the Office of Native American Programs, an agency that became an important source of funding for other unrecognized Indian groups at this time. With outside funds the PYA succeeded in maintaining a paid form of tribal organization, something the vast majority of unacknowledged groups could not accomplish during the 1960s.[76]

Despite the strides made by the PYA, dissent remained a constant companion for the New Pascua project. The major dissenting group based in Old Pascua continued to oppose the PYA at every turn well into the 1970s. As the new community was highly dependent on voluntary contributions, the negative publicity surrounding the project hurt fundraising efforts. In 1969 the whole New Pascua program collapsed for a time when funding ran out. That year opponents in Old Pascua hurled charges of mismanagement and missing funds in a series of highly negative articles criticizing the association. Hindered by insecure federal funding, yearly grant applications, and outside attacks, the entire community development experiment appeared threatened. Within the year, however, new funding ensured that the New Pascua project opened again under a new type of grant from the OEO "Indian Desk."

During the crisis and discord Valencia distanced himself from the non-Yaqui PYA advisers, while disavowing any wrongdoing. According to Valencia the money was likely misspent but "not by the PYA board. They had no say-so by then. In fact they lost control way back in 1966." In fact, William Willard had fired Valencia in 1968, believing the Yaqui leader could not handle the internal strains of the project. By this time even Spicer began seeing Valencia as a dictator type, and a rift developed between the old friends. Not surprisingly Valencia saw the issue another way: "Once they had me out of the way, the Board lost all control—once the OEO and the Anglos took over."[77] After 1969 Valencia took steps to regain Yaqui control of the housing project.

Despite controversies and growing pains, the program in community development and leadership at New Pascua was an overall success, creating momentum that would roll into the group's efforts to become a federally recognized tribe. By the middle 1970s the PYA had built ninety-six homes, a community center, and a church at the new site, as well as roads, septic tanks, and water lines. In the goal of creating independent leadership experienced in dealing with the rough-and-tumble world of local and federal bureaucracies, the continued leadership of Valencia and younger Yaquis such as Raymond Ybarra stood as testimony that the Pascua Development Project succeeded at least partially in that aim, as many Yaquis emerged as independent voices for the group. According to Roz Spicer, during this time the Pascua Yaquis grew to be very assertive in getting what they wanted, having learned to deal with the bureaucracy through the PYA. Valencia and the others, once described as "shy" and "happy" to have a little government help, had grown to demand their full rights as Native Americans. The New Pascua leadership was so successful, in fact, in achieving private and federal funding that nearby recognized tribes came to resent the Yaquis. In retrospect, however, it seems likely that without the PYA, the federal land grant, and OEO programs the Pascua Yaquis would not have succeeded in gaining federal recognition. As Spicer noted, the OEO project had "a remarkable revivifying effect on the Yaqui community" at New Pascua.[78]

As part of the Yaquis' growing assertiveness, by the late 1960s and early 1970s Yaquis throughout Arizona became involved in Indian activism and fund-raising, influenced by the Indian rights struggles and rhetoric of the day. Although the Yaqui leadership was not involved in the Chicago Indian Conference or AIM protests, it was participating in national, pan-Indian organizations such as the NCAI. Younger Yaquis became active in protesting negative portrayals of them in the media as well. As Mary Jane Martinez argued in the local paper, "I am tired of the misinformation printed in the newspapers about us—we are not a frightened people, we don't preserve the simplicity of mountain life in

Pascua . . . we aren't a primitive people."[79] In their drive for recognition the Pascua Yaquis would employ rhetoric of resistance, entitlement, and Indian pride that was a far cry from the "appeal" to the benevolence of the federal government used in the 1964.

By the early 1970s New Pascua was uniquely situated compared to other Arizona Yaqui settlements, for it had a federal land base and a tribal government developed largely under the influence of the federal bureaucracy and Great Society programs. A downside was that New Pascua was dependent on outside funding and non-Yaqui bureaucrats for its continuing functioning. According to Spicer, the growth of federal programs and "interference of bureaucrats" also inhibited supra community organization by intensifying the traditional systems of patronage and dividing the loyalties of the various Yaqui barrios. On the positive side, by the early 1970s the New Pascuans had developed a functioning administrative organization under ONAP funding, serving its approximately 1,747 members through a housing program using low-interest loans through the Farmers Home Administration. The New Pascua community was now operating politically through the formalized governing and administrative umbrella of the association, calling itself the Pascua Yaqui Tribal Council, holding annual elections, and organizing formal committees to manage housing and fund-raising. Over the years the PYA enabled several dozen Yaquis to gain experience in government and administration while others were trained in social service work. The community development workers showed Yaquis how to gain welfare, health care, and legal aid through local service organizations. During the early 1970s New Pascua was humming with outside funding and volunteer organizations, as well as through the traditional ceremonial societies.[80]

Even with its accomplishments New Pascua faced a major crisis in 1973 due to its ambiguous status under the 1964 land act. Being dependent on the federal bureaucracy also made the PYA vulnerable to the shifting tide of public policy. After his landslide victory in the 1972 presidential race Richard Nixon set out to dismantle the welfare state created during the 1960s under Johnson's Great Society by harnessing the growing "white backlash" of working- and middle-class whites. Under a policy of New Federalism Nixon sought to return poverty programs to the local level and took steps to end the largely discredited OEO program. The success of Indian activism engendered its own backlash by the early 1970s as well. As one angry Arizonan argued, "Why have so many legal actions come up before the Federal Courts demanding settlement for deeds done over 100 years ago to the Indians?" Another citizen seconded this, saying, "We have paid far too long!"[81] The association now became aware of the downside of dependence on federal funding.

By 1974 Nixon dismantled the OEO and with it the major source of New Pascua funding. The Indian wing of the Office of Native American Programs was transferred to HEW in 1973 and continued to fund the Pascua Yaqui government, yet in an era of "limits" and cutbacks reliance on these funding sources seemed precarious at best. The Pascua Yaqui Development Project was one of the few OEO demonstration projects that was considered successful at the time. [82] Despite its achievements, the OEO's demise affected the Pascua Yaquis and made their continued funding uncertain. Under Raymond Ybarra, a younger Yaqui leader groomed under Valencia within the association, the group now attempted to meet the new funding crisis.

In the mid-1970s the Pascua Yaquis faced further financial problems when Pima County officials, fearing lawsuits pending a "catastrophe of some kind," made an attempt to impose its building codes on New Pascua.[83] Because the PYA held its land subject to federal controls and because it had once been Bureau of Land Management property, the Yaquis considered it to be trust land exempt from local ordinances. Besides, they argued, they paid no taxes on the land, and as a result local agencies had never provided services such as sewer lines. Despite threats from the county, the PYA proceeded with construction at New Pascua. As the county and city did not consider the land within their jurisdiction for some purposes, while including it for others, they provided only limited law enforcement protection for New Pascua as well. In 1976 Ybarra lamented, "It seemed like all hell had broken loose because the Sheriff's department did not have and does not have any jurisdiction over our land."[84] Faced with crime and health concerns, the New Pascua settlers were in the anomalous position of having no agency to aid them.

In response to the growing crisis the PYA made attempts to secure aid from various outside sources while their status threatened to stall community development once again. Denied the ability to mortgage their land to raise money, the group's progress also was hindered by their unclear tribal status. Reflecting the varying qualifications for Indians in the federal system at the time, the Department of Labor determined that New Pascua could continue its CETA program because it was not limited to federally recognized tribes and because Congress had demonstrated intent in 1964 to create a "trust responsibility" for the group. On the other hand, when Ybarra turned to the Department of Commerce's Economic Development Administration (EDA) for help as an indigenous group, the EDA was unsure whether it could fund

New Pascua under its provisions for Indian reservations, Indian trust lands, or restricted Indian lands. Like other agencies, the Commerce Department logically turned to the BIA to determine the Yaquis' eligibility. Referring to Section 4 of the 1964 Pascua act, however, the bureau's lawyers determined the Pascua Yaqui group was precluded from inclusion under the EDA programs for Indians, just as it was precluded from BIA and IHS services. Similarly Ybarra inquired whether his people could qualify for a Department of Justice crime control grant as an "aboriginal group," only to be referred back to the "proper office," the BIA, which was dead-set against providing federal services for the group.[85]

By the middle 1970s the concerns of unacknowledged groups such as the Yaquis were more visible than ever before. Though the publicity had positive results overall, the potentially large number of groups also encouraged strong opposition from some recognized tribes and their leaders. Accepting the government's position, many reservation tribes now began actively opposing groups in fear the federal "funding pie" would be sliced too thinly if hordes of unrecognized Indians were let in the fold. In Arizona, as in many states, recognized tribes by this time had helped establish state Indian commissions to voice their concerns at the state level. By the mid-1970s the Arizona Commission of Indian Affairs operating within the governor's office began to attack the PYA's efforts to achieve funding, sending out letters to various agencies questioning the Yaquis' eligibility for funds that they were already receiving. Through Arizona governor Raul Castro, the commission sent letters to HEW and Arizona congressmen protesting the Yaquis' funding through the OEO and other programs. Although the tribes were rebuffed in this effort, being informed that the Pascua Yaquis received funding not as an Indian tribe but because of their status as low-income families, Arizona's recognized tribes harbored ongoing resentment toward the Pascuans. Not surprisingly this sentiment prompted the Arizona Indians to block an effort by the Pascua Yaquis to become a state-recognized tribe.[86]

While Ybarra and the New Pascuans searched desperately for funds, the Intertribal Council of Arizona and the Colorado River Indian Tribes went on to pass resolutions against the PYA, admonishing the governor to "refrain from recognizing the Yaquis" for the purposes of taking "funds intended for recognized American Indian tribes." Accepting the discourse and paradigms of the BIA, the tribes directly quoted Section 4 of the 1964 act stating the Pascua Yaquis were not eligible for funds or services provided to Indian tribes to make their point.[87] The sentiments of Veronica Murdock, chairperson of the Mohave Tribe of the Colorado River Indian Tribes and later president of the NCAI, represented the feelings of many recognized tribes toward both the Pascua Yaquis and others at the time. Murdock declared, "It's basic we're against having people infringe on the funds set aside for Indians. The Yaquis are not American Indians—they are 'Native Americans.' We don't question their needs for funds, but there are more programs available to the Yaquis than to Indians. We don't want them to dip into funds which are already inadequate. The Yaquis are from Mexico, outcasts from Mexico."[88] During the period Roz Spicer recalled that some officials told them, "You belong in Mexico, go on back where you belong."[89] Hearing these kinds of comments, Yaquis felt the disdain acutely. According to Yaqui José Solorez, other recognized tribes did not even "consider us Indians."[90]

Despite the opposition from reservation tribes, the Pascua Yaqui Association had become dependent on federal funding and viewed the continuance of these funds as vital to its survival. As Valencia put it, "We are afraid that if we do not have our culture together [at New Pascua] it will die. Our culture is very much alive in this village."[91] By 1975, facing organized opposition stemming from their ambiguous position, the Pascua Yaqui Tribal Council nonetheless held a meeting at New Pascua and voted overwhelmingly to seek recognition. According to Valencia, "we did not notify the other communities because, simply, they are a community within themselves. I am sure that if we had gone to the government and said that seven thousand Yaquis are here and we want to be recognized, that a portion of each community would have said no and that would have killed our chances."[92] In this light the PYA went forward to project a united front to government officials and the public.

The Yaquis in Arizona, however, were far from a small, united Indian "band." In 1971 the Guadalupe Yaquis, operating as the Arizona Yaqui Bands of Indians, independently had made an earlier determination to seek federal recognition. Reflecting the activist stance of many Arizona Yaquis, Guadalupe chairperson Antonio Coronado told Udall that his people deserved "to have the same rights as any other American Indians" because "we are Indians not Mexicans . . . the only thing that separates us from an American Indian is the name."[93] At that time the New Pascua Yaquis were not involved in this effort, having no desire to be recognized and fall under the paternalistic arm of the BIA.

Both Udall and Arizona senator Barry Goldwater inquired into the possibility of recognizing the Guadalupe Yaquis. The BIA, however, took an adversarial stance toward the group, as it did toward many other unacknowledged

Indian groups in the early 1970s. As Assistant Secretary of the Interior Harris Loesch told Senator Goldwater, "the people calling themselves the Guadalupe Band," upon investigation, "are not, in the true sense, American Indians but are descendants of alien refugee Indians. It appears that they seek Federal recognition as an Indian tribe, not from any pride in their Indian ancestry, but solely because they believe it would work to their economic advantage."[94] Because of this administrative determination, both Goldwater and Udall soon dropped the effort to recognize the Guadalupe Yaquis through legislation.

In 1975 the Pascua Yaqui Association now came to Udall seeking the same thing. With new laws such as the Indian Self-determination Act allowing for greater Indian administration and control of BIA programs, Valencia and the other Yaqui leadership now believed they could retain a degree of autonomy under the bureau. Aware of the government's views toward the Guadalupe Yaquis, the New Pascua group chose to avoid the administrative route of going through the BIA. They also realized that the language of the 1964 Yaqui act potentially ruled out an administrative decision anyway. Because of the express language of the 1964 act, Congress had precluded any services or status for the Pascua Yaquis as an Indian tribe. It seemed it would take an act of Congress to overturn the act it passed in 1964. The Lumbee Indians and Tiguas of Texas faced the same issues the following decade.

The PYA chose to try to gain full legislative recognition. Indians such as the Pascua Yaquis, however, often face difficulties accessing power because of their small size, yet the group would need to appeal again to Congress to get a recognition bill passed. Fortuitously, during the early and middle 1970s the position of Congress toward legislatively recognizing tribes was still somewhat fluid. For Indian groups with access to power and resources there existed a brief window of time to attempt legislative recognition before the Federal Acknowledgment Project swung into effect. The PYA would attempt to pass through this gap between 1975 and 1978.

Dismayed by their Indian-status limbo, Valencia approached Ned Spicer in 1975 about their need for recognition. At first Spicer "was shocked" that the Yaquis would desire to come under the BIA and lose their traditional independence. Valencia, however, explained that the Pascuans had exhausted their funding sources and that the Arizona recognized tribes were threatening the funding they already possessed. At the national level it was apparent that all tribes faced threats springing from the white backlash as well. Despite these realities, many individuals familiar with the Yaquis believed that recognition was an unwise move. As noted anthropologist Bernard Fontana remarked at the time, "I hope that [the Yaquis] will explore every means possible by which various problems people in that community feel they face can be resolved short of the drastic action entailed by federal recognition. Surely there are other ways to get bus service and sewer lines."[95]

However, this was the Yaquis' decision, and Spicer agreed to help construct a viable argument. Once again Valencia's timing was right when he approached Mo Udall for assistance. In 1975 Udall was in the ascendancy of his power in Congress. A staunch advocate of traditionally liberal causes, he was an early proponent of ending termination, and supporting the Yaquis would be a step toward recognizing federal responsibility toward tribes that had slipped through the cracks. Known for his sense of humor, Udall often used wit and his commanding presence to prevail against opponents. In 1976 he ran a close second to Jimmy Carter in the primaries for the Democratic nomination for president. More importantly for the Pascua Yaquis, he became the chairman of the House Committee on Interior and Insular Affairs, the committee responsible for Indian affairs. In a demonstration of his influence and power, in 1984 supporters and opponents alike voted him the most respected member of Congress.[96]

In the summer of 1975 Udall's office drew up legislation to recognize the Pascua Yaquis as an Indian tribe under United States law. The bill concerned only the Pascua Yaqui Association and directed the secretary of the interior to accept the association's lands in trust for the group. However, Arizona recognized tribes, still angry over the funding provided to the Pascua group, immediately attacked the bill. The Colorado River Indian Tribes passed a resolution against the measure, and lobbyists for the recognized tribes attempted to influence legislators in Washington. Undeterred by the opposition, the Yaquis proceeded to ask Arizona senator Paul Fannin to sponsor a Senate version of the bill. More so than Udall, however, Fannin was sensitive to the expressed interests of the Arizona recognized tribes and waffled on the issue. On top of tribal opposition, a new problem soon emerged to complicate the Yaquis' chances. Valencia's group faced opposition from other Tucson Yaqui communities and from Yaquis in Guadalupe. Not surprising in light of these external attacks and Yaqui opposition, the bill died unceremoniously in committee in 1975. The reason was fairly simple. As Udall told a constituent, "The main stumbling block for this legislation is the concern by other Indian tribes that funding for the Yaquis will mean decreased services for other tribes."[97]

It was also clear that Yaqui opposition to the plan severely hurt the chances of the New Pascua community. The old divisions between Old and New Pascua reemerged full force in 1975. The split between Old and New was in no way clear or absolute, however, as some in New Pascua opposed the recognition plan and Valencia's leadership, while some in Old Pascua supported it. However, a new organization formed in Old Pascua to bury the acknowledgment bill. Called MAYO (Mexican-Americans, Yaquis, and Others), the group consisted of many former members of the Yaqui Improvement Committee. Led by Mexican American Ramon Jaurigue with the help of Reverend John Swank, MAYO members asserted their point of view and in the process made the people appear hopelessly divided in the local press and other media.[98]

The effect of MAYO's actions and dissent over recognition in Guadalupe made Senator Fannin back off his support for the Pascua Yaquis. As an aide advised Fannin, there is "much opposition" and because of this, the "Senator may have some moral support in the event that he decides he can't support the Bill."[99] An article appeared in a local paper in which Jaurigue reported that many elders of the Yaqui community did not want to be forced onto a reservation and become "wards" of the government. MAYO members also stressed that the PYA represented only about 1,000 of the 3,500 Yaquis in Arizona. According to the organization, "it seems a step into the past to isolate a specific group from the rest of the community, into which they have begun to assimilate."[100] Underneath, however, members of MAYO also worried that the group's members would be excluded from the Pascua Yaqui tribe if it came into being. Despite the visible and vocal protests of MAYO, Udall's office inquired into the situation and found that the majority of Tucson Yaquis supported recognition, so he proceeded with the legislation.

In issues of legislative tribal recognition, Indian groups of necessity must appeal to the public, members of Congress, and recognized tribes. As the Pascua Yaquis experienced in 1975, groups that face organized opposition to their recognition efforts generally fail. The stance of recognized tribes has proven particularly important because in many ways they serve the function in public discourse of legitimizing "Indianness." As the "constituency" of the BIA, they also have much power over the bureau's position toward un-acknowledged groups. On acknowledgment issues Congress has tended to weigh the opinions of recognized tribes as represented by the BIA as well as public comments and scholarly evidence. Groups such as the Lumbees and MOWA Choctaw, who have faced vocal Indian opposition and doubts about their authenticity, have failed to persuade Congress to accept their legitimacy.

Like all unrecognized Indians, Valencia and the other Yaquis knew that to have any chance at acknowledgment they needed to project a strong image of themselves in public discourse as authentic Indians, participating in an organized tribal structure. They also had to overcome perceptions that they were a foreign, Mexican tribe or illegal alien "wetbacks" trying to get a piece of the Indian pie.[101] With this in mind the New Pascua leaders set out to construct an image of themselves by building upon their cultural traits detailed in written scholarship while engaging in a campaign to expose their story to the larger Indian audience.

When the American Indian Policy Review Commission (AIPRC) held hearings on the plight of unrecognized and terminated tribes, Valencia's people lobbied to get their message heard before the commission. Udall's office helped in arranging for one of the task force hearings to be held at New Pascua, and a written report of their history ended up being featured prominently in the task force's final report. During meetings with the commissioners Valencia and Ybarra presented their views of Yaqui origins, history, and culture as well as outlining the problems they experienced without recognition. Before commissioners Jo Jo Hunt, a Lumbee, and Ada Deer, a Menominee, Valencia, Ybarra, and Spicer stressed the group's sense of Indianness, emphasizing not only the unique Yaqui culture expressed in their language, deer dances, and Easter ceremonials but also their pride in being Indian. To further represent their authenticity, the association held a Yaqui fiesta for the visitors complete with dances and regalia.[102]

Despite the program, Commissioner Deer still doubted whether the group was indigenous to the United States. Clearly, earlier documentation on the Yaquis stressed they were refugees from Mexico, while Spicer's published work plotted the people's territory far to the south of Arizona. Spicer unveiled new evidence, however, that Yaquis were longtime residents of Arizona. He located a colonial-era census that showed that at least a few Yaquis lived at the first missions established in present-day Arizona as early as 1796. Although Ada Deer seemed less than convinced, Valencia and Ybarra alternately argued their ancestors were the ancient Toltecs that once lived near present-day Yuma, Arizona, a theory Spicer could not confirm.[103]

As a result of their testimony, however, and the fact that the Tucson group presented such an organized front, the Pascuans exposed their story to a wider audience through the AIPRC. In the process they succeeded in converting the image of their people as Mexican, "wetback" interlopers to something of a cause célèbre representing the federal government's failure to live up to its commitments to worthy Indian groups in the United States.[104]

In addition to reaching a larger national audience through the commission,

Valencia's group already possessed a fairly high profile in scholarly discourse that aided its effort. The continuing influential studies by Spicer left little doubt in academic circles that the group was Native American. In terms of popular images the works of Carlos Castaneda helped considerably as well. During the late 1960s Castaneda began publishing a series of tomes about a Yaqui sorcerer named Don Juan that welcomed readers to explore, with the help of mind-altering drugs, "a Yaqui way of knowledge" and different ordering of reality. The "Yaqui way" became a popular phenomenon among flower children and hippies seeking to explore Indian ways. Although Native American scholars later attacked Castaneda's Don Juan as being a "purely invented Yaqui sorcerer," Valencia reportedly kept quiet at the time because he knew the books were extremely valuable to his cause. Valencia knew that, in comparison to many other groups, the Arizona Yaquis possessed a storehouse of literature authenticating their Indianness and a high profile as Native Americans.[105]

Even with their advantages, however, the Yaquis faced lingering doubts about their Mexican origins and anger over their financial acumen. After the failure of their 1975 bill, the group launched a more concerted effort to amass evidence of their culture, history, and unity to present to Congress and the public. In 1977 Udall faithfully drafted and submitted a new bill to the House. In an effort to craft a convincing argument the PYA hired local activist-lawyer Roger Wolf and enlisted the help of the Arizona State University Law School to prepare material for their recognition attempt. The group also turned to NARF and John Echohawk for legal assistance and later acquired the aid of the American Friends Service Committee and the National Indian Lutheran Board.[106] Each of these parties worked free of charge for the Pascuans. The PYA next looked to find a sponsor for legislation in the Senate.

All Indian groups hoping to gain recognition on Capitol Hill have to prove their culture, tribal organization, and worthiness to congressional delegates as well as deal with enumerable political issues at the same time. The Pascuans proved no exception. Having the unwavering support of Udall in the House, they set out to prove their case to the Arizona senators at the time: Barry Goldwater and Paul Fannin. Although Fannin proved receptive, he told the Yaquis that they needed to establish an authentic tribal roll and "a legal justification supporting recognition" before he would introduce legislation.[107] In 1975–76 Fannin faced considerable pressures from his recognized tribal constituency and was particularly concerned with the number of potential Yaquis, especially the large population in Mexico. According to Fannin's legislative assistant, the senator wanted proof that Arizona "wouldn't be inundated with Mexican Yaquis" and wanted to consult with experts cognizant of Indian issues to document their authenticity. [108] Moreover, both senators involved followed press reports on the internal dynamics and conflicts of the Yaquis closely.

To convince Senators Fannin and Goldwater, the New Pascua group referred back to the Rocky Boys precedent while presenting a compelling legal argument that the federal government already had established a commitment to the Yaquis. They pointed out that the government had a responsibility to acknowledge them because it had an ongoing relationship with the group. As Spicer said, "It would be a rejection of the obligation established by the [1964] congressional land grant if [the bill] should not now pass." [109] As many members of Congress were lawyers, the legislators seemed impressed by the legal precedents. The Pascuans were lucky. Very few other unacknowledged groups possessed a communal land base with any form of relationship with the federal government.

Spicer and the attorneys also took pains to emphasize the Yaquis' genetic "Indianness," which seemed so important to whites, while Valencia worked to cover up factional disputes as well. As Wolf argued, "there is no question that the Yaquis are Indians. The vast majority are three quarter or full blood Indians." [110] In the end, however, it does not appear Congress investigated this fact at any time. To overcome fears of a flood of Yaquis from Mexico, Spicer and Wolf conceded that although the Yaquis' ancestral homeland was in Mexico, their membership was tightly controlled and required blood quantum. To appease the legislators and the BIA, however, the group upped its "blood quantum" to "one half" Yaqui blood, although this requirement was largely meaningless to the Yaquis. Combating fears of their financial impact on the BIA, the Pascuans argued that they represented only 1,700 of the approximately 4,500 Yaquis in Arizona and that the others did not desire membership in the association. [111]

During the Pascua Yaquis' recognition drive a fortuitous event occurred: Senator Fannin retired, and Dennis DeConcini succeeded him. The new senator was a native Tucsonan and required little persuading of the Yaquis' authenticity or their need for federal recognition. In 1977 DeConcini and South Dakota senator James Abourezk, the cochair of the Senate Committee on Indian Affairs, sponsored a bill on the PYA's behalf, while Udall sponsored its companion in the House. Valencia, Ybarra, and rising Yaqui leader David Ramirez traveled repeatedly to Washington and to pan-Indian conferences to press the Pascuans' case during this time. With Udall's help the Yaquis made the rounds at the Capitol and "met all the right people," and Udall used his influence to force a meeting between the Yaquis and reluctant Department of Interior officials. Though MAYO continued to protest, Valencia and the others managed to get the association's views across more forcefully in 1977 and 1978, providing interviews and presenting a united front in the public realm.[112]

In the spring and early summer of 1977 Udall and Senators Abourezk and DeConcini introduced bills to recognize the Pascua Yaqui group as an Indian tribe amid a growing backlash against Indian rights, tightening federal budgets, and a growing sentiment that legislative recognition was unfair. In April the Interior Subcommittee on Indian Affairs and Public Lands within the House Committee on Interior and Insular Affairs considered the Yaqui recognition bill. There was little opposition to the measure because, as a local newspaper reported, "With House Interior Chairman Udall behind the bill, it's expected to have no trouble passing the full Interior Committee."[113] As a result of Udall's initiative, the subcommittee voted in favor of the measure and sent it on to be considered by the full committee.

In early fall of 1977 the Senate committee also held a hearing on the Pascua Yaqui recognition bill with Valencia, David Ramirez, and NARF attorney Raymond Cross appearing for the Yaquis. At the hearing the Yaquis attempted to construct a positive image of themselves. During the proceedings a confident Valencia presented the Yaquis as an impoverished Indian group, utilizing rhetoric and criteria easily identifiable to the legislators as "Indian." As the Pascua leader testified, "The Yaquis are Indians in every sense of the word. We have our own language, our own culture, such as the Pascola Dancing, the deer dancing, and the coyote dancing. These dances are Indian in origin. In the deer dance, we sing to honor the great mountains, the springs and the lakes. We sing of our father the Sun, and of creatures living and dead. We sing of trees and leaves and twigs. We sing of birds in the sky and fish in the ocean." Valencia also emphasized his people's heroic resistance. He testified that whites had "tried for centuries to undermine our 'Yaquinness'; after 400 years they have not succeeded. We have retained our language, our culture, and our Indianness." To further attest to and appeal to the legal definition of Indian tribes as operating political entities, however, Valencia also stressed that the Pascua Yaqui had a functioning "tribal council."[114]

Beyond the oral testimony the Yaquis realized they would need to provide academic evidence to convince the legislators. To this end Spicer testified that after forty years of study he believed that the Yaquis formed a distinct

Indian tribe (the necessary political unit) while continuing to speak their native language and carry on traditional Indian ceremonials (the "Indian" culture component). Concerning their nationality, Spicer testified that the Yaqui may "appear to some neighbors to have merged their way of life with that of the Mexican Americans, but this is a very superficial judgment."[115] Spicer was the acknowledged authority on Indians of the Southwest, and his testimony was highly influential at meeting the scholarly proof called for by the dominant society.

In debates over the Yaqui bill a senator from Oklahoma expressed a recurring concern about future immigration from Mexico. Valencia assured him that the Immigration and Naturalization Service would control any possible immigration in the future. A more important concern of the legislators, however, was the Mexican origin of the Yaquis. Many lawmakers feared creating a precedent that would open a floodgate of potential immigration and recognition of Indians from Latin America. There was a consensus that Congress should recognize only Indian tribes with aboriginal territories in the United States. This belief was later codified in the regulations of the FAP that applied the acknowledgment criteria only to Indian tribes indigenous to the continental United States, while defining "indigenous" as tribes "native to the continental United States in that at least part of the petitioner's territory at the time of sustained contact extended into what is now the continental United States."[116]

To appease the legislators Spicer presented evidence the Yaquis had come to Arizona with the Spanish missions at least by 1796 (more than a hundred years prior to Arizona statehood), although this was long after the first sustained contact between Yaquis and Europeans as required under the BIA regulations. He also reported that it was very likely that the descendents of these Yaquis still lived in the area. Under the BIA regulations, however, Spicer would have been required to prove these assertions and link the Pascua Yaquis to the mission descendants, although Congress did not press him on this point. Spicer also went on to argue that being "indigenous" was a relative term and questioned the whole criteria for acknowledging groups. Although Spicer was persuasive, in the final analysis the tribal origins of the Yaquis did not seem to be a crucial factor to the legislators, though it likely would have precluded the group's recognition by the BIA.[117]

Upon hearing the testimony and deliberating, the Senate Select Committee on Indian Affairs met in March of 1978 and unanimously recommended adopting the Senate bill with amendments. It still needed final approval, however, from the full Congress. Reflecting the sentiments and motivations of legislators toward to Pascua Yaquis, DeConcini said, "I think the Yaqui Indians of Arizona have been identified by every recognized authority as being a major and unique American Indian tribe," were supported by the AIPRC, and descend from ancestors who lived in the Southwest "since time immemorial." DeConcini went on to state, "I have grown up in close proximity to the Yaqui villages in Arizona and can personally testify to the sense of pride and strength of culture, language, and character that has carried these people through much adversity."[118]

During the congressional deliberations the Pascua Yaquis had embarked on an intensive lobbying campaign to convince Arizona's reservation tribes of their Indian authenticity and need for federal funding. From 1976 to 1978 they produced a written appeal to the recognized tribes containing much of the discourse presented to Congress. Through numerous meetings with recognized tribes of Arizona, lobbying the American Indian Policy Review Commission, and presenting their history to the NCAI, Valencia and Ramirez largely succeeded in neutralizing Indian opposition for this second effort. In fact, the Pascuans ultimately secured the informal endorsement of the Hopi, Cocopahs, and some Alaskan groups while the Navajo, Colorado River Indian Tribes, San Carlos Apaches, and the other Arizona tribes raised no organized opposition. Eliminating the opposition of local reservation tribes was crucial because they often serve as arbiters of Indianness. Although organized tribal opposition did not develop against the Yaquis at the individual tribal level, the interests of recognized tribes were represented through the BIA, however. And the bureau proceeded to raise objections to the bill in 1978.[119]

Unfortunately for the group the Yaqui recognition bill became enmeshed in the debates surrounding the newly drafted BIA acknowledgment regulations. Although the bureau's traditional position was that the Yaquis were a non-indigenous tribe (a stance it maintained well into the 1990s), initially the agency did not oppose the bill. By 1978, however, the nascent FAP proceedings caught up with the Yaquis. Facing severe criticism for its lack of uniformity on acknowledgment cases and with the new FAP guidelines in tow, the Interior Department changed its position. In hearings on the 1978 bill Assistant Secretary of the Interior Forrest Gerard testified that the Department of the Interior was attempting to develop criteria for a "unified Indian position" on acknowledgement in order to establish an even-handed approach. Gerard therefore requested that Congress wait until the regulations were finalized so that the Yaquis could go through the administrative process. Because Section 4 of the Yaquis' 1964 law expressly prohibited a federal relationship between the

Pascua Yaquis and the BIA, the department recommended that it be removed to allow the group to petition for acknowledgment.[120]

Despite the BIA's remarks, Section 4 actually may have aided the Yaquis because the Senate referenced it as one reason the Pascuans needed legislation, especially in light of the BIA's negative stance toward the group. Even if allowed to proceed through the FAP, it was apparent that the Pascuans could expect little sympathy from the Bureau of Indian Affairs. As NARF attorney Raymond Cross noted, "the BIA was very reluctant to support a bill that had at its purpose the extension of federal services to non-indigenous tribes, which they consider the Yaqui tribe to be."[121] At this time the BIA also began arguing that the Pascua Yaquis had not "continuously existed" as a tribe, an ironclad requirement under their new rules. To make its point the BIA cited Spicer's work in which he had stated that the Yaquis came to Arizona as individual families or small kin groups, not as part of an organized tribal movement. One source reported that the bureau also opposed the Yaquis because it would increase costs for the agency.[122] Because the Yaquis had a strong congressional sponsor and because they knew the BIA's position, Valencia and the others aggressively pushed their legislation to avoid going through the administrative process.

Because of the BIA position the Yaquis now faced an uphill struggle. As American Friends Service Committee representative Bryan Michener reported at the time, "everyone is worried about setting a precedent that many other non-federally recognized groups might seize on," and many legislators were reluctant to support any tribal recognition bill.[123] Even with the opposition of the bureau and the reluctance of many legislators, Udall, DeConcini, and Abourezk skillfully pressed the Yaqui bills, succeeding in passing them in their respective committees.

As the New Pascua community waited anxiously, the Senate and House bills then went to a joint conference to hammer out the differences between them in May of 1978. Early in the process, the Pascua Yaqui Association and Udall had drafted the House bill to provide only limited recognition to appease the BIA and some members of Congress. At the insistence of NARF and Abourezk, however, the subsequent Senate bill provided full tribal recognition. Significantly, Udall's House proposal limited the Yaqui Tribe's sovereignty by abridging its ability to define its membership in the future. In particular, Udall's bill prohibited the Yaquis from admitting new members after a one-year closing date (beyond the direct lineal descendants of the tribal members at the deadline). Further, the House bill recognized the Pascua Yaquis solely for the purposes of receiving federal services and did not allow for civil or criminal jurisdiction or other governmental powers. It also precluded the Pascua Yaquis from participating in the Indian Health Service. In light of these significant concessions, the House version of the Yaqui recognition bill represented a potentially dangerous precedent of extending limited recognition to Indian tribes. Although the PYA was in a precarious position when it negotiated the House bill, Raymond Cross and Roger Wolf insisted that the Pascua Yaquis secure a reservation with the full plethora of governmental powers. [124]

Valencia and Ybarra thus pressed for the Senate bill to prevail in conference because it provided for comprehensive tribal acknowledgment. The Senate version extended the provisions of the Indian Reorganization Act to the Yaquis, allowing the tribe to exercise important governmental powers while providing protections for the tribal government as well. The Senate bill also extended the services of the IHS to the Pascua Yaquis and clearly directed the secretary of the interior to take the Yaqui land in trust to hold as a reservation. Establishing a reservation made it clear that New Pascua was Indian land, not subject to state or county jurisdiction—important because issues over jurisdiction had precipitated the recognition efforts in the first place. The Senate bill also expressly repealed Section 4 of the 1964 act while providing that the tribe would adopt a constitution within one year. It did not limit future membership or establish membership requirements for the tribe. [125]

To prevail on the stronger bill Abourezk and Udall lobbied so that sympathetic legislators would be appointed to the conference committee on the two bills. In its deliberations the joint conference drafted a compromise measure that recognized the Yaquis for all purposes yet, significantly, allowed the state of Arizona to retain civil and criminal jurisdiction over Yaqui lands and retained restrictions on membership. Under the skilled direction of Udall, Abourezk, and DeConcini the legislation now experienced relatively smooth sailing through the congressional committees, waiting only for a vote by the full Congress. [126]

Late in a long session Udall attempted to push the bill through, fearful that he might not get another chance. The only obstacle in the Yaquis' path was Congressman John Cunningham of Washington. At the time Cunningham gained notoriety for sponsoring legislation to end the special legal status of Indian tribes, and in the same vein he objected to taking up the Yaqui bill that session. Before the full House Udall now demonstrated why his colleagues considered him one of the nation's best congressmen. To Cunningham's objections, Udall interjected, "Let me say that this is a very minor Indian bill that affects only a very small number of Indians. . . . I do not think it is the kind of bill that the gentleman should be making an issue of." Udall assured Cunningham that the band totaled only four hundred, but the Washington congressman objected anyway, saying, "It is my understanding that these Indians are basically a Mexican tribe." Even though Udall conceded that the Yaquis were once political refugees from the Mexican Revolution, he chided Congressman Cunningham, saying the Yaqui group was so small and worthy that it deserved a token gesture of federal aid. To this Cunningham asked, "Could the gentleman assure me that they have ceased their revolutionary activities?" An amused Udall replied, "The gentleman can be assured that they pose no threat to the people of Washington State." Although perturbed, Cunningham withdrew his objections, but only after being reassured that the Yaquis were citizens who were proud to be Americans.[127]

With Udall's humorous and forceful treatment of this potential obstacle, the amended bill went on to pass both houses of Congress. Although members of the House and Senate seemed to have been confused as to whether the Pascua Yaquis were Mexican refugees or indigenous to the United States, their origins did not seem to be a primary concern, as they met the outside expectations as to what "authentic" Indians looked and acted like. Ultimately Udall's presentation of the group of potentially over five thousand members as a tiny band of four hundred served to carry the day.

The only obstacle left standing in the way of Pascua Yaqui recognition was a threatened veto by President Jimmy Carter. The Department of the Interior, still smarting over its failure to kill the bill, influenced the president to veto the legislation. Unlike many other unacknowledged groups, however, the Pascuans once again benefited from having an extremely powerful advocate in Udall, and the Democratic congressman used his clout with the president to overcome the threatened action. At the time the president needed Udall's support for his civil service reform bill. Out of necessity or deference to the respected congressman, Carter quickly signed the bill into law on 18 September 1978. In signing the law, however, Carter made it clear that this was an unusual circumstance and should not be viewed as a precedent for other groups hoping to circumvent the new BIA acknowledgment process. Carter's words have proven prophetic. Since 1978, tribes with no previous recognition and thus claims for "restoration" have faced little success in gaining legislative recognition.[128]

After years of effort, the Pascua Yaquis were now a federally recognized Indian tribe with all its possibilities and potential pitfalls. Though they had a strong political organization, a land base, and unambiguous Indian heritage, it is clear that without Udall the Pascua Yaquis would not have secured tribal recognition. According to C. Lawrence Huerta, a Yaqui intimately involved in the process, "it was 99% Udall" who won recognition for the tribe.[129] In this light the legislation supports a common criticism of legislative recognition, for the Pascua Yaquis were in many ways lucky to have had Morris Udall. Numerous other Indian groups that lack such a strong benefactor have failed to secure acknowledgment through Congress.

In retrospect, the Pascua Yaquis were also fortunate that Congress recognized them prior to the implementation of the FAP. Although some tribes such as the Tunica-Biloxis of Louisiana and the Jamestown S'Klallams of Washington experienced little difficulty early in the BIA process, it soon became increasingly slow and costly for petitioning groups. In light of the bureau's position that the Yaquis were a refugee group of Indians from Mexico, their chances of success seemed very unlikely under the FAP, although a similar case has yet to go through the process. Because the acknowledgment regulations require groups to have had an aboriginal territory that extended into the present borders of the United States at first contact with Europeans, the Yaquis would likely have faced extreme difficulty proving their territory extended into Arizona.

By bypassing the FAP, however, the Pascua group did not have to meet the demanding criteria required under the BIA process. The Yaquis never had to prove that they had maintained continuous political and community organization since first contact with Europeans, nor did they have to prove their descent from a historic Indian tribe in the United States. The Pascuans never had to show communications between members, the exertion of leadership, records of lineage, intermarriage rates, or a host of other types of evidence the BIA generally requires of petitioners. Significantly they also never had to show a bilateral political relationship between the various Arizona Yaqui communities—relations that largely did not exist and that have proven extremely burdensome to document for groups such as the United Houma Nation. The Pascuans only had to meet the expectations of legislators and the dominant society as being authentic and "worthy" Indians. In the Pascua case many legislators likely believed as Udall did that some recognition cases should be decided more for fairness and equity than on the ability of Indian groups to document elusive details of their tribal life. As Udall remarked on the Yaqui bill, it was "the just, right and fair thing to have done."[130]

By most gauges the Pascua Yaquis were a Native American tribe worthy of tribal recognition. They maintained their language, unique religious practices, identity, and concentrated Indian-defined communities. Even so, the Yaquis benefited from having noted anthropologists such as Edward Spicer document their history and culture and present their findings to a skeptical Congress and Indian constituency. Possessing a federal land grant given to them as Indians helped as well. Overall, the Yaquis visibly "looked Indian" and certainly benefited from not having to prove and document their Indian ancestry before the genealogists of the FAP.

In the end the Yaquis' historical timing was also key as they slipped through a brief window of time before the FAP and before Indian gaming complicated the acknowledgment picture. Since 1978 Congress has tended to defer to the BIA process and has largely ceased to grant legislative recognition except in cases tied to land claims or restoration efforts. Many legislators have come to agree with Senator John McCain (R-AZ) when he said that the congressional route operated without any criteria at all and was "a proven formula for unfairness." [131] After the Yaquis, recognized tribes (often the arbiters of "authenticity" regarding unacknowledged groups) have largely united behind the FAP in opposition to legislative recognition they perceive as unfair and political. As these developments show, the Pascua Yaqui achieved legislative recognition just in time.

With tribal acknowledgment the Pascua Yaqui Tribe now seemed able to fully realize Valencia's vision of New Pascua. Reflecting the coup he and Udall accomplished, Valencia declared, "Recognition does not conquer us, we conquer recognition." [132] In the next several years the Pascua Yaqui Tribe began working with the BIA to establish a tribal constitution, to create a tribal roll, and to operate BIA and IHS programs for the group. Immediately after securing status, however, the Pascua people also faced issues of leadership and admission of new members that would complicate their future. With the complex issues of achieving congressional recognition behind them, however, Yaquis in other Arizona communities gradually joined the Pascua Yaqui Tribe. By 1980 the tribe counted 4,000 members taking part in its federal health, education, and social programs. After opening their Casino of the Sun in the early 1990s, the Pascua Yaqui Tribe was able to run tribal courts and provide services to its membership, a group that by the end of the decade numbered approximately 15,000. Fortunately Anselmo Valencia lived to see the flowering of the tribe he helped so much. Called the "Moses" of his people upon his death in 1998, Valencia was further remembered when the Pascua Yaqui Tribe named a multimillion-dollar performing arts center after the leader in 2001. [133]

FOUR. SOMETIMES SALVATION

*The Death Valley Timbisha Shoshones of California
and the BIA's Federal Acknowledgment Process*

Travelers heading west toward Death Valley National Monument in the late 1960s would enter the California park on a lonely blacktop road through a long, winding canyon that splits the Funeral and Black Mountain Ranges. Descending steadily downward, the visitors would see the austere grays, blacks, and browns of the desert landscape whirling past, peppered here and there with sage, creosote, and an occasional barrel cactus. Perhaps a rabbit, coyote, or chuckwalla lizard would appear from the window in a passing scene stark and desolate in its beauty. Just as the travelers begin wearying the canyon breaks, revealing a scene from a mirage or old Hollywood movie; just ahead a splendid hotel emerges, set in silhouette on a knoll overlooking Death Valley, the white heart of the Mojave Desert. The emerging hotel is the Furnace Creek Inn, a lavish resort that appears strangely out of place in the wild environment. If the travelers gazed beyond the inn, however, past the palm oasis, fountains, and middle-aged couples carrying golf bags fresh from the nearby course, they would have to strain to see a small collection of crumbling adobe cottages off to the south. Set in sand dunes between the snow-capped peaks of the Panamint Range and the white sand flats of the Death Valley floor is the "Indian Village," home to the Timbisha Shoshones, the original inhabitants of Death Valley. In all likelihood, however, the travelers would not see the Shoshones or even know they existed. The Indian Village was not a tourist attraction.

Although invisible to tourists, the group's informal spokesperson, Pauline Esteves, and the rest of the Timbisha Shoshones were gathering in the village to fight an organization that had been their nemesis for several decades: the National Park Service. Since 1938 the Death Valley Indian group had lived in the village at the sufferance of the monument administrators who were attempting to evict them. The Timbisha band was in a weak position, however, because like approximately two-thirds of people identifying as Indians in California in the late 1960s, it was an unacknowledged Indian community lacking the benefits of a reservation and denied the services emanating from the BIA. In 1966, increasingly angered over the Park Service's modern-day removal policy, the Shoshones began an odyssey that would lead them to petition the BIA to acknowledge them as an Indian tribe. In the following years the Timbisha Shoshones would construct a petition representing their story as an unbroken narrative showing their tribe had existed continuously since first contact with whites. Like fifty-three other petitioners within the boundaries of California (the state with the largest number of unacknowledged groups), the Death Valley Timbisha Shoshones would enter a labyrinth of regulations in hopes of emerging with tribal acknowledgment. As of 2003, however, Esteves's people emerged as the only California-based tribe with a positive finding from the Federal Acknowledgment Process.[1]

The Timbisha Shoshones' experience provides a rare glimpse into the history of an Indian group that succeeded through the BIA acknowledgment process. Their odyssey reveals the extreme difficulties all Indian groups face surviving without clear federal status or protections. At the same time the following pages show that the band presented few of the difficult racial, cultural, or community questions that daunt many others. Although there are many ways "to be Indian" and a vast range of experiences among unacknowledged tribes, the Timbisha Shoshones' struggle to gain acknowledgment demonstrates that the FAP privileges Indian groups with previous relations with federal or state governments. Entering the process, groups that once possessed trust lands, Indian allotments, BIA schools, or other government Indian services have records generated by these very relationships that enable them to prove their tribal existence and Indianness to outsiders. As revealed here, good timing also helped Esteves's people, as the tiny band passed through the FAP before it became more exacting and burdensome—although they likely would have succeeded with more effort at a later time.[2]

In the late 1960s the Timbisha band was but one of dozens of scattered Indian communities in the harsh Great Basin, an area of almost rainless deserts and uplifted mountains that covers most of Nevada, southern Idaho, eastern Oregon, and significant parts of Utah and California. The Death Valley group was remarkable only, perhaps, because it was nonrecognized. And the Timbisha Shoshones were unacknowledged primarily because the federal government failed to create a reservation for them when it established Death Valley National Monument. Although federal officials later built the "Indian Village" for the people, the monument administrators ungraciously charged the Indians a nominal rent to live on lands they once owned, a state of affairs that continued until the "termination era" of the 1950s and 1960s, when federal officials decided it was time for Esteves's people to go.[3]

In 1957 the Park Service inaugurated a new eviction policy for all Indians within national preserves. As in Yosemite and Grand Canyon National Parks, the superintendent of Death Valley implemented a plan to gradually eliminate the Shoshones' village by limiting residence to the present occupants and their descendents. To further the removal plan, the Park Service began collecting rents, razing vacant dwellings, and evicting Shoshones who failed to pay or who left the premises unoccupied for too long. Park officials also issued regulations forbidding the occupants from making repairs or improvements to the buildings without approval and began forcing the Shoshones to apply for yearly "special use permits" to occupy their homes.[4]

From 1957 onward Pauline Esteves and a small group of mostly elderly Shoshone women had other ideas, however, and bitterly resisted the monument housing policy. Although males had traditionally served as informal spokespersons for the community, the few men still living in the village feared they would lose their jobs with the Park Service if they opposed the monument. In the absence of traditional leadership, the older women took the reins in fighting to secure their homes. In large part their intransigence stemmed from a deep spiritual attachment to Death Valley. Esteves and many of her relations were born and raised amid the date palms of Furnace Creek, a rare perennial stream in an otherwise harsh environment. They possessed a deep spiritual bond to the land, to its sacred places, and to the memories of their ancestors buried there. The people vowed never to move, refusing to pay rent or to reapply for permits to live on lands they considered their own. Faced with this resistance, the monument officials eventually stopped trying to collect rents on the property, although the policy of gradually eliminating the village remained. In the course of fighting the new policy, however, Esteves realized her people needed help. Yet because of their unacknowledged status, they could expect little support from Washington.[5]

Like many ambiguously recognized Indian groups during the 1950s and 1960s, the Timbisha Shoshones were caught in a bureaucratic "no man's land," with the various agencies involved in their situation either unable or unwilling to aid them. In fact, the Indian Service supported the monument's removal policy as it meshed well with the federal goal of terminating tribes. Also working against the Shoshones was their residence in California and the Great Basin. With its numerous small, "rancheria" reservations, California was a major staging ground for the termination policy, as officials dreamed of eliminating Indian reservations and transferring Indian responsibility to the states. In light of these realities the Sacramento Area Office of the BIA refused to help the Timbisha band, arguing it could not intervene for the group because the Timbisha band lacked a reservation base: the National Park Service was free to terminate the band's village and scatter the group as it willed.[6]

In essence both the Bureau of Indian Affairs and the Park Service supported the eviction policy because they sincerely believed it would be best for the Death Valley group to end its isolation and to assimilate into the dominant culture. To encourage what it viewed as an inevitable process, the BIA went so far as to recommend terminating "Indian Ranch," the one rancheria that existed for a segment of the Timbisha people to the west of the monument. With the acquiescence of the Park Service's Sacramento Area Office, Congress passed the 1958 Rancheria Act, a law that terminated numerous California tribes, including Indian Ranch—by some accounts against the will of the extended Shoshone family living there.[7]

Beginning in the 1950s park officials also destroyed several of the original dozen adobe homes at Furnace Creek while the occupants were away on their traditional summer migrations out of the searing heat of the valley floor. Years later Pauline Esteves still remembered the Park Service hosing down the fragile adobe walls. Pointing to the remains, she recalled, "Those are the ones the Park Service hosed down . . . the Kenedys left . . . then their house got hosed down. Those were rough years—the reason why these others didn't get washed down is 'cause we stayed on in them."[8] Faced with the Shoshones' resistance, however, and fearing a possible land claims suit or adverse public criticism, park officials refrained from outright eviction. Monument administrators simply waited, confident that the "old ladies" and the community would quietly die out.

Although the Shoshones' resistance initially worked, by the late 1960s and early 1970s their village was imperiled. At the time the Boland, Esteves, Kennedy, Shoshone, and Watterson families occupied the nine remaining houses at Indian Village, representing twenty to twenty five people whose family life centered on the core of elderly Timbisha women. Although village residents found work with the Park Service or at the nearby hotels run by the Fred Harvey Company, the majority of Shoshones were unemployed or underemployed; many of the young men and women of working age left to find jobs in nearby towns such as Beatty, Nevada, while others moved to larger California cities because of the housing shortage.[9]

Lacking secure land tenure and subject to the whims of changing National Park Service policy, the Indians had little incentive and few resources to improve their housing and general material conditions. By the early 1970s, by most accounts, the adobe *casitas* were in dilapidated shape. An ominously growing sand dune threatened to engulf homes on the edge of the village. What was most appalling to the few visitors who happened upon the Shoshone community, however, was its lack of modern conveniences at such a late date in the twentieth century. Although a power line ran a mere three hundred feet from the site, the village still lacked electrical service. As early as 1967 the group had requested a line, but a bureaucratic tangle and a lack of funds found them still waiting ten years later. By the mid-1970s most of the old adobe houses were uninhabitable, replaced by aging trailers that were becoming extremely overcrowded. All the houses lacked indoor toilets and other sanitation facilities, and none had air conditioning. Even without air conditioning, however, many families had ceased their traditional summer migrations to the coolness of nearby mountains for fear the monument officials would wash down their homes once they left. [10]

In light of these conditions the Park Service simply could not understand why the Shoshones would chose to remain in Death Valley. From their angle the Indians could not comprehend the monument officials' policy either. To Esteves's people it was inhumane to wash down their homes and prohibit family members from moving in with their relatives. In light of the impasse the two sides began meeting. Yet the discussions that occurred generally resulted in angry exchanges and frustration, rather than constructive dialogue. In the middle of one particularly heated debate with park officials, Esteves asked why the monument officials refused to allow a Shoshone man, Ted James, to move into a vacant house. "I think the worst possible thing I could do to help Ted James would be to give him that house," was the response she got from Superintendent John Stratton. "He has a lot of capabilities but he can't utilize them by staying in the village." Esteves and the other Shoshones understood the officials' true aim, however. As she asked: "Do you just want the Indians out of here? If this is true why not just go down and wash all the houses down and get it over with? Why couldn't someone else use the house . . . we do not really understand this policy. What is the Park Service gaining by washing down the houses?" [11]

Though the generally "deplorable" conditions shocked the sensibilities of visitors, what angered the Shoshones and their supporters the most was the inequity and apparent hypocrisy of the monument officials' position. The people could clearly see that they lived in squalor, tucked away on an unmarked dirt service road, while visitors luxuriated at the nearby Furnace Creek Ranch on lands once owned by the band: playing golf on its irrigated course, sipping cocktails by its swimming pools, and enjoying its air-conditioned comforts at night. There seemed to be plenty of space and resources for the visitors but apparently none for the Shoshones.[12]

Spurred by this reality, Esteves and her people reached out for support, finding a more conducive political environment by the end of the 1960s than in the previous decade. In their crusade Esteves' people ultimately secured the help of two organizations that were aiding other neglected California Indians, the Inter-tribal Council of California and the California Indian Legal Services (CILS). Like the Pascua Yaquis and Tiguas at the same time, the Shoshones' drive focused primarily on improving the group's material conditions and not on gaining federal recognition per se. Fortunately by this time many federal officials had recognized the failings of the termination policy in California and agreed to help the band secure a land base in Death Valley National Monument. Not surprisingly, however, the Park Service was not keen on creating a precedent that would set aside parklands for Indian tribes. Interior Department lawyers determined that they could not "unilaterally give away lands" without an act of Congress and argued that establishing a reservation would be contrary to the purposes of the monument to "preserve the unusual features of scientific, scenic and education interest" in Death Valley.[13]

Far from destroying the band, the National Park Service (NPS) policy unintentionally served to unify the Shoshones in opposition to an agency that treated them as "intruders" on their ancestral lands. Despite their living conditions, the Indian Village families steadfastly refused the park officials' plan to move them to the nearby Lone Pine Reservation in the Sierras or to the mining towns in Nevada where they had social ties. Members of the band went as far as to decline a compromise offer to move to better housing provided to park employees. Instead, during 1975 and 1976 Esteves's people began working with NARF in their ongoing efforts to secure a reservation, to win rights and services, and to gain access to sacred sites closed by the monument policies.[14]

Aided by NARF attorneys Edward Forstenzer and Bruce Greene and by Stephen Quesenberry of CILS, the group decided to petition the bureau to organize under Section 19 of the Indian Reorganization Act of 1934 as individuals of at least one-half degree Indian blood. Aided by the existence of several 1930s-era BIA censuses, the Timbisha Shoshones quickly succeeded in this effort. The BIA approved their petition in August of 1977, informing Timbisha spokesperson Alice Eben that her relatives of at least one-half certified Indian blood were now eligible for federal services. Unfortunately the bureau determined that until the Shoshones obtained a land base, however, they were ineligible to organize as a "tribe" under Section 16 of the Indian Reorganization Act. Until that event the government did not consider the Timbisha to be a federally recognized Indian tribe able to exercise self-government.[15]

Despite the Shoshones' lack of full status, the BIA's determination did give the group's members partial federal rights. In short order the band's leader, Pauline Esteves, executed an agreement in March of 1978 with the Indian Health Service and the National Park Service for a new domestic water supply and waste disposal facilities. With loans obtained through the Indian Service, Shoshones also purchased four trailers to augment their housing and finally received electrical service. In light of their newly confirmed legitimacy, the Park Service also began a study to ascertain the Shoshones' legal status and land rights within the monument lands.[16]

Even with these positive changes, for all practical purposes the NPS policy of phasing out the village remained. Without federal acknowledgment, the band's status on the land remained precarious. Although the superintendent and others were often sympathetic to the group's plight, Park Service officials continued to oppose the Shoshones' aspirations for a reservation. At one point the monument assistant superintendent threatened to deny the Shoshones' pending trailer permits if they "rattled cages" and contacted their congressman about securing land in Death Valley. Similarly NPS lawyers resisted the people's efforts to construct permanent houses in place of their shabby trailers. NPS lawyers went so far as to insinuate that the Shoshones were not native to Death Valley, floating a theory that a mining company imported the people to work in its mines at the turn of the twentieth century.[17]

Thus, despite some positive results from their status as a "one-half or more Indian blood community," the BIA decision clearly had not solved the band's most pressing problem: the lack of a permanent land base in Death Valley National Monument. Without a viable reservation the Death Valley group could not exercise tribal sovereignty or have any chance for economic self-sufficiency. Realizing this fact, Esteves's people decided that they needed tribal acknowledgment to have any hope of securing a reservation. Like many other unacknowledged tribes, Esteves's group decided to pursue two options concurrently: pushing for legislative recognition while also attempting the BIA's new Federal Acknowledgment Process.

With the help of Linda Anisman, an attorney for CILS in Bishop, California, the band first turned to politics to gain legislative acknowledgment. After the *Los Angeles Times* published an article on their plight, the group secured the backing of California Senator S. I. Hayakawa. In spring of 1979 the senator pressured the Department of the Interior to tell him why the group faced so many problems relative to other Indians. Although Hayakawa considered introducing legislation to recognize the Shoshones, the BIA assured him that their petition was under review, and the senator dropped the plan. The Timbisha band's hopes thereafter rested solely on the new and largely untested BIA acknowledgment process.[18]

With the California Indian Legal Services at the helm, the group constructed a petition to represent its history to the BIA project team. In late April of 1979 the inconspicuous twenty-two-page document arrived at the Federal Acknowledgment Project's small office within the Department of Interior building in downtown Washington. Shortly thereafter the Shoshones' case was placed in the hands of George Roth, an anthropologist who would become the institutional memory of FAP in later years. Along with the rest of the project team, Roth was charged with analyzing the band's submission in light of the seven mandatory criteria promulgated by the BIA in 1978.[19]

As with many unacknowledged groups, the band's history was not completely documented or clearly understood. The BAR and the band's attorneys were thus forced to piece together a historical narrative from various ethnological and historical sources. In the course of research by various parties, however, the band's dimly understood origins gradually came to light. Taken as a whole, the ethnohistorical records that emerged outlined the unique experiences of the Shoshones in Death Valley yet also contained gaps and ambiguities common to the histories of all unacknowledged groups. A sad twist to the whole affair was the fact that Indian groups such as the Timbisha band had to rely on outside experts to present their "traditional" society in a form that met the legal requirements of federal acknowledgment in the first place.[20]

What was most apparent from the Timbisha Shoshones' history was that their peaceful nature, isolation, and small size had attracted little attention from military officers or Indian agents in the nineteenth century. As a result federal officials never officially recognized the band by signing treaties with them or creating a reservation by executive order. Unlike groups such as the Pascua Yaquis and Tiguas, the Timbisha Shoshones did not develop highly visible ceremonies that outsiders used to identify them as well. Fortunately for the band, however, their Indian ancestry and location in the American West did attract the attention of anthropologists and settlers who documented their existence during the late nineteenth century.

In the 1890s pioneer ethnographers and government scientists Frederick Coville, E. W. Nelson, and B. H. Dutcher studied the ancestral Timbisha Shoshones, publishing short works on the Death Valley people in the scholarly journal *American Anthropologist*. Afterward noted authority on California ethnology A. L. Kroeber of the University of California accepted the Death Valley Shoshones (also called Koso or Panamints) as an aboriginal California Indian group, including them in his comprehensive 1925 study, *Handbook of the Indians of California*. It was not until the late 1920s and early 1930s, however, that Julian Steward conducted the first substantial fieldwork among the band's ancestors, publishing sections on them in his 1938 *Basin-Plateau Aboriginal Sociopolitical Groups*, a work that established Steward as the foremost authority on the region's Indians.[21]

Compared to most petitioners the Timbisha ancestors had extremely late contact with whites. In fact, sustained encounters essentially began with the California Gold Rush in 1849, centuries after the first dealings between eastern tribes and non-Indians. Because of this reality, the group's efforts to prove its identity from "first sustained contact" would be far less burdensome than for groups in the eastern United States. And compared to many areas of California, Death Valley's forbidding environment and lack of major mineral reserves had ensured that the group remained relatively isolated until the creation of the national monument in 1933.[22] With knowledge that sustained contact occurred after 1849, the band proceeded to present evidence of its tribal identity and community functioning from that date onward.

Scholarly reports indicated the Timbisha Shoshones were a branch of the Western Shoshone people of the Great Basin. In the nineteenth century Shoshonean groups spread over a wide area of the western United States from Southern California to Wyoming and included the Comanches of the Southern Plains and Sacajawea's people, the Lemhis. Early ethnographers referred to Panamint or Shoshone-speaking people living in the Death Valley region and specifically referenced a group living on Furnace Creek who took their name from a source of red ochre called "Timbisha" in their language. Traditionally the Death Valley people spoke Timbisha Shoshone (also called Panamint), a distinct branch of Western Shoshone, itself a part of the larger Uto-Aztecan stock of Native American languages. Speakers of Timbisha Shoshone were never numerous, however, and likely never included more than two hundred individuals. In the 1970s, thirty-five to forty members still spoke Timbisha fluently, although all of these individuals were in their eighties and nineties. Traditionally many of the people were bilingual or trilingual, however, having intermarried with culturally similar Southern Paiutes and Kawaissus, all of whom inhabited a loosely defined region that included Death Valley and its surrounding mountain ranges.[23]

Prior to the creation of the park, the Timbisha Shoshones were hunter-gatherers who practiced limited agriculture near the scattered springs in the Great Basin and Mohave Deserts. Although early explorers dismissed these peoples as lowly "diggers," the desert groups actually possessed complex subsistence strategies particularly adapted to the often-hostile desert environment. Migrating with the seasons, they utilized a great number of ecological niches afforded by the extreme topographic variety of Death Valley, a region where, within a distance of twenty miles, elevations range from over 11,000 feet at Telescope Peak to 282 feet below sea level at Bad Water. From their winter villages at Furnace Creek and other locations on the valley floor, small Shoshone groups fanned out in the summer, migrating to cool haunts in the nearby Panamints and other mountain ranges, only to migrate back again in the fall.[24]

Because of environmental conditions and limited natural resources, Western Shoshone political development, like that of many other California Indians, did not approach popular conceptions of tribal organization: a central, political leadership simply was not needed and did not exist. Instead, the Timbisha Shoshones formed small, extended family groups that spread over wide expanses of Death Valley. These families came together only at winter camps and at annual rabbit drives, pinion nut harvests, and a fall festival where certain informally recognized leaders exercised authority. In his research, however, Steward detailed the existence of several Timbisha village and community "districts" that were associated with springs and particular canyons. These districts were under certain recognized chiefs who inherited their positions patrilineally. Despite lacking centralized political structures, the Timbisha-speaking groups shared a common culture, spoke the same language, and saw themselves as the same people.[25]

Although their experience was much less harsh than in Gold Rush areas of California, the Timbisha ancestors faced significant cultural contact and disruptions during the second half of the nineteenth century. From the 1860s to the 1880s a continual stream of ranchers, miners, and homesteaders filtered into Death Valley. The settlers took the best lands, and their presence at scarce water sources prevented the Shoshones from practicing their traditional subsistence activities. In response many Indians took to raiding isolated prospectors' camps for a time, while others began working for wages or raising livestock and vegetables.[26]

Despite the Shoshones' adaptations and resistance, during the 1880s mining companies and settlers patented most of the fertile lands in Death Valley. The turn of the century thus found many Indians working at area mines and on the famous "twenty-mule teams" of the Pacific Coast Borax Company or toiling in hay fields, repairing irrigation ditches, and doing other manual labor for area ranchers. During the 1920s this situation changed, however, when Death Valley became an unlikely tourist destination promoted by health seekers and popularized in western novels by Zane Grey and others. As demand for lodging grew, the Pacific Coast Borax Company constructed several hotels, including the Furnace Creek Inn, where Shoshones found additional work.[27]

Fortunately for Esteves's community, the colorful characters of Death Valley and its environs spawned several "pioneer accounts" and other published memoirs on the "Wild West," works that noted the presence of Indians within the valley during the nineteenth century. Although there was a paucity of records for the beginning of the twentieth century, the BAR eventually located several pieces of "high evidence" on the band. Between 1908 and 1911 several documents revealed the BIA clearly recognized some of the band's ancestors as Indians under the tutelage of the Bishop Agency in California. In 1908 the Indian Service issued Hungry Bill, a Timbisha ancestor, a patent for 160 acres in a spring-fed canyon on the east slopes of the Panamint Range, while the Carson Indian Agency later granted another ancestor, Robert Thompson, an allotment at Warm Springs in a nearby canyon. There were also documents showing that several Timbisha Shoshones had attended the Carson and Sherman Indian boarding schools between 1911 and 1959 as part of a government-sponsored program to eradicate their culture, a sad reality that nonetheless provided evidence of a government relationship. Finally, researchers determined that the bureau had established a small reservation known as "Indian Ranch" for Panamint George and his family in 1928, a group who were related to the Timbisha people yet lived outside the park. Together, these documents were strong evidence the BIA once recognized individual Timbisha ancestors as Indians.[28]

While researching federal records in San Bruno, California, however, the group's attorneys Ed Forstenzer and Bruce Greene chanced upon several yellowing documents from the 1930s that represented a bombshell. The stash contained federal contracts and other records that seemed to confirm that the

Indian Service once referred to the Death Valley people as a "tribe" of Indians. Believing they had hit the jackpot, the attorneys seemed to have proof that the Timbisha Shoshones were already an acknowledged tribe.[29]

In his last days in the White House Herbert Hoover signed a document establishing Death Valley National Monument in 1933. The president created the new park following years of lobbying by the Automobile Club of Southern California, an organization that promoted its extreme and fantastic environment as a potential playground and natural treasure. The new monument encompassed lands of great contrast, containing the lowest point in the Western Hemisphere, 282 feet below sea level near Bad Water, and the place where the hottest temperature ever was recorded in the United States, 134 degrees in 1913.[30] In their initial excitement over the new preserve, monument planners gushed at Death Valley's unique animal and plant life but seemed to take little notice of the small groups of Indians living throughout the new federal park.

Although overlooked, several dozen Indians continued to range throughout the newly established preserve in the early 1930s. Shoshones inhabited all parts of the park, yet most squatted part of the year on borax company lands near Furnace Creek. During the late nineteenth century the Pacific Coast Borax Company had patented the fertile lands along Furnace Creek where many Indians had traditionally lived. Afterward its mine had acted like a magnet, drawing additional Indians from the surrounding areas in search of work. By the 1920s, many of the Valley's kinship-based Shoshone groups had converged at Furnace Creek, where they lived in traditional, brush-covered houses. The year 1933 thus found the modern Timbisha group located at a village on Furnace Creek Ranch, an operation established to produce dates and other foods for the mines.[31]

While the new monument disrupted the Shoshones' lives, the Great Depression more directly affected the band during the early 1930s. Although the Shoshones were once welcomed at the site for their labor, as the depression worsened, the Pacific Coast Borax Company found the Indians' presence less and less tolerable. Once jobs completely dried up in 1934, the company began agitating to have the Indians removed from its property. The borax company's plan found a sympathetic ally in Monument Superintendent John White, a former colonel who decided it was high time to end monument officials' "indulgent treatment" of the Furnace Creek Indians. Just as the Pascua Yaquis discovered at the same time, the Shoshones found that local non-Indians were suddenly less tolerant of Indian groups in their midst.[32]

It turned out that the borax company's plans to remove the Indians meshed well with the NPS's growing alarm over the Shoshones' traditional land uses in the park. Although not residing permanently on monument lands, the Timbisha people still utilized the valley's resources as they had for generations. From Furnace Creek, family groups continued to take their stock to summer pastures high up in the Panamint Mountains and other ranges. Following their seasonal migrations, the Indians still fanned across the sand hills and creosote flats in search of plants, moving up the slopes to gather pinion nuts and to hunt deer and bighorn sheep when the season arrived. Although Esteves's ancestors had practiced these activities for centuries and the "pristine" environment that the monument was established to protect had been affected by Indian practices for generations, this fact was missed on Colonel White. As he said at the time, the Indians needed a new home because they were "eating out the scanty herbage" and "taking toll of the sparse wild life" of Death Valley.[33] In light of these concerns, monument administrators supported the borax company's efforts to evict the people while opposing any permanent land base for the Shoshones. Monument officials also contacted the Indian Service about their newly discovered "Indian problem." To solve the immediate ecological concerns, however, the superintendent took steps to curtail the Indians' subsistence activities, measures that forced the Shoshones into further dependence on wage work and charity.[34]

Despite the clear final goal, the efforts to remove the Shoshones dragged on until 1936 and 1937, when a more sympathetic Park Service official, T. R. Goodwin, took up the Timbisha issue with the Indian Service office in Carson City, Nevada. At the time the Carson Agency was under Alida Bowler, an energetic Indian advocate and personal friend of Commissioner of Indian Affairs John Collier. The first woman to serve as a superintendent of an Indian agency, Bowler eventually succeeded in helping other "landless" Shoshones establish reservations. Beginning in 1936 Bowler and Goodwin started working together to aid the small Timbisha group as well.[35]

During the Great Depression several Timbisha families continued squatting on borax company land despite the mining conglomerate's opposition. Although the company still wanted to evict the group, its representatives did not have the heart to remove them by force. Like many forgotten groups at the time, the Death Valley Indians were in an ambiguous legal position. Stretched thin by the economic crisis, local relief agencies were reluctant to aid them, believing that all Indians were the Indian Service's responsibility. Bowler and Goodwin therefore stepped in and secured limited food, hospital care, and school funding for the group. While the agencies debated their responsibilities, Shoshones John Boland, Hank Patterson, and a Spaniard who had married into the community, Serafin Esteves, managed to secure seasonal work at the Furnace Creek Inn while quietly maintaining their traditional hunting and gathering activities. Many families, however, were out of work and going hungry.[36]

Bowler and Goodwin were plainly aware that the limited government aid they gave was not enough to provide viable subsistence for the group. They also could not ignore the growing criticism from tourists who could plainly see the "wretched hovels" of the Indians right next door to the park headquarters. As the "Indian problem" finally reached a crescendo in 1936, Bowler contacted her good friend John Collier about aiding the group. Motivated by a genuine concern for the Shoshones, she opposed the efforts to remove the Indians, arguing that they would only drift back to their traditional homeland if they were displaced.[37]

Working with Park Service officials, Bowler proposed that the BIA and the National Park Service construct a "model village" for the Shoshone group patterned upon an Indian village in Yosemite. The federal effort to create the village proved important for Esteves's people. It subsequently created both a home for the Indians and a paper trail that helped the Timbisha Shoshones document their ancestors' tribal activities. As planned, the model community was to provide modern homes for the Indians near wage work at Furnace Creek. It also would house a trading post where Indian women could market their intricate baskets and a laundry service where they could work. Superintendent White promptly signed on to the plan, hoping that the Indian Village would concentrate the Indians in one area where they could take up modern occupations and cease their traditional "nomadic" wanderings. Bowler and the others planned to carve a 160-acre reservation from private lands donated by the Pacific Coast Borax Company. Had this been accomplished, the band's history would have been much different. But the company failed to donate the land, and the Park Service and BIA eventually settled on a 40-acre tract of monument land the Shoshones could occupy but not own.[38]

To accomplish the model Indian colony, John Collier and the National Park Service executed a "Memorandum of Understanding" on 23 May 1936. This agreement would be the first of several significant pieces of evidence supporting the Shoshones' acknowledgment case. In the memorandum the BIA agreed to fund the construction of the Indian Village. To accomplish the plan Bowler and Goodwin also helped the group organize a formal tribal council to administer BIA funds and subsequently signed a "Trust Agreement" with three newly elected council members, Fred Thompson, Hank Patterson, and Tom Wilson, in 1938. Significantly the bureau compiled several censuses of the band as well.[39]

To complete the colony a federal work relief agency constructing trails and facilities in the monument, the Civilian Conservation Corps (CCC), provided labor and hired unemployed Shoshone men. By the end of 1938 the CCC had finished eleven adobe houses and a community laundry. The new houses were certainly a drastic change from the previous brush-covered dwellings, although none had plumbing or electricity; a single tap served the entire village. The absence of modern conveniences was planned, however, as Bowler and White wanted to ease the group into modern life. As White remarked, "I do not think it advisable to put them in quarters with running water, plumbing, etc. [this would] make the transition from their present method of living to one of comparatively modern standards too violent."[40] As the Shoshones moved into their new homes on the forty-acre plot, they hoped to finally have a secure, permanent community.

In 1939 the small group took further steps to make the Indian Village an Indian reservation, activities that would also aid their descendants' efforts to substantiate their tribal status in the FAP. With Bowler and Goodwin at the lead, the party hoped to transfer title to the forty-acre site to the Department of the Interior for the BIA to hold in trust for the band as an Indian reservation. If secured, the trust land would enable the band to organize as a formal tribe under the experimental Indian Reorganization Act of 1934. Because the Indian Village sat on parkland, however, government lawyers informed the parties that legislation would be needed to accomplish a land transfer. Seeing the complications involved with the NPS, Commissioner Collier let the effort simmer.[41]

As the depression decade came to a close, John Collier attempted to end the imbroglio in October of 1939 by directing the local Indian agency to enroll the band. Again citing the lack of availability of trust lands, Assistant Commissioner of Indian Affairs Fred Daiker suggested that the Indian Service could accomplish its main goal of providing services to the needy group by simply organizing the Timbisha Shoshones as a community of at least one-half degree Indian blood under section 19 of the Indian Reorganization Act. Like the earlier reservation plan, however, this second BIA solution was never accomplished, but for entirely different reasons. The band never organized as one-half bloods—not because of the lack of trust lands, but because the bureau believed it simply was not necessary. As the commissioner of Indian Affairs informed the superintendent of the Carson Agency, "The Department in the past has recognized these Indians as being entitled to benefits, [there is] no reason therefore why these Indians should not be recognized as wards of the Government." A short time later the Carson Agency received a second letter from Washington concurring that organizing under section 19 was unnecessary: "These people are entitled to the benefits and privileges as wards of the government without regard to their blood status."[42]

In light of these determinations, in 1940 the BIA entered into another trust agreement with trustees Hank Patterson and Tom Wilson, calling the band variously the "Death Valley Shoshone Indians" and "Death Valley Shoshone Tribe." Further committing itself, the Indian Service later paid the salary of a woman operating the village laundry, trading post, and craft workshop as well. Together, these actions were clear evidence that the BIA considered the group to be an Indian entity. Even with these fledgling plans, however, the group never organized under the Indian Reorganization Act during the New Deal era, although it seemed apparent to Esteves's people that the Indian Service had identified their ancestors as a "tribe" and not simply as individuals of Indian descent. If not for the land impasse, it appeared that the band would have become a recognized tribe during this era.[43]

As the United States entered World War II, federal emphasis generally shifted away from John Collier's Indian New Deal and thus away from the Shoshones' plans. During the war Death Valley National Monument became virtually deserted; the park store and Furnace Creek Inn closed, as did the band's Wa-Pai-Shone Trading Post. Funding for their nascent rehabilitation programs, including the community laundry service, dried up as well because of the war. The Shoshone women apparently did not mind these developments, however. They always despised the trading post middlemen for taking a large percentage of profits from their painstaking basketwork, and they particularly hated the laundry service. "We were supposed to wash the White man's clothes—for money; [we] quit doing that because the Park Service ladies who were supervising the thing started bossing the women around. They said, 'To heck with it. We're not going to wash nobody's clothes no more,'" recalled Pauline Esteves.[44]

Following national Indian policy trends, BIA involvement with the band essentially ended after World War II, with the exception of the bureau funding several children who attended government boarding schools during the 1940s and 1950s. The Death Valley group thus dropped from the federal radar, only appearing briefly during the sale of Robert Thompson's allotment in Warm Springs, the sale of Hungry Bill's ranch in the 1950s, and the 1957 efforts to terminate the Indian Village. In terms of documentation, the band reappeared only after Esteves spearheaded resistance to the NPS housing policy in 1966. Despite the few but important recorded contacts during the 1940s and 1950s, the government's termination policy essentially precluded any BIA involvement with the ambiguously acknowledged group. Throughout the 1940s and 1950s, however, some band members continued to live on monument lands, eking out an existence while maintaining their traditional family pursuits from their center at Indian Village.[45]

In light of existing ethnologies and federal records, the Timbisha Shoshones appeared to have an airtight case for tribal acknowledgment. After submitting its acknowledgment petition in 1979, the group waited anxiously for the FAP's initial review. Despite limited records for certain periods, the research seemed to confirm that federal officials identified the group as Shoshone and treated it as a tribe in the past. Because the time span involved was relatively short and the number of members of the group was very small, the band could document with relative certainty that the majority of tribal members could trace their lineage to people identified as Shoshones by the various federal and scholarly records that existed. Together, Esteves's people and CILS attorney Linda Anisman believed that the band had clear evidence that would meet their burden on each of the FAP's seven criteria.

In its "Obvious Deficiency Letter" to the Shoshones in July of 1979, however, the FAP team wanted further evidence concerning the four most contentious criteria. In essence the BIA researchers still had questions whether the group could prove it descended from the historic Shoshone bands of Death Valley and whether Esteves's people continued to be a functioning community with tribal leaders after World War II. The BIA asked the group to provide additional documentation identifying its ancestors prior to the establishment of the monument in 1933 and more evidence of its modern community. The BAR requested more evidence of group decision making and political authority. It also wanted more documentation establishing a genealogical link between the Indians noted in early historical accounts and the Timbisha band's specific ancestors listed on the BIA census rolls created in the 1930s. To meet this request Linda Anisman went back to Death Valley for further research and soon submitted additional historical references to Indians in Death Valley during the contact era, more data on the group's organization and culture, and two brief oral histories from tribal elders Sally Boland and Hank Patterson that corroborated the written record. Fortunately for the group both Boland and Patterson had personal links with people alive during the period of first contact, something quite rare for petitioning groups.[46]

Charged with weighing all data by the preponderance of the evidence, the FAP team set out to determine whether the Timbisha band was in fact a "tribe" and not perhaps simply an aggregation of Indians with certifiable Indian blood who somehow converged on Furnace Creek in the 1920s. As the FAP is a fact-based process, the apparently obvious existence of the band was not enough. With additional data the FAP team led by George Roth and Acknowledgment Chief Bud Shapard thus set out to make a determination that in many ways would decide the legal fate of the Death Valley people. At this early stage of the Federal Acknowledgment Process the BIA team conducted considerable research into the relatively accessible federal records near its Washington offices. In a rare occurrence they also were able to utilize a sizeable collection of materials compiled by the Park Service in regard to the band's status within the monument. On the whole this outside research greatly reduced the financial burden and time required for the Shoshones to compile and document their petition.[47]

Demonstrating its need for written proof, the BIA team was first concerned whether outsiders had consistently identified Esteves's people as indigenous and whether the Indians identified in early accounts were, in fact, the ancestors of the current band. These points would be difficult to prove in light of the paucity of records for the period prior to the creation of the monument in 1933. To meet this standard, however, the BIA called for certain types of evidence in descending level of credibility. The FAP deemed past identifications and dealings with federal officials as the best evidence on this point. Less authoritative forms of identification also included dealings with state or local governments and identification by scholars, churches, schools, or Indian organizations. For most groups, proving outside identification has proven a daunting task because it relies exclusively on evidence generated outside the Indian groups.[48]

Although historical sources were thin, the band's attorneys eventually located additional records concerning its identity over time. Overall, in trying to prove outsiders identified the band as Indians, Esteves's group was highly advantaged by its extremely late contact with whites. With first encounters in 1849, the band did not have to go far back in time. Because of their isolation the Timbisha Shoshones could confidently argue that their ancestors maintained a fairly traditional identity and culture, even though they did not possess abundant records.[49]

After weighing all the evidence, anthropologist George Roth and the rest of the FAP team agreed with the Shoshones, concluding that outside sources consistently had identified the band and its ancestors as Indians since first sustained contact with non-Indians. In his conclusion Roth relied heavily on early ethnological reports by Steward, Park Service data, and BIA records, particularly federal censuses that the BAR considered "high evidence," or the best form of documentation. In a rare occurrence Julian Steward's 1920s work with elderly informants spanned both the group's early history and linked this history to its living members. Because the early ethnographic and historical accounts apparently were untainted by motivations or advocacy, the FAP accepted their conclusions at face value at this early stage in the acknowledgment process. In establishing specific links between contact-era Shoshones in Death Valley and the modern band, the FAP team compared nineteenth-century accounts of Death Valley Indians with Julian Steward's 1920s and 1930s work, noting that they often "correspond exactly" as to specific village sites and individuals who lived there. The fact that these accounts often discussed ancestors of the Timbisha Shoshones by name, including Hungry Bill, Panamint Tom, Grapevine Dock, Tule George, and Cold Mountain Jack, and specifically noted that they were Indians or Shoshones was also invaluable for Esteves's people in proving Indian identity. In the course of its investigations the FAP team also corroborated Steward's work with several federal censuses and BIA rolls taken between 1900 and 1940 that identified specific Timbisha ancestors as Indians and tied them to traditional locations in the monument lands.[50]

For the modern period following World War II the bureau agreed that outsiders continued to identify the Furnace Creek village as an Indian enclave, although fewer records existed for this period. Apparently recognizing the government's culpability in the matter, the FAP team assumed that the Timbisha group continued to be identified as Indians throughout the termination era of the 1950s and early 1960s, despite what it called a "gap" in records. After 1966 the battle of Esteves and the others to save their homes and the paper trail it generated provided sufficient evidence that outsiders identified Esteves's people as an Indian entity. A letter provided by the neighboring Owens Valley Paiute-Shoshone Tribe and a six-day field visit assured the BAR team that other Indians of the area identified the group as Indian as well.[51]

The Furnace Creek group next had to prove more definitely that it had always existed as an Indian community. Compared with many other groups the Timbisha Shoshones ultimately faced less difficulty demonstrating this point, yet they clearly encountered problems meeting the social science definitions of the concept embedded in the acknowledgment process. Before the 1994 revised regulations the "community" criterion mandated that groups provide "evidence that a *substantial portion* of the petitioning group inhabits a specific region or lives in a *community viewed as American Indian*" and that "its members are descendants of an Indian tribe which historically inhabited a specific area."[52] To meet this requirement, the BIA suggested groups provide written evidence such as minutes taken at tribal meetings and records of tribal ceremonies or festivals. The regulations also required that groups prove they descended from a tribe native to the area or one that had migrated to its current residence as a group.

In proving their community's existence over time, the Timbisha people once again had the advantage of extremely late contact with non-Indians and the fact that they lived in relative isolation within Death Valley. Unlike many other Indians in California who were devastated by epidemics, life in Spanish missions, and the Gold Rush, the Death Valley Shoshones could argue persuasively that their community had "remained almost entirely insulated" from the dominant society until the 1930s. Because of this rather rare isolation, the band believed that its ancestors had preserved their traditional community organization relatively intact until Julian Steward documented the various "district" communities scattered around Death Valley. To the group's attorneys, it seemed clear that the harsh desert had left the band "forgotten" until the area caught the fancy of the Park Service in 1933. Overall, the Shoshones provided little evidence on this point, however, perhaps believing these facts were largely self-evident.[53]

For the modern period after World War II, many unacknowledged groups have been stymied in their efforts to prove "community," as their members moved away and married non-Indians. Unlike these groups, the Timbisha Shoshones were able to reference the physical space of Indian Village after 1933 as evidence of their "core community." Clearly, federal documents generated by the 1930s-era Village plan showed that a well-defined forty-acre space was allocated to the group in recognition of its aboriginal inhabitation of Death Valley. After its creation the Indian Village served as an unofficial Indian reservation. As historian Frederick Hoxie noted with the Cheyenne River Indian Reservation in South Dakota, the Indian Village created a place where Shoshone culture and tribal forms could exist in relative insulation from the centrifugal forces of modernization. Since the Depression the Indian Village had served as a cultural homeland and a core for the Timbisha community. As the band put it, "We did not lose our land like other Californian Indian groups; we do not have a reservation [but] we do have our village which is separate from the rest of the National Monument."[54]

Much like Indians on federal reservations, the Shoshones lacked individual title to their lands, a fact that enhanced community solidarity. Ironically, in trying to disperse the band, Park Service policy unintentionally encouraged the Timbisha group to negotiate with their common nemesis as a band and to work toward communal concerns. In stark contrast to other areas of California, the establishment of the monument had also kept development at bay, save for a limited number of concessions and developments for Park Service employees. Overall, the elderly Shoshone women's determined resistance to remain in this place, coupled with their common interests in the Indian Village, helped bind the group to the little village in the middle of the vast national preserve. Numerous other unacknowledged groups inundated by outsiders simply lack a common land base and common causes to bind individuals to a tribal entity.[55]

Despite the concentrated Indian Village, the Death Valley group soon ran into problems springing from the wording of the FAP rules and the social science methodology used by the BIA to measure "community." For the modern era the branch team wanted to know why a "substantial portion" of the group did not live in Indian Village. In computing the numbers the bureau determined that only about 35 of its approximately 150 members lived on the monument land. Because of the small percentage of members who actually lived in the "core" area, the Timbisha Shoshones had to prove that a substantial portion of their claimed membership continued to maintain social ties with Indian Village. To this issue the group's lawyers argued that the members who did not reside in Death Valley National Monument had maintained close ties and were concerned about the band and village nonetheless. Despite these assertions, the Shoshones submitted no evidence to support the argument. The group argued, however, that the Park Service's policy of limiting the number of houses had forced many of its people off the monument lands in search of work or living space. Although the BIA generally looks upon "voluntary abandonment" of tribal relations and movements away from the core community with disfavor, the Shoshones' situation appeared to have been forced upon them by the federal government. And although only 35 members resided in Death Valley, the band was able to show that many others lived in nearby areas just outside the monument lands.[56]

Compared with latter petitioners, the Shoshones provided scant evidence of actual group interaction between members living outside the monument and those at Indian Village. The band also provided little data on their distinctiveness or culture, beyond saying that many elders were still familiar "with the old ways." Even so, Esteves's people possessed what seemed to be the best evidence of the existence of an Indian community: a living language. Most experts agree that the continuing existence of an indigenous language speaks volumes to the maintenance of social ties and community. When asked, the band could show that many of its members still spoke the rare Timbisha language; for several it was their first or only tongue.[57]

As part of the BIA process George Roth conducted a six-day field visit to the area to verify the statements made by the band about its community. Despite the band's language, the branch team still was concerned about the lack of documentation of a functioning Timbisha community after 1940. Upon contemplating the issue further, however, the team seemed to take the NPS policy and traditional dispersed Western Shoshone patterns into account when judging the community's existence. Unlike some unacknowledged groups, the Timbisha Shoshones possessed an easily recognizable "core" community at Indian Village, a fact that made the determination easier. The village was isolated from both the limited park development at Furnace Creek and the nearest small town over thirty miles away—physically isolated to a degree quite rare among unrecognized tribes. In light of this fact and the common antagonist of the National Park Service, the FAP team determined that Indian Village had served as "the core" community, despite the fact that its researchers determined that only 26 of the 199 Timbisha members (13 percent) actually lived there, and despite the fact that many of these 26 migrated in and out with the seasons. As Roth noted, however, the "severely limited jobs and housing" restricted the number of Shoshones who could live in the park. The BIA also remarked approvingly that 65 percent of members lived in nearby areas "traditionally" visited by the group. In its analysis and evaluation, the FAP team thus acknowledged the federal government's culpability in restricting the size of the core community.[58]

In measuring community the BIA also looked to cultural distinctions the Timbisha Shoshones maintained vis-à-vis the surrounding society. In this case the bureau remarked approvingly upon the "considerable degree" of cultural distinction the band maintained from surrounding populations, especially as reflected in the distinct Timbisha Shoshone language. The BAR also found that the group maintained marriage taboos and clear family lines distinct from surrounding populations. In particular BIA researchers determined that until 1950, the Docks, Shoshone, Patterson, and Boland lines, and to a lesser degree the Kennedy, Button, and Thompson-Billison-Wilson lines, had continued a pattern of high intermarriage. As was common for Indians after World War II, however, the FAP team determined that intermarriage rates had dropped precipitously after that date. Unlike many other groups, however, the subsequent Timbisha band marriages were primarily to individuals from other Indian tribes and not to whites, African Americans, or other ethnic groups. The BIA did not raise the issue of whether these individuals had become somehow less Indian or less tribal after marrying outside the group.[59]

Ultimately the BIA agreed that the Timbisha Shoshones were a distinct Indian community. In proving their community existence, however, Esteves and her people had the advantage of going through the acknowledgment process early. In the early 1980s the FAP team assumed group interaction took place and accepted some of the band's assertions of group cohesion at face value—something it would not do as the process became more legalistic and detail oriented. In later years the BIA would ask groups without a clear "social core" and with a larger membership, such as the United Houma Nation of Louisiana and the Shasta Nation of California, to produce ethnographic studies and to provide phone logs of personal calls to prove group interaction. Demonstrating community has become longer and costlier as a result.[60]

After clearing these first difficult hurdles the band still needed to demonstrate that it had maintained continuous political authority over its membership. In essence the bureau demands that groups prove they were political bodies or tribes that exercised sovereignty since first contact with Europeans. Although in many ways this BIA requirement is the most central requirement for acknowledgment in terms of Indian law, it is also the most ambiguous and difficult to document. To meet this criterion, groups are required to demonstrate longstanding decision-making processes and reveal how sanctions are enforced against members. To prove political functioning, the BIA recommended that groups provide records demonstrating how they settled land disputes or otherwise regulated their members' activities.[61]

The Shoshone petition was briefest on this point at only two pages—far shorter than most petitions in the FAP. The band dismissed the lack of records of formal political organization and procedures, however, as stemming directly from the group's traditional, small band organization. Although the FAP did not technically require that groups remain static in tribal organization, the Timbisha Shoshones' traditional, loose family-based organization gave them a clear advantage. They could argue that the lack of records flowed directly from their ancestors' traditional, informal political organization.[62]

To prove political functioning, however, the BIA evaluators still wanted to see some evidence. And here the outside interference of white officials played a key role in the band's ultimate success. The group was able to reference the correspondence surrounding the BIA's creation of the Shoshones' Tribal Council in 1937. Ironically, however, the formal council was not part of indigenous organization but sprang into being to meet the needs of federal officials. As Monument Superintendent T. R. Goodwin argued in 1937, "The time is ripe for a Tribal Council and the organization of these Indians—at present there is no authority and no head."[63] Without federal intervention it is doubtful a visible council would have existed that left documentary evidence of its being. Even with this incongruence the council was clearly the representative body of the group, directed to handle trust rehabilitation funds for the band. But the council was prompted from the outside, rather than arising from the inside, and it lasted only until the late 1940s.

In light of the documentary nature of the BIA process, Roth recalled later that he and the FAP team agonized over whether the Shoshone group had proven that it exercised political authority over its members. Ultimately, however, the branch concluded the modern group had descended from kinship groups that lived under the authority of "chiefs," the last of whom died in 1943. Overlapping the influence of the traditional "chiefs" was the formal Tribal Council that functioned between 1937 and 1949. In particular Roth noted that the group's effort to create a reservation during the New Deal was prime evidence of political processes and group decision making. The BAR also determined the Timbisha Shoshones acted as a political unit after 1966 when Pauline Esteves, Grace Goad, and Madeline Esteves began spearheading Shoshone resistance to NPS removal policies.[64]

The BIA was concerned, however, over a "gap" in the records concerning political functioning between the late 1940s and late 1960s. Under the rules, if the group disbanded during these decades its descendants were precluded from acknowledgment. The BIA team therefore scrutinized the period between 1950 and 1966 for political activity. Ultimately, despite noting that there were "some significant fluctuations" in the existence of political leaders from 1949 to 1966, Roth's team concluded that leadership existed nonetheless, apparently taking the government's culpability into account when evaluating this "gap." To make up for the lack of records, the BIA examined the heroic efforts of the older Shoshone women in resisting the NPS eviction policy and viewed this resistance as strong evidence of the existence of informal political processes. As the final report noted, "the period after 1940 is the most difficult to deal with in terms of describing political processes; [however] important indirect evidence is the survival itself of the village between 1942 and the 1960s when economic opportunities were at a minimum, services from the Bureau of Indian Affairs had been withdrawn, and there was a maximum of resistance by the Park Service to the continuance of the village."[65] Although believing that Esteves's group lacked concrete evidence of its political processes for these years, the BIA team ultimately concluded that they existed nonetheless. With their pure and untainted motives, the Timbisha Shoshones had met outside expectations of what Indian bands were supposed to do in this situation, in particular, clinging to ancestral lands at all costs when there was little apparent incentive for doing so. In addition to heroic resistance, cultural retention was also important. As evidence of political authority, the BIA team pointed to the strong distinctions maintained between the band and neighboring Indian groups and to taboos enforced against marriage between relatives as well. To the BIA these culturally defined rules indicated the continuance of informal, traditional authority.[66]

Ultimately the FAP team determined that the band had met its burden of proving that it exercised political authority over its membership. In the process the BIA assumed that political mechanisms existed within the village for certain periods, something Roth admits it would not do today. These assumptions seemed to flow from the fact that this was such a small, interrelated group. The FAP team decided that the group's loosely organized band structure and informal political processes conformed to "traditional patterns" found in Western Shoshone culture, with this fact serving to explain the absence of clear written records concerning its political functioning. In the final evaluation of evidence the FAP team used common-sense assumptions that tribal authority or decision making occurred even though the record was sparse. The Timbisha Shoshones therefore had cleared another hurdle. Now Pauline Esteves and the others had to prove the seemingly obvious fact that they descended from the historical Shoshone groups of Death Valley.[67]

Having previously secured recognition as Indians of at least half-blood degree, Esteves's people seemed to have an airtight case that they were genetically Indians. In particular the Timbisha Shoshones possessed several BIA rolls that noted their "blood quantum." Proving Indian ancestry was not enough, however, as the BIA requires groups to submit a membership list containing the names of "individuals who have established, using evidence acceptable to the Secretary, descendancy from a tribe which existed historically." In light of this, the group members had to prove that they were lineal descendents of a Shoshone tribe that lived in the region at first contact with whites. To demonstrate tribal ancestry, the FAP recommended that groups submit certain types of evidence in order of significance, including BIA rolls, state or federal records, church and school enrollment records, affidavits of tribal elders, and other documents identifying their ancestors as Indians from a particular tribe.[68]

In comparison to many petitioners, proving descent would be fairly clear-cut for the band. Esteves's group simply submitted three censuses compiled by the BIA in 1933, 1936, and 1978. Because the census rolls were prepared by its own officials, the BIA considered these genealogical records highly persuasive. In examining the Timbisha bloodline the FAP genealogist also located several other government sources documenting the group's ancestry. Taken together, these records clearly proved the Timbisha group's Indian descent.[69] In this regard, however, the Death Valley group plainly benefited from evidence taken at an earlier time and place. A Depression-era letter reveals the relative ease with which groups could establish Indian ancestry at that time. During the 1930s the assistant commissioner of Indian affairs instructed a local Indian agency to enroll Timbisha individuals using existing BIA rolls or, in their absence, to rely "upon affidavits to establish the degree of Indian blood" produced by a committee of elders, "men and women of good memory and extensive knowledge of the families involved."[70] At present, oral history carries little weight in proving Indian ancestry, so the Timbisha Shoshones were fortunate to have BIA rolls prepared during a time when people were alive with firsthand knowledge of their ancestors and, more importantly, before Indian identity became increasingly scrutinized—when Indians were Indians because they said they were.[71]

Even though the Timbisha group had proven its members had the requisite Indian blood, it now needed to prove it had the right type. Again revealing the BIA's documentary focus, the FAP team next asked: Were the members listed on the 1933 and 1936 BIA rolls actually related to tribal groups living in Death Valley at first contact with whites in 1849? To this end Esteves and attorney Anisman took the depositions of tribal elders Sally Boland and Hank Patterson, individuals who had personal connections to individuals alive at first contact. It was a rare occurrence that these elders possessed memories tying them directly to nineteenth-century ancestors and to specific places in Death Valley described by Steward and others for the early historical period. Groups whose first contact occurred in the sixteenth century logically are hard-pressed to find similar affidavits.[72]

In light of this evidence the BIA team determined that the Timbisha Sho-shones did in fact descend from Shoshones native to Death Valley. Specifically the FAP researchers compared individuals noted by Julian Steward to people listed on federal censuses and Indians mentioned in the oral testimonies presented by the band. Although early federal censuses often failed to include the Indians of Death Valley, FAP researchers located a 1900 census that listed specific Shoshone family groups, including the Hanson, Panamint Tom, Grapevine Dock, Bill Dock, and Panamint Joe families who fortuitously later were informants for Julian Steward or mentioned in his work. Tribal elders Sally Boland and Hank Patterson were related to these families, and their oral testimony was able to corroborate the written record sufficiently to convince the FAP researchers that their ancestors lived in Death Valley at contact with whites.[73]

Having met the BIA's four most difficult criteria, Esteves's people still needed to meet three additional requirements to become acknowledged as an Indian tribe. Although to most groups these last rules are an afterthought, they would cause the band some concern. The first required petitioners to submit a governing document with membership criteria. This was easily accomplished. Yet two additional regulations prohibited petitioners from having a membership derived from another recognized tribe and demanded that groups prove they were not terminated or otherwise prohibited by Congress from establishing a federal-tribal relationship. Many Death Valley Shoshones resided on nearby reservations at Bishop and Lone Pine, California, and had married members of the Shoshone and Paiute tribes on those reservations. It thus appeared that the Death Valley group was composed of members of these tribes. In time, however, the band established that its members were not on the rolls of these reservations and also demonstrated its members had maintained a distinct identity and community apart from these tribes. On the usually simple termination issue the band also faced concerns over its ties to the Indian Ranch rancheria, the local Shoshone reservation that was specifically terminated by Congress in the early 1960s. Upon investigation, however, the FAP team determined that only a small number of the Timbisha members were related to individuals from Indian Ranch, and that none of these individuals were specifically listed as Indians "terminated" by the legislation. The road was now clear for the full tribal acknowledgment of the tiny Furnace Creek community.[74]

In early November of 1982, three and a half years after the group submitted its petition to the BIA, Pauline Esteves and the other Timbisha Shoshones heard the good news from the BIA. The band had met the seven criteria to be acknowledged as an Indian tribe. Because they went through the BIA process early with such a strong case, the Shoshones had what would be seen as a short wait in the annals of the BIA program. Fortunately the "comment period" came and went with no opposition surfacing. In fact, several area tribes wrote in support of the band—there seemed to be little doubt that the small group was an Indian tribe within the legal and popular definitions of the term. Department of Interior authorities sent word to the Sacramento Area Office of the BIA to begin planning services for the group. After decades of government neglect and years of being in-between, Esteves and the others could now hope to realize some of their aspirations.[75]

The question remained, however, whether federal acknowledgment would be a panacea for the group in its quest for a permanent land base within Death Valley National Monument. But for a moment, however, the Shoshones' strong sense of place and tenacity had seemingly born fruit with the federal decision to acknowledge them. In a later interview Pauline Esteves summed up the root of her persistence: "Our people have always lived here. The Creator, Appü, placed us here at the beginning of time. This valley and the surrounding places that the Old Ones frequented, is tüpippüh', our Homeland."[76]

The Shoshones immediately set out to improve their lives within Death Valley National Monument. Their first concern was the original adobe houses whose crumbling walls served as a testament to the decades of neglect. As the majority of the 199 tribal members were under twenty-nine years of age and most of their forty-acre tract was covered in sand, Esteves and the others pressed for additional land where they could place more houses for their children. Beyond living space, the band also wanted increased access to traditional resources and sacred sites within the monument. Despite their new status, the Furnace Creek people were still ineligible to qualify for grants under the Indian Self-Determination Act and other tribal development programs because they lacked a reservation. Esteves and the others quickly realized they would need a viable land base for economic and community development. To make ends meet in the meantime, however, tribal members continued working seasonal jobs for the Park Service and at the Furnace Creek Inn. As a part-time Park Service employee, Esteves seized the occasion to inform visitors of her people's plight in between presentations on Shoshone food preparation and basket making. Most tribal members such as Barbara Durham wanted more than low-paying seasonal jobs, however. "We need to secure a homeland where we can rebuild our community and overcome the dispersing of the Tribe—a place where people can live, work, and plan as a community. Our Tribe is losing its culture, deprived of being a sovereign nation, deprived of keeping traditions, songs, stories, cultural practices and kinship," argued Durham following her peoples' recognition.[77]

To this end, in 1994 the band successfully lobbied to have an amendment added to the California Desert Protection Act directing Secretary of the Interior Bruce Babbitt to conduct a study identifying lands suitable for a reservation either within Death Valley Monument or the surrounding areas. As was the case with their earlier efforts to secure a reservation, however, events outside their control hindered the Shoshones' plans. In fact, the California Desert Protection Act ultimately hurt the band's chances of securing a homeland by upgrading Death Valley National Monument to a national park. Although the park protected an additional 1.2 million acres from further use, this protection stymied the band's efforts to establish a reservation on these lands. Now approximately 80 percent of the Timbisha's ancestral territory was within Park Service boundaries, and as its history had shown, the NPS was reluctant to remit lands from its possession.[78]

Although the California Desert Protection Act quickly set aside vast areas of the Mohave Desert for preservation, the Interior Department dragged its heals on its mandate for the Shoshones. As a result the tribe initiated meetings with the NPS, the Bureau of Land Management (BLM), the BIA, the National Forest Service, and other entities, ultimately forming the Timbisha Shoshone Land Suitability Study and Committee to coordinate efforts to achieve a permanent homeland.[79] After years of effort, however, by 1997 Pauline Esteves and the other Shoshones believed the NPS and the BLM were stalling and not negotiating in good faith with the tribe. In exasperation she and younger spokesman Richard Boland turned to the media and to activist groups for help.

The band ultimately secured the aid of the Western Shoshone Defense Fund, a legal organization helping other area groups oppose nuclear waste sites planned on or near tribal lands. Esteves and the Tribal Council also joined forces with environmental groups such as Greenpeace to lobby for their right to exist within the National Park system. Together, these parties fought a proposed cyanide leach gold mine located on a potential reservation site just outside park boundaries in the Panamint Mountains. In their struggle for land the Shoshones also formed the Alliance to Protect Native Rights in National Parks with the Miccosukees of the Florida Everglades, the Hualapais of the Grand Canyon, and other tribes to lobby for the return of Native lands held by the NPS. Over time Esteves's people organized several protest marches from the Indian Village to park headquarters and held scholarly symposiums to highlight their plight as well.[80]

As the years passed, however, with no reservation in sight, the seemingly endless meetings with Park Service personnel stressed the patience of the band. After a particularly long meeting Pauline Esteves vented, "Those pasty-faced bureaucrats knew from the beginning that they would not restore ancestral lands to us—we were stonewalled." Richard Boland seconded this, saying, "The National Park Service promotes the image of being stewards of the land. We want the world to hear the real story of how the NPS views Indians. When most people think of the Park Service they think of the happy smiling ranger wearing a Smokey the Bear hat in Yellowstone or Yosemite. We have a different tale to tell."[81]

By the late 1990s the tribe had spent an estimated $600,000 to document their historical encampments, burial sites, hunting grounds, and other sites of occupation or religious significance in support of their aspirations for a reservation. Despite the Desert Act's mandate and efforts of the group, the NPS maintained that there was simply not enough land or water within the park for the group. As they had in the 1960s, the Shoshones pointed to the plush hotels, RV campgrounds, and irrigated golf course as symbols of the Park Service's hypocrisy. Unmoved by these facts, however, Death Valley Park officials still resisted creating any precedent that would give away lands within the park. Particularly wary of a potential Indian casino in the middle of the park, NPS spokespersons suggested that the group establish a reservation on federal lands outside park boundaries or continue living under a long-term residential lease. The prospect of continuing to live under NPS rules and restrictions was unacceptable, however. As Richard Boland said, "If the Park Service thinks they're going to continue to dictate to our people how they live their lives, they're crazy. They may as well put back the barbed wire around this relocation camp they forced us into in the 1930s."[82]

Band members were in essentially the same position as their ancestors when the Death Valley National Monument was established in 1933, although with a few more legal rights. As a recognized tribe, the band was entitled to enter negotiations with other recognized governmental entities under several federal acts. Yet in light of their travails and treatment, dealing with Park Service officials would be a trying experience. Barbara Durham expressed the group's dilemma: "It has taken a lot for our people to sit across the table from the federal government—that distrust has been there for many, many years."[83] To the Timbisha Shoshones it seemed they were continually having to prove their identity and right to exist as Indian people on their traditional lands and were caught in a bureaucratic tangle from which there often seemed no escape. Despite the growing tensions, tribal members Grace Goad, Ed Esteves, Ken Watterson, and Pauline Esteves formed a group called the Historic Preservation Committee and hired Catherine Fowler, a noted authority on Great Basin ethnology, to produce a study documenting their history. The NPS also commissioned and funded a cultural affiliation study to comply with the Native American Graves Protection and Repatriation Act and other federal mandates.[84]

As these studies converged, the Shoshones and the Department of the Interior reached a breakthrough, agreeing on a proposal for a tribal homeland. In essence, the plan called for establishing several parcels totaling approximately 7,500 acres of land to be held in trust as a reservation for the tribe. The proposed reservation included 300 acres at Furnace Creek and several parcels of BLM land adjacent to the park. In the process of negotiating, Department of the Interior officials agreed to recognize the Shoshones' traditional use of lands within the park, to acknowledge their water rights, and to work on highlighting the band's contribution to the area's history and ecology. For its part the Timbisha tribe agreed to ban gambling within the park. The group reserved the right to open casinos on reservation lands outside the park, although this would be of dubious value considering the location of Death Valley on the Nevada border. For economic development the tribe planned to build a hotel and museum and made plans to construct a permanent tribal center and larger housing complex. Although the Park Service was behind the proposal, legislative action was required to accomplish the plan.[85]

While Pauline Esteves, now in her eighties, waited for a reservation, the newly recognized Timbisha Shoshone Tribe succeeded in obtaining funds from the Indian Health Service and other sources to renovate the remaining adobe houses, to purchase additional trailers, to install electricity, to pave village roads, and to improve the settlement's water system. The Tribal Council also began working to revive and promote Shoshone culture within the park. By the late 1990s these physical improvements enabled approximately fifty tribal members to move back to Indian Village to live in seventeen homes. By 1999 the group had grown to approximately three hundred members, yet the continuing restrictive housing policy prevented the growing membership from living in the park or developing Indian Village further. As was evident, the tribe's ambiguous position on National Park Service lands continued to thwart its aspirations. In contrast, other tribes acknowledged through FAP have rather quickly established reservations.[86]

As the new millennium dawned, however, the Timbisha Shoshones achieved their long-awaited justice. At the end of 2000 President Bill Clinton signed the

Timbisha Shoshone Homeland Act restoring lands to the tribe in accordance with the earlier proposals. After almost two decades of tribal status, Pauline Esteves's ultimate crusade was rewarded. On a brisk January day in 2001 the tribe gathered to celebrate their victory at the old Indian Village at Furnace Creek. To the sounds of Shoshone songs and tribal drums, Timbisha elders and Park Service personnel held a barbeque together to symbolize a new, hopeful era. Although lingering distrust remained, a new relationship clearly was emerging. It remained to be seen how quickly federal bureaucrats would act on the new law.[87] Even so, federal officials were one step closer to living up to their obligations toward the long-suffering Death Valley Timbisha Shoshones.

In the end the Death Valley group's odyssey illuminates several key facts about the BIA acknowledgement process. Although no fault of the BAR, perhaps the most telling point is that it took so long for the government to acknowledge the status of this fairly unambiguous Indian group. Clearly, some unacknowledged entities such as the Timbisha Shoshone band are among the most unassimilated and "traditional" Indians in the United States and yet have remained unrecognized largely because of historical circumstances. Even so, Esteves's people had several advantages relative to other petitioners in California and elsewhere. Like all groups acknowledged through the BIA process, the Timbisha band had ongoing relations with non-Indian governments, entities that recorded and substantiated their Indian identity, ancestry, politics, and communities in the years prior to formal acknowledgment. Unlike many others, however, the Death Valley group had a de facto reservation within a vast national park that served to protect and even enhance community solidarity and survival. Compared to many groups in California, in particular, their isolated village allowed the Shoshones to be easily recognizable and distinctly visible as an ethnic community. Although the Timbisha Shoshones had a strong case and almost certainly would have succeeded at a later date, they clearly had the fortune of going through the FAP in its early years when the levels of proof and burdens were not so onerous. As BAR evaluations are historically situated, Alogan Slagle, an expert on tribal recognition in California, guesses that the Shoshones' twenty-two-page petition would not survive the FAP today. Slagle's point is on the mark because FAP evaluators assumed certain aspects of community and political authority existed for Esteves's group—assumptions that they would not make today.[88]

In the final analysis, beyond having a core village, federal records, and good timing, the Timbisha Shoshones also faced few of the racial, cultural, or economic issues and challenges that many groups encounter. Because the band was small in size, was racially unambiguous, and spoke a native language, it did not engender organized opposition from either reservation tribes or from segments of the dominant society. In fact, the band possessed considerable moral authority stemming from the poor treatment meted out by the NPS. Because non-Indians generally expect "real" Native Americans to be impoverished or isolated people who are tied to the land, the Death Valley group met many of these ideals in their quest for federal status.[89] The band seemed to have pure motivations while lacking any racial ambiguity that would have influenced the subjective decisions of the FAP team.

As the twenty-first century begins, however, cases like the Timbisha Shoshones' will become increasingly rare. We can only guess at the outcome if the Shoshones no longer spoke their language or if the Park Service evicted the core group in the 1950s and dispersed them. As linguist Jon Dayley noted, a brief ten years after the band petitioned for acknowledgment fewer than a half-dozen people still spoke Timbisha Shoshone fluently or used it daily, and all these individuals were over eighty. Only a couple of people still remembered enough of the old ways and the Death Valley environment to relate the traditional names for them. Certainly the acknowledgment team's task would have been much more difficult had the band not possessed a living language as well as a communal land base, a common nemesis, and a central homeland that helped promote high intermarriage rates. Without these features and indigenous survivals, it is unclear what symbols of tribalism and what level of documentation the FAP would have required. In 1995 approximately one-half of all people claiming an Indian identity lived in urban areas. In light of the continuing processes of modernization, what will be the symbols of ethnicity and tribalism relied upon by the BAR in the future? Down the road the majority of acknowledgment cases almost certainly will present greater conceptual difficulties to BIA teams. Just as the image of tribalism enshrined in the 1978 FAP criteria is not timeless and is subject to endless interpretation, the evaluation of the criteria and standards imposed will undoubtedly evolve as well—just like the groups the regulations seek to define.

FIVE. A MATTER OF VISIBILITY

The United Houma Nation's Struggle
for Tribal Acknowledgment

Sometime in the first half of the nineteenth century, the historic Houma Tribe that once lived along the lower Mississippi River of Louisiana disappeared from known historical records. Over 150 years later, a group claiming descent from this tribe, the United Houma Nation, petitioned the BIA for federal acknowledgment. In December of 1994, after nearly a decade-long wait for a proposed finding, the animated leader of this group, Kirby Verret, received word from the Branch of Acknowledgment and Research (BAR) in Washington. His organization had failed to convince the BIA that it was a tribe within the meaning of the federal acknowledgment regulations. The BAR determined the group failed three of its criteria, finding that it did not prove it descended from the historic Houma Tribe, that it was not a community for certain periods of its history, and that it was not a functioning political unit for the modern era. As a people of Indian, European, and African ancestry, the United Houma members were accustomed to skepticism and challenges to their Indian identity from local people. But to hear from the experts of the federal government that tribal members were not who they said they were was a difficult blow for Verret and the others. Based on his experience with the BIA process, a disgusted Verret says that the "BAR" really stands for the "Branch Against Recognition" as far as southern Indian groups are concerned. Even with the BIA's negative ruling, the United Houma Nation still pushed forward into the new century. "The federal government cannot take away our spirit," Verret says. "Whether recognized or not, we know who we are and that won't change."[1] As its rebuttals and appeals lurched forward into 2003, the long-waiting group still hoped for a positive final determination on its tribal status.

While devastating to Verret and the others, the encounter of the United Houma Nation (UHN) with the BIA acknowledgment process was, in many ways, representative of the troubles many southern and eastern Indian groups face in using historical documentation to prove their Indian tribalism. In particular the Houmas' experience represents the failure of one petitioner to succeed through the Federal Acknowledgment Process (FAP) because, like many other eastern groups, it did not neatly fit the model of tribalism contained in the federal regulations. In their ongoing quest for recognition, Verret's people apparently presented an ambiguous scenario to federal officials, challenging deeply held western conceptions of Indian tribes in terms of race, culture, community, and political organization. Although the United Houma Nation is recognized as Indian by nearby tribes and respected scholars and possesses documented Indian ancestry, it still failed to convince the BIA that it was a tribe within the meaning of the acknowledgment regulations. In light of their history, the United Houmas' experience reveals the subjective nature of the FAP and the difficulties of relying upon Euro-American records when dealing with preliterate, Native societies. As detailed here, the United Houmas are an Indian people or "nation" sharing common descent, Indian identity, history, and territory. [2] Yet at the present they have failed to convince the federal bureaucracy that they are a "tribe" of Indians. As the following pages reveal, the complex issues of history and oral tradition in their case expose the puzzle that is so often the work of the BAR in deconstructing, decoding, reconstructing, and then resurrecting the obscure and often invisible histories of unacknowledged peoples. When issues of specific tribal identity and racial motive bled into the process with the Louisiana group, the BAR team repeatedly asked: Was the United Houma Nation essentially an acculturated, multiracial enclave that chose to claim an Indian identity over the alternatives? Because the BAR researchers determined that this was in fact the case, the BIA is reluctant to acknowledge the United Houmas as a tribe of Indians. Beyond issues of proof, the United Houmas' struggle also reveals the difficulties large petitioners experience in exhibiting the characteristics of tribal governments when they clearly lack formal, sovereign powers. With over 17,000 members, the group was the largest to go through the process, leaving many observers to wonder whether the federal government would acknowledge such a large entity. Clearly, it seemed difficult for such a people, without tribal lands or formal governmental powers, to exhibit the attributes of a "tribe" required under the government criteria.

Although Verret's people were devastated by the initial determination, members of the group were accustomed to waiting through adversity. Centered in Golden Meadow, Louisiana, just south of the city of Houma, Verret's people were generally less educated and poorer than their white counterparts. Denied public education because of their Indian racial status until the 1960s, Houma people have continually struggled to wrest a living from the swamplands sixty miles west of New Orleans: fishing, shrimping and oystering, or working at gritty jobs on oil rigs in the Gulf of Mexico. Beginning in World War II, however, other United Houma members began migrating to New Orleans to work in its industrial plants and factories. Even with their financial travails, United Houma people maintained a vibrant, Cajun-influenced culture, with many speaking French, performing traditional subsistence practices, and attempting to maintain their Indianness amid the growing oil boomtowns of their homeland.[3]

Although obtaining recognition is an ongoing affair, the modern Houma group began its formal struggle with the FAP in 1979. After years of painstaking research by a well-respected scholarly team, partially funded by the Administration for Native Americans (ANA) and partially completed through volunteer labor, the United Houma Nation crafted a voluminous petition in hopes that the Branch of Acknowledgment and Research would come to see that the people had descended from the historic Houma Tribe of the Mississippi River and were a functioning tribal community. After submitting the petition in December 1985, the group was optimistic about the document's chances with the Bureau of Indian Affairs. Yet the UHN would wait almost ten years to hear that it failed in the preliminary stage of the BIA process.[4] After the Houmas received the initial report, it was clear that there were points of contention between the two parties that would be difficult to reconcile.

Both sides agreed that there was a historic Houma Tribe that once lived on the Mississippi River several miles above the present site of Baton Rouge. From tradition Verret's people believed they descended from the historic tribe, while the bureau surmised that the Houma Tribe had become extinct and thus that the modern group could not have descended from it in any possible scenario. French adventurer René-Robert Cavelier, Sieur de La Salle, mentioned this people on his trip down the Mississippi in 1682, but it was not until 1686 and 1699 that Chevalier de Tonti and Pierre Lemoyne, Sieur d'Iberville, visited the Houma Tribe on the Mississippi near its confluence with the Red River. Because the modern United Houma had a tradition of calling themselves "Houma," they logically set out to prove that they were connected to this tribe that once lived within a hundred miles of their present settlements. Like other groups in the eastern United States, however, they had a daunting task ahead because under the FAP regulations it was from these early dates that the United Houmas had to prove all facets of their tribal existence.[5]

Ironically, because of the importance of Indian nations to European alliances and trade, there were more data on the historic Houma Tribe in the early colonial period than there would be during the nineteenth century under American rule. Late-seventeenth-century and early-eighteenth-century accounts of Iberville, André Pénicaut, M. Le Page Du Pratz, and others all reported the Houmas living on the east bank of the Mississippi River, approximately twenty leagues above New Orleans. A Muskogean-speaking people, the Houmas interacted frequently with the neighboring Bayogoula, Acolapissa, and refugee Muskogean-speaking tribes streaming in from West Florida. According to the early reports, they planted a red post (*baton rouge* in French) to mark their territory, a marker that sat near the present site of the capital of Louisiana. Early French adventurers noted that the Houmas called themselves the "red nation," for "Houma" meant red in their language, and that they had a red crayfish as their war emblem. When they arrived in 1700, Jesuit priests remarked that the tribe possessed a rich culture and that it engaged in a mixed economy of hunting, farming, and gathering. The early accounts also noted the presence of both hereditary male chiefs and female leaders within the tribe.[6]

The tribe never numbered more than 1,500 individuals, and European contact progressively took its toll on the Mississippi River Houmas. Diseases introduced by the French and Spanish would make the tribe at once much smaller, less significant, and thus less visible to the European powers vying for supremacy in the lower Mississippi Valley. At the earliest stages of colonial contact observers remarked that the tribe was the victim of an "abdominal flux" that took half the population. Coupled with slave raiding and warfare, European colonization wrecked havoc on the group and other "petit nations" along the lower Mississippi River. A plague of another kind also affected the Houma nation. According to Louisiana's first historian, M. Le Page Du Pratz: "Upon first establishment of the colony, some French went and settled near them; and they have been very fatal neighbors, by furnishing them with brandy, which they drink to great excess."[7]

Despite these fatal encounters, the Houmas were a resourceful and adaptive people. In their struggle to survive they became fast allies of the French, welcoming them into their villages and intermarrying with them. The tribe and other "petit nations" also incorporated members of related Indian groups into their communities and began the process of accommodating the Europeans by learning French, trading in food, furs, and slaves, and defending New Orleans against other Indian tribes.[8] In this way the small nation eked out an existence during the colonial period.

Plagued by enemies, in the early eighteenth century the Houmas migrated southward down the Mississippi River to be closer to French protection at New Orleans. Records from 1722 indicate, however, that there were two Houma villages: Grand Houmas, on the east bank, and Petit Houmas, a smaller settlement located near where a significant waterway, Bayou Lafourche, divides from the west bank of the Mississippi River approximately fifty river miles above New Orleans. By 1733 the Houmas moved the larger village to the west bank of the great river and had apparently incorporated the related Bayogoulas and Acolapissas.[9]

There is evidence that during the colonial era French and Spanish officials presented medals and other regalia recognizing the sovereignty of the Houma Tribe. Following traditional French and Spanish Indian policy, however, these acts apparently were never written down, and the regalia have disappeared. When the Spanish succeeded the French in the Louisiana colony after 1763, the Houmas secured new alliances and new contacts that soon generated records confirming the tribe's historical existence. Yet the divided nature of the tribe and the records that survive would make pinpointing the Houma people's exact whereabouts extremely difficult.

In significant correspondence written between 1773 and 1775, a local Spanish commandant, Louis Judice, reported that the Houma people had three chiefs at three different villages near the Mississippi. In 1774 one chief, Calabee, sold his village site on the east side of the river to local setters who were inundating that area. The following year Commandant Judice wrote the governor, saying that "Since this tribe has sold its village site, it has divided to the point that it currently consists of three villages, Calabee, with about twenty men, remains on the village site that he sold to Mr. Conway; the chief [another besides Calabee], with about as many men, retired to a site two and one-half leagues above, and established a village twenty arpents distance from the river, upon the land of the district settlers who are greatly disturbed by it; one Tiefayo, with eight families, has withdrawn to the Lafourche, where they have done quite well." Judice recommended concentrating all the Houmas on the Lafourche, "where they will be very well, out of harm's way, and too distant to cause numerous disorders."[10] From the wording of the letter, this last location was apparently down the bayou away from the growing white settlements. Written records reveal, however, that Judice was unsuccessful in his effort to concentrate the people and that the Houmas remained divided into different villages.

For this time period both the bureau and the United Houma Nation sought to determine by a reasonable likelihood where these three bands eventually settled. And in a scenario common in the acknowledgment process, despite diligent research the United Houma researchers failed to locate written evidence confirming the exact place where Houma chief Tiefayo ultimately ventured. After the initial BIA ruling, however, they did find an important document indicating that the entire drainage of Bayou Lafourche from the Mississippi to the Gulf of Mexico was within the Houmas' territory, indicating the Houmas easily could have settled in the modern Houma area. Certainly the United Houmas had an oral tradition that their people migrated down Bayou Lafourche to neighboring Bayou Terrebonne at this time and established their present settlements after that date.[11]

In trying to prove its ties to the historic Houmas and the whereabouts of Tiefayo's band, however, the United Houma Nation soon learned the limits of oral tradition and vague historical references when used in the FAP. In its 1994 finding the acknowledgment team conjectured that *all* the Houmas remained on the Mississippi River near its confluence with Bayou Lafourche (near modern-day Donaldsonville) and never migrated down the bayou as the modern group claimed. The bureau guessed that Chief Tiefayo resided at the place where Bayou Lafourche "forked" from the main river, despite the fact that locals referred to the entire bayou as Lafourche, for the "fork." Although the BIA's theory is certainly possible in light of the existing records, the BAR was not able to account for a reuniting of the three villages or to explain why, if the "fork" was near the Mississippi and European farms, Judice would want the group to retire there. The existing records only indicate that Tiefayo's group retired to "the fork"—a location that may have been where the BIA believes it was or further down Bayou Lafourche in the region of the United Houma ancestral settlements.[12] Rejecting the United Houma position, the BAR team surmised that the entire Houma Tribe eventually became extinct through the effects of intermarriage, disease, and excessive alcohol consumption. The modern group could not possibly descend from an entity that was extinct—to the BIA the case was closed, although it went on to make preliminary conclusions on the United Houma Nation's history after that time frame.

During the late Spanish colonial period both sides agreed that three United Houma ancestral families secured land grants on Bayou Terrebonne near present-day Montegut, a town approximately ten miles south of modern-day Houma, Louisiana. Here several ancestors including Houma Courteau, Louis le Sauvage (a last name likely meaning "the savage" in French), Jean Billiot, and Alexander Verdin settled together. As was common in this case, however, the two sides differed markedly on the character of this founding group. To the United Houmas it was a tribal community composed of Houma and other Indian refugees and their European relatives. To the BIA the community was nontribal: more European in orientation than Indian, although with acknowledged Indian members.[13]

Shortly after the United Houma ancestors were settling along the bayous, Spain transferred Louisiana back to France. Napoleon Bonaparte then abruptly sold the colony to the fledgling United States with the Louisiana Purchase in 1803. It was during the next twenty years that the actual recognition problems of the surviving Houmas and the United States began—a time when the BIA believed the tribe became extinct. Shortly after taking possession of the new territory, the newly arrived governor from Mississippi, W. C. C. Claiborne, contemplated securing lands for the Indians of lower Louisiana. Unfortunately Congress never acted upon his suggestion, however, and it is a sad reality that had the United States lived up to its treaty obligations to honor previous Spanish and French policies, many of Louisiana's small Indian nations would still exist today.[14]

Records reveal that in 1806, shortly after the transfer to U.S. control, a delegation of Houma leaders visited New Orleans. Before the War of 1812 another group led by Houma chief Chac-Chouma also traveled to the Crescent City to meet the governor. On these two occasions, Governor Claiborne unambiguously recognized the Houmas in a manner common at that time. As he wrote to another official in 1811: "At the present day, the number of this Tribe is greatly diminished; it does not exceed 80 souls—but their conduct is exemplary and the late visit of the Chief being the first he paid me, I thought it a matter of policy to make him a small present."[15] The governor's correspondence contained both important data and omissions: it noted that the tribe was recognized as an indigenous nation, yet the surviving correspondence left precious few details on who was present at these ceremonies.

At this point in history the modern group once more ran headlong into the problems of relying upon oral tradition in proving tribal ancestry and former acknowledgment. United Houma Nation oral tradition recalled that one of their known founding community members, Louis le Sauvage, was present at one of these ceremonies. The correspondence that exists, however, discusses only Chief Chac-Chouma by name and not le Sauvage or other known UHN ancestors. The records also clearly reveal that Chac-Chouma and the other Houma delegation apparently resided on the Mississippi near the junction of Bayou Lafourche and the Mississippi River in proximity to Donaldsonville,

Louisiana, the location where the BIA believes all the remaining Houma Tribe lived at that time. The presence of Louis le Sauvage at these meetings remains unsubstantiated.[16]

Despite this limited official correspondence, a central question was still unanswered: what became of the three bands of Houma Indians? There is certainly evidence pointing to the BIA's theory that at least a portion of the historic Houma Tribe remained near "the fork" of the Mississippi River and Bayou Lafourche and gradually assimilated into the surrounding non-Indian society. In his *Historical Sketches of the Several Tribes in Louisiana* (1806), Dr. John Sibley, the territory's first Indian agent, reported that "there are a few of the Humas still living on the east side of the Mississippi [across from Donaldsonville], but scarcely exist as a nation."[17] That same year American explorer William Dunbar likewise recorded that approximately sixty Houmas still lived on the east bank of the Mississippi, while adventurer Henry Brackenridge (likely relying upon Sibley's report) declared the tribe extinct by 1811.[18] These reports thus provide key evidence that during the early American period at least a portion of the Houma Tribe still resided on or near the Mississippi and was declining in numbers.

Clearly, these surviving reports do little to support the United Houma Nation's position, yet they are far from conclusive as to the non-existence of other Houma bands. Dr. Sibley admitted his findings were not comprehensive, and it is clear his report did not include all Indian groups in the state. In light of controversies surrounding the agent, the United Houma Nation argued that Sibley purposefully overlooked the group on the lower bayous because he had land claims in the region. Although Sibley cataloged only one group of Houmas, anthropologist Emanuel Drechsel later argued that three separate Houma clusters existed in the early American period: one near Pointe Coupée north of Baton Rouge (a group that may have included Louis le Sauvage at one time), another in St. James and Ascension Parishes midway between Baton Rouge and New Orleans (the traditional locations noted by Governor Claiborne), and the last along Bayous Terrebonne and Lafourche in the modern United Houma area. The BAR team rejected the United Houmas' arguments on the Indian agent's report, however, and countered that it was more probable that Sibley failed to mention Houmas living on Bayou Lafourche simply because they were not there. Reliance on outside records, therefore, brought the UHN face to face with a common dilemma many groups encounter in the acknowledgment process: in some cases records simply do not exist that document Indian peoples in frontier areas of the United States. Because these

Indians had no written languages and lived outside American governance, many aspects of their internal lives during this era seem destined to remain obscured from modern-day chroniclers.[19]

Despite the BIA's theory, the modern Houma group appeared to possess strong evidence of an ancestral land claim near Houma, Louisiana, evidence that would help place the historic Houma people in their core area. Over the years the United Houmas had maintained an oral tradition that their people once possessed a Spanish land grant near Houma, Louisiana. In fact, while researching a government series, *The American State Papers*, modern researchers discovered a claim recorded in approximately 1814 stating that "the Homas tribe of Indians claims a tract of land lying on bayou Boeuf, or Black bayou, containing twelve sections."[20] Although this is strong evidence, the BAR researchers erroneously dismissed the United Houma Nation's document on this point, arguing that the "Homa" claim was for a tract of land on another Bayou Boeuf in central Louisiana, not the Bayou Boeuf near Houma, Louisiana. In fact, the claim was brought in the Eastern District of Louisiana, an area that encompassed the lands of the present-day United Houma settlements; the Bayou Boeuf in question actually flowed approximately twenty miles west of the modern town of Houma. Relying upon this mistaken conclusion, however, the BIA determined that the Houma Tribe of the Mississippi River most likely drifted to central Louisiana and thus away from the lower Bayou country. There is little evidence, however, to support this position. In any case the BAR team took a highly literal approach to the claim, arguing that because it contained no data tying the land claim group directly to the United Houma ancestors living approximately thirty miles east in Montegut, it could not provide them with evidence of a tribal link.[21]

The 1814 "Homa" claim was the last known official record of the Houma Tribe in the lower bayou region. Upon losing its land claim, this entity apparently lost its land base and any hope of tribal acknowledgment during the nineteenth century. With the establishment of the Natchitoches Indian factory in 1805 in northwest Louisiana, American attention gradually shifted to this area and thus away from the lower bayous. After the Indian removals of the 1830s federal officials generally assumed that the remaining southern and eastern Indian remnants would eventually assimilate into American society, and they ignored these Indians, leaving currently recognized tribes in the South such as the Mississippi Band of Choctaws, the Florida Seminoles, and the Louisiana Chitimachas to wait until the early twentieth century for federal recognition.[22]

Although there were apparently three villages in the 1770s, it is clear that the BAR team always conceived of the Houma Tribe as a single unit that had a single fate. It denied the possibility that a segment of the Houmas migrated to the swamps around Houma, Louisiana, arguing instead that the single tribe became extinct. Without concrete records it also rejected the possibility of interaction between the known UHN Indian ancestors near Montegut and the declining Houma group living near Donalsonville on the Mississippi, a distance of approximately sixty to seventy miles directly downstream on Bayou Lafourche and Bayou Terrebonne. Although the BIA's negative findings are designed to accentuate the negative evidence against groups, it seemed in this case that the Houma remnants could have gone anywhere but the undesirable swamps south of Montegut. Clearly, absent additional written data, the BAR team would not accept the modern group's theories as to its tribal origins.[23]

This brings up a central question in the United Houma case: without concrete records of a group migration to the Houma City area, could the non-acknowledged group convince the BIA of its origins using possibilities and probabilities rather than written certainties? In the 1940s and 1960s historian Marc Bloch and anthropologist Claude Lévi-Strauss dismissed the historian's search for pure origins and beginnings as folly. Could the BIA's insistence on pinpointing an originating strain be such an undertaking?[24] For this time period, however, the Branch of Acknowledgment and Researach clearly possessed the power to make the judgment call whether there was a "reasonable likelihood" that a segment of the Houma Tribe migrated to Bayou Terrebonne, and it believed that no band of Houmas had done so.

In the absence of clear tribal migration documents the two parties next turned to scrutinizing the founding settlement at Montegut. In particular, if the United Houma Nation could find genealogical evidence that its ancestors were from the Houma Tribe, it could use this data to convince the BIA of its links to the historic entity. Once again the two sides differed markedly on the nature of this settlement and its origins, however.

Both sides agreed that ancestors of the modern Houma group began settling near present-day Montegut between 1790 and 1830. In this delta region the marshlands contain narrow strips of arable land right along the bayous, and it was on these cypress- and oak-covered banks that three families with documented Indian ancestry and possibly other Indian ancestors of the United Houma Nation settled under Spanish land grants. Below Montegut the inhabitable land progressively fades to open marsh, and much of this land was classed as public swamplands and not surveyed until the 1870s. Scholars conjecture these marshes, like the Florida Everglades and swamps of North Carolina, served as havens for remnant Indian groups such as the Houmas and related groups after sustained contact with Europeans.[25]

As all groups must do in the FAP, the modern Houma petitioners had to document the historical outlines of the founding settlement at Montegut to prove that it was essentially an Indian enclave. Historical records were incomplete, so it became apparent that only vague outlines of the community could be sketched. All sides agreed, however, that during the first decades of the century a documented Indian, Houma Courteau, also known as Courteau Houma, Joseph Abbe/Touh-la-Bay, or Shulu-shumon, settled near modern-day Montegut. Noted in records as a "Biloxy medal chief," this man would prove central to the modern group's case. At that time Houma Courteau obtained land in the area with his wife, Nuyu'n or Marianne Courteau, and her brother, Louis le Sauvage, both of whom were likely Indians. Near them settled Jean Billiot and Marie Enerise or Iris, both of whom lack existing evidence that would confirm their Indian ancestry. In 1811, however, Jean Billiot's brother Joseph married a documented Indian noted in a record as "Jeanet, an Indian woman." Another ancestral family composed of Frenchman Alexander Verdin and Marie Gregoire (noted as a *femme sauvage*) also settled in the immediate area near a man who may have been Marie's brother and thus Indian. Verret's people trace their confirmed Indian ancestry to these individuals.

Significantly, however, none of the genealogical records stated that these individuals were Houma Indians, although a lack of specificity as to tribal origins is common in records for this period. This fact severely hurt the United Houmas' petition in the eyes of the BAR evaluators. It is certainly possible that the individuals listed as generic "Indian" and their relatives were Houmas or from an amalgamated people that contained a Houma element. Yet the only individual with a specified tribe was Houma Courteau, who was apparently Biloxi, a people who nonetheless had long associated and intermarried with the Houmas. It is also possible that undocumented Indians (who may have been Houmas) interacted with these individuals from the surrounding countryside and swamps, although records of these contacts have yet to surface. In essence both sides agreed the settlement was of multiracial ancestry, yet it clearly contained at least one apparently full-blood Indian family. Despite these facts, genealogical evidence ultimately left the modern group without concrete proof that it descended from the Houma Tribe or tribes, although these omissions certainly did not mean that the people did not derive from that people.[26]

In looking for the origins of the Indians who settled the UHN's founding community, the Branch of Acknowledgment and Research team conjectured that the Houma Courteau family was likely from the Biloxi, Mississippi, area. It based the theory on testimony that ethnologist John Reed Swanton took from a local Indian informant in 1907. Garnered from a granddaughter of the Courteaus, the information was somewhat contradictory, however, and thus of dubious use. In particular the informant said that her mother, Rosalie Courteau, was Attakapa, a tribe near the Texas-Louisiana border, while also stating the confusing proposition that this woman's parents were Biloxi and Acolapissa, tribes from the east and not Attakapa. Because Spanish records from the mid-eighteenth century indicate that the Acolapissa tribe had combined with the Houma, this data does not damn the United Houmas, especially in light of the fact that most Indian groups of the lower Mississippi were composites of numerous precontact indigenous peoples.[27] Yet in terms of conclusive written proof, the few surviving genealogical records do little to pinpoint the specific origins of the modern group.

Despite the fact that a few documents listed Houma Courteau as a Biloxi medal chief (and the later discovery of a document noting he was Houma), what were evaluators to make of the name "Houma?" Was it a tribal appellation commonly affixed to Indians as witnessed with Timbisha Shoshone ancestors such as "Shoshone" Doc, or was it something else? And what were evaluators to make of the fact that the nearby town of Houma was named after a band of Houma Indians that apparently lived near the town sometime prior to its founding in 1834? In unraveling the mystery both sides closely scrutinized the founding settlement; one side ultimately relied upon incomplete written records for answers, whereas the other relied on oral tradition and significant circumstantial evidence.

Just as questions arose as to how the UHN's ancestors got to Bayou Terrebonne, the two sides fiercely debated the founding settlement's tribal nature. Although the United Houmas acknowledged the settlement was a composite in terms of race, to them it was also clearly Indian in other senses. Oral tradition held that Houma Courteau's brother-in-law Louis le Sauvage was a Houma Indian and chief of the tribe. Records exist indicating le Sauvage may have migrated from the Houma cluster near Pointe Coupée, while land records confirm that he obtained title to a tract of land in the community before 1803. Modern Houma members also maintain an ongoing tradition that Rosalie Courteau, a niece of Louis le Sauvage, succeeded him as leader of her people. In a common scenario involving individuals who did not read or write, however, the United Houma Nation failed to locate written evidence of the functioning of this group during the course of the nineteenth century.[28]

In finding that the founding settlement was not an Indian community, the BAR team pointed out that all the key United Houma ancestors appear to have owned land in fee simple and not as a communal body. Clearly, specific references noting that a "tribe" lived in the area on tribal land early in the century have not been unearthed. Yet this land tenure arrangement was likely a necessity, and as J. Anthony Paredes notes, those looking for a "smoking gun" saying unambiguously that a "tribe" lived in many areas of the South may be searching in vain; most groups simply did not appear as such to outsiders.[29] In the group's oral tradition, however, the settlement was tribal and served as a haven for refugee Indians and other indigenous peoples hiding out in nearby swamps. It incorporated various peoples yet always remained first and foremost Houma.

As with tribal migration, however, the FAP team rejected the United Houma Nation's position, concluding instead that the founding community was more European in orientation than Indian. BIA researchers pointed to the assimilation levels of the known founding families as evidence. Citing probate records, the BAR noted that United Houma ancestral families—the Courteaus, Billiots, and Verdins—were farmers and slaveholders, growing grain and sugar while raising domesticated animals on lands owned in fee simple. The BIA concluded they were of multiracial ancestry, spoke French, and were culturally non-Indian. Although acknowledging that these families lived next to each other among non-Indian neighbors, the BIA determined that these families intermarried and socialized widely with surrounding non-Indian individuals. To the BIA team, the founding community did not constitute an Indian community during its time of constellation between 1790 and 1830. Evidence of interaction from two centuries past was thin, but the acknowledgment office cited the fact that the multiracial families often utilized white witnesses to their baptisms and court transactions as evidence of the nontribal nature of the settlement.

As with many unacknowledged groups, however, there is little evidence indicating exactly how these people identified themselves, how they interacted, and how they functioned as a community for this early period. Clearly, as seen with the Pascua Yaquis, Indian communities routinely interacted with the dominant society without giving up the attributes that made them Native American. Ironically the UHN ancestors with known Indian connections were clearly the ones who most closely played by the European rules and thus showed up in records. Were these adaptations now being used hundreds of years later to show that they assimilated and were not Indians in a tribal sense? Or were these adaptations an indication that the French-speaking United Houma forebearers were little different than their neighbors without Indian blood?

Even with the deficiencies in their written record, the BAR seemed to scrutinize the United Houmas' early history to a degree unseen in several earlier cases. By producing its "Proposed Finding," the bureau came to control much of the written discourse on the group, often making the United Houma Nation appear less Indian in the process. A quote by BIA genealogists reveals the odds the petitioning Houmas faced in proving their case. Regarding the families with undisputed Indian members, the BIA concluded that "Virtually nothing is known about the ancestors of these early families." [30] Yet it later reported that these individuals did not know each other before coming to the Houma area and were largely non-Indian in culture, ancestry, and political organization. The BIA team surmised that the Indian ancestors of the UHN migrated independently of each other to what was essentially a "frontier," non-Indian settlement. While this conclusion is possible, it is contrary to the fact that most immigrants during the nineteenth century traveled within kinship groups. The entire scenario certainly begged the question: How did so many Indian individuals end up in the same small bayou community? In fairness, there is simply little more probability that the Indians of the UHN ancestral community were unrelated, detribalized pioneer individuals than that they were refugee Houma Indians. [31]

Also revealing the scrutiny Verret's organization faced, the bureau discounted any connection between the name of the nearby town of Houma and the petitioning group. In the absence of concrete records indicating a link, the BAR team again maintained a strict reading of the facts. As the BAR historian wrote: "Since the ancestors of the petitioner had been living over 20 miles south of the location of the city of Houma for 30 to 40 years by the time the city was founded in 1834, this does not indicate a connection between them and the [Houma] band camped for some time northwest of the city location." [32] Adding to the United Houmas' woes, the BAR researchers also took an extremely literal approach to evaluating the Indian ancestry of the group. They conjectured that Marianne (Nuyu'n) Courteau, wife of Houma Courteau, was likely an Indian based on the fact that her granddaughter reported to Swanton that she was Native American. In their published report, however, the BAR researchers concluded:

BAR genealogists speculate that Marianne may have been of Indian descent.

However, no direct evidence was provided or found to confirm this. It seems unlikely that an Indian man would have married a non-Indian woman in the late 1700s due to marriage patterns of that time period. In addition, [her granddaughter] report[ed] that Marianne had an Indian name, "Nuyu'n," when she was baptized, which, along with her sibling relationship to Louis Sauvage/le Sauvage (whose name could be translated as Louis, "the Indian") would suggest that she may have been of Indian heritage. *However, even when taken collectively, this circumstantial evidence is not sufficient to credit Marianne with Indian ancestry at this time.*[33]

The genealogist went on to conjecture that the name "le Sauvage," while meaning "the savage" (or Indian) in French, was potentially an unrelated Flemish family name as well.

Although the modern Houma group certainly had gaps in its record, the BAR seemed to have taken a literalistic and adversarial stance toward the group in printed discourse. In this case it had whittled down the "known" or conclusively recorded Indian ancestors of the UHN to three—making its Indian ancestry appear less than it likely was, while concluding that the Indian individuals and families did not immigrate together when there was little evidence to support this conclusion.[34] Absent concrete linkages, the BAR also rejected any possible connections between the ancestral group and Houma bands living in the region as well.

Like many southern and eastern unacknowledged groups the United Houma Nation had come face to face with the burdens of proving its visibility during periods in the distant past. Clearly, a major obstacle for the United Houma was documenting the tribal heritage of its members using Euro-American records, documents that were riddled with omissions or patently inconsistent regarding racial identities during the nineteenth century. Even so, throughout the century many ancestors of the UHN were identified as "Indians" in federal censuses, records considered high evidence in the BIA. In the 1860 and later federal censuses several individuals born in the eighteenth century either identified themselves as Indians or were identified by enumerators as such.[35] The group's ancestors thus clearly had a longstanding identity as Native American, but pinpointing specific tribal origins for these individuals currently is difficult using Euro-American documents.

Reflecting a major obstacle that all southern Indian groups face, the Byzantine race laws of the antebellum period often served to obscure racial identity and discourage the assertion of Indian identity. Despite frequent interracial and inter-ethnic marriages and unions in French and Spanish Louisiana, with the advent of the American era Louisiana law avoided the finer points, generally classifying all nonwhites, including Indians, as "free persons of color." During the territorial period a small number of individuals from the free African American community in New Orleans married into the ancestral United Houma community, adding some African ancestry and much racial confusion to the group's history. Consequently some United Houma ancestors were listed as black, although they were at least partially Indian. Compounding the confusion was the fact that until 1972, except for a brief moment during Reconstruction, Louisiana state law prohibited interracial unions. Since many of the United Houma ancestors were individually classified as free persons of color, white, or Indian, most marriages within the ancestral group were technically across racial lines and thus illegal. As a result most United Houma ancestors did not legally sanction their marriages. Unfortunately their descendants are left with few written records of this key life event and the race of the individuals involved as a result.[36]

Although not insurmountable, vague and inconsistent racial categories have caused modern Indian petitioners such as the United Houma extreme difficulty in establishing their Indian identity, particularly when using the high evidence of federal censuses. During the nineteenth century it was up to the individual census enumerator to decide the racial classification of individuals. In the binary racial system of the South, in particular, people of mixed race defied the social order by challenging seemingly fixed and immutable social constructions of race. Thus many census takers simply followed the "one-drop rule" of classifying anyone possessing a degree of African ancestry as black. Based on phenotype or marriage status, census takers could use more specific categories such as Indian or mulatto if they chose. The entire scenario, however, left a legacy of confused and often contradictory racial designations. For example, in the 1860 federal census many UHN ancestors appeared as "Indian," whereas in the 1900 census they simply appeared as "black." In many cases in the Houma region the racial status of women followed the status of their husband or was based on their last name rather than phenotype or actual racial origin, engendering further problems for modern researchers. In a particularly perplexing case UHN ancestor Manette Renaud, who incredibly married four separate Billiot brothers, appeared as "M" for mulatto in the 1850 census, as "Ind" for Indian in 1860, and as "W" for white in 1880. She could not be found at all in the 1870 census. In light of this chaotic system, modern groups such as the United Houma Nation often find it difficult, although not always impossible, to establish their Indian ancestry and much less a specific tribal ancestry by referring to official records.[37]

Despite the ambiguities and inconsistencies, research by the BIA and the United Houma Nation confirmed the Indian ancestry of many UHN ancestors. During the nineteenth century the core ancestral families had intermarried, with their children often classified as Indian. Federal censuses from 1860, 1870, 1880, and 1910 listed Indian individuals residing on the lower bayous. A special 1890 federal census of Indians taxed and not taxed also listed fifty-five Indians living in Terrebonne Parish. Between 1810 and 1860, federal census takers were specifically instructed to omit "Indians not taxed" from their records, however, and several documented Indian ancestors of the UHN do not appear in these records. The United Houmas also believe that census takers loathed venturing deep into the swamps and thus missed many of their ancestors.[38]

Adding to the visibility puzzle was the possibility that unassimilated Indians may have inhabited the frontier swampland and interacted with the founding settlement. As late as the 1930s an Indian Office anthropologist reported that many United Houma ancestors squatted on marshlands and rarely, if ever, attended Catholic church. It is certainly possible, if not likely, that a century earlier other Indians may have existed in these same swamps, squatting on marshlands while pursuing avoidance strategies for survival. These individuals, ironically, would be the least likely to have left records. Owning no lands, they would be absent from land, probate, and tax records; having no Catholic ties or access to churches, they would have undocumented marriages. In light of the racial laws of the period, certainly there would have been little incentive for isolated Indians to take part in the system at all.[39] As Virginia DeMarce, a Stanford-trained historian who worked on the UHN case, concluded, "our estimate overall as genealogists is that 90 percent of the population of the world throughout history has lived and died without leaving any records."[40] It is certainly possible that the least assimilated ancestors of the UHN fell into this category. Yet the acknowledgment criteria required more than possibilities.

In a somewhat unique scenario the Branch of Acknowledgment and Research agreed that the group's ancestors formed a distinct community between 1830 and the 1880s, although it questioned whether any individual ever exerted leadership over the Montegut settlement during this era. Even so, Verret's organization had met its burden for proving "community" for this time period. Once again, however, the two parties looked to different forms of evidence when making this determination: one to family traditions, the other to Euro-

American records. In United Houma oral tradition, a prominent leader, Rosalie Courteau, daughter of Houma and Marianne Courteau, emerged as chief of the tribe at this time. Passed down through the generations, oral tradition held that local Cajuns burned Rosalie and her band out of their homes at the site of Houma and forced them to relocate further down the bayous in the early nineteenth century. At the present, however, no records have surfaced confirming their land ownership at Houma or the leadership activities of Rosalie. Records show, however, that during this time many Frenchmen married into the people, introducing the names Billiot, Dardar, Dion, Dupre, Gallet, Naquin, Parfait, Verdin, Gregoire, and Verret. In time these names became "Indian" names that locals used to identify the people as a separate ethnic group.[41]

Although discounting the group's oral tradition, the BIA used statistical evidence to confirm the existence of a UHN ancestral community during the mid to late nineteenth century. The BAR team agreed that from 1830 until the later parts of the century, ancestors of the United Houma Nation lived in a community near Montegut composed almost exclusively of the group's ancestors. The BAR determined that the United Houma Nation had proven that it formed a distinct community with over 50 percent residency rates from 1830 until 1880. Under the revised acknowledgment regulations of 1994, by meeting its burden of showing community for this period the United Houma automatically met the more daunting criteria of demonstrating political authority during the same time period. Therefore, in an unusual scenario, the BAR determined that the United Houmas' ancestors were not a community during their early history yet became one in later years through extensive racially prescribed intermarriage or endogamy.

In the last decades of the century, however, the group's expanding population pushed many from the core community. This fact caused the United Houmas' descendants further complications in the FAP. After 1880 the BAR team concluded that, once again, the United Houma no longer constituted a unified community. It found that after that date the modern group's ancestors had fanned out, forming several communities and dispersed homesteads stretching southward from Montegut along the various murky bayous. Although these settlements were almost entirely Indian, the BAR researchers concluded that the communities were never united as one unit in the political sense. The origins of these settlements have not been completely detailed, but by 1910 there were eight related villages on the lower courses of the bayous. The settlements of Bayou Dularge and the town of Dulac on Bayou Grand Caillou sat on the western end. In the center was the original settlement of Montegut on Bayou Terrebonne, while Point Barre, Point aux Chenes, Isle Jean Charles, Grand Bois, and Golden Meadow trailed down Bayou Lafourche on the eastern edge of the territory. Located on strands of land near the Gulf of Mexico, these villages shared kinship ties, Indian identity, and common cultural traits, but the BIA believed that they did not share a common tribal structure.[42]

Although acknowledging that their ancestors lived dispersed in the swamps, the modern Houma Nation argued that these extended families and communities were essentially one unit, maintaining contact by traveling along hand-dug canals or *trenasses*. The UHN reported that these extended families also trapped and fished together while engaging in other social activities. In effect, for the modern era the United Houma Nation argued that its members had always been united in a complex web of family ties and marriage. Respected *noncs*, *tantes*, and *traiteurs* (herbal healers) exerted informal leadership at the local level while being aware of similar people on other bayous and interacting frequently with them. In particular, the *traiteurs* commanded wide respect and authority among the various communities. Overall, the group argued that its ancestors maintained a sense of solidarity by taking part in communal efforts such as fish drying, digging canals, and fighting discrimination. Verret's group pointed out that in later periods members who moved to New Orleans nonetheless maintained ties with their home territory. As one individual put it, "the road runs both ways. And I always come home." The group failed, however, to produce written documentation of much of these traditions and activities.[43]

Therefore, to further demonstrate the group's unity, anthropologists pointed to folklore and cultural practices the UHN maintained. The Louisiana people continued to relate tales of *feu-follets* (false fires) that led travelers astray and stories of tricksters called Lutins and l'*homme de bois* who lived in the trees and caused mischief, which the group argued had indigenous roots. Unfortunately the United Houmas apparently lacked colorful and stereotypically "Native" religious ceremonies that could be used to identify the group. Although in the earlier Timbisha case the BIA accepted the proposition that informal contacts and loose, family-based social organization would logically produce few records of tribal activity, the FAP team rejected the United Houmas' position in this instance. In the Houma finding the bureau implied that United Houma ancestors left no records of tribal activity or unity precisely because they were not a tribe during the century.[44]

The government's stance raises a central issue for large petitioners such as the United Houma Nation. Although it is perhaps a questionable and virtually impossible requirement for large, dispersed groups, the BIA requires that petitioners demonstrate substantial political connections between all segments of a population over time. The United Houma ancestors, however, who lived at land's end dispersed along the bayous of the delta during the nineteenth century, kept to themselves and clearly did not have federal sanction that would have given them easily identifiable tribal structures. Ironically the very isolation that helped these people of color survive makes it very difficult for their descendents to document possible communal activities decades later.

Because the United Houmas presented little evidence as to the functioning of these eight communities and their ties to each other, the BAR determined that the UHN had failed to prove it was a single community that maintained political authority over its membership between 1880 and 1940. In a rare finding the BIA determined that the group's ancestors were not a community between 1790 and 1830, were a community between 1830 and 1880, and were not a unified community once again after this last date. The BIA finding did not mean, however, that the United Houma Nation's ancestors were not an Indian people in the looser sense. Yet, in the BIA's opinion, the Houma people did not exhibit the attributes of a formal Indian tribe or sovereign political unit— features that not surprisingly are most easily recognizable by noncommunity members. In another unique scenario the bureau suggested that each of the eight settlements might meet requirements for community and political authority independently because settlements such as Isle Jean Charles and Point aux Chenes were apparently isolated and composed of at least 50 percent United Houma ancestors. Assistant Secretary for Indian Affairs Ada Deer, a Menominee, found that the people as a whole, however, did not maintain an overarching tribal political organization.[45]

Although modern BAR researchers and some officials in the late nineteenth century believed that the historic Houma Tribe had become extinct, the UHN's ancestors continued to exist as a people identifying themselves as Houma Indians. Because of this, in 1907 noted ethnologist John Reed Swanton of the Smithsonian Institution's Bureau of American Ethnology visited the people in Terrebonne and Lafourche Parishes. His work forever would be linked to the UHN's aspirations. Trained in linguistics and ethnology at Harvard and Columbia, the former student of famed anthropologist Franz Boas came to be regarded as an expert on Southeastern Indians. During his stay in south Louisiana, Swanton took numerous photographs of the Houmas, showing them living in thatched palmetto houses along the bayous. He found them engaged in hunting; trapping otter, muskrat, and mink; fishing and gathering shellfish; and working on the area sugar plantations. Swanton described them as fairly prosperous, living off the abundance of the land and the sea, and concluded they were a remnant of the Houma people. A year later another anthropologist, M. Raymond Harrington, also wrote about the Louisiana group, reporting that the "Houma tribe, near Houma, Terrebonne Parish, is now nearly extinct; French is the prevailing language to-day, and the Houma live like the white people about them." [46] Harrington also went on to report, however, that they possessed surviving Indian arts, including fine double baskets of apparently Indian type and a unique cypress wood blowgun, and that they fashioned dolls stuffed with Spanish moss and decorated with gar scales. At the turn of the century the scholars noted Houma men continued to produce dugout canoes, or *pirogues*, using them to traverse the network of area canals. [47]

On his trip Swanton's principal guide was Bob Verret, who claimed to be a Houma tribal leader although others considered him a scoundrel. Traveling the bayous with Verret, the ethnologist collected a population estimate of the Houma communities that revealed that the group or groups were fairly small and isolated, with between 876 and 890 individuals living in six settlements. After conducting interviews among the bayou people, Swanton was the first to identify three central families as progenitors of the Houmas: the Courteaus, Billiots, and Verdins. Although they shared common surnames, Swanton remarked that Verret apparently did not know the people in the other villages. This statement prompted the BAR team to question the group's cohesiveness. While on the bayous, Swanton also collected genealogical and linguistic data on the group that would serve as the crux of contention in the later acknowledgment case. [48]

Félicité Billiot, a daughter of Rosalie Courteau, was Swanton's primary and oldest informant. Although few in number, her words would provide the BIA with what it saw as further evidence that the group was not Houma. Her testimony, while correct on many points, was contradictory however. Félicité reported that the parents of her mother, Rosalie Courteau, were Houma Courteau of the Biloxi Nation and Nuyu'n Courteau, an Acolapissa, yet somehow her mother was an "Atakapa from Texas." [49] Significantly Billiot also remarked that her grandmother's people were associated with the badge of the red crayfish, an emblem long reported by early explorers to be associated with the Houmas. [50]

The bureau used this testimony to conclude that the group's own oral tradition revealed origins in the Mobile area, not with the Houma. While potentially correct, this finding dismissed the fact that the Biloxis and other Mobile area tribes had lived in the lower Mississippi region since the eighteenth century, while the Acolapissas had apparently merged with the Houmas by the 1750s.[51] It appeared that the researchers seemed to have missed the discrepancy regarding Rosalie Courteau's tribal origins as well. In any case Swanton and others reported that the historic Houma Tribe had incorporated elements of all sorts of Muskogean tribes in the colonial era; therefore the mix of tribal groups in the testimony of Félicité would not be inconsistent with this history.

Although the BIA correctly reported that Swanton's notes pointed to partial tribal origins near Mobile, the ethnologist was aware of the multiple and often confusing tribal ancestries of the United Houma people. While analyzing his data from his office, Swanton wrote that although the Indians on the bayous "call themselves 'Houmas,' or, rather 'Hômas,' it has been intimated above that remains of several other tribes, such as the Bayogoula and Acolapissa, have been incorporated with them. To these must be added Biloxi and Chitimacha (pronounced by them 'Sitimasha'), who were often introduced in the capacity of slaves, and probably remnants of the Washa and Chuwasha, besides individuals from a number of other Louisiana and Mississippi peoples." Based on his knowledge of primary sources, linguistics, ethnology, and oral tradition, Swanton concluded that only a portion of the ancient Houmas settled along the bayous and had likely drifted down at the end of the eighteenth century. According to Swanton, "remnants of all sorts of tribes joined the Houma . . . though it is certain that most of these were Muskogean, and that the Houma was always the dominating element."[52] Despite the ambiguity, Swanton concluded that the Louisiana people descended from the Houma and other tribes, based on the group's self-proclaimed identity and his review of the colonial sources.

Swanton also collected important linguistic data on the people that seemed to reveal important links between the bayou people and the historic Houmas. Out in the field the ethnologist collected a Houma language vocabulary that he featured prominently in his influential work, *Indian Tribes of the Lower Mississippi Valley and Adjacent Coast of the Gulf of Mexico*. Significantly Swanton reported that at least two old Indian women knew elements of the language in 1907. A year later Harrington noted that an old woman knew Indian songs as well. Swanton recorded approximately ninety words that he classified as being from the original Houma language as well as a number of local Houma placenames, including the term *Chit na tsebu*, the name for Bayou Lafourche. The people's word for fire, *lua'k*, was apparently identical to both the Choctaw term and to the historic Houma word for fire as reported by the Jesuits in 1700. Their word for themselves was *ho'ma*, which meant "red." Based on his collection and his expertise in linguistics, Swanton concluded that Houma was a Muskogean language, closely related to Choctaw and other tongues.[53]

For Verret's people Swanton's linguistic data seemed to provide an important link between the United Houma Nation and the historic Houma Tribe. According to Swanton, their ancestors called themselves Houma. They also knew elements of an Indian language and had traditions pointing to ties to the red crayfish emblem of the Houma Tribe long before tribal acknowledgment became an issue. Certainly Swanton classified both the people and their language as Houma. Yet although earlier BAR teams had relied upon Swanton's work in positive findings on the Tunica-Biloxis, Poarch Creeks, and others, the UHN team set out to debunk his theories in the Houma case. In terms of the language known by the elderly women, the BAR conjectured that it was actually Mobilian Trade Jargon, a lingua franca used by Indians of the region, or potentially Choctaw, but not Houma. They enlisted an expert who seemed to support this belief, although it was later revealed that he never directly challenged Swanton's conclusions. Overall, although it was correct that Swanton noted the close similarity between the informants' words and Choctaw, he was intimately acquainted with both Choctaw and Mobilian Trade Jargon and nonetheless concluded that the language was Houma, not these other tongues. Significantly, several years after the BIA preliminary finding Cecil H. Brown and Heather R. Hardy published an article titled "What Is Houma?" in the respected *International Journal of American Linguistics* (2000), which concluded that the words collected by Swanton were in fact Houma, a unique language, and not part of Choctaw or the trade jargon. If accepted by the BIA, these findings would provide a definitive link between the modern group and the historic Houma.[54]

The BIA's doubts about Swanton and the United Houma Nation rested largely on the bureau's questioning of the group's motives for asserting an Indian identity in the first decade of the twentieth century, a time of Jim Crow segregation and institutionalized racism in the South. Although it has never been made clear why a group's reasons for maintaining an Indian identity are in any way relevant to the BIA process, it is certain they play a part in deliberations. Because of the area's racial codes, the BIA believed that the Houmas chose to claim an Indian identity to separate themselves socially and legally from their African American neighbors even though they were culturally and socially non-Indian. Despite the fact that Swanton said the bayou people called themselves Houma, BIA researchers implied that it was Swanton who gave the name to the group; the appellation was thereafter accepted by the UHN's ancestors and subsequent scholars. According to the federal government, outsiders such as Swanton invented the Houmas as Indians, a fact that enabled them to pass as Indian in the dominant society. The BIA believed that land claims and greed were potential motives as well. As a branch historian noted, "During this period, as recounted in the UHN oral histories, the assertiveness of the petitioning community as to its Indian/Houma identity personalized in Rosalie Courteau, emerged in the context of claims to certain land."[55]

Lacking irrefutably Indian cultural attributes, the United Houmas were exposed to attacks impugning their motives and identity. Although a consideration of motives does not appear in the BIA acknowledgment regulations, it is clear from past decisions that groups with purer, apparently less materialistic and more stereotypically "Indian" motives have succeeded more often than others. Apparently possible financial, social, and racial questions surrounding the Houmas' Indian identity were clouding their claims within the BIA channels. Even so, the bureau found that outsiders such as Swanton and census takers had clearly and consistently identified the petitioning group as Indian since 1900. Despite the skepticism shown by the BIA reports, the Houma group therefore met the difficult "identification" criterion under the regulations.

Over time the UHN people clearly had assimilated many visible characteristics of the surrounding Cajun society, raising a central, confounding issue: when do people such as the United Houmas assimilate to such a degree that they cease being Indian? As the BIA essentially is recognizing a distinctive ethnic and political community, groups must be unique and separate to some extent. Yet in many cases like the Houmas', distinctive Indian survivals are difficult to pinpoint. Certainly many of the Cajun/Houma traditions that the people maintained contained Indian elements that are difficult to separate from their European parts. It is patently impossible to decipher how much, if any, of the Houma hunting, fishing, and agricultural practices included Indian antecedents without further academic study. While the bureau seemed cognizant of the fact that culture is a living organism that continually changes and evolves, it also seemed to be searching for indigenous survivals, an endeavor steeped in controversy within academia.

From Swanton's visit until the 1920s the bayou people faced a gradual erosion of their lands and livelihood as fur and oil companies closed traditional fishing and trapping lands to the group. Although the federal government did not recognize the Houmas as an Indian tribe at that time, local officials and area residents certainly did identify them as a distinct racial and social class, separate from both whites and blacks in the dichotomous segregated system of Louisiana. This racial distinction was most apparent in the realm of education. During the first half of the century the governments of Terrebonne and Lafourche Parishes prohibited Indian children from attending "white only" schools. In turn, the Houmas refused to attend segregated schools for African Americans. As a result, Houma children simply did not attend school. By the 1930s, however, in a humanitarian gesture for the Indians, the Methodists and Baptists established church schools on houseboats at Bayous Grand Caillou and Point aux Chenes. Later that decade Terrebonne Parish relented and provided a substandard one-room public school for Indians at Montegut on Bayou Terrebonne as well.[56]

The existence of Indian schools provided the modern group additional evidence of its Indian identity but did not solve its acknowledgment dilemmas. Although classified as Indians, locals also considered them to be mixed-bloods. The tripartite racial system of the bayou parishes presented an anomalous situation in the traditional black and white regime that prevailed in the South. Local residents thus began calling the Houmas "Sabines," an offensive term that denied their Indian identity by implying they were the product of illicit sexual liaisons between African Americans and whites. Because the Houmas' physical appearance ranged across a broad spectrum, it was generally difficult for residents to classify the people by appearance. In the Houma communities a visitor could find many individuals with darker skin, dark eyes, and straight black hair, some with light hair and eyes, and some with apparent African features. Because of the vagaries of genetics, some families had members possessing all these traits. In this light, United Houma ancestors were identified by family names that came to be associated with a separate Indian racial class with acknowledged, multiple ancestry.[57]

Within this climate some Houma "passed" as white and denied their Indian heritage if their phenotype appeared light enough. This fact led the BIA team to question their longstanding Indian pride and identity. Yet the government's stance seemed to downplay the prevailing racial stigma of the region. Explaining why they may have denied their heritage, anthropologist Ruth Underhill reported in the 1930s that "the Houma feel their inferior position keenly and many would not at first admit to the writer that they had Indian blood."[58] In this environment the group's members also carefully maintained social distance from nearby African American populations with whom locals associated them. Individuals who married African Americans thus generally found themselves cast out from the Indian community. Others who migrated to New Orleans for economic opportunities escaped the racial stigma of Terrebonne and Lafourche Parishes and for practical reasons did "pass" as white to attend white schools.[59]

During the early years of the Great Depression several United Houma ancestors made concerted efforts to secure federal services or recognition for their people for the first time. From this point until the end of the century, however, the Terrebonne-area Houmas experienced periodic federal opposition to recognizing them as an Indian tribe largely because, as in earlier eras, the enclave continued to challenge embedded cultural and political assumptions regarding indigenous peoples. During the 1920s and 1930s Charles and David Billiot began working with lawyers and writing the Indian Service in hope of gaining assistance for their people, variously calling their associates the "Houma Tribe" or "Houma Indians." Largely as a result of the Billiots' activity, during the New Deal officials of the Indian Service recognized the United Houma ancestors as Indians worthy of limited federal services. Unlike the Timbisha Shoshones, however, the Indian agency apparently never attempted to organize the people as a tribe.[60]

From the late 1920s until the 1940s, David, Charles, and Marice Billiot persuaded white patrons and Houma children to write to the Bureau of Indian Affairs for them. Much like the Yaquis at the same time, these three secured influential allies who believed they were Indians worthy of support, including anthropologist Frank Speck of the University of Pennsylvania and Oliver La Farge of the Association on Indian Affairs.[61] Even so, unlike the Yaquis and the Death Valley Shoshones, their people had racial issues to overcome. In 1938 David Billiot, a boat builder by trade, told Speck that locals were working hard "to have it said that there aren't any Indians here . . . are trying to say we aren't Indians but Negroes; I can show you and prove to you we are not that but we are white Indians."[62] After years of chicanery it seemed that turning to outsiders was the Indians' only hope. As Marice Billiot noted, "We can't read and we don't trust anybody here."[63]

For obscure eastern Indians, opportunities for securing federal acknowledgment generally followed the curve of federal Indian policy; the Houma people were no exception. In 1931, while assimilation agendas still reigned in federal circles, the BIA begrudgingly responded to the Billiots' pleas. That year the Indian Office dispatched Special Indian Commissioner Roy Nash to examine the remnant Indians in Louisiana. His report, "Louisiana's Three Thousand Indian Outcasts," concluded that the Houmas and other Louisiana groups (several of whom later secured acknowledgment) were all "mixed bloods" and too scattered to make it practicable to provide federal educational services to them. Apparently Nash was influenced by Terrebonne Parish school superintendent H. L. Bourgeois, who took the BIA agent aside, telling him that the Houmas were not really Indians at all but mulattos, pointing to the fact that early documents referred to them as "free men of color" as proof. After his trip, however, Nash did call for a detailed ethnological report but notably began using the term "Indian" in quotations to describe the group. Unfortunately for Louisiana's Indians, federal officials never conducted the study.[64]

The Indian Service did not fund the ethnological study because it was ideologically and financially opposed to acknowledging Indians at that time. As Commissioner of Indian Affairs C. J. Rhoades noted in 1932, "it would seem that since these Indians have been independent for so many years the problems of providing school facilities belongs to the State of Louisiana rather than the Federal Government."[65] At the time most non-Indians agreed with Commissioner Rhoades's hard-nosed approach. As the commissioner said, "A main objective of the Federal government for the Indian is to bring him to the point where he can stand on his own feet. Without Federal aid the Indians of Louisiana exist, free of the handicaps of wardship; to impose wardship upon them would be to turn the clock backward."[66]

In the seesaw of federal Indian policy, however, the momentum soon swung against assimilation agendas and efforts to destroy tribalism during new commissioner John Collier's Indian New Deal. With the Wheeler-Howard Bill federal policymakers took a renewed interest in Indian groups in the South. Sympathetic director of education W. Carson Ryan Jr. noted in 1934 that the southern Indian groups were not "scattered" as reported by Nash and that the federal government had a duty to assist all Indians of at least one-fourth Indian blood under the bill (this was later increased to one-half). Referring to the landless, neglected groups, Ryan said, "We sometimes refer to Indians as adequately 'adjusted' when what we really mean is that they are resigned to a discrimination that is neither fair nor socially desirable."[67] Because of the blood quantum requirement of the Indian Reorganization Act, Collier dispatched cultural anthropologists to the South to determine whether groups such as the Lumbees of North Carolina and Houmas of Louisiana had the prerequisite blood flowing through their veins.[68]

In 1938 the Indian Service sent anthropologist Ruth Underhill, who was well versed in her discipline and an associate of both Swanton and Speck, to investigate the Louisiana Indians. In October Underhill visited both the Houma and Tunica enclaves in the state. During the field trip she concluded that the bayou people were Indians and rejected the previous government position that the Louisiana groups were too mixed and scattered to be considered for federal assistance. As Underhill wrote, "the subject is reopened as far as the Houma and Tunica are concerned." Ultimately, however, her work would cast a cloud over the UHN's subsequent acknowledgment efforts as she reported that there "are some 300 people of Indian descent calling themselves Houma, though not organized as a tribe." [69] Although perhaps correct, this was a common assessment of anthropologists at the time. Albert S. Gatschet said the same thing about the presently recognized Chitimacha Tribe of Louisiana as early as 1881, and federal officials noted the Timbisha Shoshones were not organized as a "tribe" in the 1930s. In these cases federal bureaucrats took steps to organize these groups but apparently did not do the same with the United Houmas. [70]

Ultimately Underhill recommended providing federal aid to the bayou group, pointing to the fact that the Houmas had a definite tradition of tribal descent, had retained some Indian legends, and produced some distinctly Indian crafts. A major obstacle Underhill perceived, however, was the fact that Houma marriages lacked official sanction. As a result she felt the government could not adequately determine the Houmas' degree of Indian blood. Basing her assessment on phenotype, however, she agreed with her colleague Speck, saying "the physical appearance of some 100 is decidedly Indian, comparing favorably with that of the Choctaw and Creek in general." [71]

Despite Underhill's belief that the UHN ancestors were Indians, local circumstances severely complicated the Houma situation. In her efforts to find justice and secure education for the group, Underhill met with Superintendent H. L. Bourgeois, who told her to stop agitating for the Houmas, warning it might lead to bloodshed. Besides, Bourgeois argued, the courts had already settled the matter; they were "Negroes." Even so Underhill went on to convince the local parishes that federal educational aid would benefit everyone involved. The BIA scholar also recommended that the Indian Service develop a cooperative shrimp cannery, establish a system for marketing furs, and hire a federal worker to serve the Indians in Louisiana. Had these programs been instituted, they would have established a federal relationship with the groups in Terrebonne and Lafourche Parishes, ties that may have dovetailed into full acknowledgment.

As witnessed with the Pascua Yaquis, however, financial concerns soon clouded the picture. While sympathetic to the Houmas, Dr. Willard Beatty of the Department of the Interior noted that the limited educational aid already extended to the nearby Coushattas had snowballed into obligations for medical and economic assistance. With this in mind, he recommended treating the

Houmas in a "gingerly fashion." [72] Although correspondence from this era clearly reveals that the Indian Service generally did not question the fact that the Houmas were Indians of at least partial Native American ancestry, it did resist incurring a financial burden by taking on the group. [73]

In the early years of World War II, the Billiots' persistence paid off, and their people attained some acknowledgment of their indigenous status from the BIA. At Beatty's urging, in 1942 Collier agreed to allocate Indian Service money to support Indian education in Terrebonne Parish—provided that Congress fund the endeavor. Finally it seemed federal Indian schools would end the vexing issue of education in the Louisiana parishes. As planned, the Houmas would agree to attend segregated schools if labeled "Indian" under federal auspices; federal support would relieve the parish of providing education for its Indian citizens. Unfortunately, in the midst of World War II the plan was dropped, and with the advent of the termination agenda after the war, federal officials never again seriously reexamined the approved plan. [74] Although the war stymied their plans, some bayou Indians moved to New Orleans during the 1940s to work in defense industries. Although these individuals clearly saw their economic and social circumstances improve as a result, the Branch of Acknowledgement and Research would see this as further evidence of the dispersal of the United Houma community.

For the period 1920 through World War II the BAR team refused to accord the Billiots' and New Deal workers' efforts for "the Houma Tribe" any significant weight as evidence of unified tribal activity. Again following a strict approach, without data on exactly who these individuals represented (if any), the branch team conjectured that the Billiots were acting alone or for their own ends and not for the Houma people as a whole. While this may or may not have been the case, the BIA proposed finding concluded that the United Houma Nation was not a community with leaders who represented the various settlements from 1880 to 1940.

Revealing the complexity of the case, Steve Austin, an affable anthropologist who worked on the United Houma finding, originally concluded the United Houma Nation had met its burden of proving that it was a community with political authority from 1940 until 1994. After reconsideration, however, the official team changed this position, with the BIA proposed finding concluding that the group was not a community with recognized leaders after World War II. The group thus failed to meet its burden of demonstrating community for the modern period. [75] Proving it was a modern, unified tribe would be the final obstacle the United Houmas would encounter in the BIA acknowledgment process. Ultimately the Houmas' experience raises serious doubts whether a large group without a land base, governmental powers, and high Indian blood quantum across its membership can appear to be a functioning governmental unit or "tribe" as envisioned by the dominant society.

Not surprisingly the two sides were diametrically opposed as to the existence of the modern Houma tribal community. To make its case that it was a tribal unit throughout the modern era, the UHN turned to scholarly studies produced after the war. Although federal officials ignored the group after 1945, scholars in the fields of anthropology and sociology had continued to turn their occasional gaze upon the unique social group in southern Louisiana. Respected anthropologist Frank Speck had started this trend in the 1930s, and ethnologists continued studying the Houmas as an example of the surviving Indian remnants in the Southeast. Sociologists likewise turned their attention to the Houmas as an example of a recently "discovered" phenomenon of mixed-race communities they described variously as "little races" or "tri-racial isolates."

Based on his understandings of Indian society and culture, Speck argued forcefully that the Houmas were an Indian people; Tulane University anthropologist Ann Fisher seconded this view during the 1960s. Ultimately, however, both would hurt the United Houmas' chances in the BIA process by writing that the bayou Indians were not integrated as a tribal unit. A student of southeastern Indians, enthnologist Speck was fully cognizant of the dynamic nature of Indian culture and believed that their loose social organization was the result of environmental adaptation. To Speck, the group had logically adapted itself to the conditions of modern society and life in the marshes, adopting French-Cajun traits while spreading out in family units along the waterways. Speck reported that this process had progressed to the point where, "It may be found, broadly applied, that the entire Houma group is now a distended consanguineous family." [76] Along with a later study conducted by anthropology student Max Stanton, Speck's statements on the bayou people's tribal organization and racial identity would make for rough travel in the BIA channels. After visiting the lower bayous Speck bluntly recommended that the group fight the "Negro" label in favor of an improved Indian status, while Stanton reported that the people had apparently stopped calling themselves "Houma" in favor of the generic "Indian" by the late 1960s. Taken together, these conclusions would leave Verret's people vulnerable to charges they were not a tribal unit as well as to skepticism regarding their Houma identity. [77]

Contemporaneous studies by sociologists on the "triracial isolates" of the

South also engendered questions as to the group's tribalism. The genre's theories could be summed up by the title of a work by one of its practitioners, *Almost White*. As author Karen Blu detailed on the Lumbees, the local assumption here was that these groups would rather be white, but lacking acceptance in this class, they "settle for Indian." It appeared to some BIA researchers that the United Houmas were in this class. [78] In light of their lack of major Indian cultural traits, were the United Houmas basically a multiracial people choosing to claim an Indian identity in preference to the alternatives? Clearly, after centuries of cultural contact most southern and eastern Indians did not fit the stereotypical Indian portrayed in Hollywood westerns. As University of Georgia anthropologist Charles Hudson noted, however, there are many ways to be Indian: culturally, socially, and genetically. And although the Houmas had lost many Indian cultural traits by the twentieth century, Hudson considered them among several groups with "unimpeachable Indian identities." [79] Yet, depending on the bent of the scholar, peoples such as the Houmas could be classified many ways.

In fact, the status of the ambiguous "triracial isolates" varies tremendously. Hundreds of these groups exist, classified as "racial islands" and known locally as "Redbones," "Brassankles," "Cajuns," and other appellations. Some maintain an Indian identity while others do not. In 1950 an article in the "triracial isolate" vein appeared on the Houma Indians, calling them "Sabines." The article concluded that the Houmas were a marginal people "doomed to racial isolation" and focused on the people's ambiguity rather than their Indianness. Clearly, this emphasis flowed directly from the theoretical bent of the researchers who were emphasizing the triracial nature of the people. Beyond referring to the Houmas by the pejorative term "Sabine," which impugned their Indian heritage, this work, like others, served to foster scholarly questions regarding the people's identity. Although not "doomed" to racial obscurity per se, when outsiders viewed the United Houmas through the prism of these articles they certainly could appear less than Indian. [80]

By the 1960s, the United Houma people began a concerted struggle for recognition of their rights as Native Americans, a battle that soon became enmeshed within the larger civil rights movement. Once again, however, the BAR refused to afford these activities much weight. In any case, a major focus of organized Houma activity during the 1950s and 1960s was a drive to end legally sanctioned discrimination and segregation, particularly in public education. Although some Houma villages were fairly isolated, with houses strung in lines along the stream banks, others existed in close proximity to their African

American and Cajun neighbors. Even in these lower bayou communities such as Dulac, however, the area settlements were highly segregated along racial lines. Houma families at Dulac lived on one side of the bayou, while white and African American communities lived on the other bank, separated by a narrow waterway jammed with docks and fishing boats. Overall, a three-way system of segregation existed in the area, with Houma people forced to sit in separate areas of churches and theaters and often denied service at local establishments because of their race. As current UHN chair Brenda Dardar, a warm and intelligent woman, recalled, locals often would refuse her people haircuts and other basic accommodations simply because they were "Sabines."[81]

Because of racial stigma and their pride in Indian ancestry, United Houma members continued to maintain the color line (or ethnic boundary), avoiding social contact with area African Americans, refusing to attend "colored" schools, and excluding members of their communities who participated in interracial marriages. Although the Houmas were more amenable to area Cajuns with whom they shared language and cultural traits (and who not surprisingly sat at the apex of area race hierarchies), Verret recalled that many Cajuns looked at the Houmas as "people of the marsh"—almost subhuman. Generally the Houma villages accepted unions between whites and Indians, although Helen Gindrat remembers a bit of "yak-ity-yak" when she married a white man from New Orleans. Through these social mechanisms and community mores the United Houmas thus maintained their identity as a distinct group in southern Louisiana. Yet, as before, the BAR would view increased inter-ethnic marriages after World War II such as Gindrat's as evidence of the lack of community and social cohesion.[82]

During the 1960s Tom Dion, a well-respected man from Dulac, led efforts to integrate public schools and to have his people reclaim lands lost in preceding generations. With the help of Ann Fischer and the Association on American Indian Affairs, some Houmas secured the services of noted civil rights attorney John P. Nelson of New Orleans. After finding the land claims virtually impossible to pursue, these Houmas turned their focus to desegregating the area schools. As Verret recalled, this effort posed a dilemma for some, however, as the schools were exclusively Indian and a focal point of the Indian community. On the bayous (as in the Lumbee areas of North Carolina) some individuals opposed to closing the exclusively Indian schools taught their children to chant, "Five, six, seven, eight, we don't want to integrate," but they eventually realized their schools were so substandard that integration was the best alternative. Despite their torn emotions, Houma communities eventually mobilized for integration, with more than fifty Indian children on Bayou Terrebonne, Bayou Point aux Chenes, and Isle Jean Charles signing on as plaintiffs. In the ensuing case, *Margie Willa Naquin, et al v. Terrebonne Board of Education* (1963), the Houmas won a court order mandating school desegregation. The people now had a chance for an equal public education through high school. Ironically school officials later named a new school for H. L. Bourgeois, the Houmas' old nemesis, and adopted the mascot "the Braves" after the Houmas, a scenario Kirby Verret finds amusing. Despite the Houmas' success, the BIA later determined that the desegregation efforts were never coordinated across Houma community lines and thus were not evidence of supra-tribal activities. The BAR apparently considered that concurrent land claims activities by leaders in Dulac and New Orleans were tainted by financial motivations and rejected these activities as persuasive evidence of group actions. [83]

As with other eastern Indian groups, the 1960s were clearly an emergent decade for the modern Houmas. Activities begun at this time would lead directly to the UHN's ultimate petition for federal acknowledgment. Taken together, the civil rights movement, assertive Indian activism, and rising educational levels all had an impact on Houma individuals. Once isolated from the larger Indian world, new leaders who gained education in New Orleans such as Helen Gindrat now kept abreast of the human rights discourse of the time. With lessons learned in the era, she and others would push for full federal rights in the 1970s. [84]

The American Indian Chicago Conference was certainly central to the United Houmas' growing ethnic activity. In 1961 Bayou Terrebonne leader Frank Naquin, who at that time had worked for decades to gain education for Indian children, heard about a forum being organized in Chicago by anthropologist Sol Tax and the NCAI. He soon raised money to send two future leaders of the UHN, Helen Gindrat and Dolores Terrebonne, to the conference. For these young women and other eastern Indians, the Chicago conference was a watershed, resulting not only in the "Declaration of Indian Purposes" that came out strongly in favor of the rights of unacknowledged Indians but also in spurring them to fight for their civil rights. Excited after meeting with similar people in Chicago, Gindrat and Terrebonne returned to the Houma area and with Frank Naquin began organizing their people. [85]

In the wake of Chicago, Gindrat and Naquin realized they needed a more formalized government structure if they were to successfully assert their ethnic identity and take advantage of the growing list of anti-poverty programs emanating from the Kennedy and later Johnson administrations. Gindrat, continuing a tradition of strong female leaders, simply felt that her people should fight back. "It was time for us to do something," she recalled later.[86] Although Tom Dion and Frank Naquin continued to lead many Houmas, the time commitments and unpaid labor required for such social activism resulted in women taking many key leadership roles in the subsequent decades. Beyond providing satisfaction and power, current UHN chairperson Brenda Dardar believes that women lead from tradition and also because it is largely an unpaid "labor of love."[87] By the early 1970s many Houma women and men moved forward, becoming involved with other Louisiana Indian groups pressing for various causes.

In 1972 Gindrat and others formed the Houma Tribe, electing Frank Naquin as chairman. This formal body would evolve into the modern United Houma Nation. The Houma Tribe, however, generally served the eastern Houma areas in Lafourche, Jefferson, and eastern Terrebonne Parishes by focusing on adult education. In 1974 the western Houma along Bayou Grand Caillou, feeling underrepresented, broke away, creating the Houma Alliance under Howard Dion, Tom Dion's son. The Houma Alliance's primary goal was to improve economic conditions for Indians in the area. The BIA, however, would look upon this division as further evidence of the traditional lack of unity among the various Houma settlements.[88]

In the dramatic days of the early 1970s Gindrat and others became involved with the newly established Coalition of Eastern Native Americans (CENA), an organization that was instrumental in pressing for recognition of the forgotten Indian enclaves outside the American West. Activities by Houma people at this time would provide the modern UHN additional evidence of tribal activity necessitated under the FAP rules. Yet the actions of CENA raised questions as well: was CENA now helping to create tribes much like the BAR team believed Swanton did decades earlier? Established in 1972 with the aid of NARF, under Lumbee W. J. Strickland, CENA set out to locate and mobilize over fifty-three "lost tribes" of the East, estimated by the organization to encompass at least 250,000 individuals.[89] Together with other legal aid groups, CENA undoubtedly invigorated eastern Indians who often felt insecure in their Indian identity. As Strickland admonished, "We Indians should not be too concerned with the age-old question of 'Who am I?' We Indians know who we are and know where we are going."[90] Despite this confidence, BAR evaluators would be less sure of the status of many groups mobilized with the help of CENA and other legal aid groups.

Despite the BIA's later skepticism, many Houma individuals were inspired by the hope offered by these new organizations and the larger civil rights struggles of the era. As the momentum grew, in the early 1970s a Louisiana Red Power organization called the Indian Angels helped establish the Louisiana Intertribal Council that included Houma representatives Tom Dion and Helen Gindrat along with members of the Coushatta, Tunica, and Chitimacha Tribes. Through protest marches they ultimately goaded flamboyant Louisiana governor Edwin Edwards to establish the Governor's Commission on Indian Affairs in 1972. Although the commission was concurrent with the larger civil rights movement, Kirby Verret recalls his people generally remained apart from the African American struggle, fearing they would become lost within its larger goals. [91]

By the mid-1970s there was an Indian ethnogenesis and pan-Indian renaissance going on all over the Bayou State. Beyond political actions, Louisiana Indians sponsored pan-Indian powwows, inviting Oklahoma tribes to come and demonstrate their dances and ceremonies. Although Houma people took part in these activities, the FAP team came to doubt whether enough of them were involved to provide evidence of tribal activity. Additionally, with the cultural borrowings and revivals, the BIA seemed to give little weight to these activities as evidence of Indian tribalism, perhaps viewing them in the same vein as the actions of the rising number of "drugstore Indian" and "wannabe" groups entering the FAP. [92] Overall, the BIA researchers implied that all this ferment had simply created new tribal activity where there once was none.

In the middle of the decade, however, the two Houma tribal groups and their supporters were intimately involved with the groundswell that culminated in the congressionally sponsored American Indian Policy Review Commission (AIPRC) and the subsequent Federal Acknowledgment Project of the BIA. In 1976 the AIPRC's Task Force on Terminated and Non-federally Recognized Indians traveled to Louisiana to conduct hearings on the problems of Louisiana Indians. By then tribal acknowledgment was a major goal of most groups who hoped to use this status to achieve Indian rights. Meeting with the task force at the old Indian school in Dulac, Houma Alliance leader and former navy sailor Howard Dion helped expose the Houmas' plight to a larger national audience much like Anselmo Valencia did with the Pascua Yaquis. As Dion reported to the Indian commissioners, most Houmas were illiterate and impoverished. Although institutionalized racism had declined, its effects still lingered. Most Houmas remained uneducated, forced into low-paying and uncertain seasonal jobs, gritty work in factories, jobs on shrimp and fishing boats, or roughneck employment in the oil fields. Their lack of education and transportation hampered communication and organization as well. By this time the area marshes also lay victim to an unprecedented subsidence as the Gulf of Mexico encroached upon the shrinking mainland, threatening the very land on which the Houmas lived. Overall, observers found that many lived without plumbing in substandard housing placed on stilts to avoid the frequent flooding from hurricanes.[93] Local Indian educator Coreen Paulk summed up the feelings of many when she told the task force: "It's hard to be Indian."[94] While certainly correct, the Houma people maintained larger than average families, with these extended family webs helping to temper the hardships of poverty, seasonal employment, and weather. The Houmas reported that the various networks of family and support nurtured a positive outlook on life among the people.[95]

In light of these chronic problems, in the mid-1970s the Houma Tribe and the Houma Alliance attempted to gain assistance for their people. Ultimately these organizations secured grants to establish education and job-training programs under War on Poverty organizations such as CETA and VISTA and a Community Action Program. Kirby Verret and Coreen Paulk set up special Indian cultural and education programs for members of the organization under the more inclusively defined Indian Education program of HEW. The Houmas ultimately garnered several grants from ANA to help prove their tribal identity as well. Under these grants Houma leaders secured minor salaries and payment for their work for the first time. With this aid Houma tribal organizations developed formal government structures for holding meetings and electing representatives. These were highly visible actions, but FAP researchers once again doubted whether these activities were significant enough to rise to the level of widespread community concerns.[96]

At the same time, Gindrat and the others also secured tribal acknowledgment from the state of Louisiana. With this status the Houma groups ultimately gained minor financial funding from the state legislature, yet this aid paled in comparison to benefits flowing to federal tribes. State acknowledgment did bring some psychological benefits, however, as Louisiana issued identification cards that Indians could pull out to validate their ethnic status to doubting acquaintances. State recognition also enabled groups such as the Houma to qualify under several federal Indian programs within the OEO and HEW.[97]

Despite the fact that the state government and other Louisiana tribes including the federally recognized Louisiana Coushattas and Chitimachas accepted the Houma people as a tribe, a palpable suspicion still existed among certain non-Indians about their cultural and racial identity. Pejorative terms such as "so-called Indians" and "Sabines" continued to accompany references to the group. Because he has light skin and hazel eyes, United Houma leader Kirby Verret was privy to the accusations. "I wonder how many are real Indians?" is a question he has heard too many times from both African American and white individuals who did not realize they were talking to a Houma Indian.[98] As some United Houma members appear to be "white," this questioning is a logical response. Clearly, despite adopting some pan-Indian ways in modern times, the United Houmas' "race" continues to baffle some observers. Yet even those whose phenotype appeared "Indian," such as Helen Gindrat, but who dressed in modern fashions inevitably faced questions about their Indianness. "You're an Indian? You don't look like an Indian," is a remark she has heard repeatedly over the years.[99] While less common by the 1980s, the term "Sabine" still lingered, reminding the Houmas that many locals still believed they were some strange amalgam of black and white.

Still desiring official recognition of their Indian heritage, in the middle 1970s the Houma Tribe secured the aid of two Mennonites, Jannel Curry and Greg Bowman, who began helping the group pursue its new goal of gaining federal acknowledgment. Realizing their goal would be better accomplished as one organization, the two Houma tribes merged on 1 June 1979, establishing the United Houma Nation with Kirby Verret as chairman. Within a few years the UHN drafted its constitution, a document that established formalized government structures, including blood quantum for membership, election procedures, and five parish voting districts. Individuals who were recognized as Indian by the council and who could trace their heritage to the core Houma ancestors could join the organization. The United Houma Nation began leasing the old Indian school at Golden Meadow on Bayou Lafourche as its organizational headquarters. It also gained title to the former Indian school in nearby Montegut and began using the former school building and community center at Dulac on Bayou Grand Caillou in the western Houma area. The organization held monthly meetings at rotating locations to achieve greater participation, while administering the limited federal programs and grants secured by the nation. Over the next years Verret, Gindrat, and tribal registrar Dolores Dardar would become the backbone of this tribal organization.[100]

As with other petitioners, United Houma motivations for seeking recognition varied widely. Reflecting goals construed by the BIA as positive, some members hoped it would bring improved health care and better living conditions. Yet clearly others dreamed that it would mean a "check in the mail." After centuries of government-sanctioned discrimination, however, leader Kirby

Verret expressed a sincere motive for seeking acknowledgment: "In our tribe, the number one thing that we stress is that the U.S. government finally realize and recognize a people that has been denied an identity."[101]

Beyond issues of justice the UHN's sheer size made for difficult analysis in the Federal Acknowledgment Process. When the United Houma Nation submitted its petition for acknowledgment in 1985, the group was fairly large for an unacknowledged Indian entity, with 8,715 enrolled members. The greatest concentration of members resided in the Parish of Terrebonne (3,847), followed by Lafourche Parish (1,950) and Jefferson Parish (1,489). Spurred by growing interest and a concerted registration drive, the United Houma Nation soon swelled to over 17,000. At approximately the same time the 40,000-member Lumbee Tribe of North Carolina also submitted a lengthy petition that was later disqualified before a full review. Thus the modern Houma group was the largest entity to face full review in the FAP. In light of the numbers, the modern Houma organization's genealogical data was voluminous, with the historical documentation and supporting articles eventually covering over seventeen feet of storage space in the BIA vaults. Overall, the group's size and residential locations would make for difficult analysis within the BIA process, especially in the modern era.[102]

Throughout the UHN's initial review, it seemed apparent that the group's history and social organization challenged the ability of most outsiders to get a firm sense of the people's community and political sinews. As with anthropological community studies, the acknowledgment process certainly worked easiest and best when dealing with small, more or less insular enclaves rather than more complex societies and ethnicities.[103] Although consistent with the state of certain traditional Indian societies, apparently the United Houmas' historical and modern social arrangements did not comport well with the fixed, insular image of Indian tribes held by most non-Indians.

While awaiting a BIA finding that was slower in coming than expected, the UHN Tribal Council continued to run limited programs for its members. Since the 1970s the group had developed a summer youth job-training program, had administered a Reading Is Fundamental Program, and had managed a local state park. Adult education programs and efforts through the Governor's Commission on Indian Affairs and the Inter-tribal Council of Louisiana continued to be focal points of UHN activity. After Hurricane Andrew devastated the area in 1993, the tribal organization received a major grant of $2 million dollars to administer relief to tribal members. Under the Department of Health and Human Service's ANA grants the United Houma Nation secured funding to support the work of researchers, run the tribal government, and pay limited funds to UHN officers. For its BAR petition and later rebuttal, the UHN was able to enlist the aid of top acknowledgment experts Jack Campisi and William Starna and an experienced NARF team that included Arlinda Locklear, Richard Dauphinais, Faith Roessel, and Mark Tilden.[104]

Throughout the 1980s and early 1990s the group attempted to raise its cultural visibility as an Indian people. Whether for individual or political reasons, the UHN promoted a cultural revival and pan-Indian exchange. These efforts, while certainly important to individual group members, have generally had little or no effect on the BIA process, however. In fact, pan-Indian borrowings more often seem to cause doubts about a group's history and motivations. Even so, the United Houma participated in numerous powwows, holding their own pan-Indian events periodically during the 1970s and after. Under Verret, John Parfait, and later chairpersons Laura Billiot and Brenda Dardar, the UHN worked to revive community spirit and pride overall. In light of the cultural revival, anthropologist Charles Hudson remarked that the group, like others that were genetically and socially Indian, was becoming culturally Indian in the growing pan-Indian sense. When outsiders and some UHN members asked why they promoted Plains Indian–style dances, drum corps, and powwows that were not traditional, Verret replied, "it's to show our Indian pride, we can bring back anything we want." According to Verret, "A Chippewa friend told me 'I know you lost a lot of culture but if you start it now, one hundred years from now, it'll be a tradition.'"[105]

Despite these positive cultural programs during the 1980s and 1990s, much of the UHN's energy, like that of other unacknowledged entities, went into fighting for tribal recognition, a fact that also seemed to damn the group in the BIA's estimation. In a process characterized by layer upon layer of bureaucracy, the Houma case was even more complex than most. After an initial review, the BIA asked for more details on the group's modern community and politics in addition to its questions about the UHN's ancestry. In response the United Houmas and Jack Campisi conducted an ethnological study to document the social cohesion of the seven communities. By 1990, however, as the requests in the bureau's "obvious deficiency" letters mounted for more and more genealogical and historical records of their ancestry and tribal government, many Houmas grew weary of working with the federal bureaucracy. Verret expressed his frustration at the time. "In a peculiar twist of logic known only to government bureaucracies, we are now being required to prove our tribal status with genealogical records, historical documentation, anthropological studies, demonstration of uninterrupted political authority and minutia that is nearly impossible to come by. The records which do exist consist almost exclusively of studies by non-Indians."[106]

As the years passed, the UHN and its researchers grew increasingly angered by the bureaucratic regimen. Throughout the review process, however, the BAR team repeatedly assured Verret that they were "maintaining the objective and independent nature of the evaluation process."[107] Yet by 1990 NARF attorney Faith Roessel publicly questioned whether you could trust the BAR to be fair and objective. Although they were still within the initial review process, Campisi and Houma leader Helen Gindrat began testifying at congressional hearings against the BIA process. As Campisi told BIA deputy Ronal Eden, "These regulations are not revealed truth, and the staff is not above error. The sad but immutable fact is that no one with knowledge of the system today believes that it is possible to get a fair and impartial review."[108] Many United Houma members agreed with Helen Gindrat when she testified in 1989, "We are a poor tribe and cannot continue to support what amounts to sort of a fishing expedition on the part of the BAR. There needs to be some limitations placed on their continuous requests for information."[109] Although the BAR staff was guarded in its response, it was clear an unbiased review would be difficult in this environment. Speaking generally about the lack of documentation on most groups, BAR researcher Steve Austin later commented that his branch could "shut down [all petitioners] if we wanted to."[110]

Mired in what it saw as an impossible bureaucracy, the group pursued an alternative route to acknowledgment. With Verret at the lead, the UHN approached its congressional delegates in 1989 for help in introducing legislation that would acknowledge its tribal status. Being well known in the state, the group had little trouble convincing longtime Democratic senator J. Bennett Johnson, rising Democratic senator John Breaux, and Republican congressman W. J. "Billy" Tauzin from their district to support a bill that would recognize Verret's people as a federal Indian tribe. In fall of 1989 Johnson introduced a bill for the group that would acknowledge the United Houmas and end the seeming bureaucratic purgatory where they existed. The local community roundly supported Verret's efforts. Yet the legislation faced strong opposition from the BIA and from oil company executives who feared potential land claims. The bill and subsequent efforts went nowhere in Congress.[111]

Verret and the rest of the United Houma Nation were thus resigned to waiting for a proposed finding from the Bureau of Indian Affairs. As before, the United Houmas ultimately learned that the BIA decided the group had not proven with a "reasonable likelihood" of the facts that it descended from the historical Houma Tribe nor demonstrated its historical community and political authority since historical contact with Europeans. It had shown, however, that it was identified as Indian since 1900. In a rare scenario, because of endogamous practices approximately 84 percent could prove Indian descent but not from a named tribe that lived in the United Houmas' ancestral area. Because it rejected the group based on its descent from the Houma Tribe as a threshold issue, the BIA admitted its rulings on the other criteria were preliminary. Under the rules the group had time to respond. Yet the proposed finding set the group into turmoil, spawning splinter groups that fractured the organization. In particular the BAR's statement that six of the UHN communities may have maintained social integrity as separate entities but were never linked in a "bilateral" political relationship with a unifying core soon prompted these settlements to break away and petition separately.[112]

At some level it was apparent that the BAR team was probing for evidence of organized and documented supra-tribal structures that may or may not have existed at all times with the Houmas. Revealing its formal bent, even in the isolated individual settlements, the BAR noted disapprovingly that the leadership that did exist was primarily ad hoc or family based. The BIA finding said these leaders dealt primarily with what it referred to as "limited issues" such as desegregation and lobbying for federal recognition. For the period after 1880 the BIA concluded that there was scant evidence of political authority exercised over the satellite settlements by a central core and little evidence that a core entity dealt with any issues of concern to the entire group of people.

For the modern period after 1940, a major issue in the BAR's negative finding was the fact a segment of the UHN lived in New Orleans. Using statistical sampling, the BIA analysts concluded that two-thirds of the United Houma Nation's membership actually lived in New Orleans, including individuals who listed bayou-area addresses. Although the city was only approximately an hour away, the BAR found no evidence that these migrants maintained a social or political relationship with the Houma organization in Terrebonne and Lafourche Parishes. Even if they had, the BIA believed that the modern United Houma Nation was not a tribe as it envisioned one. Despite the fact that the Houmas had had an organized governing structure since the 1970s, the BAR determined that there was no broad-based relationship between it and the membership. According to the bureau, the UHN primarily consisted of a handful of close relatives presiding over meetings attended by only a handful of members who discussed issues "staged" by the council that were of little consequence to Houma people. Using tribal minutes, the BIA produced evidence that as few as eleven members attended some meetings, although this number rose to several hundred during the 1990s.

In a balancing test that judges have used since the late nineteenth century, the BIA evaluators attempted to decide whether the United Houma Nation was a political unit or merely a social club—a slippery and difficult endeavor at its very best. In this task the acknowledgment branch ultimately determined that the modern entity did not deal with matters deemed important by the bureau. The BIA researchers found that issues the council discussed during the 1980s— such as education, equal representation, land claims, beauty contests, crafts classes, and genealogical work—generally fell into the category of insignificant matters, more akin to the activities of a "social club" than a "governing body" typical of a tribe. Beyond this usurping of a group's ability to define its own concerns, it seems doubtful many reservation tribes, including small bands in the Southwest, could stand up to the scrutiny and challenges to what constituted viable motives and tribal concerns posed by the government. It was apparent, however, that the BAR had searched for a central, unifying government structure for 17,000 individuals and found it wanting. [113]

In its conclusions on the United Houma Nation the BAR often referenced the nearby Tunica-Biloxis, a tribe acknowledged via the FAP in the early 1980s, as an apparent model of a functioning tribal community. And it seemed clear that the Houma group lacked many of the records and evidence of tribalism possessed by the small Tunica-Biloxi community. Although Louisiana anthropologist Hiram Gregory views the groups as essentially similar in race and culture, he believes the crucial difference in their current fates is the fact that the Tunica-Biloxis played the European "game" masterfully since the nineteenth century while the Houmas had not; and the Tunica-Biloxis played the game because they had tribal land to protect. [114]

Unlike the ancestors of the United Houmas, the much smaller Tunica-Biloxi Tribe possessed a 127-acre tract of land confirmed in a letter from Spanish governor Estevan Miro in 1786. In the course of legal challenges the tribe had hired lawyers and developed a paper trail showing its tribal identity on several occasions during the nineteenth century. As with the Timbisha Shoshones, the proof of the Tunica-Biloxis' continuing tribalism rested on the tribe's having a communally held land base. Because the chiefs allocated use of the tract, control of the land promoted formalized procedures and political authority needed to administer the land. Beginning in the early part of the century, Tunica-Biloxi leaders actually began to notarize and record their offices and changes of authority in the local courthouse. Basing its decision largely on this fact, the BIA determined that the group was a tribe. As for its Indian ancestry, the bureau used rolls partly prepared by Swanton and Underhill, requiring levels of proof that paled in comparison to the detailed genealogies completed for the UHN. In the end, however, the tribe was able to secure acknowledgment precisely because it existed in a form easily recognized as a political body to outsiders. The Tunica-Biloxis passed the BAR process despite the fact that the BIA determined that only 15 of the 200 members lived on tribal land, that the Tunica-Biloxi chief lived four hours south in New Orleans, and that over half of the members actually lived outside the state. The Tunica-Biloxis passed with relative ease through the process before the BIA "ratcheted up" its requirements in fear of lawsuits and before, as Verret says, "the FAP became more efficient at finding errors in petitions, got better at denying and criticizing."[115]

Unlike the happily recognized Tunica-Biloxi Tribe, the United Houmas' negative finding set into motion a series of legal appeals by the group and its attorneys. In a matter still pending, the UHN case inspired the Native American Rights Fund to challenge the entire federal criteria for acknowledging Indian tribes. In addition to the lawsuit, the United Houma Nation soon produced a rebuttal that attacked the seeming certainty and finality of the BAR conclusions on its organization. The factional dispute, however, threatened the UHN's chances by engendering negative publicity about the group and its status as a tribal body.

Prior to the negative finding, it was apparent to some United Houma members that the BAR and its lead anthropologist, Holly Reckord, believed that their people did not descend from the historic Houma Tribe and that each community had a better shot on its own. "The United Houma Nation already had its epitaph on its tombstone and it says 'You're not going to get recognized,'" remarked Reggie Billiot, a leader from Dulac at the time. [116] Knowing that their chances for recognition as separate tribal communities would be precluded upon a negative final ruling on the whole tribe, the leaders of several dissident groups severed their relationship with the UHN body.

Although related to the BIA findings, the factional disputes actually predated the BAR influence and had been brewing for some time. Yet the controversy clearly hurt the larger organization's acknowledgment chances. In its reports the BAR team pointed to these divisions to make its case that the group was not united as a tribe. After 1988 a generally younger and vocal group of Houmas from the western area of Dulac led by forceful and articulate spokesman Reggie Billiot, along with Jim Liner, Ernie Dardar, and Joseph Billiot, among others, began challenging the leadership of Gindrat, Verret, and Gindrat's niece, Laura Billiot. Charging mismanagement of hurricane relief funds, nepotism, and at various times despotic rule, this group eventually severed its ties with the main UHN body and then proceeded to carry on friendly correspondence with the BIA prior to its proposed finding.[117]

In general the BAR looked favorably upon the emergence of the faction as representative of true tribal concerns and government. The BIA team praised the factions for challenging what it referred to as the "old guard" leadership that was concerned more with gaining acknowledgment and appearing united than with other matters. An additional plus for the dissidents was the fact that they "freely refer to African as well as Indian ancestry."[118] Although functioning tribes have factions as a matter of course, the BAR team in this instance revealed its generally unflattering opinions about the United Houma leadership.

Bypassing a separate petitioning process that would have placed them at the back of the waiting list and decades from consideration, eventually two factional groups, the Biloxi, Chitimacha Confederation of Muskogees (BCCM) under Reggie Billiot and the Point au Chien Indian Tribe (PACIT) under Steve Charamie were able to separate themselves from the UHN petition in 1996 yet be considered under its related final ruling. Strong and opinionated, Reggie Billiot became the early leader of BCCM and a lightning rod of contention. In a tumultuous time following the BIA's negative determination, Billiot led approximately two thousand UHN members to resign from the tribal organization, although some later returned.[119]

For a time the BIA's initial ruling affected the group's organization and altered its sense of its own identity and history. Billiot and the others generally accepted the BAR finding that their people did not descend from the Houma Tribe but rather were an amalgamation of Biloxi, Chitimacha, Choctaw, and other battered colonial tribes who coalesced on the lower bayous. Inquiring on his own after the BIA finding, Reggie Billiot went around asking about tribal members' identity, learning surprisingly that elders on Bayou Grand Caillou had long thought they were Chitimacha, Biloxi, Choctaw, or perhaps just generic "Indian" and not Houma.[120]

In 1995, Billiot and others formed a loosely aligned organization centered on the lower bayou communities of Grand Caillou, Point aux Chenes, Isle Jean Charles, Bayou Dularge, and Montegut. Members of the BCCM accepted the BIA conclusion that the United Houma Nation was too centralized and autocratic, and that its large membership maintained little real contact with the main tribal organization. Billiot clearly believed his organization should be based at the local level and should work closely with the BIA. He also rejected what he saw as the UHN's theory that it should admit as many members as possible to project an image of strength. To Billiot, this goal was bound to fail, especially since the United Houmas had tied their hopes to a faulty base beginning with Swanton's theories. By 1997, however, the BCCM had its own splinter group, as Albert Naquin and the Isle Jean Charles community made overtures to separate themselves from the BCCM, believing ironically that Billiot was now too autocratic and out of touch with their local community.[121]

The Houmas' protracted encounter with the legal process had brought them face to face with the realities of proving ethnic identity in the modern world. The federal government had wielded the power to tell them they were not who their traditions said they were. Not surprisingly many United Houma members came to dislike the BIA, while Reggie Billiot came to hate NARF and the group's scholarly experts, who he believed had "leached off" the Houma people in the BIA process. "The best thing for the tribe is for them to go out of business," Billiot said in 1999.[122] For his efforts Billiot has been called a traitor to the cause and has faced community hostility. Clearly, the federal finding had started a snowball rolling, stymieing the United Houmas' efforts to define for themselves who they were without outside interference.

Emblazed by the BIA proposed ruling, the tribal divisions served only to add credence to the government's belief that the Houmas were far from united. Current UHN chairperson Brenda Dardar argues quite correctly that the divisions have prejudiced her people in the acknowledgment process. Dardar believes, however, the splinter groups simply have fallen victim to the old government "divide and conquer" strategy. She and United Houma member Pat Arnould of the Governor's Office of Indian Affairs view the factions as little more than disaffected leaders who lost power in tribal elections and then broke away for individual opportunity. Both Dardar and Kirby Verret genuinely believe the BAR intentionally interfered with their internal politics by encouraging these groups to fissure from their organization, luring them with the carrot of eventual acknowledgment. At times the internecine strife brought out painful accusations. One faction reported that the members of the UHN lacked any Indian ancestry and were not really Indians at all or were "apples" and not "true Indians." Likewise, Reggie Billiot was accused of "having a white mentality" for accepting the conclusions of the government and not following the "traditional" Indian way by seeking personal fame and fortune.[123]

As happened to the Lumbees, the major factions made the Houmas appear to be a questionable tribal people in public discourse. The divisions also affected the appearance of the United Houma Nation in the FAP. Prior to its negative finding, the BAR closely followed a series of negative articles in a local paper on the UHN's alleged mismanagement of funds, despotism, and lack of standards for verifying Indian ancestry. Coming from members of the factions, these reports did little to support the United Houma case before the BAR. The resulting BIA reports on the group, in fact, seemed to mirror the negative views of the UHN published in these articles, images that portrayed the group as a small cadre of individuals who worked primarily for recognition and personal gain. The emergence of factions clearly distressed many United Houma leaders, however. Pleading for unity, Verret summed up the feelings of many when he argued, "We are the same people. Remember when we could not go to school because we are Houma Indians? Now some people say they are not Houma Indians and they have taken a real long name and claim to be something else. A tribe is a large family. Even the ones who claim to be different from us are still our relatives! How can we separate our blood? We can not."[124] Many eventually returned to the United Houma Nation.

Beyond these emotional issues of identity and ancestry, the Point au Chien splinter organization further complicated the UHN's acknowledgment hopes by inciting opposition from powerful oil companies. In 1993 the leaders of the faction brought suit in federal court under the 1790 Nonintercourse Act to restore their rights to several hundred thousand acres of oil-rich lands in the Houma area. While perhaps a valid claim, this suit ignited the wrath and legal firepower of the Louisiana Land and Exploration Company (LLE), one of the largest landholders in the region. To the oil company it was clear that tribal acknowledgment would give the Houmas standing in court to press land claims under federal Indian laws. In response LLE attorneys took depositions, trying to cast doubt on the race of all Houmas. Calling them "so-called" Indians, oil company lawyers dug for further evidence that they were not a tribe within the meaning of federal law. Beyond problems stemming from its large membership and its documentation, the United Houmas now had a large oil company gunning for them. The oil company lawyers made it all too clear that they were reviewing the same documents as the BAR, thus raising the stakes a notch on a potential positive finding for the group.[125]

In 1996 the activities of the former UHN factions, now independent tribal petitioners, bled into a second effort by the United Houmas to bypass the BIA process by securing legislative recognition. By this time Senator Breaux had internalized the negative conclusions about the Houmas' tribal status and no longer supported the UHN. Because of Breaux's position, the United Houmas turned to Congressman Tauzin to introduce legislation on their behalf. When the factions lined up with the Bureau of Indian Affairs to oppose the United Houma Nation's effort this time, its bill stalled in committee.[126]

The United Houmas' only real chance for acknowledgment now rested with challenging the BAR findings and eventually the entire BIA process. In November of 1996, approximately two years after learning of the negative finding, the United Houma Nation's attorney, Mark Tilden of NARF, and Jack Campisi submitted a voluminous rebuttal to the BIA's proposed finding. After spending hundreds of thousands of dollars conducting statistical analyses and hundreds of hours researching area records and historical writings, the UHN was ready to challenge the BIA's opinion that it was not an Indian tribe within the federal acknowledgment regulations. The UHN rebuttal, still pending in 2003, presented compelling new evidence that raised serious issues regarding the BIA's initial finding. Yet it also seemed apparent that the group did not possess certain written documents that would have closed its case once and for all. Concerning its migration, the UHN had to rely on statements such as "these families may also have found their way into the lower bayou regions" and "it is conceivable that . . ." to document its case for the key early period of its petition. In light of the existing evidence, however, the group's arguments as to its origins are certainly logical. The United Houmas and the BCCM also were able to locate documents supporting Indian ancestry for additional ancestors. Importantly, they found an 1832 death notice that listed a key ancestor, Houma Courteau/Joseph Abbe, as Houma.[127]

In its rebuttal the United Houma Nation argued that its case compared favorably with prior positive acknowledgment decisions. A major problem with the BIA acknowledgment process, however, has been comparability between past decisions. Clearly, groups need to know what standards need to be met in order to make their cases. Yet the BAR has long said that it needs flexibility in its determinations, a need that makes close comparability between cases impossible. Because the FAP's burden of proof is not "absolute certainty," its determinations have always required the subjective decisions of the BAR researchers. This fact has left the bureau wide latitude on its determinations, yet open to attacks on its methods and potential bias in individual cases like the Houmas.

In past cases with less ambiguity on certain issues, the BAR had shown an ability to assume certain facts, assumptions that it did not make with the United Houma Nation. In the Tunica-Biloxi case, for example, the fact that this tribe possessed a communal land base and solid leadership records resulted in the

BAR accepting documents by anthropologists and group testimony as to their descent—modes of evidence it subsequently rejected from the UHN. Lacking records on some aspects of the Tunica-Biloxi migrations, the BIA also assumed that because the group possessed a tribal structure at a later time, the people logically moved from point a to point b as a group. Securing acknowledgment in 1995, the Jena Choctaw of Louisiana likewise passed the BAR's tests, in part, because the small group maintained its language and apparent high Indian blood quantum. These attributes allowed the BAR to overlook the fact that local records generally were sparse concerning the Jena Choctaw's origins, migration to the Jena area, and tribal ancestry.[128]

Lacking key legal records of their tribal existence like the Tunica-Biloxis or cultural symbols of Indianness such as the Jena Band, the United Houmas faced a daunting challenge verifying their tribalism and ancestry to modern judges. Apparently the lack of conclusive written evidence on several criteria left the group open to skepticism on all of them. As the UHN pointed out in their rebuttal, however, many other tribes do not possess detailed written records of their tribal existence, forcing them to rely heavily on the reports of early ethnographers to prove their tribalism. In fact, a debatable aspect of the bureau's initial finding was its attacks on the scholarship of John Reed Swanton. When piecing together the fragmented histories of unacknowledged southern Indians such as the Jena Choctaw, Tunica-Biloxis, and Poarch Creeks, the BAR had relied heavily upon Swanton's work. In other cases such as the Timbisha Shoshones, the BAR also accepted the firsthand, primary source accounts of tribal origins, ancestry, and political organization provided by informants. In the UHN case, however, several BAR researchers set out to "debunk" the theories and work of Swanton, in particular. Why was this so?[129]

Because it rested so highly on challenges to Swanton, the UHN case posed complex questions regarding the BIA process. Did the bureau team have strong footing to attempt such a debunking effort? And did it truly refute Swanton's theories as claimed? The UHN pointed out that two BAR anthropologists working on the Houma case lacked Ph.D.s in their discipline yet were directly challenging the primary source work and observations of a figure noted as a leading scholar in his discipline. According to some, Swanton, while not infallible, was the most distinguished member of the Bureau of American Ethnology and had conducted varied fieldwork and historical research over a lifetime on the southeastern Indians. Swanton had served as a founding member of the American Anthropological Association and its president and editor and later received the highest honor of the profession.[130] Were attacks on his work the inevitable and healthy products of time as modern researchers logically attempted to refine and build upon work done in earlier eras? Or, as the UHN implied, do some individuals within the BIA lack the scholarly background to challenge the work of scholars long dead and unable to defend themselves against the allegations? Perhaps because they hold the purse strings, the answer is obvious that the BIA team has this power, yet the debunking effort was far from complete. In the end, however, the attack on Swanton's work in the Houma case clearly raises issues as to why the bureau did not scrutinize his work in the petitions of smaller groups such as the Tunica-Biloxis.

Beyond questioning the propriety of the challenges to Swanton, the UHN also challenged the methodology used by the BIA to find that its people lacked a functioning community after 1940. Much of the thrust of the BAR's argument on this point rested on its assertion that two-thirds of the United Houma Nation's membership lived and continue to live in New Orleans, a fact that, if true, would raise doubts about the social solidarity of any group. The UHN presented evidence, however, that the BAR's own analysis revealed that only 16 percent actually lived in the city, while over 50 percent resided within a social core area within a twenty-mile radius of Montegut, Louisiana. The United Houmas based this conclusion on statistical sampling and work completed using standards set by the BAR in earlier positive cases on the Mohegan Tribe of Connecticut and other written BIA standards. If the FAP team accepts these statistics, evidence of a 50 percent rate of residence in the core area would be enough proof under the regulations to demonstrate that the UHN existed as a community with political authority for the modern era. In reality, however, it seems likely that the BAR team would challenge the UHN's statistics by arguing that the population of the "core" area is too heterogeneous to assume that it was a United Houma community. Beyond residence in a geographic core area, however, the United Houma presented additional evidence of community cohesion for individuals living outside the core area. Using new data, the UHN argued that at least 75 percent of its members were closely associated with the Montegut core community. According to Verret's group, 75 percent of its members were living in the UHN parishes, were born in the core area, had primary kin still living on the bayous, or could show actual interaction with UHN members inside the core region. It remains to be seen, however, whether the BAR will accept these figures.[131]

As the statistical wrangling continues on the facts of the case, the United Houma petition certainly raises some serious theoretical questions as to the acknowledgment process. It seemed apparent that the BAR had followed a strict construction of the rules for acknowledging Indian tribes in the United Houma case. It may be that the UHN made a tactical error, if entirely logical and just, in admitting all blood relatives into its ranks. Clearly, without federal sanction, reservation lands, major tribal resources, or government powers, it would be difficult (although not impossible) for any organization to exert the kind of influence and achieve the level of participation the BAR appeared to require over such a large group. Even on reservations containing more than ten thousand individuals, certain scholars have acknowledged that functioning social units capable of group tasks and social unity are often considerably smaller than the membership of the entire tribe, while many recognized tribes have populations scattered over vast distances as well. Because of poverty and outside preemption of governmental authority, overarching political integration often fails to develop even on large federal reservations.[132]

In the Houma case, BAR researchers clearly took a skeptical stance toward the motives of the organization and its group concerns. The BIA apparently felt that the pursuit of acknowledgment, land claims, local relief work, and pride in Indian identity were not viable reasons for a tribal organization to operate and exist. But the BAR's position neglects the fact that the political and governmental activities on many reservations center upon administering federal programs and land use. As principal chief of the Cherokee Nation, Chad Smith, notes, more than 75 percent of his tribe's budget comes from the federal government.[133] The entire milieu seems to beg the question: Why would an organization exist except to pursue immediate issues of concern regardless of its motivations? And for groups without federal acknowledgment, gaining this status is a foremost priority from which other benefits would flow.

As of 2003, the United Houma Nation still waits for a final determination on its case. Despite the continuing state of legal limbo, the fight for acknowledgment has served to energize the group. The UHN continues to administer Indian Education programs in the public schools that provide limited scholarships and to hold workshops where Houma children are able to interact with Navajos, Kiowas, and other Indians. The organization also sponsors an "Elders Fest" and remains active in area powwows, including fielding a pan-Indian–inspired dance troop, the Bayou Eagles. Some United Houma members continue working to revive their ancestors' distinctive basketry, arts, and history as well. Prejudice and struggles with the oil companies remain, but the UHN has helped foster resistance to these concerns. And the United Houma Nation continues to receive ANA funding to push for acknowledgment. Chairperson Brenda Dardar says she will continue to make acknowledgment a priority for material as well as psychological reasons. "Recognition would be an admission or recognition that they did us wrong," she says.[134]

The crusade for acknowledgment has taken a toll on all Houmas while engendering strong opinions on the subject. Like many unacknowledged tribal leaders, Dardar has come to feel that the BIA process is unfair. She has grown frustrated that working for recognition has come to consume almost all her time. Although Reggie Billiot of the BCCM argues that the BAR process is slow but generally fair, most UHN members believe that the government branch is manifestly aligned against them. "They gave the impression they were going to help you—when it's really a bureaucracy to work against you getting it," Kirby Verret tells visitors. He believes that some of the BIA's continuing resistance comes from reservation tribes. "Recognized tribes don't want new groups to come in and take a piece of the pie. Even some who made it don't want new groups now."[135]

Kirby Verret particularly hates the fact the BAR will not recognize his people's traditions as to their origins. He wonders why they will not accept the proposition that people calling themselves "Houma" in 1900 logically came from that obscure tribe. Despite his protestations, his people's case seems to show that the BAR process, born in the Western legal tradition, is loath to accept oral traditions of Spanish land grants, tribal medals, and family heritage as proof of tribalism. "It is a struggle of attrition—they would like us to just go away," Verret has ultimately concluded on the process.[136]

Beyond other issues, the United Houma Nation is mired in controversies over its sheer size. Because of its numbers current chairperson Brenda Dardar genuinely believes that the BIA is biased against her organization. Helen Gindrat seconds this: "It's all politics . . . the BIA is scaring them to death with all the numbers. We're the only tribe that had to answer three different deficiency letters . . . everywhere it was nitpicking."[137] Is it correct that the size of the group is a major concern? Although it was never admitted publicly by federal officials, in 1993 the congressional budget office estimated that health and education outlays for the UHN membership alone would amount to $53.7 million per year. Beyond federal costs, numerous gaming concerns have approached the UHN as well, and Verret sees gaming as a negative issue that has complicated his group's chances for acknowledgment. All these concerns, coupled with the opposition of large oil companies, present the BAR and the UHN with confounding complications to the organization's tribal acknowledgment quest.[138]

What is clear about the UHN case is that nothing is entirely clear about the

Houma case—except the BIA's initial negative determination against them. When faced with social and descendancy questions and major consequences of a decision, the BAR can and will scrutinize every aspect of an Indian group's record. In early cases with less at stake the Branch of Acknowledgment and Research employed its burden of proof of a "reasonable likelihood" of the facts in a liberal fashion in favor of petitioning tribes. This stance acknowledged the reality that Indians, especially unacknowledged groups, were often truly a "people without history." Previous BIA researchers accepted the fact that unacknowledged Indians, living peripherally to the dominant society, may have existed unrecorded by white officials. Even though the BIA designed the acknowledgment rules in a narrow fashion to exclude "wannabe" groups with dubious claims, it also engineered the rules with flexibility to acknowledge groups with unique and varying circumstances. Yet the United Houmas believe, with some cause, that the bureau is using the subjectivity and flexibility of the process against them.

Although the history of the United Houma Nation has gaps in the record that make its case more ambiguous than that of some groups acknowledged via the FAP, modern observers may never really know the exact circumstances of the Houma ancestors' lives and origins along Bayou Terrebonne. Clearly, the current BAR team has the discretion to make judgment calls based on its reading of all the evidence. The lack of a document or letter specifically referring to the United Houmas' ancestors as a "band" under a "chief" on Bayou Terrebonne has thus far allowed the BAR to take a highly positivist stance toward their history. Although certain BIA officials and professional scholars recognized the UHN ancestors as Indians on an equal basis with many other southeastern Indian tribes, the ancestral Houmas' failure to secure acknowledgment in an earlier era continues to haunt their descendants. Even nearby recognized tribes who once supported them are now lukewarm to their aspirations.[139]

Clearly, however, the United Houma people are not among the "Johnny-come-lately" Indians that the federal regulations were intended to prevent from taking needed resources from reservation tribes. In 1999 BAR anthropologist Steve Austin remarked that the UHN case was indeed different from other petitions declined by his office. The BAR conceded that the United Houmas presented it with a "unique" and perplexing scenario. With 84 percent of its members possessing verifiable Indian ancestry and having several well-delineated Indian communities along the lower bayous, the United Houma Nation continues to remain a uniquely anomalous group, even in the annals of recognition cases. Lacking surviving Indian cultural traits such as language and religious ceremonies and copious documents of its specific tribal ancestry, the United Houma Nation does not neatly fit the model of tribalism held by the dominant society and many reservation tribes. Living in a marginal environment without substantial tribal resources, the group also may have lacked the ability to maintain political forms that BAR researchers could easily recognize under the regulations, criteria that tend to favor small, previously acknowledged tribes. The United Houma Nation thus continues to present outsiders with challenges to embedded assumptions about Indian racial identity, culture, and tribal forms.

These facts, however, do not mean that the United Houma Nation is not an Indian tribe. Yet whether it is a tribe clearly depends on who is doing the evaluating, and who has the power to decide. Historically the United Houmas have been, in a loose sense, an Indian nation or people sharing common origins, history, territory, and Indian identity. Currently, however, the federal government does not believe they have possessed a state-like, governmental organization required under the FAP rules. Because the stakes rose markedly for acknowledgment decisions in the 1990s, issues of evidence and documentation seem destined to present the UHN and similar groups with greater challenges to securing a status they believe they once held yet lost because of federal neglect and local malfeasance.

Ultimately it may be that everyone is quibbling over a name. The regulations clearly require groups to show that they descend from a named tribe that exercised sovereignty over its members since contact with Europeans, the essential basis for federal Indian status. Numerous recognized tribes, however, do not have documentary evidence demonstrating their sovereignty and political organization since historical contact with Europeans, although this data is now required of groups such as the UHN. At this point it is clear, however, that at least three, perhaps more, Indian people settled together along Bayou Terrebonne at the end of the eighteenth century. Handed down over generations, United Houma oral tradition has recounted that these people were from the Houma and other tribes. In 1907 a few older people still recalled an Indian language that certain scholars believe was Houma. They called themselves Houmas and had a tradition of having descended from that group on the Mississippi River. As of 2003 the descendants of these people wanted tribal acknowledgment, but the BIA was reluctant to grant it. Before the presidential election of 2000 there was a trend for denied groups to overcome negative BIA findings. Perhaps the United Houma Nation will do so.

SIX. FROM PLAYING INDIAN TO PLAYING SLOTS

Gaming, Tribal Recognition, and the
Tiguas of El Paso, Texas

In late 1985 Texas state comptroller Bob Bullock, who was legendary for both his tax-collecting prowess and a temper that a colleague described as "a woeful and awful thing to behold," had turned his wrath on the Tigua people in the far western corner of Texas. Bullock was directing his considerable political power and influence to stopping the Tigua and Alabama-Coushatta tribal restoration bill dead in its tracks over the issue of Indian gaming because he was worried that federal status for these groups would open the door to casino gambling in the state. The comptroller, described by Texas governor George W. Bush as "the largest Texan of our time" upon his death in 1999, vowed to pressure Texas senators to "kill" the bill if he was not appeased, and raised the battle cry against the alleged ills of Indian bingo. "If this bill passes like it's written we might as well get the highway department to put up a sign at the state line that says, 'Gangsters Welcome,'" warned Bullock at one point.[1] To the declarations that the Mafia was waiting in the wings for its chance, Tigua tribal superintendent Raymond Ramirez shot back that the comptroller's allegation of organized crime infiltration was simply a red herring. "The majority of the Indian tribes in this country have the ability to make sound and moral decisions that reflect the integrity of their communities," he said.[2] Unfortunately for the two Texas Indian communities, however, the once fairly innocuous Tigua and Alabama-Coushatta restoration bill, designed to restore federal status to the terminated Alabama-Coushatta Tribe and to provide full tribal acknowledgment to the Tigua Pueblo of Ysleta del Sur, had run afoul of the contentious debates swirling around Indian gaming.

As the following pages show, the Tiguas' battle with the state over the gaming issue was only the last in a long line of obstacles the group faced in trying to survive as an Indian community in modern America. In a larger sense, their story brings this work to the present by exposing how Indian gaming has come to complicate tribal acknowledgment decisions. Yet the Tigua people's history reveals much more about the experiences of other unacknowledged Indian communities. From its origins among the Pueblo people of New Mexico the Texas tribe's struggles as an unacknowledged band largely encapsulated the issues many nonrecognized groups have faced in the past century. In particular the Tiguas became a "state recognized tribe" and pioneered a non-BIA tribal program, a common, if rarely studied, Indian experience and status. Along the way the Texas group's lack of federal acknowledgment meant that its members had to "play Indian" to a host of audiences, most importantly to its Pueblo relatives, to prove it was a viable, ethnic community and to gain its rightful place among other acknowledged tribes. Ultimately the Tiguas' ongoing problems with Texas officials sadly speak volumes about the inherent conflicts between tribes and state governments. Although the group ultimately secured acknowledgment, this outcome was never a foregone conclusion. As revealed here, the tribe's odyssey shows that anti-tribal, assimilationist ideologies still linger in modern America, although often disguised within debates about Indian bingo.

By the time of their troubles with Bob Bullock, the Tigua Indians and the Alabama-Coushattas had operated a reservation for almost two decades under the auspices of the Texas Indian Commission. During the 1960s the tiny, unacknowledged Tigua group became something of a cause célèbre for the NCAI under Vine Deloria Jr. as a symbol of the survival of tribalism and "the modern era of Indian emergence." The Tiguas were featured prominently in Deloria's work, *Custer Died for Your Sins: An Indian Manifesto*, and the author worked to have Congress acknowledge the Tiguas as Indians. Responding in 1968, Congress passed a limited recognition bill that placed the Tiguas in a legal position much like the Lumbees of North Carolina. In essence the federal act recognized the Tiguas as Indian people, yet at the same time it denied them services provided to Indians because of their status as Indians and transferred any federal responsibility to the State of Texas.[3]

At the same time the Texas state legislature also recognized the Tiguas as a "state Indian tribe" to enable it to provide special programs for the group. As a state Indian tribe, the Tiguas became eligible for a tax-exempt state reservation as well as special state programs. Unfortunately, however, the Texas programs lagged far behind concurrent movements toward Indian self-determination and tribal sovereignty at the federal level. From the late 1960s through the 1970s the Tiguas struggled to find their voice and preserve tribal self-government in the face of often-paternalistic state commission programs. By the early 1980s, however, the state was facing a mounting budget crisis, and the once romantic and glamorous notion of having "real Indians" in Texas waned. In this light the state government was determined to get out of the "Indian business" itself, and in the early 1980s many Tiguas were not too upset by the new plan. One-time tribal governor Joe Sierra and others were growing weary of dancing and "performing" before the Texas legislators every two years to prove they still were really Indians. As the years had passed, the Tiguas tired of the state legislators forcing them to act, as Sierra said, like Indians in Buffalo Bill's Wild West Show to gain needed funding. Under the state program, however, this was the political reality the tribe faced because, as Sierra recalled, the state lawmakers "only saw an Indian" when he was wearing "feathers like a savage."[4]

Although the Texas tribe possessed an act of Congress declaring them "Tiwa Indians," like many Indian groups in the United States the small El Paso group had persisted for hundreds of years without any aid or protection from the federal government, struggling to survive in the unenviable status as an "unrecognized" tribe. The Tigua people, like many unacknowledged Indians across the United States, lacked status through no fault of their own. Over time the community remained unacknowledged largely because of historical accidents and oversights. Because the tribe never fought wars with the United States, the Tigua band lacked a treaty establishing a reservation for it, while geopolitical shifts separated the community from its Pueblo ancestors, leaving the Tiguas in the proverbial "lost" tribe status until well into the twentieth century. As was the case with other Indian peoples straddling the United States border such as the Cocopah, Rocky Boys Cree, Tohono O'odham, and Mohawk nations, an arbitrary border drawn by modern nation-states divided the Pueblo people. By the mid-nineteenth century, the Tiguas became separated jurisdictionally from the other Pueblos in New Mexico and excluded from the federal rubric.[5]

At the time of contact with Europeans the ancestors of the Tiguas of Ysleta del Sur resided primarily at a pueblo thirteen miles south of modern-day Albuquerque, New Mexico. Because the community sat on or near an island in the Rio Grande, the Spaniards called it Isleta, for "little island." The people of Isleta spoke a Southern Tiwa language, a branch of the Kiowa-Tanoan language family, and like other Pueblos the Isletans lived in compact settlements of multistory stone and adobe houses and practiced irrigated farming, supplementing their diet with wild game. Many of the Texas Tiguas continued aspects of this agricultural and hunting life well into the late nineteenth century near El Paso.[6]

Shortly after contact in the early seventeenth century Franciscans established a mission complex at Isleta, attempting to convert the Pueblos to Christianity and otherwise completely reorganize their society. Fired by millennial dreams, the Franciscans often brutally suppressed indigenous religious practices and regularly impressed the labor of their Indian subjects. Facing forced conversion, the Isletans and other Pueblo peoples accommodated the colonial powers by showing outward acceptance of Christianity while carrying their indigenous religion underground. Through a process of compartmentalization, the Pueblos maintained Native belief and rituals separately from Catholic forms. Most scholars have concluded that after a century of effort the Franciscans failed to convert the Pueblos fully, although they may have been more successful at Isleta. By the late seventeenth century most Pueblos faithfully performed the external rites of Catholicism but chose not to internalize all Catholic concepts and beliefs. Centuries later, elements of these Native beliefs survived at the Tigua community and would provide solid evidence of its indigenous heritage.[7]

More relevant to the Tiguas' later recognition efforts, however, was the fact that the Europeans also attempted to alter indigenous political organization into more formalized structures. The Spaniards established town governments at all the Pueblos by the early seventeenth century, having the people elect a *gobernadorcillo* (petty governor), *alguacil* (sheriff), *mayordomos* (ditch bosses), sacristans, *fiscales* (church wardens), and a *capitan de guerra* (war captain). In addition, the Pueblos also maintained their indigenous government. Incredibly, most of these positions and structures would survive in the Texas community. A core of traditional sociopolitical and ceremonial leaders headed by a cacique, or chief, continued to be the de facto governing group, however, selecting the civil officers and controlling Pueblo affairs.[8]

By the late seventeenth century a combination of religious repression, excessive labor demands, drought, disease, and increased raids from Apaches brought the Pueblos of colonial New Mexico to the breaking point, resulting in the Pueblo Revolt of 1680. This is where the Tiguas' modern history began. That year San Juan Pueblo leader Popé succeeded in uniting more than two dozen independent Pueblo communities in an effort to expel the Spaniards. The resulting Pueblo Revolt, considered by many scholars as one of the most successful Indian rebellions against the Spaniards in the Western Hemisphere, succeeded completely. Within weeks the rebels drove all the colonists from New Mexico. The Pueblos killed over 400 colonists and 21 of the 33 missionaries, destroying churches and all vestiges of Spanish rule in the process. Retreating southward from Santa Fe, over 2,000 Spaniards and Indian slaves and allies initially took refuge at Isleta, only to flee again to El Paso. Although many Isletans escaped to nearby settlements, it is clear that the core of Isleta and several Piro Pueblos did not take part in the rebellion. Although the reasons are lost to history, scholars speculate that Isleta Pueblo may have hesitated to join the rebels until it was too late, may have been sympathetic to the Spaniards, or may have feared retaliation from the rebels for its initial reluctance. Whatever the reasons for their lack of participation, it is clear that Spanish refugees took over 300 Tiwa, Piro, and Tompiro people to the El Paso area in their flight.

The following year New Mexico governor Antonio de Otermín attempted to reconquer the Pueblos. Although the expedition failed, on their journey north the Spaniards overtook the reoccupied Isleta Pueblo (one of the southernmost Pueblo settlements), ultimately taking an additional 400 Isletan captives back to El Paso del Norte. By 1682 the Franciscans had reestablished three new pueblos south of modern-day El Paso: Senecu, Socorro, and Ysleta, christening them with their previous names and the designation *del sur*, meaning "of the south." Over time the Tiguas of Ysleta del Sur maintained the older Spanish spellings for both their name and village. In contrast the people of Isleta in New Mexico later adopted "Tiwa" for Tigua and "Isleta" for Ysleta.[9]

From the beginning, Governor Diego de Vargas planned to return the Pueblos upon his reconquest of New Mexico. The Tiguas, Piros, and Tompiros never relocated to New Mexico after the Reconquista in 1693, however, likely fearing retaliation from the northern Pueblos who viewed them as traitors. During the next century the Pueblo immigrants appear to have prospered in the El Paso area. Under Franciscan tutelage the Tiguas reestablished the Isleta mission, dedicating it to San Antonio de Padua. They reportedly received a land grant from the Spanish Crown in 1751 and reestablished their ceremonial and political life around the mission church at Ysleta del Sur. During the Spanish and later Mexican periods the Tiguas appear to have lost contact with their Isleta relatives as their histories began to diverge considerably.[10]

Beginning in the nineteenth century the Texas Tiguas' lives became entangled in the intrigues of territorial expansion. In terms of federal recognition it seemed the group was always in the wrong place at the wrong time throughout much of its history. Although there is evidence that the Spanish Crown granted the Tigua community approximately thirty-six square miles of rich farmland surrounding Ysleta Mission in 1751, this act did not ultimately result in United States recognition as it did for the New Mexico Pueblos. After Texas independence from Mexico in 1836 the Tiguas' land lay in disputed territory between the two nations. As the group peacefully farmed its valley plots, Texas became a state in 1845; through negotiations it entered the Union retaining all its public lands like the original thirteen colonies, a fact unique among western states. As in the original thirteen states, the lack of a federal presence had severe consequences for the area's Indians. Although Congress had exclusive jurisdiction over Indian affairs under the Constitution, the federal government could not establish reservations for Indians in Texas from public domain as it did in other areas of the American West. In the 1850s federal troops removed the vast majority of the state's indigenous peoples. Thereafter, as in most eastern states, no federal Indian reservations existed in the state of Texas. Following these removals, only the Alabamas and Coushattas remained on a small state reservation in the eastern part of the state while the Tiguas clung to their lands in the far western fringe of the territory—ironically, neither was native to the state.[11]

After the U.S. victory in the Mexican-American War in 1848 much of the American West passed to the United States, including the disputed El Paso region. Although Texas was already a state by this time, in 1850 Congress passed an Organic Act as part of the Compromise of 1850, settling the Texas boundary at its present borders; El Paso became part of Texas, unfortunately leaving the Tiguas separated jurisdictionally from the other Pueblos who were living in the newly created New Mexico Territory. Even so, in 1849 the federal government had inventoried the El Paso Pueblos and recommended establishing an Indian agent and federal jurisdiction for the groups. Regrettably for the southern Pueblos, the Organic Act of 1850 intervened, and the groups fell under Texas jurisdiction. It was not until the Civil War that President Abraham Lincoln confirmed the New Mexico Pueblos' sovereignty and land claims. Ultimately Isleta Pueblo in New Mexico grew relatively prosperous, retaining 211,000 acres for its 3,401 members. In another historical twist of fate, however, during the Civil War the Tiguas were in Texas, a part of the Confederacy, and thus were omitted from consideration. Because of its location, the Tigua tribe thus remained unacknowledged after the Civil War.[12]

Unlike other Texas tribes, during the course of the nineteenth century the Tiguas managed to avoid removal by helping defend El Paso against Apache and Comanche attacks while peacefully farming their lands. Although they avoided expulsion, the Tiguas gradually lost their lands. By the end of the century land speculators and corrupt Texas legislators apparently acquired and sold the vast majority of Tigua farms. Because they lacked federal status and protections, the Tiguas became a landless people, working as laborers on farms that they once had owned while a growing population of Mexican Americans and Anglos gradually surrounded them.[13]

Despite the change of circumstances, the Tiguas continued their ceremonies and traditions carried with them from Isleta centuries earlier. During this period the Tiguas maintained their traditional alliance with the larger Mexican population by intermarrying and helping to defend the area. To this end, the United States Army hired several Tigua men to serve as Indian scouts against the Apaches, actions that explicitly recognized the indigenous status of the group. In the late nineteenth century the Indian Service also acknowledged some trust responsibility for the Tiguas, sending several children to the Albuquerque Indian School.[14] Decades later the group's lawyers discovered census data that confirmed that its members continued to identify as Indians throughout the nineteenth century while local newspapers routinely reported on the group's tribal elections and primary religious ceremony on St. Anthony's Day.[15]

By the turn of the century the Tiguas and other El Paso Pueblos also attracted the attention of pioneer ethnologists then fanning out across the country to salvage bits of Indian culture that they believed were vanishing rapidly. Since the late nineteenth century members of the nascent field of American anthropology had often heard rumors that descendents of the Pueblos lived near El Paso. Along with U.S. Army chronicler J. Bourke, ethnologists Ten Kate, A. F. Bandelier, James Moody, and, most importantly, Jesse Walter Fewkes of the Smithsonian Institution ultimately followed these leads to the El Paso area. The scholars were generally disappointed with what they saw at Ysleta, however. The early anthropologists studied the Tiguas only briefly, primarily to document their apparent advanced stage of assimilation or "Mexicanization," a process that they believed was the future of all area Indians. "One fact seems certain," reported Bandelier at the time, "the Indian, as an Indian, must disappear; he may keep his language and traditions, but his social organization and his creed are out of place in the march of civilization, and they must perish."[16] Although Bandelier and the others documented Indian political and social survivals, by declaring that the El Paso Indians were "fast disappearing as . . . tribe[s]," their works contributed to the misperception that the Tiguas had become "extinct" after the turn of the century. The salvage ethnologists, however, did produce valuable work; their studies unintentionally provided key evidence of tribal existence that the Tiguas presented to policymakers in later decades.[17]

Most important to the Tiguas' later acknowledgment efforts was the work of Jesse Walter Fewkes. Best known for his subsequent excavations of Mesa

Verde in Colorado, Fewkes visited the Tiguas in 1901 as part of a trip to study the New Mexico Pueblos. In references to the ostensibly more "pure" New Mexico Pueblo culture, Fewkes wrote that the Tiguas had "practically become Mexicanized," yet he went on to provide the most complete ethnographic account of the Tigua culture yet written. As Fewkes found them, the Tiguas had in fact become more Hispanicized than the New Mexico Pueblos, who themselves varied considerably in their level of acculturation. Living on the border surrounded by Mexican society and lacking a federal reservation, the Ysleta del Sur community clearly had adopted certain cultural practices from the Hispanics. Most spoke Spanish, dressed in Mexican-style clothing, and lived in adobe dwellings almost indistinguishable from the surrounding society. Overall, the Tiguas' isolation from the other New Mexico Pueblos largely had closed off cross-cultural contact between the groups that may have staved off Mexican influence.

Despite their historical situation at the turn of the century, Fewkes found the Tiguas still living in El Barrio de los Indios (Indian quarter) near the Ysleta Mission, calling their community by a Tiwa name, Chiawipia. The Tiguas still considered St. Anthony their patron saint, although years earlier Catholic priests had rededicated the Ysleta church to another saint. Fewkes recorded the names of about twenty-five individuals who spoke Tiwa, noting that many more could understand, but not speak, the language. The Tiguas still faithfully practiced religious ceremonials containing elements of both indigenous and Catholic practices and beliefs. On various saints' days, group members performed ceremonial dances, or bailes, in front of the church; the feast day celebration of St. Anthony was the most important, although the Indians also celebrated the feast days of St. John, St. Andrew, and St. James. Although tied to Catholic saints' days, the Indians performed dances that mixed elements of indigenous spirituality with the Catholic rituals. Departing from traditional Catholic observances, the Tiguas performed a mask dance referred to by the Tiwa name newafura, or baile de tortuga (for the turtle shell rattles used), a rattle dance (Shiafuara), and the "red pigment dance," among several others. Tiguas also remembered the Kufura, or scalp dance, though after the cessation of warfare they ceased to perform the dance for obvious reasons. In the course of many of these bailes, Tiguas wore face paint and buffalo skin masks of red and yellow and used the ancient tribal drum and gourd rattles to maintain a beat. Upon seeing them, Fewkes noted the direct similarities between the Tigua cultural forms and those of the New Mexico Pueblos.

The ethnologist also found signs that the Ysletans maintained a matrilineal descent system and myths about their origins in a Shipapu, or ancestral opening of the earth in a lake to the north, that were similar to the traditions of some of the New Mexico Pueblos. Apart from the distinctive ceremonials and speech, however, Fewkes reported that the Tiguas' clothing, physical appearance, and dwellings were indistinguishable from their Mexican American neighbors. The ethnologist reported that by the end of the nineteenth century the nearby Piro settlement of Socorro had largely ceased to exist as a tribal organization while the Piros of Senecu still maintained a tribal structure and dances. As Mooney had noted earlier, it seemed that the various Indian groups of the area—Piros, Sumas, Mansos, and Tiguas—had widely intermarried and amalgamated into the Tigua community at Ysleta. After 1910 the Mexican Revolution apparently disrupted the communities on the Mexican side to such an extent that the refugees fled to the United States, with many joining the Tiguas.[18]

For the Tiguas' subsequent efforts to secure tribal acknowledgment, however, the most significant aspect of Fewkes's work was the fact that he recorded the group's governmental or tribal structure. Although currently there is little consensus on what constitutes a "tribe," tribal acknowledgment has long been predicated on the federal government recognizing Indians as a political entity or "tribe"—not as individuals of Indian descent. In essence United States Indian law and Indian status derive from the notion of tribes as political units retaining elements of sovereignty. Incredibly, despite land loss and assimilation pressures, when Fewkes found the Tiguas they still maintained a strong tribal political organization that closely resembled the governments of the New Mexico Pueblos.

Central to the group's later efforts, Fewkes published a formal document that the Tiguas had drawn up and notarized in 1895, setting forth a "compact" of government. The Compact of 1895 detailed Tigua rules and regulations while including signatures of tribal members who agreed to abide by punishments and fines imposed by the "native authorities." A second document set forth the duties of the tribal offices of cacique, lieutenant-cacique, governor, lieutenant-governor, war captain, and subordinate captains. In 1901 Fewkes wrote that the cacique was José Tolino Piarote, who served for life as Tigua chief and spiritual leader. Mariano Manero served as governor, as well as "justice of the peace," and represented the Tiguas in secular matters and outside contacts. Significantly, Manero carried a baton or staff of office just like the governors of the New Mexican Pueblos. War captain Tomal Graneo (Granillo) and his assistants preserved order at the public dances and regulated hunts. As in other pueblos, only males chose tribal officials; women were excluded from formal political participation. Overall, from Fewkes's work it appeared, incredibly, that the Tiguas had maintained the dual form of government organization established in the seventeenth century under Spanish rule—and had it notarized. Few unacknowledged tribes—or recognized tribes, for that matter—likely ever had or developed such formalized political organization without manipulation by federal officials.[19]

Despite dire predictions that the Tigua were a vanishing breed, the tribal organization continued throughout the early twentieth century, although the last Tiwa speakers appear to have died in the 1930s. Although Fewkes had called for further studies of the Tiguas "at once, for it will soon be too late," these studies never materialized, and the scholarly world assumed the Tiguas had become extinct—a fact the Tiguas apparently did not notice. For many unacknowledged Indian groups that lacked a federal land base and trust status, the possibility of "tribal extinction" was a constant possibility, however. Even recognized tribes faced assimilation policies such as the Dawes Severalty Act that sought to destroy them, while forces of industrialization and modernization impinged on Indians from all sides. Although ostensibly under federal protection, the New Mexico Pueblos fended off laws such as the federal Code of Religious Offenses and boarding schools that sought to eradicate their cultures. For recognized and nonrecognized tribes alike, the assimilation trend would not wane until the Great Depression and John Collier's Indian Reorganization Act of 1934, a tribal plan that was generally modeled on the New Mexico Pueblos.[20]

As was noted with the Pascua Yaquis, Houmas, and Timbisha Shoshones, many unacknowledged Indian groups sought to organize under the Indian Reorganization Act. There is no evidence, however, that the Tiguas ever attempted to secure federal aid during this period. Although they were somewhat obscure by this time, in 1936 the Tiguas did take part in the Texas Centennial Celebration opening the National Folk Festival in Dallas. By this late date the once-loathed Texas Indians had been safely vanquished, and the dominant culture was ready to resurrect the Tiguas and other Indian peoples. Incorporating their Indianness into the great pageant of state history, one tribal patrón noted proudly that the Tiguas had been "a docile, exemplary tribe" that was so manly that there was "no record of the Tigua man of the house donning an apron to do the dishes."[21] Having suddenly found their place in the sun, the Tiguas dressed up, decorated a bus with the banner "Tigua Indians," and made President Franklin D. Roosevelt "honorary cacique" and Eleanor Roosevelt "honorary squaw."

Through the Great Depression, World War II, and the "termination era" that followed, the Tiguas maintained their identity, faithfully performing ceremonials that were regularly noted by the El Paso press. Group members clung to their culture for its intrinsic value despite racism and pressures to assimilate. During these decades the surrounding Mexican American and Anglo cultures were ambivalent about the Tiguas. In the 1940s and 1950s mainstream ideology continued to predict that small Indian groups such as the Tiguas would join the great American "melting pot." Yet at the same time non-Indians also exalted Indianness—at least in its colorful and mythic forms. During this period individuals such as Pueblo scholar Edward P. Dozier and Tigua leader Joe Sierra noted that Anglo-American culture provided an incentive structure for the maintenance of an Indian identity, with whites attending the Pueblos' ceremonies and showing an ongoing interest in their colorful performances. As Dozier detailed in New Mexico, Anglo-Americans also tended to place Indians in a higher social status than the Mexican American population. During the 1950s the Pueblos' strong commitment to their culture and the dominant society's interest in Indians each served to encourage the retention of ethnic identity at a time when policymakers were promoting cultural and economic assimilation through the "termination" policy.[22]

Despite public interest in the group, by the late 1950s and early 1960s the independent Tiguas faced considerable threats to their continuing existence. Like the nearby Pascua Yaquis, the greater danger arose from the rapid urbanization of the Sunbelt. The imminent threat came from the City of El Paso's decision to annex Ysleta, raising taxes to ten times their previous levels. The annexation seriously imperiled the Tiguas' dwindled community land base near the Ysleta Mission because the majority of Tiguas lived in poverty and could scarcely afford the previous taxes, much less the raised rates.[23] Having survived in relative obscurity with no outside aid for centuries, the steadily declining Tigua core now faced the painful realization that it might need outside assistance to continue as a people.

Like the Pascua Yaquis discovered in Arizona at the same time, the Tiguas found a favorable social and political climate for their efforts to gain outside relief. Buoyed by an era of unprecedented prosperity, Americans heeded the call of Presidents John F. Kennedy and Lyndon Johnson that the country should help minorities and the poor who were excluded from full participation in American life. Most liberals as well as conservatives, however, also had joined in the postwar call to "free" the Indians from the BIA and their isolated reservation life in order to allow them to compete in the mainstream. In the early 1960s many policymakers still believed that the termination of the federal relationship with Indian tribes was a worthy goal. Even so, in 1961 the mayor of El Paso wrote the BIA hoping to acquire aid for the small Indian group. Because many bureaucrats still believed in termination, the BIA denied any obligation to the Tiguas. Deflecting responsibility, the bureau articulated its position that, with the exception of the Alabama-Coushattas, the federal government had not assumed responsibility for any Texas tribes.[24] In light of the BIA's stance, the Tiguas seemed destined to face urban encroachment alone.

Although the Tiguas historically were unrecognized, they had maintained a strong ethnic identity and community in the face of continual economic and cultural pressures to assimilate. In the first years of the 1960s a small core of Indians had persisted in the midst of urban sprawl, coalesced around the ancient tribal political organization in the Barrio de los Indios. Except on saints' days, however, few outside visitors could distinguish the Tiguas from the surrounding Mexican Americans, whom the Tiguas called *vecinos*, or neighbors. The Tiguas had no trouble distinguishing between themselves and the *vecinos*, however, and the Mexican Americans had no trouble distinguishing either. Although Tiguas spoke Spanish, the dominant language of the surrounding area, and had lost all but perhaps a hundred Tiwa words and the majority of Indian arts and material culture, they still possessed a strong sense of themselves as Tiguas.[25]

Until the 1960s the Tiguas maintained their community by clearly delineating its membership, although the boundaries of the ethnic enclave were fluid and always changing. For membership the Tiguas recognized ancestry and blood quantum to some degree but placed more emphasis on ceremonial participation. Nicholas Houser, an anthropology student who studied the group in 1966, determined that there were approximately 166 persons in thirty-two households in the Tigua community. Of these, a "core" group of approximately twenty families living near the Ysleta church and the Tigua ceremonial center called the *tuhla* (kiva) was actively involved in all ceremonial affairs. Showing the group's adaptability over time, the *tuhla* eventually had relocated to the rear bedroom of War Captain Trinidad Granillo's tiny adobe home. Overall, this core group was less integrated into mainstream culture, was more likely to be unemployed and poor, and had chosen to emphasize a Tigua identity over others or, in the alternative, was unable to pass as Mexican in the surrounding city. There were ten to fifteen additional families who had Indian ancestry and identified themselves as Tiguas but were inactive in the community. These peripheral Tiguas had either left the area for steady employment, had married

Mexican Americans, or had moved from the barrio because of the poor living conditions. Over time many other Tigua, Piro, Manso, and Suma Indians had assimilated into the larger Hispanic population.[26]

Around the old mission complex, however, Tigua elders maintained group norms that enhanced Indian community and identity. To be Tigua, individuals had to respect the power of an ancient drum (tombe) kept by Trinidad Granillo and used in Tigua ceremonies. Tiguas believed that the drum had spiritual powers—anyone who abused it would incur not only the wrath of the community but also potentially would be struck by lightning. Members also had to show respect for St. Anthony, the group's patron saint, whom the Tiguas believed protected them in times of sickness and health. It was imperative that Tiguas participate in the St. Anthony's Day ceremonies and other saints' day celebrations. Young members learned Tigua ritual chants and dances and performed them during the various ceremonies. The Tiguas also incorporated the fictive kinship system of compadrazgo (godparents) that served to integrate individual families into the larger community. Overall, although the community recognized blood and ancestry, it was said that one drop of Tigua blood canceled out any other admixture. "Tigua blood is stronger than Mexican blood," Nicholas Houser was told. Although the core families frowned upon marriages with outsiders, they did occur. Outsiders who married into the community were welcomed as members yet could not assume office or call themselves Tigua. The families considered children of these unions full members of the community nonetheless. According to Tigua leader Ray Apodaca, the Tiguas still maintained traditional elements of matrilineal organization, with women owning the houses and the children being named by their mother's relatives and trained by their maternal aunts and uncles.[27]

Because both the dominant Hispanic and Anglo-American cultures surrounded the group, being Tigua was both a conscious choice and a racial status imposed by pressures from outside. Having deep roots in New Mexico and the El Paso region, race consciousness was pervasive in Hispanic society. Since the colonial period people of Spanish descent had maintained a fictive racial identity as "pure" Spanish, although people in the region had long intermingled. Because Mexican society largely stigmatized being Indian, people of multiple racial descent, mestizos, often constructed their racial identity as European, denying any Indian ancestry whatsoever. In Ysleta many Hispanics considered the Tiguas inferior to themselves. When conducting a survey of Tiguas in 1966, Nicholas Houser recalled that one Tigua woman, upon being asked if she was Indian, exclaimed, "I'm Castilian!" and slammed the door in his face. [28]

Because of centuries of miscegenation, racial identity in many Hispanic areas such as El Paso was both a matter of personal identification and stigmatization, as the majority of individuals in the area were mestizos. Tigua Miguel Pedraza recalled the often heart-wrenching experiences his people faced trying to maintain an Indian identity in Ysleta instead of blending into the larger Latino population. "When I was a kid, the white kids and the little Mexicans would grab me by the hair, call me names, and sometimes give me a good beating," he said. To avoid trouble, Pedraza asked his father to cut his hair, only to experience the flip side of society's expectations of "Indianness." While marching in a 4th of July parade in full Tigua dress Pedraza recalled a Mexican boy seeing his short hair and shouting, "Say, you're not an Indian!" [29] Experiencing such personal identity issues, Tiguas had long faced the wrenching decision whether to move away, marry non-Indians, or otherwise deny their heritage and "pass" as Mexican American in the dominant culture. Indeed Vicente Ordoñez, a Mexican American resident of Ysleta, recalled that most Hispanics felt stigmatized by the dominant culture yet could at least feel they were "above" the local Indians. As a boy, Tigua Joe Sierra recalled being called a "dirty Indian" and facing racism, although he felt the stigma derived mostly from the group's poverty. In return the Tiguas maintained an animosity toward Mexicans and Mexican Americans and expressed feelings of superiority over Hispanics. Although Latinos often ridiculed the Tiguas' dancing and ceremonies, "that didn't stop us from having our ceremonies!" Sierra recalled with pride. [30] Overall, Apodaca remembered that the Indians and Hispanics of Ysleta, although living in close proximity, lived very separate social lives. The two may have been phenotypically indiscernible, yet every Tigua and Mexican American "knew" who was Tigua in Ysleta based largely on family lines. [31]

Along with family and racial lines, a major factor keeping the community together was the colonial government structure. In the mid-1960s José Granillo was cacique, and like earlier chiefs, he saw himself as a "father" of his people. Granillo presided over religious matters in the community and had considerable knowledge of herbal medicine. Although Tigua caciques once held power over irrigation allocations, this function disappeared as the group lost farmlands. In the early 1960s Trinidad Granillo was war capitan, an office that once had been central in matters of defense against the Apaches but had been reduced to keeping order at the fiestas and protecting the drum and ritual paraphernalia in the *tuhla* in his home. The Tiguas continued to elect officials annually, although the cacique served for life. In 1966 Salvador Granillo was assistant cacique, while Antonio Silvas, Rodolfo Silvas, Santiago Granillo, and Concepción Granillo served as assistant captains.[32]

Despite these unifying attributes, in the early 1960s the group faced imminent tax foreclosure and other serious social and economic problems. Although Tigua elder Miguel Pedraza could remember when his family owned abundant farmland in Ysleta, by this period the members of the group had been divested of all but approximately three acres. As a result, most Tiguas were migrant farm workers on area cotton and produce farms, yet few Tiguas maintained regular employment. Out of economic necessity most Indian children dropped out of school to work, and the fact that most teachers had low expectations for the children did little to discourage the trend. Because of their poverty, the majority of Tiguas subsisted on a diet of beans and tortillas. Few had regular medical attention, while many continued to rely on medicinal *yerbas* (herbs), the traditional folk medicine practiced by Cacique Granillo. Women worked in the fields and also ran the homes, cooking all meals on wood-burning stoves and doing washing by hand. Tigua women also served as midwives and prepared the dead for burial. Most families lived in one- or two-room adobe homes that lacked electricity, their dirt floors and outhouses serving as testaments to the group's poverty. In fact, the majority of homes were so small that all family members slept in one room on the floor using blankets and burlap sacks for bedding.[33]

In spite of their poverty, the Tiguas' maintained a rich social life revolving around the old mission church at Ysleta. From cradle to grave, Tiguas were christened, baptized, married, and interred by Roman Catholic priests at the church. Despite the considerable economic hardships, the community faithfully contributed substantial time and expense to staging the saint day fiestas at the church, particularly the central festival of St. Anthony on June 13th. Like many Native American groups, the Tiguas felt spiritually tied to the Ysleta mission and cemetery, considering it sacred ground because their ancestors were laid to rest there. By the early 1960s, however, the cemetery was full, a highly distressful situation because few could afford the cost of burying their dead in a new cemetery. At this time it seemed outside crises would serve the death knell of the group.[34]

Lacking federal aid provided to recognized Indian tribes and generally unwilling to ask for public assistance, Tigua elders looked for other ways out of their crisis in the early 1960s. Like the Pascua Yaquis, urban encroachment and tax foreclosures ultimately prompted the Tiguas to seek federal support. In order to secure assistance the Tiguas, like many unacknowledged Indians, would have to "play Indian" to prove they were an authentic and worthy indigenous group. Although scholars Rayna Green and Philip Deloria have detailed how Europeans and Anglo-Americans have dressed up and "played Indian" since the colonial era, it is less known that unacknowledged Indians often have to "play Indian" to gain access to valuable state and federal resources.[35] For unacknowledged tribes, their "Indianness" is not a given and must be constructed to meet the expectations of the dominant culture.

On 4 July 1965 local newspaper writer Jack Salem approached a young attorney, Tom Diamond, hoping he would help the Tiguas with their tax problems. Diamond, like many Anglos, seriously doubted there were "really Indians" in El Paso, but he agreed to check into the situation. At the time he was the El Paso Democratic Party chairman and had worked on the campaigns of John F. Kennedy and Lyndon Johnson, where he developed a strong belief that society should help minorities left out of the "American Dream." Even so Diamond still was skeptical that the Tiguas were really Indians, believing that if they were truly Pueblos the federal government would be taking care of them. At the same time, a city tax collector of partial Tigua heritage, Alex Candelaria, also was looking into the Tiguas' tax problems. Candelaria, a member of a prominent Ysleta family that had served as the group's informal *patrones* since the nineteenth century, took an active interest in helping the group. Through his godchild, Tigua Pablo Silvas, Candelaria arranged a meeting between Diamond and Cacique José Granillo, tribal elder Miguel Pedraza, and Trinidad Granillo, the Tigua war captain.

After hearing countless stories of past chicanery and exploitation, the Tigua leaders were skeptical about Diamond and avoided meeting him, wary that he was just one more in a long line of people trying to take advantage of the group. With Candelaria's help, however, the Tigua leaders eventually met with Diamond. At these first tentative meetings the Granillos showed the attorney their grandfather's discharge papers from the U.S. Calvary, sang a few of their Indian language chants, and showed him poll-tax receipts marked with the phrase "Exempt-Indian." Less skeptical now of their Indianness, Diamond began to research the Tiguas' ancestry and origins. When Diamond heard their oral tradition that the tribe originated way to the north, he, Candelaria, and others made a trip to Isleta Pueblo, where they met the pueblo governor, Andy Abieta, who had become well known for ejecting a priest from the pueblo in 1965. Even after the long separation, when asked about the origin story of the Ysletans, Abieta said, "Yes, those are our people down there. The last time I visited them was in World War II when I was stationed at Fort Bliss." Despite the governor's easy acceptance, other Isletans questioned whether the Tiguas were still Indian and considered them traitors or witches (*brujos*) for their role in the Pueblo Revolt.[36]

At the delegation's request Abieta came down to El Paso in November of 1965. At an initial meeting the Tigua leaders were reluctant to reveal their culture and claimed that they did not know the Tiwa language or dances. War Captain Trinidad Granillo even ordered Abieta and the rest of Diamond's party off his property. At Miguel Pedraza's insistence, however, Granillo reluctantly invited the party into the Tiguas' sacred *tuhla* in the back room of his home. Although it was awkward at first, once Abieta began beating the moon-decorated Tigua drum and chanting in the Tiwa language, Pedraza and the others joined right in and began dancing. Back in front of the war captain's house after this encounter, Pedraza admitted to the Isleta governor that he often denied being Indian because people laughed at him. The two embraced and openly wept.[37]

After this meeting Tigua leaders became aware of the Indian Claims Commission and hired Diamond as their tribal attorney and Candelaria as their agent in 1966 to help them secure federal aid and pursue a land claim. From the start Diamond began uncovering evidence that the Tiguas had once possessed a Spanish land grant that unscrupulous state and local politicians had gradually usurped during the nineteenth century. Diamond now realized that the Tiguas had a strong land claim case that would gain the attention of policymakers. Presented with Diamond's evidence, the Tiguas held a junta at Trinidad Granillo's house and voted to pursue a land claim case. Although the claim held financial potential, the Tiguas pursued the action primarily to provide leverage to work a recognition deal with the state and federal governments. This was a wise move, as other groups' experiences with the Indian Claims Commission demonstrated that any monetary gains would be long in coming. With evidence in hand, Diamond began working with Representative Richard White (D-Texas) to secure some form of justice for the Tiguas. In 1966 the Tiguas approached Bernard Fontana, an anthropologist at the Arizona State Museum of the University of Arizona, asking him to document their culture and tribal status as well.[38]

Fontana, a well-respected ethnologist, had worked with a related group of Tiguas in Tortugas, New Mexico, and encouraged Diamond to collect as much oral history and surviving language and genealogical data as possible, saying, "if these groups have survived in any recognizable manner, it will be more startling than the saga of the Mohawk Indian high steel workers who have kept [an] intact community in the heart of Brooklyn." Fontana found the Tiguas startling because several anthropologists in New Mexico had told him that the group was extinct. After hearing of the Ysleta Tiguas, Fontana remarked that he was "frankly astounded" that Tiguas continued to exist: "this is exciting anthropological news, to put it mildly."[39] Like many action-oriented anthropologists of the 1960s, the ethnologist clearly wanted to help Native Americans with their current concerns, and he enthusiastically entered into an informal partnership with the Tiguas to help them document their culture. In a greater sense Fontana and other anthropologists saw the Tiguas as an untapped "mine" of ethnological data that could demonstrate Indian ethnic persistence in urban environments. The Arizona scholar soon went to Ysleta, where he met with Miguel Pedraza, Salvador Granillo, Pablo Silvas, and other Tiguas. Here he first observed the group's political structures and witnessed the Tigua dances and chants. Fontana inventoried the Indians' ceremonial articles, including a tribal drum, feathered prayer sticks, bows and arrows, and kachina masks. After several visits Fontana remarked, "the fact that these Indians have survived as well as they have is indeed a minor miracle. And there can be no mistake they are Indians."[40] With the Tiguas' blessings, Fontana and Diamond secured an OEO grant in 1966, sending University of Arizona anthropology student Nicholas Houser to conduct a thorough ethnographic study that summer.[41]

At this time pan-Indian groups such as the NCAI, the National Indian Youth Council, and nascent Red Power activists made new demands on the federal government. In 1966, by good fortune, the NCAI Board of Directors was meeting in El Paso. Prior to the conference Diamond had contacted NCAI president Wendell Chino, a Mescalero Apache, and arranged a meeting between the Tiguas and the board. Upon seeing the eight Tiguas gathered for the occasion, Chino asked them to sing some of their chants for him. Chino's wife was a Pueblo, and he soon recognized one of the chants and the Tigua scalp dance, traditionally performed after battles between the Pueblos and Apaches. After the performance the NCAI leaders were convinced that the Tiguas were Indian and accepted the people into their organization, agreeing to help them secure federal status and provide funding.[42]

The fact that this tiny Indian group had survived was startling and gratifying to the Indian leaders. Executive Director Vine Deloria Jr., a Standing Rock Sioux, embraced the Tiguas, seeing their existence as a symbol of the survival of tribalism in the modern world. In his groundbreaking book, *Custer Died for Your Sins: An Indian Manifesto*, Deloria declared "the modern era of Indian emergence had begun" with this meeting with the Tiguas in El Paso. As he stated, the "discovery of the Tiguas rocked Indian people in several respects. Indians had been brainwashed into accepting the demise of their tribe as God's natural plan for Indians. Yet the Tiguas plainly demonstrated that Indian tribal society had the strength and internal unity to maintain itself within an alien culture."[43] Working for the group, Deloria and the NCAI believed that securing acknowledgment for the Tiguas would be symbolic of a change in federal emphasis and set out to contact as many unacknowledged groups in the eastern United States as possible. As NCAI officer Oswald George, a Coeur D'Alene from Oregon, put it, "It is gratifying at this time [to see the Tiguas about to be recognized], especially when the Colville Tribe of the state of Washington is in the process of being terminated—a reversal of this trend does give the Indian people of this nation some hope that there are people in our government that do care."[44] Although they became symbols, the Tigua elders did not consider themselves "Indian activists" in any way and especially rejected Red Power tactics that they considered "radicalism" and against the "Pueblo way."[45]

Realizing the broad public support for civil rights and armed with evidence of land grants, the Tiguas contacted the BIA through their attorney Tom Diamond. At this time the bureau had no clear policy on recognizing Indian tribes. Although the Kennedy and Johnson administrations started questioning the termination ideology, there was still much intransigence toward acknowledging additional Indian groups in the 1960s. Facing initial BIA skepticism, Diamond enthusiastically trotted out evidence that the Tiguas had attended the Albuquerque Indian School, had served as Pueblo Indian scouts, and had been inventoried in 1849–50 by the U.S. Indian agent. Faced with this evidence, the BIA nevertheless denied having any trust responsibility, reiterating that the federal government never possessed public domain in Texas and had never had dealings with the Tiguas. BIA officials told Diamond that dishonorable land dealings, if they had in fact occurred, had been by the State of Texas and, if proven, would place trust responsibility for the group with Texas. The bureau suggested that the Tiguas avail themselves of local, state, and Great Society programs for citizens at large. Overall, Diamond recalled that the BIA "fought us like Hell" at every turn. Faced with this position, a few parties batted around the idea of having the Tiguas relocate to Isleta, New Mexico, a "solution" clearly not acceptable to the group.[46] Ultimately, the Tiguas hoped Congressman Richard White and Governor John Connally could end the impasse.

Responding in 1966, White's office drew up legislation to recognize the Tiguas by designating them the Tiwa Indians of Ysleta del Sur, a name later changed to Tigua to differentiate them from the Isleta Tiwas. Working through Diamond's Democratic Party connections, the Texas group secured the assistance of liberal Democratic senator Ralph Yarbrough, who agreed to submit a bill to the Senate. Knowing the BIA's position, White advised that the Indian Bureau would oppose any bill that established trust responsibility for the federal government and suggested the state could help the Tiguas. The State of Texas had a long relationship with the Alabama-Coushattas and had established the Texas Commission for Indian Affairs to provide assistance to the group after Congress "terminated" the tribe in 1954. The Tiguas' attorney thus used the threat of a lawsuit to prod either the state or the federal government to accept responsibility.[47]

After seeing the evidence, members of the Texas state government agreed to assume responsibility for the group. However, Attorney General Crawford Martin and his assistant, Alan Minter, believed that the Texas Constitution prohibited the state from providing aid to individual groups, especially Indians whom they believed were the responsibility of the federal government. Martin suggested the Tiguas secure federal and state legislation acknowledging them as Indians that specifically transferred federal jurisdiction to the state. At this time Indian leaders such as Georgeann Robinson, an Osage and vice president of the NCAI, agreed that Texas had an effective program for the Alabama-Coushattas, while tribal adviser Bernard Fontana cautioned the Tiguas to avoid dependence on the often-paternalistic BIA. After weighing their own feelings and outside advice, the Tigua Council agreed to pursue the transfer of any potential federal obligation to the state and set out to prove to state and federal legislators that they were "authentic Indians."[48]

Armed with additional legal and anthropological evidence collected by Diamond, Houser, and Fontana, the Tiguas went to Austin in April 1967 to prove their identity. To this end Diamond assembled a panel of experts, including NCAI executive Georgeann Robinson and Isleta governor Andy Abieta, to present Indian validation, as well as Nicholas Houser and Bernard Fontana to present scholarly reports. In addition to the experts, Tigua leaders José Granillo, Miguel Pedraza, Trinidad Granillo, and others came ready to "play" Indian for the legislators, bringing with them Indian foods and Indian corn—plucked from Diamond's garden—while donning headbands, feathers, and ochre paint. At the hearing the Tiguas sang their songs to the rhythm of the Tigua drum and gourd rattles. As Fontana recalled, "neither Houser nor I had to say very much because Andy Abieta, Governor of Isleta Pueblo, stole the show." As the Tiguas danced, Abieta thumbed through pages of a report by Elsie Clews Parsons containing watercolor drawings of Isleta ceremonies. Pointing to specific watercolors, Abieta told the legislators that these were indeed the same ceremonies his people performed at Isleta, New Mexico. As Fontana noted, "What further proof of the Ysleta's ancestry could be needed? Anything Houser and I had to say was simply gilding the lily."[49] The Tiguas' performance, coupled with Abieta's and the NCAI's confirmation of their Indianness, had clearly met the expectations of the Texas legislators as to the group's "authenticity." The Tiguas also possessed visible Indian ancestry that met the racial expectations of the dominant culture. The bill sailed through the Texas legislature. Reflecting the mood of the time, Fontana recalled both liberals and conservatives leaving the hearing saying, "By God! Isn't that something! These people have been ignored all these years but have managed to hold on to their culture without any help from anyone. They certainly deserve recognition!"[50]

At a later bill signing ceremony with Governor John Connally, Diamond wanted the group to look the part. When several Tiguas showed up sporting mustaches, the attorney recalled, "after they got their war paint on ready to go in the governor's office," I told them, "while I didn't doubt that they were Indians, I didn't want press coverage with people with Mexican type mustaches on."[51] The Tiguas, willing to look the part to gain what they felt was rightfully theirs, promptly shaved. After assuring Governor Connally that the paint would come off, Cacique Granillo made Connally "honorary Cacique" by applying paint to his face. The event made for a colorful press opportunity with the cameras catching the awkward-looking governor surrounded by Indians dressed in war paint and feathers. A Dallas paper reported enthusiastically on the "noisy bill-signing ceremony complete with drums, chants and real live Indians."[52] It was plain that Texans were pleased to discover they had some "real" Indians and were ready to help them.

Using Diamond's political connections with Marvin Watson and Bill Blackburn in President Johnson's office, the Tiguas next worked to secure federal legislation for their plan. From the start LBJ took a personal interest in the Tiguas, an interest stemming from his deep commitment to minorities and his pride in Texas as well. The Tiguas and the NCAI soon orchestrated an effective letter-writing campaign to show support in Indian Country for the legislation. Around El Paso there was clearly a "buzz" that the locals had found a "lost tribe" that spurred sympathy, excitement, and hopes of a tourist windfall. Some El Pasoans expressed a desire to "preserve" the Tiguas, much like they would a historic home, while others expressed hopes of creating a living Indian "village" as an educational and tourist attraction for the city. As local support was vital for the success of any legislation, the Tiguas secured letters of endorsement from many segments of the El Paso community and submitted them to Congress. Working with LBJ's office behind the scenes, NCAI executive Vine Deloria Jr. was instrumental in helping the BIA to draft an acceptable bill.[53]

Once they became convinced their departments would incur no financial responsibilities or loss of revenue, the Department of the Interior and Treasury Department quickly dropped their opposition to the Tiguas. At the insistence of the BIA, however, Congressman White and Senator Yarbrough added a clause to their bills, lifted from earlier Lumbee and Pascua Yaqui acts: "Nothing in this Act shall make such tribe or its members eligible for any services performed by the United States for Indians because of their status as Indians." They also added a provision stating that, "responsibility, if any, for the Tiwa Indians . . . is herewith transferred to the State of Texas."[54]

In hearings on the legislation before the House Subcommittee on Indian Affairs and Public Lands of the Committee on Interior and Insular Affairs, the Tiguas came prepared with an ethnological report and comprehensive legal brief, although Houser recalled that the legislators were much more impressed with the Tiguas' appearance and the support of the Pueblos than anything legal or scientific. Even Wayne Aspinall, the crusty committee chairman who initially opposed the Tigua bill, changed his mind upon seeing José Granillo and hearing the cacique's heartfelt statement. With Aspinall's nod, the Tigua bill easily cleared the House, only to languish in the Senate. As Diamond recalled, New Mexico senator Clinton Anderson was holding up the legislation to respect the wishes of some New Mexico Pueblos who felt that the Tiguas were "Mexicanized traitors" and brujos for their role in the Pueblo Revolt. Apparently the Pueblos' historical memory was very long, yet after a night of politicking over a bottle of whiskey, Senator Yarbrough convinced Senator Anderson that the Tiguas were worthy of assistance, and the New Mexico senator withdrew his opposition. With this obstacle lifted, the Senate passed the tribe's legislation. On 13 April 1968 President Johnson signed a bill recognizing the Tiguas and transferring trust responsibility to Texas.[55]

The Tiwa Act was symbolic of both Indian emergence and survival, yet like the earlier Lumbee and Pascua Yaqui acts, the legislation was also in keeping with the termination-era goals of transferring federal responsibility for Indians to the states. Although certain historians believe that termination ideology was fading by the early 1960s, it was far from dead. Reflecting its continuing survival, Commissioner of Indian Affairs Robert Bennett advised LBJ assistant Marvin Watson in 1967, "The emphasis in more recent years in Congress has been on bringing to an end the need for these special services of the Indian Bureau, as the various tribes become able to provide for themselves and as the local and state governmental services are extended to them."[56] Agreeing, the Tiguas and the Texas legislature also viewed the state trust status as temporary, believing that the Tiguas would ultimately become self-sufficient and on "equal par" with other citizens of the state.

Like the Pascua Yaquis in Arizona, the Tiguas were attempting to create their own "third way" to self-sufficiency by no longer going it alone as before yet avoiding BIA paternalism at the same time. Under the state, the Tiguas seemed ready to develop their experiment toward self-sufficiency and ethnic survival. While passing the Tigua bill, the Texas legislature also approved a bill establishing a revamped Texas Commission for Indian Affairs to administer trust responsibility for the Tiguas and Alabama-Coushattas. In 1968 the Tiguas thus became a "state recognized" Indian tribe, a status held by many U.S. Indian groups that few scholars have studied in any detail. During the termination era many legislators hoped to scrap the BIA, and the Texas efforts for the Tiguas fit nicely with this trend. The state recognized the group as Indians only to provide social services and a temporary tax-exempt reservation that would help them ultimately become self-sufficient. The Tiwa Act gave the group no legal status as Indians under federal law, and thus the Tiguas continued to be subject to state civil and criminal laws.[57]

The Texas Indian program was a small part of a larger national trend. By the early 1970s federal programs such as termination and relocation and economic opportunities had swelled the number of Indians residing in urban areas. Now generally ineligible for BIA services, these urban Indians pushed states to establish Indian commissions. By 1970, twenty states had created Indian commissions, a number rising to thirty-eight by 1989. At the time of the Tigua activity, however, all but two of the state commissions had very limited roles, serving primarily as liaisons between state leaders and Indians. Most, like North Carolina, had enacted legislation recognizing tribes such as the Lumbees yet provided no special programs for them.[58] Unlike other state Indian programs of the 1960s, the State of Texas set out to provide fairly comprehensive assistance to the Tiguas and Alabama-Coushatttas. When the Tiguas came on board in 1968, the Texas Commission for Indian Affairs was composed of non-Indians who appointed a superintendent for each of the two reservations at opposite ends of the state. The governor selected the commissioners while the Texas legislature appropriated funding to support seventeen employees at the Alabama-Coushatta Reservation and eight at the newly created Tigua Reservation. Now that the Texas legislature had recognized the Tiguas, the Commission for Indian Affairs began developing programs the bureaucrats felt would best help the group. The state commission, with good intentions, hoped that in a few years its programs would enable the Tiguas to become self-sufficient, supporting their own programs in health, education, housing, and economic development.[59]

In its planning the commission hoped to exploit the dominant culture's heightened interest in Indians. As Philip Deloria has noted, during the Cold War Americans were "playing Indian" with increased vigor. By the late 1960s it was "in" to be Indian, and white Americans could be seen jumping in their vans heading for powwows dressed up as Plains Indian warriors, although now with an increased emphasis on participating with "real" Indians to add "authenticity" to the experience. Unfortunately, however, the vast majority of Native Americans were not profiting from the "Indian fad" in popular culture. As 1960s folk singer and Cree Indian Buffy St. Marie put it, "Everyone's cashing in on the colorfulness of the Indians" except the Indians![60] With this in mind the Texas commission set out to create a program through which the Tiguas could market their Indianness.

Despite the commission's plans, the Tiguas' early goals had nothing to do with tourism. From the start Tigua leaders José Granillo, Trinidad Granillo, and Miguel Pedraza expressed concerns that outsiders would exhibit them "as freaks" and that the tribal council would lose control if they reached out for help. Presciently, the leaders feared that outsiders would interfere with tribal government and ceremonies as well. In joining the state program, the Tigua men wanted nothing more than to help their people become self-sufficient and independent, as quickly as possible. Tigua Ray Apodaca later expressed a common sentiment: "I'm an Indian and proud of it, [but] I can do it on my own by myself." The band hoped only to acquire a small, tax-exempt reservation where it could build a new tuhla and preserve its cultural heritage. The leaders also wanted some form of educational and medical assistance, and at the Tiguas' insistence Diamond worked to have the federal government set aside a hunting preserve on federal lands in New Mexico and to reacquire Hueco Tanks, a sacred site in the mountains east of El Paso. Nick Houser also developed a plan to create a community center, adult education and cultural programs, and a greenhouse agricultural project to provide jobs for the group.[61]

Early on it appears the state commissioners paid little attention to the Tigua leadership. Hoping to benefit from the popularity of Indians, the commissioners ignored Houser's plan and modeled a tourist complex at Ysleta on their successful tourist program at the Alabama-Coushatta Reservation. In 1968 this program had attracted 113,414 visitors to the isolated "Big Thicket" reservation who spent close to $200,000. The commission's decision was not novel, as both the Johnson and Nixon administrations and many Indian communities were promoting tourism as a source of economic development. The commission's plan also melded well with the dreams of El Paso civic leaders who hoped to create an economic boom for the larger community. As one university report concluded at the time, "Image studies indicate that the pleasure traveler expects an 'Old West' atmosphere in El Paso. Few tourists attractions presently here meet this expectation and the proposed Tigua facilities would help fill this gap." [62] By the mid-1970s the Alabama-Coushattas had a 1,500-seat amphitheater built with a grant from the Economic Development Administration (EDA), where tribal members and hired employees performed a drama, "Beyond the Sundown," modeled after a similar pageant produced by the Eastern Cherokees in North Carolina. The Alabama-Coushatta model also included camping and fishing facilities as well as a tribal museum and gift shop. [63]

With state funding and outside grants the Tiguas proceeded to purchase lands near the old mission, including the nineteenth-century hacienda of the Candelaria family. On these sites the Commission on Indian Affairs under Executive Director Walter Broemer planned to develop a tourist complex, with all the Tiguas living in a re-created cliff-type Indian pueblo that would showcase their lives in a vibrant "Indian village." As one article pronounced at the time, the "cliff-type pueblo for the Indians [will bring them] full circle to the sort of multi-story their ancestor used." [64] Without consulting the tribal council, the commissioners planned to build a community tuhla to serve as a living ceremonial center complete with bathrooms built to resemble sacred Pueblo kivas. Newly appointed tribal superintendent Alton Griffin, a retired grocery store executive, set out to establish a formal tribal roll as well, using blood quantum criteria—again without consulting the tribal council. For the first time the state needed to establish formal membership criteria to delineate those eligible for services, and because they held the purse strings, the commissioners believed they should decide on eligibility. The commission also worked to establish a formal, written constitution, which the traditional leaders opposed vehemently. [65]

The Tiguas felt the commissioners were pushing the tourism program and community development plans on them right from the start. The Tigua elders did not want to come "full circle," it seemed. At one particularly heated junta the Tigua Tribal Council protested the actions of the commission, especially the policies of Superintendent Griffin, whom they believed was using his control of outside funding to dictate policy. Cacique José Granillo objected to Griffin's unilateral decision to purchase Alex Candelaria's adobe hacienda for a museum and site of the tuhla. As Granillo said, "we don't want to use the tusla . . . it's his. We're going to do the dances when we are together here in the house of the War Capitan." Agreeing, Trinidad Granillo also worried about the commercialization of the St. Anthony's day fiesta and performing sensitive dances at the Candelaria house complex and Boy Scout jamborees as Griffin planned. According to Trinidad, the complex could not serve as a religious center as it "was made for those souvenirs . . . for when tourists come." The multistory pueblo replica seemed particularly ridiculous. "Griffin wants to move us from our barrio to another barrio [that] isn't an Indian barrio . . . we aren't going to leave here like they want and be pushed around . . . it would be better if they left us like we were before!" The Tigua leaders also objected to the commission's new membership criteria and policy. According to the cacique, "I don't want them to bring more Indians that aren't Tiguas—Mr. Griffin is bringing in many Mexican Indians that are not Tiguas." The Tigua leaders felt they were losing something basic to tribal authority—the ability to decide and control membership. As Trinidad Granillo argued, "When we first started the tribal program we were no more than 150 Indians and now there is more than 300." Cacique Granillo summed up his resentment of Griffin's plans: "We don't want him to bring in other Indians [to dance]—he has to talk to me, I am Cacique . . . and if we give him permission to bring other dancers he can bring them. The ones who give orders are us."[66]

As the leaders' comments revealed, the early administration of Griffin was "authoritarian" in the most basic sense. Ironically, the Texas commission's paternalistic policies coincided with a period of increased Indian self-government and control of federal programs at the national level with newly passed legislation such as the Indian Self-determination and Education Assistance Act. Unfortunately, however, the Texas commissioners had to relearn many of the policy errors of the federal government. From the start the superintendent of the Tigua Reservation ignored the Tigua leaders, making all management and reservation policies himself. On the central issue of membership, the superintendent ignored Tigua traditions of basing membership more on ceremonial and community participation than blood quantum and opened the rolls to anyone of Tigua ancestry. The religious core of Tiguas worried that an influx of descendants—people Joe Sierra referred to as "those that only believe in the money," would destroy the customs that had maintained the group for centuries. Many Tiguas resented former *vecinos* coming forward now to claim the benefits of new state programs and potential gains from an Indian Claims Commission suit. Ray Apodaca recalled the Tigua leaders asking, "Where were you when we had nothing?"[67]

In 1969 Diamond reported that the Tiguas were "very resentful" of plans for putting their culture on display. The council adamantly rejected the idea of having Tiguas don Plains Indian dress and perform other tribes' dances. Instead, Tigua leaders preferred a crafts program and perhaps charging a small admission fee to enter their mission. Diamond agreed that creating a "Barnum & Bailey" carnival atmosphere at their sacred mission and peaceful barrio was particularly distasteful. "Had I known what the administration of Indian Affairs meant, I would never have undertaken to help them in their battle for recognition," Diamond said.[68] Ultimately, however, young Tiguas such as Joe Sierra saw tourism as a "survival issue." As he recalled years later, the group's predicament came down to basics. "We needed to feed the family," Sierra said. Ray Apodaca seconded this opinion, believing the tourist program was the only real economic alternative available to the Tiguas at the time. Therefore, despite trepidations, the junta gave the go-ahead to the state program.[69]

Even with their initial reservations about the tourism venture, under the commission the Tiguas soon embarked on a significant cultural regenesis. In time the tribe reintroduced Pueblo Indian culture previously lost during centuries of cultural contact with Mexican and Anglo society. They also proceeded with a partial ethnogenesis by introducing cultural practices from other Native American groups, ultimately producing an element of a pan-Indian cultural identity among the Tiguas. The tribe began a program to teach children the Tiwa language, and many tribal youths enthusiastically joined the program, hoping to revitalize their culture while enhancing their visible "Indianness" to outsiders. "My mom and dad were never given the opportunity to learn their native tongue, I don't want that to die out. I don't want to be an Indian in name only," remarked Darlene Munoz.[70] Before the program Apodaca remembers that many Tiguas felt "shy" around the other Pueblos, feeling they lacked enough traditions and culture. However, the elders told them to be proud that their ancestors had clung to as many of their traditions as they had in the face of extreme pressures to assimilate. As Apodaca said, "it would have been much easier to blend into the Mexican culture; and after all they went through, to still be Indian is a pretty damned good accomplishment."[71]

Under the new state program the Tiguas started recording religious chants and dances. In the early 1970s the community also hired a man from Isleta Pueblo in New Mexico to teach pottery, art, silverwork, and basketry to the Tiguas. This effort to reintroduce traditional Pueblo culture seemed a good way to provide a sustainable career for their people, and Tigua craftspeople soon began to sell their wares at Ysleta. With a grant from the OEO and EDA funds, the Tiguas soon completed an Arts and Crafts Center, where for the first time Tiguas charged admission to enter the historic Ysleta mission complex and witness their ceremonies and dances. The council also began hosting an intertribal powwow, with cash prizes for dancers representing the Sioux, Zuni, and other groups. They also established an herb and spice business, drawing on tribal knowledge of herbal medicine and foods. During the early 1970s the group ultimately formed the Tigua Tribal Enterprise to operate an Indian craft shop, museum, and restaurant, businesses that provided employment for thirty-five members.[72]

Although many Tiguas objected to having tourists watch them working—it was, as one Alabama-Coushatta put it, like being a "monkey in a cage"—others accepted the tourist program as necessary for Tigua survival by providing jobs and reinvigorating Pueblo culture. And by most accounts the Tigua program was an early success. In promotional literature the Tiguas constructed themselves as "the oldest ethnic group in Texas," while touting the Ysleta mission as the second oldest continuously used church in United States. Largely with federal grants, the Tiguas reconstructed their *tuhla* or kiva near the old mission and built beehive ovens (*hornos*) complete with demonstrations of the group's bread making. The tribe constructed a restaurant where it marketed mostly Mexican dishes with an Indian flare, such as chicken tacos (christened *pollo indio*). Tigua artisans marketed newly learned crafts that ranged from Pueblo pottery to ceramic lamps, decorative peace pipes, and cartoon-like Indian heads. Ultimately, however, tribal artisans had trouble competing with cheaper crafts from just across the border in Mexico.[73]

By the mid-1970s the Tiguas were offering a full plethora of Indian cultural experiences, from the arts program to living displays of Indian farming, weaving, and bread making. In a five-hundred-seat amphitheater Tigua youth performed less sensitive tribal dances wearing both Pueblo and pan-Indian dress. The Tiguas' efforts attracted the attention of the press, with numerous pieces appearing that promoted the Ysleta Mission complex. One 1977 article beckoned visitors to "listen for the call of the drums and visit one of Texas' most exciting new attractions."[74] With commission support the Tiguas had succeeded in marketing both their Indian culture and their place in Texas history. Articles appeared touting the new complex as "an authentic repository of Tigua history and culture," that in a short drive "transports the visitor to another era."[75] The Tiguas had created a historical experience, convincing tourists and journalists alike that they had been taken back in time to a primordial Indian space. One reporter created this scene: "watch as the Tigua farmer works his way down neat rows of flowering squash, beans, and waist-high Indian corn, as two tawny Tigua children, befeathered and red-sashed, chase through zebra-striped shadows cast by a brush arbor."[76] Clearly, members of the group had grown facile at projecting an Indian identity. One Tigua even attracted the attention of Princess Diana of Wales, who upon meeting the Tigua man in London remarked, "It's a pleasure to meet a red Indian. I've never met one before."[77]

Besides developing the tourist complex, the Tiguas began purchasing land for a residential reservation soon after recognition. With commission help and federal grants the group eventually acquired a twenty-seven-acre main reservation and approximately seventy other acres scattered around El Paso. In the early 1970s the group's most pressing need was modern housing to replace aging adobe structures that lacked plumbing and utilities. In 1972 the Tiguas succeeded in securing outside grants of approximately $1.7 million dollars for housing to add to $237,151 provided by the state. With a Department of Housing and Urban Development (HUD) grant the group built a 113-unit housing complex on the reservation and a multipurpose community center complete with laundromat and recreational facilities. The grant required "sweat equity," with each family performing 250 hours of work in order to move into the new homes.

Despite the Tiguas' significant progress, the federal and state largess created tensions between Indians and their Hispanic neighbors. Many Tiguas now heard grumbling that they were riding a government "gravy train," as jealousy inevitably emerged. In spite of the murmurs, at the housing dedication ceremony in 1976 many Tiguas beamed with pride at their new white stucco homes, built to resemble Pueblo architecture and placed close together to enable community interaction. The homes were completed ahead of schedule, and at the dedication ceremony Joe Sierra glowed, "Our dreams have finally come true, and now we can work together as Indian people." Besides providing modern housing, the new houses "changed the scope of education," Sierra recalled, because now Tigua children could study in private, lighted rooms for the first time.[78]

The Tiguas' state tribal status enabled them to join the West Texas Council of Governments, a membership that helped the group compete for federal grants and programs. With federal and state funds the El Paso tribe implemented federal programs such as CETA, Head Start, Neighborhood Youth Corps, and other adult education and youth programs. The group also administered its housing complex under the newly created Tigua Indian Housing Agency managed by the Texas Indian Commission. Their status also helped in efforts to acquire Hueco Tanks, an area of rocky crags, water holes, and petroglyphs that the group considered sacred. Paralleling efforts of other Indian nations, the Tiguas briefly ran Hueco Tanks as a state park and then closed it to rock climbing, an activity they found highly offensive.[79]

With tribal status and reservation cultural programs, the Ysleta del Sur Pueblo emerged from its relative isolation, taking greater pride in its identity and becoming involved in national Indian issues. Following the lead of East Coast groups, the Tiguas pursued an Indian Claims Commission case while later pressing a land claim under the 1790 Trade and Intercourse Act. Younger leaders emerged such as Ray Apodaca, who became involved in efforts to pass Texas legislation to protect Native gravesites, while others became active in the Governors' Interstate Indian Council. Some Tiguas were vocal opponents of the negative portrayal of Native Americans in films and as sports mascots as well.[80]

By the early 1980s the Tiguas had made noticeable economic and cultural improvements under the renamed Texas Indian Commission. The Tigua Tribe achieved modest success with their Pueblo Restaurant, Arts and Crafts Center, Cultural Center, and pottery operation that together employed forty-four people, twenty-three of whom were tribal members. The group's Spice Plant and Indian Handicraft programs, however, had largely failed, while draining reservation resources in the process. Yet overall the tourism complex was successful, promoted by the El Paso Chamber of Commerce as one of the city's premier tourist attractions. In 1985 the tribe's young governor, Manny Silvas, reported that the Tigua membership had grown to 1,124, with 468 living on the reservation. Ray Apodaca noted that the average Tigua family income had risen over two times since the late 1960s, and average education levels had increased from second grade to sixth grade. Even so, Silvas reported that "funds for the basic health, human services, and education have been nonexistent."[81] Unlike the BIA, the State of Texas had never provided funds for higher education, and the Tiguas realized they needed educational assistance to manage their own affairs. "We have to have our own professionals—as long as this is being done for us and not with us, we will never be self-sufficient," Ray Apodaca surmised. [82] Although superior to most, the Texas commission ultimately could not provide programs in any way comparable to the federal services provided to federally recognized tribes.

Well into the late 1970s and early 1980s the Texas Indian Commission continued to operate in a paternalistic frame, although it did help the Tiguas achieve noticeable successes nonetheless. While onetime tribal governor Bernie Ortiz credited the Texas program with the tribe's economic gains, most Tiguas accused the commission of treating the Indian people "like children." As early as 1978 tribal governor Joe Sierra protested the dictatorial methods of the commission director Walter Broemer, while members of both the Tigua and Alabama-Coushatta tribes accused Broemer of sidestepping the tribal councils by making plans and decisions alone. At the time Broemer defended himself against charges of paternalism, although in a strange way: "I do try to sell my program, but at any time the Tribal Council can vote it down. Yes, I push people [because] sometimes it's very difficult for an Indian to assume the responsibilities a position requires."[83] Ending his controversial tenure, Broemer retired in 1982, and the Texas governor appointed Tigua superintendent Ray Apodaca as the first Native American executive director of the Texas Indian Commission. Commissioner Ed Fifer noted that hiring Apodaca was "mainly what the Indian tribes wanted. They don't want any non-Indians telling them what to do."[84] Under the youthful Apodaca the commission would be less paternalistic in the future, yet divisive issues remained.

In the late 1970s the most pressing concern the Tiguas faced was the Texas legislature's threatened termination of the Indian Commission altogether. Since the late 1960s Joe Sierra recalled that every few years the state legislature required his people to travel to Austin and perform their sacred dances and songs to "prove" they still were really Indians. "Every two years we had to do our 'dog and pony show' for the legislators, to prove that we had something unique from the other people," Sierra remarked. [85] As early as 1971, Commissioner Dempsie Henley promised the state it could terminate all aid to the Texas Indians in three years. By the late 1970s state legislators were wondering how long the state would have to spend tax dollars on the Tiguas. At the time Broemer remarked, "Working with the state legislature is like pulling teeth."[86] Unlike most state Indian commissions, however, the Texas commission had appropriated moderate funds for the Tigua Reservation, averaging between $200,000 to $300,000 per year from 1976 to the mid-1980s, although Texas's share of the millions spent on the Tigua Reservation never amounted to more than one-quarter of the total. At this time Ray Apodaca thus felt that the state was providing only token funding for the reservation and that the group was languishing under the commission. Indian Commission chairman Dempsie Henley revealed the pressure the Tiguas felt. According to Henley, every year "we had to show a termination date to the Legislature or we wouldn't get funded . . . and it's always been our hope to terminate state funding, replace all the white (administrators) with Indians and let them run their own affairs."[87] Faced with budget shortfalls in the late 1970s, the legislature slated a 1982 termination date. Many Tiguas, however, including Joe Sierra, claimed they were never informed of the 1982 cutoff date and feared the group's tribal enterprises would fold.

In spite of Indian protests the state went forward, arguing that perpetual funding was never contemplated for the groups. Tom Diamond believed a major reason for the state's actions stemmed from the fact that the romance and excitement of having "real Indians" in Texas had faded, and legislators now saw the tribes as a financial burden. Faced with this threat, Alabama-Coushatta chair Morris Bullock and Tigua governor Miguel Pedraza Jr. protested the state's actions, arguing they were "a repudiation of the trust duties assumed by the State in 1954 and 1967. . . . The very survival of our Tribes and their lands is threatened."[88] Ray Apodaca, however, really was not surprised by the state's actions, recalling during this time that "we found very little sympathy in Texas with the Texas Legislature for our problems."[89]

Despite the looming specter of state termination, many Tiguas looked back with pride on their accomplishments. "They thought we'd disappear but we're still here," proclaimed elder Miguel Pedraza in 1984. Economically, however, few Tiguas were riding the "gravy train." Most continued to work as laborers or at clothing manufacturing plants, although approximately 30 percent now graduated from high school, and some were moving into the middle class. Dismaying to the tribal elders, some of these high school and college graduates gradually drifted away from the community. Overall, although the reservation provided employment, many Tiguas continued working other jobs; Pedraza was a school bus driver in addition to his service in the tribal council; Joe Sierra did maintenance work for the reservation. Some such as elder Ramona Parras Paiz still lived in their crumbling adobe houses without electricity, continuing life as their ancestors had always done. Parras Paiz summed up her long struggle: "I got married because life was difficult and I worked most of my life cleaning other people's houses."[90]

Even with the significant gains made by the Texas Indians under the commission, the threatened "termination" plan came as promised in 1983. It all came to a head in the spring of that year when a Texas Parks and Wildlife game warden arrested two Alabama-Coushatta men while they were field-dressing a deer on tribal lands in the pinewoods of east Texas. The warden charged the Indian men with violating state hunting laws for shooting game out of season, despite the fact that the Alabama-Coushatta Tribe had its own wildlife regulations. This was not an isolated incident, however, as Indian tribes and states have a long history of legal problems stemming from hunting and fishing rights. In response to Texas Parks and Wildlife requests, Attorney General Jim Mattox issued a legal opinion that no Indian reservations existed in Texas, arguing that the state's Equal Rights Amendment made it unconstitutional to treat one group of Texans differently than other citizens. According to Mattox, the state could no longer appropriate tax dollars for Indian programs. The Tiguas and Alabama-Coushattas responded by filing suit in federal district court to force the state to acknowledge its trust responsibility.[91]

The Texas Indians now were painfully aware of the limits of state status and found themselves at odds with local officials, locked in an adversarial position common in Indian-state relations throughout the United States. The deer-hunting incident ultimately set off a chain of Texas attorney general opinions that held that the Alabama-Coushatta Tribe (and, by extension, the Tigua Tribe) no longer existed as a political body or had a reservation. Because of the attorney general's opinions, the entire existence of the Texas Indian Commission fell under a constitutional cloud. It seemed apparent to members of the Texas Indian communities that the state was following a policy and taking actions reminiscent of the federal termination efforts of the 1950s. As Tigua leader Raymond Apodaca remarked, "The state of Texas is gradually going out the Indian business."[92]

Under the spell of the popular Reagan-era ideology of scaling back big government by cutting social programs, the Texas state government also passed a bill ending state funding for the Texas Indian Commission. Facing an economic downturn (and without consulting the tribe), the state cut all funding for the Alabama-Coushatta Reservation while seizing the group's mineral royalties to fund programs for the tribe. The legislature also scaled back funding for the Tiguas. The Alabama-Coushatta's tribal land base and economic programs were now in serious jeopardy as local agencies instigated procedures to tax tribal land and programs. Taken together, the state's actions painfully showed the limits of state recognition and programs, while being an eerie flashback to the termination era of the 1950s. Because of the state's position, the Texas Indian people believed they had no choice but to seek full tribal acknowledgment or restoration of their federal status and services and turned to their congressional delegates for aid.[93]

In 1984 Tigua leaders approached their lawyer Tom Diamond and NARF attorney Don Miller to draw up legislation to restore their tribal status along with the status of the Alabama-Coushattas. The Tiguas also contacted their local congressional representative, Ronald Coleman (D-Texas), asking him to introduce legislation on their behalf. Together with east Texas representative Charles Wilson (D-Texas), Coleman introduced bills in 1984 and again in 1985 to restore federal status to the two tribes.[94]

With Don Miller the Tiguas crafted a legal strategy arguing that Congress had a moral and legal responsibility to restore the two tribes to federal status. As Miller noted, high federal officials from Richard Nixon to Ronald Reagan had repudiated the termination policies of the past. With the exception of several hard-fought battles to restore the Menominees and other tribes in the early 1970s, Congress thereafter readily acquiesced to bills seeking to restore the tribal status of terminated groups by invoking its plenary power over Indian affairs. Because there was much less opposition to restoration legislation than to recognition bills, the Tiguas took the stance that they were in fact recognized as an Indian tribe in the 1968 bill and pursued restoration jointly with the Alabama-Coushattas.[95]

In drafting the bill, however, NARF attorney Don Miller realized that Congress had passed clear termination legislation only for the Alabama-Coushattas. Yet he lumped the two groups together because he felt that the average legislator would not be aware of the fine distinctions. According to Miller, calling the Tiguas' effort "restoration" would be a far easier sell to Congress. At this time lawmakers on Capitol Hill were reluctant to sidestep the BIA acknowledgment process, although they believed it was their duty to "restore" tribes terminated by their own repudiated policy. By going for restoration legislation the Tiguas also would avoid the scrutiny of recognized tribes, who generally took a more jaundiced view of acknowledgment bills than restoration acts.[96]

Consistent with its stance toward federal acknowledgment legislation, however, the BIA opposed the bill, arguing that it had not evaluated the Alabama-Coushattas under the department's restoration criteria to determine whether the group still was maintaining tribal relations since termination. The BIA also argued that the Tiguas were piggybacking on the Alabama-Coushatta bill because the two groups held entirely different statuses under federal law. The Branch of Acknowledgment and Research stated that the federal government had never acknowledged the Tigua Tribe as it had the Alabama-Coushattas. The bureau felt that the 1968 Tiwa Act simply had recognized the El Paso group as "Tiwa Indians" in order for the State of Texas to assume trust responsibilities for the group. In the BIA's estimation the federal government never assumed jurisdiction for the group nor evaluated its existence as a tribe. "We view this bill as proposing to give the Ysleta del Sur Pueblo a Federal status it never had; this group should be required to meet the same basic criteria the Department of the Interior uses in determining whether any group should be acknowledged as a Federally recognized Indian tribe," Deputy Assistant Secretary for Indian Affairs Hazel Elbert testified at hearings on the measure.[97]

The Tiguas responded by providing more scholarly evidence of their political organization and continuing tribal relations, much of which was obtained in their Indian Claims Commission research. Despite the Tiguas' evidence, an exasperated Tom Diamond sighed, "we are just getting buried in red tape; now we are fighting the same old battle we once fought with the initial recognition effort where the Washington bureaucracy constantly nitpicks and objects to item after item."[98] Because of the economic doldrums of the early 1980s, the Tiguas faced opposition from the Office of Management and Budget as well as the Interior Department. Not surprisingly, their bill died an unceremonious death in committee in 1984. All the while, although the state continued to fund the Tigua Reservation, the group's status remained in jeopardy. Knowing the slow pace of the BIA's process and sincerely believing that Congress had already acknowledged them, the Tiguas chose to ignore the BIA recommendation and to continue to pursue legislative restoration.[99]

In their favor, the Tiguas had considerable support for their restoration bill in the community of El Paso, where the Tigua Reservation had become one of the city's top tourist draws. The group also had backing from their congressional representative, Ronald Coleman, who, according to Don Miller, was willing to "bust his butt" for the tribe. To members of Congress, local support was central to their decisions regarding Indian legislation. They generally considered Indian bills involving small numbers of people and low financial costs to be local matters and deferred to state congressional delegations unless larger policy issues arose. Knowing this, the Tiguas drafted and secured numerous letters from all sectors of the El Paso business and civic community, including the Convention and Visitors Bureau, praising the Indians' economic and cultural contributions to the city.[100]

Despite the local support, the tribe knew it had to convince the Pueblos and other Indians of its authenticity to have any chance at success. As recognized tribes are often the arbiters of authenticity for Indians seeking federal tribal status, the Tiguas worked to secure the support of Indian groups. Working against them, however, was the fact that many Pueblos, including some people at Isleta Pueblo, still privately believed the Tiguas were "Mexicans" trying to pass themselves off as Indians. This perception persisted well into the 1990s. Reflecting this view, Verna Williamson, the tribal governor of Isleta Pueblo, candidly told a production crew: "Over three hundred years things have slowly eroded [with the Tiguas] as far as keeping in touch with the language, the traditions, the ceremonies, all those things. Of course, they have been inter-breeding with non-Indians—to where I personally question the blood quantum of [those] down there."[101] Ray Apodaca recalled many people in Isleta saying, "yes, you are descendants—but are you Indians? Do you still have traditions, culture?"[102]

The Ysleta group clearly had to prove different attributes to an indigenous audience than the racial and often-stereotyped images they had to display to state officials and tourists. To overcome lingering suspicions, the Tiguas arranged personal visits with the All Indian Pueblo Council, members of the Kiowa tribe, and other Indian groups to secure their support. As Apodaca recalled, "this was the natural route for us, going back to the Pueblos in New Mexico, arranging visits and reestablishing relations with them." According to Apodaca, "the important thing was to have the tribal elders sit down and talk with each other so they could see we are Indians on more than just paper. We wanted them to see that though we had lost substantial things, there were enough [elements of culture] that they could recognize us as Indians and more specifically as Pueblos from Isleta."[103]

After various meetings elders of the Indian groups found that they shared much in common. The Kiowas and Tiguas discovered that both groups had oral traditions of a battle their ancestors fought at Hueco Tanks in the nineteenth century. As Miller recalled, the Tiguas handled these relations skillfully by establishing personal contacts that demonstrated their traditions and culture and by avoiding misunderstandings and red tape. Upon meeting the Ysleta group, the other Indians "just knew" the Tiguas were Indians. As Ray Apodaca recalled, with us "it's almost like having a crust of Hispanic culture, once you scraped it away, you have Indian culture underneath."[104] Through this effort the Tiguas worked to project an image that they were "real Indians," while also promoting the message that the Spaniards took them as slaves and burden bearers to El Paso during the Pueblo Revolt to dispel any lingering Pueblo opposition and animosity. Through their diplomacy the Tiguas ultimately secured the support of Isleta Pueblo, the All Indian Pueblo Council, the Kiowas, the NCAI, and the National Tribal Chairmen's Association, who understood the impact of history upon the group. With local congressional support, national Indian backing, and the Tiguas' determination, the outlook looked good when Representative Coleman reintroduced the bill in 1985.[105]

Unfortunately, however, in this go-around the Tigua bill became entangled in the national debates raging on Indian gaming, propelling the legislation from a local restoration bill involving a small number of Indian people to a complex measure of national significance. After the landmark Indian victory in *Seminole Tribe of Florida v. Butterworth* (1981), gaming was forever raising the stakes and changing the meaning of tribal acknowledgment. Although Indian gaming became an important source of tribal revenue, it also added substantially to the obstacles facing unacknowledged Indians, groups that already encountered considerable opposition to their efforts. It certainly affected the Tiguas' plans.[106]

By the mid-1980s Indian gaming had grown exponentially from the initial success of the Florida Seminole Tribe, an Indian group the federal government officially acknowledged as a sovereign nation only in 1957. The phenomenon began somewhat inauspiciously when, during the mid-1970s, Seminole leaders opened a smoke shop and bingo hall on their reservation, fortuitously located near a large retirement community in southern Florida. As the reservation was exempt from state civil regulations and taxation, the tribe was able to offer cigarettes for $4.75 a carton, $2.15 less than local vendors, while offering bingo jackpots ten times higher than the limit for charity games in the state. Although the profits from these enterprises provided valuable economic resources for the tribe, many locals were not pleased by these developments. Goaded by local merchants and charity groups, state officials moved to shut down the gaming operation, arguing that Seminole bingo violated state criminal laws. In most states, state officials have no jurisdiction or control over Indian activities on reservations; however, Florida was one of twenty-one states where Congress had specifically limited tribal sovereignty by granting the states limited civil and complete criminal jurisdiction through a termination-era piece of legislation, Public Law 280.[107]

The Seminoles brought suit to enjoin the state from enforcing its laws on the reservation. The case turned on whether Florida bingo laws were criminal/prohibitory or civil/regulatory in nature—if they were criminal, the state would have authority to close the Seminole operation. In a significant finding for Indians, in 1981 the United States Court of Appeals, Fifth Circuit, ruled in the tribe's favor, holding that Florida did not forbid bingo as a criminal activity. The Seminoles were free to continue their operations. After the Seminole case, if states allowed a form of gambling, the tribes could do so as well—without limits imposed by the states. By the late 1980s other federal circuit courts followed the Fifth Circuit's "civil/regulatory" test, ruling in favor of Indian tribes in California and Wisconsin. Although the tribes had won victories in various federal courts, states and interest groups continued to press Congress to regulate or terminate Indian bingo.[108]

In these halcyon days of Indian gaming the Tiguas and other tribes debated the benefits and consequences of gambling on their reservations. In fact, religiously conservative elements within both the Alabama-Coushatta and Tigua Tribes strongly opposed gaming. It was a common feeling among many Indians that gaming only encouraged hustlers, experts, and lawyers to descend upon Indians, promoting "get rich quick" schemes. As one Oneida warned, these pipe dreams simply enticed tribes to assimilate and embrace American materialism. Some culturally conservative tribes such as the Hopi and Navajo thus consistently opposed gambling on their lands. Many others, however, including most New Mexico Pueblos, opened bingo halls.[109]

Beyond debates among the Tiguas and other tribes, Indian gambling was igniting heated controversies in the non-Indian world as well. Organizations as diverse as the National Association of Attorneys General, the Nevada Resort Association, the National Sheriffs' Association, and religious organizations were aligning against the Indians, lobbying against Indian gaming or, in the alternative, for state regulation of the activity. Interest groups ranging from the Humane Society to the Religious Right rallied against gambling, claiming it was an immoral vice that the government should not sanction. In response to the fears raised about the issue, in 1985 Arizona congressman Morris Udall and Arizona senator Dennis DeConcini introduced legislation to provide federal oversight and statutory authorization for Indian gaming. While Congress debated, however, there was a serious threat that appeals working through the courts would culminate with the Supreme Court overturning the Seminole decision and other cases.[110]

In 1987, however, Indian tribes won what Morris Udall called "a surprising victory" in the Supreme Court. [111] In the case *California v. Cabazon Band of Mission Indians*, the justices upheld the rulings of the circuit courts, finding that without specific congressional authorization and with few exceptions, states that allowed gambling could not regulate gaming on Indian lands. In this context members of Congress and state officials now were willing to compromise on Indian gaming. The resultant Indian Gaming Regulatory Act of 1988 (IGRA) generally removed the threat of state regulation over certain types of gaming and appeared to be a satisfactory compromise to most parties. IGRA created the National Indian Gaming Commission to oversee and regulate gaming on Indian lands based on three classes of gaming. Only in Class III gambling, which included all forms of "casino" gambling and pari-mutuel betting, would Congress require tribes to sign compacts with states giving the state governments some control and share of the profits. By the mid-1980s Indian gaming became one of the fastest-growing sources of economic development on reservations, prompting some to call it "the new buffalo." Gaming provided jobs as well as funding for health, housing, and tribal government programs, while enhancing Indian political power.[112]

In 1985, however, when the Tiguas ran headlong into the controversy, the future of Indian gaming was far from settled. It was then that the once hard-living and hard-working tax collector of Texas, Bob Bullock, set his sights on stopping the Tigua bill and the potential Pandora's box it represented. Bullock mobilized his legendary political acumen in opposition to the bill, launching a concerted media and political campaign to stop the establishment of federal reservations in Texas, enclaves he believed would serve as beachheads for Indian gaming in the state. Not taking the comptroller's actions lightly, the Tiguas fought back with the help of Diamond, NARF, the NCAI, and the American Friends Service Committee. In their efforts the Texas tribes' earlier politicking bore fruit, as former Texas senator and governor Price Daniel, an "honorary chief" of the Alabama-Coushattas and former senator Ralph Yarborough, an "honorary" governor of the Tiguas, agreed to work pro bono and lobby the Texas delegation against Bullock's position. Both Yarborough and Daniel felt an obligation to the Texas Indians, especially since Daniel had sponsored the Alabama-Coushatta termination act in the first place.[113]

In light of the support for the Tiguas, Bullock took his case to the public, sending out a warning cry against the bill, arguing that restoration would bring problems to the state that it had avoided by not having federal reservations in its borders. Mirroring larger national debates and fears, Bullock argued that the Indian bill "would lure organized crime to Texas to muscle in on high-stakes bingo games." As the Texas politician warned, "unregulated Indian bingo games are a law enforcement problem in virtually every state that has them because organized crime sees them as easy money."[114] Bullock offered as evidence a resolution of the Conference of Western Attorneys General that concluded that Indian gaming was a threat not only to the "public welfare" but also to the tribes themselves. The Texas comptroller pointed out that the recently recognized Pascua Yaqui Tribe ran bingo games that he said "haven't made a dime" for the tribe. "With the money problems they have," warned the comptroller, the Texas tribes could not resist temptations to gamble. [115] At this time the Justice Department did in fact conclude that Indian bingo, if unregulated, could attract the Mafia, while the huge sums generated by Indian games could become targets for money laundering from drug transactions as well. Bullock noted that Indian bingo "is no little old church ladies operation" and would likely bring alcohol and crime problems—and even had led one "curly-haired Wisconsin housewife" to murder her husband for bingo money. [116]

To gain allies Bullock attempted to mobilize the state's charity bingo operators against the bill, arguing that Indian games with jackpots as high as a million dollars would quickly put out of business the state's 1,500 charity operators, who were limited by state law to a maximum jackpot of $500. Some observers felt that Bullock's real concern, however, was the loss of millions in tax revenue from the charity games and that he simply was playing on fears of crime to win his case. Even so, Bullock also warned that tribes would acquire off-reservation lands and begin operating bingo parlors in major cities across Texas. A rumor soon circulated that the Tiguas were contemplating opening a casino in downtown Houston after restoration. In the midst of the controversy Bullock expressed the growing public resentment of the newly found Indian success by saying, "Indians should be subject to the same damned laws as everybody else in Texas! I call it fair play." [117]

Showing how the gaming issue had clouded tribal acknowledgment and restoration, Bullock argued, "I'm all for the Indians. I'm all for the status they want—but I'm flat out against unregulated, high-stakes bingo games." [118] In a neighboring state the rise of Indian bingo had prompted Louisiana officials to go so far as to question the federal status of the Louisiana Coushatta reservation previously established by administrative action in the early 1970s. It also led to antagonism between once friendly groups. In the early 1990s the unacknowledged MOWA Choctaws in Alabama charged the recently recognized Poarch Creeks with financing opposition to their BIA petition in fear of gambling competition. [119]

The irony of the entire debate was that the Tiguas and Alabama-Coushattas had a highly religious and conservative leadership that adamantly opposed gaming. NARF attorney Don Miller recalled that gaming was never even considered by the tribes; broaching the issue would have been "political suicide" at the reservations. Having converted to Presbyterianism in the late nineteenth century, the Alabama-Coushattas were especially against the practice on moral grounds. The two tribes deeply resented Bullock's remarks, and Alabama-Coushatta chair Morris Bullock countered that their primary motivation was to secure tribal lands, not tribal casinos. As the Alabama-Coushatta chair told Texas officials, his people had "a very strong government" that was insulted by insinuations that "we would not be capable of managing our own affairs and regulating matters that strike at the very heart of tribal religious and cultural beliefs."[120] Incensed that Comptroller Bullock made no effort to speak with the tribes, Tigua superintendent Ray Ramirez told him, "you know as well as I that these issues have nothing to do with the alleged infiltration of organized crime into Indian bingo, but are simply a red herring for the issue of state regulatory control versus tribal regulatory control." Ramirez expressed the feelings of many Texas Indians by saying, "it is the kind of thing that makes you wonder why, every time we turn around, the state is attacking us."[121]

Though the restoration attempt became enmeshed in politics, the Tiguas were favorably situated to play the game. The two Texas tribes put their restoration efforts "in high gear" with a two-prong strategy, lobbying both politicians and Indian groups. In correspondence with state legislators, Texas Indian Commission director Ray Apodaca crafted a historical narrative that portrayed the Tiguas and Alabama-Coushattas as "church going, law-abiding citizens" who helped protect Texas settlers against Apaches and the Mexican dictator Santa Anna during the Texas Revolution. Their rhetoric incorporated the tribes within the great historical mythology of Texas, while arguing that the Texas Indians were independent, worthy people. In this vein Price Daniel and Ralph Yarborough argued, "It is a mockery of our Texas Sesquicentennial for us to be celebrating our freedom from Mexico while reneging on our state's responsibilities to these Indians whose forbearers helped us win that freedom."[122] The Texas Indians also stressed that federal reservation status would enable the tribes to continue their tourist programs that were good for the El Paso and east Texas economies while the federal government would assume responsibility for the social and education programs for the two groups, a fact that appealed to local governments.[123]

With their place in history emphasized, the Tiguas and NARF began working on a compromise solution over the contentious gaming issue. Ronald Coleman ultimately persuaded the Texas delegation to the House to line up solidly behind the legislation. In response, Bullock took his campaign to the Senate, where his chances of blocking the bill were greater. Negating the gambling issue, Texas Senators Lloyd Bentsen, a Democrat, and Phil Gramm, a Republican, generally opposed the bill anyway: Senator Bentsen was against what he saw as special status for groups in general, while Gramm, best known for his Gramm-Rudman-Hollings Deficit Reduction Act, wanted to reduce government spending on social programs to balance the federal budget. After several weeks of lobbying, Bullock's office secured promises that the two senators would kill the Tigua bill unless gaming was prohibited in the restoration legislation. The issue put the Tiguas and Alabama-Coushattas in a quandary. Both tribes opposed gaming, yet to agree to a total ban or state regulation of gaming on reservation lands would incur the opposition of Indian groups and national attention for the precedent it would set.[124]

In the midst of these problems the Tiguas secured a breakthrough with the Department of the Interior in 1986. During hearings in 1984 and 1985, the Interior Department had adamantly opposed the Tiguas' position, insisting that the group go through the BIA acknowledgment process. Despite the department's objections, the House had passed the Tigua/Alabama-Coushatta bill due to strong support from the Texas delegation and Morris Udall, chairman of the Interior and Insular Affairs Committee. When the Senate did not take up the legislation that year, however, the two groups redoubled their efforts to present more evidence of their status during the next legislative session. Using data collected for their land claim and supplemental research, the Tiguas presented a "petition" to the BIA modeled on the acknowledgment regulations. The Tiguas' research helped convince the BIA that the group was indeed an Indian "tribe." At hearings on the bill in 1986, Assistant Secretary Ross Swimmer withdrew the department's objections. Swimmer noted that "though this documentation nor our evaluation of it has approached the level required of other Indian groups seeking Federal acknowledgment," the department felt that the Tiguas' case warranted a special exception. According to Swimmer, the BIA reversed its position for several reasons, including new evidence the Tiguas presented, the existence of the 1968 Tiwa Act, the tribe's relationship with the State of Texas, and, most importantly, the fact that the other Pueblos, who, Swimmer said, "are among the most traditional of Indian tribes," had accepted the Tiguas as Pueblos.[125] With the BIA endorsement, the Tiguas had cleared a major obstacle in the path of their restoration effort.

Working with NARF, the Tiguas and Alabama-Coushattas next turned toward countering opposition to their legislation on the gambling issue. The bill that passed the House in 1985 contained an apparent compromise section stating that tribal laws on gaming were to be identical to Texas law until amended. However, state officials noted correctly that, although it appeared that Texas bingo regulations would apply to the Tigua reservation, recent federal cases made it clear that state "civil/regulatory" laws were inapplicable to Indian reservations. As to the tribal position against gaming, Bullock remarked, "they can say they have a law, but that doesn't mean another Indian can't change it. You put a headdress on another Indian and you get another set of laws."[126] The comptroller proposed a provision in the legislation specifically providing for state regulation of gaming on the reservation. The Tigua Council responded that the state's position was "wholly unacceptable to the Tribe in that it represents a substantial infringement upon the Tribe's power of self government, and would set a potentially dangerous precedent for other tribes." To avoid state regulation and the wrath of recognized tribes, Tigua governor Miguel Pedraza Jr. and the Tigua council decided simply to pass a tribal resolution banning all gaming on the reservation. The Tiguas asked the House to amend their bill to prohibit all gaming as defined by Texas law on their lands. As Pedraza said, "the controversy over gaming must not be permitted to jeopardize this important legislation."[127]

Still facing opposition from the Texas senators, however, the Tiguas secured the aid of Hawaii senator Daniel Inouye, who introduced a Senate bill on their behalf. Senators Gramm and Bentsen appeared to want to wait and see how the national Indian gaming debates came out before making a commitment on the Tigua/Alabama-Coushatta bill. During negotiations in the Senate Select Committee on Indian Affairs the Tiguas accepted compromise measures suggested by the Department of the Interior. Both tribes passed tribal resolutions completely banning gaming while agreeing to an unusual provision limiting membership. Tribes normally set their own membership criteria, yet to pass the bill the Tiguas agreed to limit membership eligible to receive services to individuals of one-eighth blood quantum. Ross Swimmer of the BIA testified, "we realize this procedure is a departure from our general policy of providing federal services to federally recognized Indians as determined by tribal membership, but we think that this solution meets our concern of having to provide services to increasing numbers of tribal members; Congress should place some limit on the potential service population of tribes being made eligible for Federal benefits for the first time."[128] The Tiguas also agreed to state civil and criminal jurisdiction over their lands. With these significant compromises, the Tigua restoration bill passed both houses in the fall of 1986—their battle appeared over.

After the Tigua bill passed the Senate, however, Phil Gramm asked Senate Majority Leader and later presidential candidate Bob Dole (R-Kansas) to vitiate the vote through an unusual Senate administrative procedure. Apparently Gramm believed he had not received adequate notice of the vote on the bill and had not been given answers to the question of the potential costs of the bill. Although Senator Gramm later denied being behind the vote that killed the bill, sources believed he may have pulled this maneuver to deny Democrat Ronald Coleman a popular victory in his home district of El Paso during the election year, while the unsettled state of Indian gaming appeared to be a major concern as well. Despite the setback, Gramm's unusual tactic struck a sour chord in Indian Country. Through NARF and the NCAI the Tiguas and Alabama-Coushattas mobilized opposition to the senator's actions. The bad press prompted Gramm to negotiate with the Texas Indians.[129]

In early 1987 the Tiguas began working with Senator Gramm's office to secure passage of their bill. During this time the United States Supreme Court issued its opinion in the *Cabazon* case, settling the issue that states could not impose laws and gambling regulations on Indian lands unless the activity was completely prohibited by state law. In Texas, bingo and other forms of gaming for charities and other purposes were clearly legal. By this time, however, it became apparent to legislators that federal regulations would soon be in place ensuring that states and the federal government would have some regulation of Indian gaming. The Tiguas and Alabama-Coushattas continued to agree to a ban on all gaming, putting a tribal resolution to this effect into their legislation. After intense negotiations Senator Gramm ultimately insisted on freezing the membership criteria for twenty years and agreed to support the Tigua bill.[130] Ironically, it was Gramm who introduced the Tigua/Alabama-Coushatta bill in 1987, becoming an unlikely champion of the Texas tribes in the Senate.

With the Tiguas' former foe, Senator Gramm, at the helm and with compromises in place, Bob Bullock and the state government withdrew their opposition. The bill passed both the House and Senate. On a momentous day for the two Texas tribes, President Ronald Reagan signed the restoration bill on 18 August 1987, adding the Tiguas and Alabama-Coushattas securely to the list of federally recognized tribes. A relieved Miguel Pedraza Jr. remarked that the bill "protects our land and will give us the same opportunity to compete with other tribes for federal grants."[131] Approximately three hundred years after being separated from the other Pueblos, the Tiguas now took their place beside the other federal tribes.

After the phenomenal gaming-fueled success of recently acknowledged tribes in the Northeast, groups following the lead of the Tiguas have had to overcome a pervasive idea that many, if not the majority, of unacknowledged peoples were assimilated Indian "pretenders" lining up to cash in on the gaming bonanza. Within a few years of the Texas bill, Atlantic City mogul Donald Trump went so far as to complain that certain Indians, who, he said, "don't look like Indians to me," were coming forward primarily to secure unfair advantages in the gambling industry.[132] By the late 1980s articles routinely appeared on the East Coast linking tribal acknowledgment and Indian casinos, an unfortunate pairing that negatively influenced public perceptions about the motivations of all petitioning groups. Although beliefs about "wannabe" groups are highly exaggerated, the potential benefits of tribal status undoubtedly have affected the number of groups seeking this beneficial designation. In Texas alone, Tigua attorney Tom Diamond estimates that over twenty groups hoping to open casinos have contacted him since the tribe's victory, including one group with a plan to open a casino complex next-door to the Alamo.[133] Indian identity and status has indeed become a highly valuable commodity—a fact that only assures that it will be more and more tightly regulated.

Compared to the Tiguas, subsequent groups have faced even stronger opposition to their attempts to bypass the FAP. Added to a host of other issues, gaming clearly has prompted vocal and powerful opposition from local interests and tribes that are apparently trying to protect their gaming "turf" against potential competition. Near New York City, legislators such as Robert Tortecelli of New Jersey have opposed recognition of the Ramapoughs primarily because of gambling concerns. Although this group received major funding from gambling firms, according to the group's chief, Ronald Red Bone Van Dunk, the casino issue caused the group's political support to wilt from pressures from casino titans. "Our problem is that we're too close to Atlantic City to be recognized [via legislation]," he complained after being denied by the BIA.[134] Local legislators, state attorneys general, towns, and anti-gambling organizations, in fact, have produced legal briefs to refute the tribal status of many groups, while Indian casino windfalls have cast a cloud of suspicion over all unacknowledged communities. In testimony during a hearing on a Mohegan land claim and acknowledgment bill, Senator John McCain summed up the mood of Congress: "I have to tell you, there will be a suspicion that this tribe sought recognition in order to start gaming operations; not by me, but by others—I do not predict [an] easy path for this legislation."[135] In a sad irony, even recently acknowledged tribes now get in line to oppose efforts of groups that they once supported before gaming, taking pains to travel to Washington to testify against the bills of once kindred peoples.

In their journey toward acknowledgment, the Tiguas' experience reflects many of the issues unacknowledged Indian communities have faced in the past forty years. Beginning in the 1960s the tribe overcame severe obstacles to achieving tribal status while struggling to maintain its tribalism in modern America. Because the group had a tribal structure that closely resembled the stereotypical "model" of tribalism held by non-Indians, the tribe gained a form of federal acknowledgment in a simpler era. The Tiguas then translated this status into a pioneering non-BIA program that helped the group survive in a modern urban environment. Despite gains under the Texas program, the small tribe came to realize the limits of state recognition and nonfederal Indian status. Hoping to gain full recognition as a result, the Ysleta group then ran headlong into debates over ethnic authenticity and Indian gaming that almost derailed its efforts. Uniquely situated to play politics, however, the El Paso tribe parlayed its visible Indian ancestry, strong political structures, and surviving religious ceremonies into support from legislators, local non-Indians, and, most significantly, other Indians. In the end, the Pueblos' acceptance of the Tiguas went a long way toward authenticating their racial and cultural "Indianness."

After the Tigua Restoration Act of 1987 the tribe began to administer federal Indian programs on its newly authorized federal reservation at Ysleta. Like other recently acknowledged tribes, the Tiguas faced daunting new issues and promising new opportunities. In time, however, debates would rage over whether to allow women to vote and whether to succumb to lucrative casino offers. These concerns nearly split the tribe in two. Ultimately, however, the Tiguas opened their Speaking Rock Casino in 1993, an enterprise that by the end of the decade had become a top tourist draw in El Paso while bringing in $60 million in revenue that the Tiguas used to fund community programs.[136] Because the casino supported the area economy and local charities, the vast majority of El Paso residents backed the Tiguas' Speaking Rock venture.

Even with the Tiguas' success, however, the problems with the state did not abate. From the casino's opening, Texas governors Ann Richards and George W. Bush opposed the Tiguas' gambling enterprise. Although the tribe won early victories, the state-tribal conflict came to a head in 1999 when Texas attorney general John Cornyn sued to shut down the Tiguas' gambling hall once and for all. Following his predecessors, Cornyn challenged the tribe by saying that the group had agreed to abide by state gambling laws in its recognition legislation. In October 2001 U.S. District Judge Thomas Eisele agreed, saying that the Tiguas, unlike other tribes, had made a legally binding contractual agreement to ban gambling in their 1987 Restoration Act. It seemed the tribe was once again in an anomalous status vis-à-vis other tribes. Despite the fact that Texas operated a billion-dollar lottery, the United States 5th Circuit Court of Appeals saw no hypocrisy in the state's position, affirming the lower court's ruling and ordering the El Paso casino closed in February of 2002. "I don't see why the state is coming down on us this way. Why do we have to close a casino that is benefiting the tribe, making it self-sufficient?" protested tribal leader Miguel Pedraza Jr.[137] Although the Tigua Tribe mounted protests and further legal challenges, their progress once again seemed in serious jeopardy, subject to the whims of a hostile non-Indian political climate. As of 2003, however, one thing was clear: the tribe would persist with or without a casino or state support.

CONCLUSION

On a winter's day in January 2001 Utah sheriff deputies raided the home of James Warren Flaming Eagle Mooney and seized a computer, ceremonial pipe, and thirty-three pounds of peyote cactus. In the roundup the State of Utah arrested the leader on a dozen counts of drug trafficking and one charge of racketeering. Law enforcement officials soon charged Mooney with operating a church and illegally administering the hallucinogenic plant to his devoted followers. Only members of the Native American Church who are also members of a federally recognized tribe can use peyote as part of their religious ceremonies. Had Mooney possessed this status, his actions would be legal. Yet, although he claimed to be an erstwhile member of the nonrecognized Oklevueha Seminole Band of Oklahoma, the "Peyote priest" was now facing a long prison term. In battling the charges Mooney found little support from other peyote users. Leaders of the Native American Church shunned him, believing renegades such as Mooney were tarnishing their people's reputation.[1] Unfortunately for him, Mooney discovered the ongoing importance of the acknowledgment issue, as federal tribal status remained central to a wide range of Native activities—including the use of peyote.

THE OPPOSITE OF EXTINCTION

As revealed in this work, tribal recognition is a pivotal development in postwar Native American policy. It is also one of the most ambiguous, acrimonious, and controversial methods for defining and measuring Indian identity and tribalism in modern America. By and large the federal government is not dealing satisfactorily with the rising number of unacknowledged Indian groups and their demands for status and identity as tribal peoples. Although the BIA process allows for significant differences in community organization and blood quantum, like earlier federal programs such as the Dawes Act and the Indian New Deal, the FAP still seeks to apply a single model to all groups, despite their differences. As my writings show, when officials designed the BIA process in the late 1970s, the tribal recognition program was a welcomed confirmation of tribes and their right to exist in modern America. The overall purpose of the project should be applauded today. Yet the ambiguous and contested concepts enmeshed in the Federal Acknowledgment Process have generated a continuously whirring controversy. In light of the significant indigenous rights and federal resources at stake, this situation is not likely to change in the near future.

As I show, a small but important body of scholarship has painted the FAP as an inequitable policy. A dozen congressional hearings and a dozen or more testimonials from knowledgeable academics also seem to bear witness that the process is "broken." Yet no viable alternatives have seen the light of day. By detailing the historical development of the BIA's policy, however, it has been my purpose to show that, in some respects, the FAP has served the interests of many parties. At the close of the 1970s many tribes and federal officials designed the BIA process as a bulwark against the growing number of nonfederal Indian groups coming forward to claim an Indian identity. When judged against the understated wishes of many reservation tribes, members of Congress, segments of the non-Indian public, and the BIA, the recognition program has functioned as it was intended. Its slow, exacting, and burdensome procedures have matched the goals of many parties interested in the issue. That said, the BIA program has clearly failed to live up to its promise as well as to its stated goals. As the decades have passed, it has not always provided an expeditious, fair, and objective remedy for many groups left out of the federal fold. Currently, tribal groups with strong claims remain stuck in an Indian status limbo from which there often seems no release.

Alternatives to bureaucracy once existed. During the 1970s, however, the BIA and recognized tribes rejected more liberal and inclusive modes of acknowledging Indian entities, instead insisting upon prodigious amounts of written proof of ancestry, political leadership, community functioning, and outside verification of Indianness. The BIA dismissed self-identification, oral testimonials, and a people's own unique sense of community and social organization as proof of tribal identity. Instead, the bureaucracy designed a comprehensive template for federal tribalism. By the close of the 1990s it appeared that most skeptical non-Indians supported the FAP, believing it reflected the outlines of "bona fide" tribes, while others attacked it, believing it already was too lenient. Like the dominant society, reservation tribes also tended to back the BIA program. Many agreed with the National Tribal Chairmen's Association when it argued the federal government had already recognized almost all bona fide Indian tribes. To them, many of the petitioning groups were unacknowledged simply because they were not tribes. Because of the stakes involved and BIA hegemony, it has remained clear that federal officials will not relinquish control over their service population. As it seems to represent the wishes of the majority of reservation tribes, the "in house" Bureau of Indian Affairs program is consistent with the current federal emphasis on having Indian tribes direct policy and exercise self-determination. In sum, the BIA process has gained preeminence over congressional and judicial alternatives because it seems to represent the wishes of presently recognized tribes.

Despite the apparent conflict of interest, the BIA and recognized tribes have long faced a serious dilemma in deciding which groups are "tribes" worthy of joining the federal circle. This fact should not be discounted. In fairness, the FAP has acknowledged a wide range of tribal groups, some bearing little resemblance to stereotypical Plains Indians. Yet unlike its stated goals, the FAP is not entirely objective (no process can be) nor above politics. Over time its functioning has been affected by underfunding, assimilation ideologies, and the palpable reluctance of the BIA to acquire additional tribes. As demonstrated here, the process has become increasingly legalistic, detail-oriented, and adversarial toward petitioners. In light of these facts, many knowledgeable individuals believe an independent commission would be preferable to the BIA regimen. Although this option is inherently political, it seems to make sense.

When first examining the issue, I came to realize this vexing policy could not be comprehended without witnessing its functioning on the ground level, within the petitioning communities themselves. In brief snapshots, my writings on the Yaquis, Timbisha Shoshones, United Houmas, and Tiguas provide telling glimpses into the challenges all petitioners face. The histories of these groups plainly demonstrate that the Indian peoples involved in the process were actors and agents of change. The varying community attributes and agendas of these peoples also provide a window into the issues facing BIA and congressional evaluators, as well as the range of racial identities, cultural systems, and political organizations found among the numerous nonfederal groups. Ideally, it is in the messy details that the complexities of the FAP emerge. Yet it is clear that the Indian people I met, studied, and wrote about can serve only as a sample of the vast range of experiences among groups.

As a whole, the groups I chose to write about represent both successful and unsuccessful groups. Contrary to a common criticism, the BIA has not declined every group that has come forward. The FAP has welcomed over a dozen groups into the federal fold. Nonetheless, although the majority of communities I wrote about gained status, it must be remembered that the majority of groups in the FAP and groups looking for acknowledgment by Congress have failed to pass through the gates. It is an old joke in Indian Country that when Indians die, they must first pass through the BIA and "get approval" before being allowed to enter Heaven. Sadly, unacknowledged groups must pass through the BIA *before dying* if they hope to survive as tribal entities in the modern United States. Some do not make it through.

All the members of the Native groups I met, researched, and detailed are enduring Indian peoples. Each group survived for generations without federal verification and without the federal protections afforded other Native communities. All possessed long histories, strong familial ties, and ways to separate themselves as ethnic groups from outsiders. At various times each group also lived in communities defined as "Indian" with some form of leadership, although their leaders often remained invisible to outsiders. All had Indian blood flowing their veins, despite the fact that blood quantum was often difficult to quantify and certainly less relevant to them than to the non-Indians judging their authenticity.

Prior to the BIA program, tribal acknowledgment of smaller, forgotten groups was reliant on historical accidents, stereotypes, outward appearances, or chance encounters between neglected groups and powerful benefactors. Where would the tiny Chitimacha Tribe of Louisiana have been if a Tabasco Sauce heiress had not "discovered" it in the first decades of the twentieth century and helped the tribe secure recognition? Surely with the Pascua Yaqui Tribe, this once dispersed constellation of communities would not have secured congressional recognition without the help of Congressman Morris Udall and others in the late 1970s. Then as now, congressional acknowledgment is highly dependent on the ability of groups to maneuver through the politics of Capitol Hill. It also has been reliant on a group's agility in projecting images that conform to non-Indian stereotypes about Indians, particularly beliefs that Indian tribes are united, impoverished, and culturally and racially homogenous. As shown here, fortuitous historical timing also helps. In the end the brilliant leadership of Anselmo Valencia allowed the Pascua Yaquis to manipulate the system to gain status as American Indians, despite the fact that their ancestral homeland was in Mexico. The Yaquis also benefited from a non-BIA tribal program supported by President Lyndon Johnson's War on Poverty. Although by most indicators Valencia's people are a genuine tribal group possessing aboriginal culture, language, kinship structures, and social organization, without outside power the Yaqui people likely would have remained unrecognized. Overall, despite the fact that congressional recognition relies upon stereotypes, it can be a fair and equitable means of handling certain acknowledgment cases. The Yaquis would be the last group, however, to go this route prior to the new BIA program. Subsequent groups would face much stiffer challenges.

Even if we acknowledge problems with legislative recognition, a nagging question still remains. Is the Federal Acknowledgment Process an improvement over the overtly political and cursory congressional route? In some cases the answer is yes. The FAP undoubtedly is more equitable in certain respects. Groups with varying ancestries and few visible cultural attributes or symbols of Indianness have succeeded through the FAP when they likely would have languished in the older system. By replacing the political intrigues with more overt and objective written criteria, the FAP is clearly more research-based than earlier modes. Yet it has never been completely insulated from political concerns. As revealed here, as controversies have mounted, the BAR process has produced higher and higher obstacles that groups must overcome to secure status.

Former Timbisha Shoshone tribal attorney Linda Anisman remarked that their experience with the FAP "was not protracted and went relatively well without any real difficulties."[2] Few modern petitioners would say the same. Although the Death Valley band had a strong claim to Indianness in terms of heritage, community integrity, and group cohesion, the band's twenty-two-page petition would appear extremely thin today. Like most of the noncontroversial cases decided in the FAP's first ten years, however, the Shoshones' history presented few of the racial, cultural, or community issues that challenge other groups and BIA evaluators.

Even with a strong case in terms of documented Indian blood quantum and former federal recognition, the Shoshone band, like most others, still faced skepticism over whether it was a "political" unit within the meaning of the BIA rules. In essence, the BIA questioned whether the Death Valley band operated like a political body, particularly one that enforced sanctions and controlled the activities of its members. It seemed apparent in my examination of the Death Valley case that the BIA looked for fairly organized political structures, although it ultimately was willing to acknowledge looser, family-based forms because these structures were in keeping with traditional Shoshone patterns. Overall, like most other successful groups in the process, the band had vocal leaders such as Pauline Esteves and outside legal aid from NARF and other groups. Yet without former governmental recognition and the written documentation generated by this very acknowledgment it is possible the band would have languished much longer in the process. The band is thus representative of all groups that have succeeded through the FAP: it possessed previous government acknowledgment as a tribal group. This non-Indian sanction, in turn, provided concrete genealogical evidence that the band used to prove its Indian identity. Not surprisingly, these documents were generated before outside parties began to widely question the authenticity of unacknowledged groups.

In addition to the rather unambiguous Timbisha history, the Branch of Acknowledgment and Research has analyzed more complex cases. These undertakings, however, have raised additional questions. Particularly, can Indian groups that pose racial, cultural, and community questions gain acknowledgment through the BIA? In many cases the answer is yes. As before, tribes with varying "racial" ancestry and acculturation levels have gained status via the FAP. Yet, as in the Death Valley case, the deciding factor was these groups' links to earlier non-indigenous governments and ties to former colonial reservations. In many ways these legally sanctioned bonds provided the "glue" that held these peoples together through centuries of repression, fraud, and assimilation pressures. Without white-sanctioned tribal spaces, many other tribes became extinct, succumbing to centrifugal forces of modernization and urbanization. Others, however, clung to tribalism by a thread. They assimilated some aspects of the dominant culture while maintaining their integrity as Indian communities. These tribes now have descendants scouring local records in hopes of finding some documents that prove they are what they say they are: Indian peoples that have always existed.

As revealed in this book, the presence of ambiguous "wannabe" groups continues to confuse and confound the acknowledgment process in all its manifestations. There are dozens of groups claiming to be Indian tribes that few knowledgeable parties accept as Native American. Although a highly exaggerated presence, these self-proclaimed "tribes" have provided many parties with a justification for maintaining the strict BIA process in its essential form. Since 1978 the FAP has worked to screen out several pretenders, with these denials raising few eyebrows. These "wannabe" groups have largely served as an exaggerated "boogeyman," however, which only helps to justify opposition to any perceived easing of the acknowledgment standards. It has been an aim of my work, therefore, to show these groups are not the only face of unacknowledged Indians in the United States, even if the general public continues to see them as such.

Despite the fact that the BIA process has succeeded in denying several dubious groups, the specific question still lingers whether it has been true to its goal of acknowledging all bona fide Indian communities. In the case of the United Houma Nation the answer appears to be no. Although many of the dubious groups could produce few, if any, links to historical Indian people in terms of ancestry, culture, or political organization, this was not the case for the large Houma group of Louisiana. Even with its strong claims to Indianness, the BAR rejected the group.

With the United Houma case its seems apparent that over time the FAP has grown more detail oriented and adversarial toward petitioners. Although BIA teams once accepted the conclusions of anthropologist John Reed Swanton with earlier cases such as the Tunica-Biloxis, the BAR challenged and scrutinized his assertions on the United Houmas. The failure of this southeastern group to prove its tribal ancestry and Native American identity therefore raises important questions regarding the scientific detachment of the FAP scholars and the methodology employed by the bureau. In particular, will the BIA acknowledge Indian groups like the Houmas that lack profuse historical documents, clear "Indian" cultural traits, and former tribal acknowledgment when the costs of such a decision will be high? As revealed in this work, the answer is apparently no. The UHN's dilemma stems from the fact that the Branch of Acknowledgment and Research is document- and precedent-bound. Unfortunately, the group's traditional invisibility, illiteracy, and multiracial composition has left the modern organization without "high" evidence of its tribal origins and Indian bloodlines. It is certain, however, that the Louisiana group is an Indian people, but apparently not an indigenous group with the types of evidence required by the BIA. The historic Houma Tribe may have become extinct, as the bureau surmises, yet this conclusion is simply a theory.

Although the United Houma Nation lacks profuse and incontrovertible evidence of its historical tribal existence and ties to the elusive historical Houma Tribe of the eighteenth century, it is clearly not among the Indian "wannabe" groups against which the FAP was designed to protect the BIA and reservation tribes. Since the eighteenth century the group's ancestors have considered themselves to be at least partially Indian, although they clearly assimilated many of the cultural and economic modes of the surrounding Cajun society. Yet, because their ancestors never possessed a documented tribal land base, having instead dispersed in family groups along the bayous, the modern group is left with few records of any "tribal" activities. Despite these ambiguities, however, the bayou enclave clearly possesses a long history as a group identified as Houma Indians.

This raises an important issue: even though the United Houmas are an Indian people, are they a "tribe" within popular or bureaucratic understandings of the concept? As their case shows, they apparently are not a "tribe" in the eyes of the BIA. Unlike the successful Timbisha band, the United Houma Nation's multiple racial heritage meant that federal officials sometimes found them to be "not Indian enough" to qualify as federal "wards" or beneficiaries. Because for over a century they have appeared to be economically assimilated, outsiders also have traditionally deemed them not economically "dependent" enough to be recognized as a Native American tribe. And unlike the nearby Tunica-Biloxis, they have historically lacked a community-held land base from which larger tribal leadership and group concerns traditionally flow. As of 2003, the United Houmas do not possess abundant evidence of a supra-tribal political organization that closely resembles BIA conceptualizations of how a tribe appears and functions.

In terms of race and tribal heritage, however, all the United Houmas' questions could be swept aside and additional analysis conducted if they could find data linking them to the historic Houmas. Clearly, the group has compelling linguistic data tying it with the historic Houma Tribe. Yet it remains to be seen how much weight the BAR team will accord this evidence. Overall, the Louisiana organization's experience with the BIA process raises questions about the FAP's emphasis on written documentation and ultimately about its fairness. In terms of firm genealogical evidence, however, the UHN lacked records the BIA deems persuasive. Because they do not have acceptable birth or death records linking them to the historic Houmas, in the eyes of the BIA the modern group is not who it says it is. In terms of community and political organization, the group also could pass through the FAP if its members had records of a common land base or common antagonists. Even if they lack these elements, the United Houmas do have a longstanding sense of themselves as Houma Indians, with an oral tradition linking them to a common history and origin. They clearly possess kinship ties, common names, and other ways that they distinguish themselves from outsiders. For over a century outsiders also have identified the group as indigenous. Even so, despite the fact that they are an Indian people of some sort, they are apparently not one that meets the federal template. Because they are a somewhat dispersed entity with over

17,000 members, the group's outline raises doubts whether it or similarly situated groups can convince the BIA that they are tribes. As the costs of a decision are high, it appears the group's size affected the scrutiny meted out in the Houma case.

Together, the questions raised in each of these group histories are significant. Of necessity, racial and community issues are central to determining tribal authenticity in the FAP and elsewhere. Groups with no Indian ancestry, group norms, or community histories clearly do not match most conceptions of what an Indian tribe looks like. The federal government cannot accept all self-proclaimed Indian groups into the BIA fold. However, the emphasis of the Branch of Acknowledgment and Research on documentation, on past identification by outside sources, and on visible political activities has led to the denial of several groups such as the United Houmas that have strong claims to recognition. They are at least as deserving as many currently acknowledged tribes.

The first three Native peoples discussed in this book illuminated the complex racial, cultural, and community issues that are entwined within the federal process. But no issue has stymied and confused the acknowledgement process more than the rise of Indian gaming. Surely the Tiguas of the Ysleta del Sur Pueblo in Texas experienced its stinging effects.

Compared to many groups, the Tiguas appeared to have a strong claim to tribal status. Even so, the tribe faced doubts about its ethnicity. Some outsiders believed the Tiguas simply were Mexicans "playing Indian" for personal gain. Despite this challenge, the small tribe possessed Indian ancestry, strong oral and cultural traditions, and, most importantly, an unusually documented government structure that survived from its Pueblo ancestors. The group used these traits to prove its identity to the conservative Pueblo tribes of New Mexico. Despite these positive factors, the Tiguas' experience with Texas state officials reveals the inherent conflicts that arise from the existence of Indian tribes within state borders. Although the band attempted to plow new ground under a state tribal program with War on Poverty aid, ultimately Tiguas' experience with state officials explains why tribes are better served with federal status and protections. The Tiguas had strong claims to Indian status, but like other similarly situated nonfederal tribes, they found their once innocuous restoration bill entangled in the controversies over Indian gaming. As was witnessed in later years with many Northeastern petitioners, non-Indian fears of casino gambling and organized crime have aligned powerful forces against unacknowledged Indian groups. Despite their ultimate success, the Tiguas' battle brings the acknowledgment story to the present: showing how Indian gaming has complicated the tribal recognition issue and severely hurt many groups in the process.

As these pages reveal, tribal acknowledgment ultimately presents few easy answers or solutions. Representing a strange alchemy of modern Indian concerns, including Indian identity, ethnic status, federal resources, self-government, and political posturing, recognition decisions have affirmed the tribal status of many groups while leaving others struggling and unacknowledged. As the building blocks of the process are ambiguous and contested, the recognition of tribes seems destined to remain contested territory for judging Indian authenticity in modern America. Overall, the BIA has played its traditional role as villain in some quarters, but the conundrum of deciding which groups are "bona fide" tribes is itself a bona fide issue that begs to be resolved—ideally in the near future. By revealing the power of recognized tribes in the process, my writings complicate the picture of the BIA as a white-dominated institution. Because there is no agreement on what a "tribe" is and because several apparently inequitable cases have been handed down, the FAP has drawn a firestorm of criticism—even when compared to other BIA programs. Despite this fact, the FAP's strange admixture of written rules and slow, exacting administration satisfies the wishes of many parties who have vested interests in the subject. Yet, overall, the BAR process clearly has failed to meet its stated goals of providing a fair and expeditious remedy for many long-suffering tribal communities.

In light of the almost impenetrable issues involved, the FAP continues to resist major reform or threats to its continuing existence. It has supplanted the obvious plenary power of Congress to decide the acknowledgment issue because the legislature has failed to devise an alternative solution. The BIA process reigns supreme because its burdensome nature provides what a skeptical public sees as a workable solution to the rising number of ambiguous and apparently non-Indian groups hoping to get federal approval. Many parties must feel as the NTCA has said, that most deserving tribes have already been recognized, or they would not be unacknowledged. Joining them, many non-Indians simply fail to see the point of recognizing new groups, or "turning back the clock," when it appears that nonreservation peoples are well on their way to eventual absorption into mainstream society (if they have not been already). Represented by Congress, many non-Indian parties thus have proven highly reluctant to ease the burdensome process.

By not acknowledging past government repression and by forcing unrecognized groups to shoulder the burden of proving their identity, the BIA process represents continuity in federal Indian policy, maintaining the restrictive and skeptical stance federal officials traditionally have taken toward groups existing outside the fold. Even so, the policy emphasis and set procedures for acknowledging tribes are clear improvements over the previous government agenda of termination that sought to deny and end tribal rights. Once FAP teams decide against groups, however, the resulting adversarial proceeding only continues the traditional government policy of opposing the rights and status of groups that do not clearly fit the government's model of tribalism.

As the twentieth century ended, however, signs of change emerged in the acknowledgment arena. There was a real possibility that the FAP would find its terminus in an independent commission that potentially would ease the criteria's dates and lessen the amount of evidence required of groups. Former assistant secretary Kevin Gover and most petitioners pushed for an independent commission. To them, a new board potentially would allow groups with longstanding histories as Indians to gain acknowledgment as tribes rather than requiring them to produce evidence that they may not possess.

By 2003 interested groups came to realize it was less and less likely Washington officials would make the plight of unrecognized Indians a top priority. Yet despite increasing uncertainty, forgotten Indian communities maintain moral authority that is hard to deny. As the descendents of California's unacknowledged tribes have argued, they never had to prove they were Indians when vigilantes massacred them during the Gold Rush or when they were forced into indentured servitude during the 1880s. "Nobody asked me to prove I was Indian when I was kidnapped from my home at age five and taken across state lines to the Stewart Indian Boarding School in Carson City, Nevada—and now I have to prove it? That's disgusting to me," noted sixty-two-year-old Clara LeCompte of the Mountain Maidu in 1997.[3] In light of the mounting inequities and the indignation expressed by LeCompte and others, change is certainly possible, yet it is extremely doubtful that federal officials will ever accept the testimony of unacknowledged peoples at face value. Because of the benefits involved, it also seems certain that groups will continue to undergo the often demeaning process to secure what they feel is their birthright as indigenous peoples on their native soil.

NOTES

ABBREVIATIONS

AIPRC   American Indian Policy Review Commission
BAR   Branch of Acknowledgment and Research, Bureau of Indian Affairs,
     Department of the Interior, Washington DC
     BCCM   Biloxi, Chitimacha Confederation of Muskogees Files
     DVTS   Death Valley Timbisha Shoshone Files
     GHP   Golden Hill Paugussett Files
     HF   History Files
     JC   Jamestown Clallam Files
     PACIT   Point au Chien Indian Tribe Files
     TB   Tunica Biloxi Files
     UHN   United Houma Nation Files
BIA   Bureau of Indian Affairs
Dardar   Brenda Dardar, Chairperson, United Houma Nation, Personal
Files   Files, Raceland, Louisiana
Diamond   Tom Diamond, Personal Files, Law Offices of Diamond, Rash,
Papers   Gordon and Jackson, El Paso, Texas
Domenici   Peter Domenici Papers, Center for Southwest Research, University
Papers   of New Mexico, Albuquerque, New Mexico
Dorman   Caroline Dorman Collection, Cammie G. Henry Research Center,
Collection   Watson Memorial Library, Northwestern State University,
     Natchitoches, Louisiana
DVNP   Death Valley National Park, Central Files, Furnace Creek, California
Fannin   Paul J. Fannin Papers, Arizona Historical Foundation, Hayden
Papers   Library, Arizona State University, Tempe, Arizona
Goldwater   Barry Goldwater Papers, Arizona Historical Foundation, Hayden
Papers   Library, Arizona State University, Tempe, Arizona
Greenway   Isabella Greenway Papers, Arizona Historical Society, Tucson,
Papers   Arizona
ITC   Institute of Texan Cultures, University of Texas, San Antonio, Texas
Johnston   J. Bennett Johnston Papers, Special Collections, Louisiana State
Papers   University, Baton Rouge, Louisiana
LBJ   Lyndon Baines Johnson Papers, Lyndon Baines Johnson
Papers   Presidential Library, Austin, Texas
     IA   Indian Affairs Files
     WHC   White House Central Files

NAB	National Archives Building, Washington DC
	CCF	Central Classified Files
	Collier Files	John C. Collier Files
	RG 75	Record Group 75, Records of the Bureau of Indian Affairs
NACP	National Archives, College Park, Maryland
	CCF	Central Classified Files
	CCM	Chronological Correspondence and Memorandum Files, 1930–1938
	GCR	General Correspondence and other Records Files, 1937–1958
	RG 48	Record Group 48, Records of the Office of the Solicitor
	RG 79	Record Group 79, Records of the National Park Service
	RG 220	Records of Special Commissions, Records of the American Indian Policy Review Commission

Painter Papers — Muriel Thayer Painter Papers, Arizona State Museum, Tucson, Arizona

Provinse Papers — John Provinse Papers, Arizona State Museum, Tucson, Arizona

SLU Papers — Stewart Lee Udall Papers, Special Collections, Main Library, University of Arizona, Tucson, Arizona

Spicer Papers — Edward Holland Spicer Papers, Arizona State Museum, Tucson, Arizona

Steiger Papers — Sam Steiger Papers, Department of Archives and Manuscripts, Cline Library, Northern Arizona University, Flagstaff, Arizona

TIC — Texas Indian Commission Records, Texas State Archives, Austin, Texas

Udall Papers — Morris King Udall Papers, Special Collections, Main Library, University of Arizona, Tucson, Arizona

White Papers — Richard C. White Papers, Sonnichsen Special Collections, University of Texas, El Paso, El Paso, Texas

INTRODUCTION

1. Kirk Johnson, "Tribe's Promised Land Is Rich but Uneasy," *New York Times*, 20 February 1995, A1; Joseph Treaster, "Connecticut Indians Feel 'Forgotten,'" *Akwesasne Notes*, 2, no. 5 (1970); Kirk Johnson, "Pequot Indians' Casino Wealth Extends the Reach of Tribal Law," *New York Times*, 22 May 1994, A1. Despite failing to examine issues of ethnic identity and the effects of discrimination on the Pequots, books by Jeff Benedict and Kim Isaac Eisler were popular nonetheless. Benedict, *Without Reservation*, 32–35, 57–63, 145–49; Eisler, *Revenge of the Pequots*, 20, 52–59.

2. The judicial route, a rarely used third method, is not discussed in detail here. Several works have examined its controversies and complexities in telling detail. See Clifford, *Predicament of Culture*; Campisi, *Mashpee Indians*.

3. This study uses the terms "acknowledgment" and "recognition" somewhat interchangeably, both because many Indians, scholars, and government officials do so and also to avoid word repetition. Many unacknowledged groups prefer the term

"acknowledgment," however. Whenever possible the study will use this term in the place of "recognition." The word "tribe" is also a vague and misused concept. This study thus refers to "groups," "entities," and "petitioners" when referencing nonrecognized groups. The work also avoids the terms "descendant organizations" or "descendants" because many petitioners find these terms offensive, particularly because the terms seem to imply that they are no longer tribal or Indian.

4. BAR, "Summary Status of Acknowledgment Cases," 29 October 1999, http://www. doi.gov/bia/bar/indexq.htm (accessed 6 April 2000).

5. For some of the strongest criticism see Campisi, "New England Tribes," 179–93; Starna, " 'Public Ethnohistory,'" 126–39; Starna, "We'll All Be Together Again," 3–12; Campisi and Starna, "Why Does It," 1–17; Paschal, "Imprimatur of Recognition," 209–28; and Slagle, "Unfinished Justice," 325–46. For supportive views see: Paredes, " 'Practical History,'" 209–26; Paredes, "In Defense of the BIA"; Quinn, " 'Public Ethnohistory?'" 71–76; Quinn, "Southeastern Indians," 34–52; and Weatherhead, "What Is an 'Indian Tribe'?" 1–47. This list is not exhaustive; additional sources are noted elsewhere.

6. BAR, "Summary Status of Acknowledgment Cases," 29 October 1999, http://www. doi.gov/bia/bar/indexq.htm (accessed 6 April 2000).

7. Suttles, *Social Construction of Communities*, 9–13; Anthony P. Cohen, *Symbolic Construction of Community*, 7–9.

8. Berkhofer, *White Man's Indian*; McCulloch and Wilkins, " 'Constructing' Nations within States," 363.

9. Snipp, *American Indians*, 27–61; Deloria and Wilkins, *Tribes, Treaties, and Constitutional Tribulations*, viii, 7–12; Wilkins, *American Indian Politics*, 41–62.

10. Snipp, *American Indians*, 36.

11. Moermon, "Being Lue," 161, and Dole, "Tribes as the Autonomous Unit," 83–94; Axtell, *Indians' New South*, 3; Asher, *Beyond the Reservation*, 4–7; Foster, *Being Comanche*, 5; Campisi, "Iroquois and the Euro-American," 455–72; Fried, *Notion of Tribe*; Fried, "Myth of Tribe," 12–20.

12. Kroeber, "Nature of the Land-Holding Group," 304; Lurie, "Problems, Opportunities, and Recommendations," 357–75; Rosenthal, *Their Day in Court*, 124–25.

13. Fried, "Myth of Tribe," 12–20; Fried, "On the Concept of 'Tribe,'" 1–11; Green, "Cultural Identities," 3–4, 28; Greenberg and Morrison, "Group Identities," 75–102; Atkinson, "Evolution of Ethnicity," 19; Karen Anderson, *Changing Woman*, 18.

14. Barth, introduction to *Ethnic Groups and Boundaries*, 9–17; Albers and James, "On the Dialectics of Ethnicity," 1–21; Moerman, "Being Lue," 153–67.

15. Felix S. Cohen, *Handbook of Federal Indian Law*, 268, 272–73; "Constitution and By-laws of the Gila River Pima-Maricopa Indian Community."

16. Albers and James, "On the Dialectics of Ethnicity," 6; National Congress of American Indians (NCAI), transcript, National Conference on Tribal Recognition, statement, Sam Deloria, 197, HF, BAR; Lafollette Butler to Henry M. Jackson, 7 June 1974, HF, BAR; Dole, "Tribes as the Autonomous Unit," 91.

17. McCulloch and Wilkins, " 'Constructing' Nations within States," 361–69.

18. Blu, "Region and Recognition," 71–74.

19. Fields, "Slavery, Race and Ideology," 95–118; Pascoe, "Miscegenation Law," 202–4.

20. Snipp, *American Indians*, 27–35; Harmon, "Tribal Enrollment Councils," 175–200.

21. Starna concludes that emphasis on intermarriage rates and use of terms such as "mixed bloods" reveals a continuing racist bias among BAR evaluators. Starna, "Southeast Syndrome," 496–97. Regarding the greater racial issue see Blu, "Region and Recognition," 71–83.

22. Royce, *Ethnic Identity*, 219, 17–19; Paredes, "Kinship and Descent," 166–73; Levine, *Our Prayers*, 123.

23. Nagel, *American Indian Ethnic Renewal*, 8–9; Barth, *Ethnic Groups and Boundaries*, 9–17.

24. Snipp, *American Indians*, 37.

25. Barth, *Ethnic Groups and Boundaries*, 12–13; Foster, *Being Comanche*, 2, 16–26; Loretta Fowler, *Shared Symbols, Contested Meanings*, 2–5; McCall and Simmons, *Identities and Interactions*, 2, 137; Aronson, "Ethnicity as a Cultural System," 9–19; Anthony P. Cohen, *Symbolic Construction of Community*, 13, Spicer, *Pascua*, xv–xviii, 6–10; Spicer, and Thompson, *Plural Society*. Studying Los Angeles, Joan Weibel-Orlando found that a vibrant urban Indian community existed, although it lacked the often-cited "markers" of community such as a territory, language, and common ethos. Weibel-Orlando, *Indian Country, L.A.*, 2–5, 43.

26. Hobsbawn and Ranger, "Introduction: Inventing Traditions," *Invention of Tradition*, 1–14.

27. Nagel, *American Indian Ethnic Renewal*, 20–21, 41–46; Hoxie, *Parading through History*, 4, 167, 295.

28. Connor, *Ethnonationalism*, 90–92.

29. Robin D. G. Kelley, *Race Rebels*, 35, 52; Lawrence M. Friedman, *Horizontal Society*, 4–6; Henry, introduction to *Ethnicity in the Americas*, 3–11.

30. Nagel, *American Indian Ethnic Renewal*, 26.

31. Asher, *Beyond the Reservation*, 16; Nagel, *American Indian Ethnic Renewal*, 70. For a similar argument see Field, "Complicities and Collaborations," 193–209.

32. Wolf, *Europe and the People*, 7–11, 388.

33. Former assistant secretary of Indian affairs Kevin Gover admitted to the subjective nature of his process in 2001. According to Gover, "What is subjective about it is the evaluation of the evidence . . . as you look at the evidence supporting any of these petitions, people can reach very different conclusions about whether the evidence is strong enough." Matt Connor, "Against All Odds," *Indian Gaming Business* (fall 2001), available in *Indian Gaming Business*, http://www.gemcommunications.com/Publications/currentpubs/indiangamingcoverstory.htm (accessed 2 February 2002).

34. Nichols, *Indians in the United States*. The present study is indebted to Richard

White for providing a model of a cultural, case-study approach in his influential work on dependency and Native American subsistence systems; see White, *Roots of Dependency*. It also benefited from a reading of David Rich Lewis's subsequent study on Indian environments; see Lewis, *Neither Wolf Nor Dog*.

35. BAR, "Summary Status of Acknowledgment Cases," 29 October 1999, http://www.doi.gov/bia/bar/indexq.htm (accessed 6 April 2000); BIA, "Indian Entities Recognized and Eligible to Receive Services from the United States Bureau of Indian Affairs," 15 July 1998, http://www.doi.gov/bia/tribes/telist97htm (accessed 28 April 1999); BAR, memorandum, "Federal Acknowledgment Project," n.d., HF, BAR.

36. BAR, "Summary Status of Acknowledgment Cases," 29 October 1999, http://www.doi.gov/bia/bar/indexq.htm (accessed 6 April 2000).

37. Porter, introduction to *Nonrecognized American Indian Tribes*; Slagle, "Unfinished Justice," 325–45.

38. Alexie, "Recognition of Distance," 49.

1. ADRIFT WITH THE INDIAN OFFICE

1. "Former First Lady Stymied on Dunes," *New York Times*, 29 January 1989, sec. I (Northeast Journal), p. 42.

2. *Procedures for Establishing That an American Indian Group Exists as an Indian Tribe*, 25 C.F.R. Part 83.1 (1997); Janet Riddel, "Those Non-Indian Indians," *Boston Globe*, 11 April 1971, 15; Earle, *Report to the Governor*, 92–127.

3. Travers, *Wampanoag Indian Federation*, 13–24, 126–38; Stone, *Metamora*, x–32; Senate Select Committee, *Indian Land Claims in the Town of Gay Head*, 9 April 1986, 33, 84–88; "Wampanoag: Totem of the Wolf," *Akwesasne Notes*, early spring, 1976, 19; Laurence H. Mirel to Robert Pennington, 17 October 1978, HF, BAR.

4. "Wampanoag," *Akwesasne Notes*, 19; "House Authorizes Spending $2.25 Million to Settle Land Battle," *New York Times*, 30 July 1987, sec. I, p. 20. On the Gay Head's struggles to convince whites of their Indianness see Grabowski, "Coiled Intent."

5. George M. Crossland to Assistant Secretary for Indian Affairs, 18 October 1977, HF, BAR.

6. Deloria and Lytle, *American Indians, American Justice*, 4, 35–36; Quinn, "Federal Acknowledgment: Historical," 331–39; Quinn, "Federal Acknowledgment: Authority," 68; Wilkins, "U.S. Supreme Court's Explication," 349–68; *United States v. Kagama* 118 U.S. 375, 381 (1886); "Draft Regulations," 16 November 1976, HF, BAR; Felix S. Cohen, *Handbook of Federal Indian Law*, 268. For comprehensive treatments of federal acknowledgment and recognition as a legal concept see Quinn, "Federal Acknowledgment: Historical," and Weatherhead, "What Is an 'Indian Tribe'?"

7. *Cherokee Nation v. Georgia*, cited in Quinn, "Federal Acknowledgment: Historical," 344; Deloria and Lytle, *American Indians, American Justice*, 27–33.

8. Nonintercourse Act, quoted in Weatherhead, "What Is an 'Indian Tribe'?" 9; Quinn, "Federal Acknowledgment: Historical," 339; Quinn, "Federal Acknowledgment: Authority," 38–39; Prucha, *Great Father*, 31, 32, 38–45.

9. *Snyder Act*, 42 Stat. 208 (1921) (codified at 25 U.S.C. sec. 13).

10. *United States v. Candelaria* 271 U.S. 432 (1926); Felix S. Cohen, *Handbook of Federal Indian Law*, 272; Spicer, *Short History*, 125; Hoxie, *Final Promise*.

11. Biolsi, *Organizing the Lakota*; Kelly, *Assault on Assimilation*.

12. *Indian Reorganization Act of 1934*, 18 June 1934, ch. 576, 48 Stat. 984 (1934) (codified as amended at 25 U.S.C. sec. 461). From 1935 until 1946 the Solicitor's Office of the Department of the Interior issued at least nine decisions on whether bands or tribes were groups eligible to organize under the IRA. U.S. Department of the Interior (DOI), *Opinions of the Solicitor*; memorandums to the Commissioner of Indian Affairs, 27 August 1935 and 28 October 1935, box 8, CCM, RG 48, NACP; Quinn, "Federal Acknowledgment: Historical," 356; memorandum, October 1977, HF, BAR; Oscar L. Chapman to the President, 22 August 1946, box 64, fd. (folder) "Indian Claims Commission Act," RG 48, NACP; Felix S. Cohen, *Handbook of Federal Indian Law*, 270.

13. Senate Select Committee, *Federal Acknowledgment Process: Oversight*, "Overview of the Federal Acknowledgment Process," 26 May 1988, 61.

14. *Montoya v. United States*, 180 U.S. 261, 266 (1901).

15. Felix S. Cohen, *Handbook of Federal Indian Law*, 271–72.

16. Felix S. Cohen, *Handbook of Federal Indian Law*, 268; "Constitution and By-laws of the Confederated Tribes of the Umatilla Reservation in Oregon"; Morrissey, *Mental Territories*, 81–86.

17. Felix S. Cohen, *Handbook of Federal Indian Law*, 271.

18. Felix S. Cohen, *Handbook of Federal Indian Law*, 272.

19. The Indian Service determined that several ambiguous or seemingly terminated, allotted, or disbanded groups were eligible to organize tribal governments in the 1930s. Nathan R. Margold to Commissioner of Indian Affairs, memorandum, "Status of Wisconsin Winnebago," 6 March 1937, and "Status of St. Croix Chippewas," 8 February 1937, in DOI, *Opinions of the Solicitor*, 732, 724; George Crossland to Assistant Secretary, 18 October 1977, HF, BAR; *Maynor v. Morton*, 510 F.2d 1254 (1975); Senate Select Committee, *Indian Federal Recognition*, 22 October 1991, 53; Senate Committee on Indian Affairs, *Pokagon Band of Potawatomi Indians Act*, 10 February 1994.

20. Commissioner of Indian Affairs to Chairman, Senate Committee on Interior, 10 January 1974, HF, BAR; George M. Crossland to Assistant Secretary for Indian Affairs, 18 October 1977, HF, BAR; Nichols, "Indians in the Post-termination Era," 84.

21. Lafollette Butler to Senator Henry Jackson, 7 June 1974, HF, BAR; Solicitor, memorandum on Minnesota Chippewa, 28 October 1935, box 8, fd. "Oct 1935," RG 48, NACP; N. R. Margold to Commissioner of Indian Affairs, memorandum, "Ft. Bidwell—Adoption of Constitution," 12 November 1935, box 8, fd. "Nov-1935," RG 48, NACP; "Status of the St. Croix Chippewas," in DOI, *Opinions of the Solicitor*, 724; Felix S. Cohen

to Commissioner of Indian Affairs, memorandum, "Whether Burns Paiute Indians Constitute Band," 31 May 1946, in DOI, *Opinions of the Solicitor*, 1394.

22. Fixico, *Termination and Relocation*, 183; Burt, *Tribalism in Crisis*.

23. "Summary of the ICC Act," n.d., box 64, fd. "Indian Claims Commission Act 1946–1947," RG 48, NACP; C. Lenoir Thompson, Creek Nation East of the Mississippi, to Walter Jenkins, 12 August 1964, IA, LBJ Papers; Rosenthal, *Their Day in Court*, 112, 121–45; *Upper Chehalis Tribe v. United States*, 155 F.Supp. 226, 140 Ct. Cl. 192 (1957); Rafert, *Miami Indians of Indiana*, 233–48.

24. Senate Committee on Interior, Subcommittee on Indian Affairs, *Establishment of the American Indian Policy Review Commission*, 19 and 20 July 1973, 35; American Indian Chicago Conference, "Declaration of Indian Purpose," 13–20 June 1961, box 35, RG 220, NACP; Vine Deloria Jr., "White Society' Is Breaking Down around Us . . . Even Its Myths—Like the Melting Pot—Are Dead," *Akwesasne Notes* 5, no. 1 (1973): 43; "NIYC: Historical Indian Policies and Priorities, 1900–1975," box 30, no folder, RG 220, NACP.

25. Stewart L. Udall, Oral History Collection, AC 74–259, interview no. 3, 29 July 1969, LBJ Papers; Spicer, *Short History*, 124, 144; "Return of the Red Man," special issue, *Life*, 1 December 1967; "Unmelted Lumps in the Melting Pot," *United Scholarship Service News* 1, no. 5 (1969).

26. Lyndon B. Johnson, "The Forgotten Americans," Address to Congress, 3 March 1968, box 8, SLU Papers; "Report to the Secretary of the Interior," 10 July 1966, box 8, SLU Papers; Amey, "Indian Affairs," 4, 134; "Report of the Interagency Task Force on Indian Affairs," 23 October 1967, box 20, fd. "American Indians—1968," LBJ Papers; Nagel, *American Indian Ethnic Renewal*, 6, 12, 114; "Indian Education Act, Part B," *Federal Register*, 40, no. 226 (21 November 1975): 54,253; *Indian Education Act*, 86 Stat. 345 (23 June 1972). For more on Indian education policies and inclusive definitions of Indianness, see Marie Annette Jaimes, "American Indian Identification."

27. "A Free Choice Program for Native Americans," 23 December 1966, box 3, LBJ Papers; Prucha, *Great Father*, 395–96; Wampanoag Tribal Council of Gay Head, "National Indian Lutheran Board Proposal," 31 October 1975, box 118, RG 220, NACP; Federal Regional Council of New England, "Federal Recognition Position Paper," 30 January 1975, box 277, RG 220, NACP. While unacknowledged tribes were ineligible for BIA and Indian Health Service programs, they were eligible for the following programs: Office of Native American Programs (ONAP) within the Community Services Administration, the successor of the Office of Economic Opportunity (OEO) in 1975; Comprehensive Employment and Training Act (CETA) of the Department of Labor; some Department of Justice programs for Indians; Indian Education Act programs in Health, Education and Welfare (HEW); and all Housing and Urban Development (HUD) programs. Various memos, box 277, fd. "Region I," RG 220, NACP.

28. Josephy, Nagel, and Johnson, *Red Power*; "Indian Rebirth," *Black Panther Party*, 25 May 1969, printed in *Akwesasne Notes* 1 (July 1969); "The Angry American Indian: Starting down the Protest Trail," *Time*, 2 February 1970; Steiner, *New Indians*; "Indians bury 'That

Rock' at Plymouth," *New York Times*, 27 November 1970, reprinted in *Akwesasne Notes*, 3 (January/February 1971).

29. "Declaration of Indian Purpose," 18, RG 220, NACP; Lurie, "Report on the American Indian," 478–500; Helen Gindrat, interview by author; Hiram Gregory, interview by author; Deloria, *Custer Died for Your Sins*, 239–47; NARF *Announcements* 1 (June 1972) and 2 (January–February 1973).

30. NCAI, Program, 34th Annual Convention, HF, BAR; Gregory interview.

31. C. Lenoir Thompson, Creek Nation East of the Mississippi, to Walter Jenkins, 12 August 1964, IA, LBJ Papers; NCAI, Program, 34th Annual Convention, HF, BAR.

32. House Committee on Interior, Subcommittee on Indian Affairs, *Federal Recognition*, 10 August 1978, 170.

33. House Committee on Interior, *Federal Recognition*, 10 August 1978, 169.

34. House Committee on Interior, *Federal Recognition*, 10 August 1978, 176.

35. Small Tribes Organization of Western Washington (STOWW), Position Paper, n.d., box 277, RG 220, NACP; Federal Regional Council of New England to David W. Hays, 30 January 1975, box 277, RG 220, NACP; NCAI, Program, 34th Annual Convention, HF, BAR.

36. *United States v. Washington*, 520 F.2d 676 (1975), 692–93; George Roth, "Issues for AS-IA," 20 September 1982, HF, BAR.

37. *United States v. Washington*, 520 F.2d 676 (1975); "Appeals Court Reaffirms Washington Fishing Rights; Officials Angry," *Akwesasne Notes*, late summer 1975, 40; "Fishing Rights Turmoil in the North-West," *Akwesasne Notes*, early autumn 1976, 17; "Federal Recognition Act, Original Briefing Paper," n.d., HF, BAR; Wilkinson, Cragun, and Baker, memorandum to NCAI, "Indian Hunting and Fishing Rights," Diamond Papers.

38. *Passamaquoddy v. Morton*, 528 F.2d 370 (1975), 371, 376; "The Maine Land Claims," *Akwesasne Notes*, late spring 1977, 20; "Legal News," *Akwesasne Notes*, late spring 1972, 14; Thomas N. Tureen, "Federal Recognition and the *Passamaquoddy* Decision," n.d., box 277, RG 220, NACP; "Briefing Report on Tunica-Biloxi, (LA) Litigation Request," September 1981, HF, BAR.

39. Grace M. Sterling, letter to the editor, n.d., HF, BAR.

40. Reid P. Chambers to Duard Barnes, 1 March 1974, HF, BAR; Joseph E. Brennan to Director, Office of Indian Affairs, 25 August 1977, HF, BAR; NCAI, Program, 34th Annual Convention, and "Number of Petitions on File as of May 1982," 24 May 1982, HF, BAR.

41. *Mashpee Tribe v. New Seabury Corp.*, 592 F.2d 575 (1979). For additional information on controversies regarding eastern Indian tribal identity, racial Indianness, and law, see Clifford, *Predicament*, 8–17, 278–319; Campisi, *Mashpee Indians*, 151–58; Carrillo, "Identity as Idiom," 43–45; Calloway, "Introduction," 8–14.

42. "Mashpee Wampanoags Lose," *Akwesasne Notes*, late spring 1978, 15.

43. Senate Select Committee, *Federal Acknowledgment Process: Oversight*, 26 May 1988,

61; "Stillaguamish People Still Seeking Recognition," *Akwesasne Notes*, summer 1975, 41; *Stillaguamish Tribe of Indians v. Kleppe, et al.*, no. 75–1718 (D.D.C., 24 September 1976); David Lindgren to Charles E. Trimble, 20 October 1975, HF, BAR; AIPRC *Meetings of the American Indian Policy Review Commission*, vol. 4, 19–23 November 1976 (Washington DC: U.S. Government Printing Office, 1976), 195.

44. Senate Committee on Interior, Subcommittee on Indian Affairs, *California Indian Oversight Hearings*, 27–28 August 1973, 1, 3; Senate Committee on Interior, Subcommittee on Indian Affairs, *Establishment of the American Indian Policy Review Commission*, 19–20 July 1973, 1; American Indian Policy Review Commission (AIPRC), *Final Report*, 3; Thompson, "Nurturing the Forked Tree," 7, 18; Kickingbird and Duchenaux, *One Hundred Million Acres*.

45. "American Indian Policy Review Commission Selects Task Forces," *Akwesasne Notes*, late summer 1975, 20; NCAI, Program, 34th Annual Convention, 1977, HF, BAR.

46. AIPRC, *Report on Terminated and Nonfederally Recognized Indians*, 8, 462–67, 476–79; Chief, Division of Tribal Government Services, to Assistant Secretary, December 1977, HF, BAR.

47. Senate Select Committee, *Recognition of Certain Indian Tribes*, 18 April 1978; Senate Select Committee, *Bill to Establish an Administrative Procedure*, 15 December 1977; House Committee on Interior, Subcommittee on Indian Affairs, *Federal Recognition*, 10 August 1978; "Report of a Meeting with Senate Select Committee," Denis L. Petersen, n.d., "S. 2375," 15 December 1977, HF, BAR; Rick Lavis, memorandum, 14 April 1978, HF, BAR.

48. House Committee on Interior, Subcommittee on Indian Affairs, *Federal Recognition*, 10 August 1978, 14–16.

49. House Committee on Interior, Subcommittee on Indian Affairs, *Federal Recognition*, 10 August 1978, 157; AIPRC, *Final Report*, 37–39, 481–83; Senate Select Committee, *Recognition of Certain Indian Tribes*, 18 April 1978, 5–14, 23, 26, 133–35.

50. Chief, Division of Tribal Government Services, to Assistant Secretary, 20 December 1977, HF, BAR; William Quinn, interview by author; BAR, "Briefing Paper," 24 April 1980, HF, BAR; Scott Keep, memorandum, 25 March 1976, HF, BAR; *Federal Register* 42, no. 116 (16 June 1977): 30,647; Senate Select Committee, *Oversight of the Federal Acknowledgment Process*, 21 July 1983, 115; Office of Tribal Government Services to Rep. James G. Ward, 18 May 1978, HF, BAR.

51. NCAI, Program, 34th Annual Convention, 1977, HF, BAR; NCAI, transcript, National Conference on Tribal Recognition, 209, HF, BAR.

52. House Committee on Interior, Subcommittee on Indian Affairs, *Federal Recognition*, 10 August 1978, 157.

53. House Committee on Interior, Subcommittee on Indian Affairs, *Federal Recognition*, 10 August 1978, 32, 38; NCAI, Program, 34th Annual Convention, 1977, HF, BAR; Deloria, *Custer Died for Your Sins*, 247–50.

54. House Committee on Interior, *Bill: Native Americans Equal Opportunity Act*, 12 September 1977; "The Confusing Specter of White Backlash," *Akwesasne Notes*, Decem-

ber 1977, 22; House Committee on Interior, Subcommittee on Indian Affairs, *Federal Recognition*, 10 August 1978, testimony of Congressman Teno Roncalio, 27.

55. NCAI, transcript, National Conference on Tribal Recognition, 209, HF, BAR.

56. NCAI, transcript, National Conference on Tribal Recognition, 118–32, HF, BAR; "National Indian Lutheran Board Proposal," 31 October 1975, box 118, RG 220, NACP.

57. NCAI, transcript, National Conference on Tribal Recognition, 124, HF, BAR; Bud Shapard to Peter S. Markey, 30 January 1978, and Charles E. Trimble to John Shapard, 10 March 1978, HF, BAR; special issue on tribal recognition, *American Indian Journal* 4, no. 5 (1978).

58. Downs, "National Conference," 2.

59. NCAI, transcript, National Conference on Tribal Recognition, statements of Veronica Murdock, 132, 118–20.

60. NCAI, transcript, National Conference on Tribal Recognition, unidentified speaker, 172.

61. NCAI, transcript, National Conference on Tribal Recognition, 311.

62. NCAI, transcript, National Conference on Tribal Recognition, 259–60.

63. *Preference in Employment*, 25 C.F.R., secs. 5.1–5.4 (1997); Gamino, "Bureau of Indian Affairs," 111; Getches, Wilkinson, and Williams, *Federal Indian Law*, 265; *Indian Self-Determination and Education Assistance Act of 1975*, Public Law 93–638 (1975), 88 Stat. 2203 (1975); 25 U.S.C, secs. 450–58).

64. Senate Select Committee, *Recognition of Certain Indian Tribes*, 18 April 1978, "The National Congress of American Indians Declaration of Principles on Tribal Recognition," 31, 20.

65. Senate Select Committee, *Indian Federal Recognition*, 22 October 1991, 31, 36.

66. NCAI, transcript, National Conference on Tribal Recognition, 198; Small Tribes Organization of Western Washington (STOWW), "Draft Bill," 14 November 1974, box 278, fd. "TF #10—Recognition," RG 220, NACP; Deloria and Lytle, *American Indians, American Justice*, 4.

67. "Procedures for Establishing That an American Indian Group Exists as an Indian Tribe," *Federal Register* 43, no. 106 (1 June 1978): 23,743.

68. *Procedures*, C.F.R. Part 54 (1978); redesignated *Procedures*, 25 C.F.R. Part 83 (1997); BIA, Reid P. Chambers to Solicitor, 20 August 1974, and George M. Crossland to Assistant Secretary for Indian Affairs, 18 October 1977, HF, BAR; Quinn, "Federal Acknowledgment: Authority," 68–69; Bud Shapard, memorandum, 5 December 1978, HF, BAR.

69. C.F.R. Part 54 (1978).

70. House Committee on Interior, Subcommittee on Native American Affairs, *Federal Recognition*, 22 July 1994, 107; "Briefing Paper," 24 April 1980, HF, BAR.

71. House Committee on Interior, Subcommittee on Native American Affairs, *Federal Recognition of Indian Tribes*, 22 July 1994, 135; Quinn interview; BAR, "Briefing Paper," 24 April 1980, HF, BAR.

72. "House Authorizes Spending $2.25 Million to Settle Land Battle," *New York Times*, 30 July 1987, sec. I, p. 20; "Final Determination for Federal Acknowledgment of the Wampanoag Tribal Council of Gay Head, Inc.," *Federal Register* 52 (10 February 1987): 4193.

2. BUILDING AN EDIFICE

1. Senate Select Committee, *Federal Acknowledgment Administrative*, part 1, 5 May 1989, 76; BAR, "List of Petitioners by State," 8 September 1997, http://www.doi.gov/bia/pet908.htm# (accessed 24 November 1997); Steve Austin, interview by author.

2. House Committee on Interior, Subcommittee on Native American Affairs, *Federal Recognition*, 22 July 1994, 127.

3. House Committee on Interior, *Federal Acknowledgment*, 8 July 1992, 493; Bud Shapard to Chief, Division of Tribal Government Services, 30 November 1978, HF, BAR; Senate Select Committee, *Federal Acknowledgment Process: Hearing*, 2 June 1980; Senate Select Committee, *Oversight*, 21 July 1983.

4. Bud Shapard to Dennis Petersen, 1979, HF, BAR; BIA memorandum, 8 November 1978, HF, BAR; "Information about Acknowledgment," n.d., HF, BAR; Ruby B. Ludwig to Assistant Secretary, 8 August 1978, HF, BAR; BAR, "Index to Federal Acknowledgment Petitioners," 8 September 1997, http://www.doi.gov/bia/indx908a.htm (accessed 24 November 1997).

5. Quinn interview; Austin interviews; BIA, "You Asked about Acknowledgment," n.d., HF, BAR, 71–76; George Roth, interview by author; Senate Select Committee, *Oversight*, 21 July 1983, 4.

6. *Procedures*, 25 C.F.R. Part 83 (1997); Austin interviews; Quinn interview.

7. Quinn, " 'Public Ethnohistory?'" 76; Quinn interview; Kevin Gover, "The Eastern Pequots Overcame the Big Lie," *Indian Country Today*, 17 July 2002; "Proposed Finding for Federal Acknowledgment of the Eastern Pequot Indians of Connecticut," 2000, http://www.doi.gov/bia/bar/epfr.htm (accessed 6 April 2000); "Proposed Finding for Federal Acknowledgment of the Paucatuck Eastern Indians of Connecticut," 2000, http://www.doi.gov/bar/pepfr.htm (accessed 6 April 2000).

8. Senate Select Committee, *Federal Acknowledgment Process: Oversight*, 26 May 1988, 2; John Lewis, "Reaganomics and American Indians," *Indian Affairs*, December 1982, 7; Austin interviews.

9. Senate Select Committee, *Federal Acknowledgment Administrative*, part 2, 5 May 1989, 196; Senate Select Committee, *Oversight*, 21 July 1983, 55; Austin interviews.

10. "Quality Stats Report," 1 April 1982, HF, BAR; "Accomplishments of Branch of Federal Acknowledgment," 11 February 1982, HF, BAR; Senate Select Committee, *Federal Acknowledgment Process: Oversight*, 26 May 1988, "Testimony of Joseph G. Jorgensen," 245; Campisi and Starna, "Why Does It," 6, 13.

11. Senate Select Committee, *Oversight*, 21 July 1983, "Statement of the National In-dian Lutheran Board," 40; Quinn interview; Roth interview; Austin interviews; Gregory interview; House Committee on Interior, *Indian Federal Acknowledgment*, 15 September 1992, "Statement of Bud Shapard," 64.

12. "Determination for Federal Acknowledgment of the Grand Traverse Band of Ottawa and Chippewa Indians as an Indian Tribe," *Federal Register* 45, no. 59 (25 March 1980): 19,321; "Petition of the Jamestown Clallam Tribe of Indians," n.d., and "Proposed Finding for Federal Acknowledgment of the Jamestown Band of Clallam Indians of Washington pursuant to 25 C.F.R. 54," 16 May 1980, JC, BAR; "Petition for Recognition of the Tunica-Biloxi Indian Tribes," n.d., and "Proposed Finding for Federal Acknowledgment of the Tunica-Biloxi Indian Tribe," 4 December 1980, TB, BAR; "Final Determination for Federal Acknowledgment of Narragansett Indian Tribe of Rhode Island," *Federal Register* 48, no. 29 (10 February 1983): 6,177; "Final Determination for Federal Acknowledgment of the Poarch Band of Creeks," *Federal Register* 49, no. 113 (11 June 1984) 24,083; Paredes, "Federal Recognition," 120–32.

13. "Final Determination for Federal Acknowledgment of the Wampanoag Tribal Council of Gay Head, Inc.," *Federal Register* 52 (10 February 1987): 4,193, http://www.lexis-nexis.com/congcom (accessed 4 March 1998); Gregory interview; "Summary Status of Acknowledgment Cases," 29 October 1999, http://www.doi.gov/bia/bar/indexq.htm (accessed 6 April 2000). The Narragansett petition, at fourteen volumes including supporting documents, was an exception to the generally small size of early petitions. Senate Select Commission on Indian Affairs, *Oversight*, 21 July 1983, 20.

14. *Southeastern Cherokee Confederacy News*, March 1980; "Proposed Finding against Federal Acknowledgment of the Southeastern Cherokee Confederacy, Inc. (SECC), Northwest Cherokee Wolf Band, SECC, Inc. (NWCWB), and Red Clay Inter-tribal Indian Band, SECC, Inc. (RCIIB)," "Final Determination That the United Lumbee Nation of NC and America, Inc., Does Not Exist as an Indian Tribe," *Federal Register* 50, no. 85 (2 May 1985): 18,746; "Proposed Finding against Federal Acknowledgment of the Kaweah Indian Nation, Inc." 13 June 1984, Kaweah Indian Nation files, BAR.

15. J. Anthony Paredes, interview by author; "Final Determination That the Lower Muscogee Creek Tribe—East of the Mississippi, Inc., Does Not Exist as an Indian Tribe," 17 September 1982, Lower Muscogee Creek Tribe files, BAR; "Proposed Finding against Federal Acknowledgment of the Machis Lower Alabama Creek Indian Tribe," *Federal Register* 52, no. 175 (10 September 1987): 43,319; "Creeks East of the Mississippi and Lower Muscogee Creek Tribe—East of the Mississippi, Inc., Clarification of Previous Notices," *Federal Register* 47, no. 66 (2 May 1985): 14,783; "Summary Status of Acknowledgment Cases," 29 October 1999, http://www.doi.gov/bia/bar/indexq.htm (accessed 6 April 2000); "Proposed Finding against Federal Acknowledgment of the Munsee-Thames River Delaware Indian Nation of Pueblo, CO," 9 February 1982, Munsee-Thames River Delaware Indian Nation files, BAR; Roth, "Overview of Southeastern Indian Tribes," 183–201.

16. "Summary Status of Acknowledgment Cases," 29 October 1999, http://www.doi.gov/bia/bar/indexq.htm (accessed 6 April 2000).

17. House Committee on Interior, Subcommittee on Native American Affairs, *Federal Recognition*, 22 July 1994, 78, 116; BAR, "Summary Status of Acknowledgment Cases, 29 October 1999, http://www.doi.gov/bia/bar/indexq.htm (accessed 6 April 2000); Senate Committee on Indian Affairs, *Federal Recognition Administrative*, 13 July 1995, "Statement of Hon. John McCain," 1, "Statement of Hon. Daniel K. Inouye," 54; House Committee on Interior, *California Tribal Status*, 10 October 1991, "Opening Statement of Hon. Eni F. H. Faleomavaega," 1; Jill Peters, interview by author.

18. *An Act to Settle Certain Claims of the Mashantucket Pequot Indians*, Public Law 98–134 (18 October 1983), 97 Stat. 851; Senate Select Committee, *Oversight*, 21 July 1983, 57; BAR, "Briefing Paper on Legislative Recognition of New Tribes," n.d., HF, BAR; Cynthia Brown, "Vanishing Native Americans," 384–89. Since 1978 the following groups have submitted bills for acknowledgment to no effect: the United Houma Nation, MOWA Band of Choctaws, Jena Band of Choctaws, Lumbee Tribe of North Carolina. See, for example, Senate Select Committee, *Federal Recognition of the* MOWA, 26 June 1991. Other tribes have succeeded through legislation during this time frame, however, including the Aroostook Band of Micmacs, Pokagon Potawatomi Indians, Little Traverse Bay Band of Odawa, the Little River Band of Ottawa, and the Cow Creek Band of Umpqua. "Summary Status of Acknowledgment Cases," 29 October 1999, *http://www.doi.gov*/bia/bar/indexq.htm (accessed 6 April 2000).

19. *Miami Nation of Indians v. U.S. Department of the Interior*, 255 F.3d 342 (7th Cir. 2001); Evan St. Lifer, "Ramapoughs Seek Federal Tribal Status," *New York Times*, 6 September 1987, sec. XI, p. 3.

20. Holly Reckord, interview by author.

21. Quinn interview; Austin interviews; "Notice of Final Determination That the San Juan Southern Paiute Tribe Exists as an Indian Tribe," *Federal Register* 54, no. 43 (15 December 1989): 51,502, http://www.lexis-nexis.com/congcom (accessed 4 March 1998); *Masayesva v. Zah*, 792 F.Supp. 1165 (D. Ariz. 1992); Bunte and Franklin, *From the Sands*. The Cherokee Nation also sued the Department of the Interior over the acknowledgment of the Delaware Tribe outside the FAP. *Cherokee Nation of Oklahoma v. Babbitt*, 117 F.3d 1489 (DC Cir. 1997).

22. House Committee on Interior, *Indian Federal Acknowledgment*, 15 September 1992, 64; House Committee on Interior, Subcommittee on Native American Affairs, *Federal Recognition*, 22 July 1994, 165–66; Quinn interview; Roth interview; Gregory interview; Austin interviews.

23. "Summary Status of Acknowledgement Cases," 29 October 1999, http://www.doi.gov/bia/bar/indexq.htm (accessed 6 April 2000).

24. Quinn interview; "Acknowledgment of Unrecognized Indian Tribes," n.d., and "You Asked about Acknowledgment," n.d., HF, BAR; "Final Determination against Federal Acknowledgment of the Golden Hill Paugussett Tribe," n.d., http://www.doi.gov/

bia/ghpfinal.html (accessed 15 January 1998); "Proposed Finding against Acknowl-edgment of the Duwamish Tribal Organization," n.d., http://www.doi.gov/bia/bar/duwamishsum.html (accessed 15 January 1998).

25. Paula E. Rabskin, Yale University, to John A. Shapard, n.d., HF, BAR; Quinn interview; Nagel, *American Indian Ethnic Renewal*, 23–30; Peter Novick, *That Noble Dream*; Senate Select Committee on Indian Affairs, *Federal Acknowledgment Process: Hearing*, 2 June 1980, 47.

26. McCulloch and Wilkins, " 'Constructing' Nations within States," 361–67; House Committee on Interior, Subcommittee on Indian Affairs, *Federal Recognition*, 10 August 1978, testimony of Charles Trimble, NCAI, 37; Senate Select Committee, *Federal Recognition*, 27 September 1977, James Allen, chief, Seneca-Cayuga Tribe, 33.

27. House Committee on Interior, *Federal Acknowledgment*, 8 July 1992, 92–105; Senate Select Committee, *Indian Federal Recognition*, 22 October 1991, 153–55. Jack Campisi and Vine Deloria declined requests to comment on the process. The Lumbee bill in 1988, in particular, provides many of the opinions of these scholars in one publication. Senate Select Committee, *Federal Recognition of the Lumbee*, 12 August 1988.

28. House Committee on Indian and Insular Affairs, *California Tribal Status*, 10 October 1991, 158.

29. *Procedures*, 25 C.F.R. Part 83 (1997); Greenbaum, "What's in a Label?" 107–24; Quinn, "Southeastern Indians," 42; "Final Determination—Mobile-Washington County Band of Choctaw Indians of South Alabama," 16 December 1997, http://www.doi.gov/bia/mowanew.htm (accessed 15 January 1998); "Final Determination against Federal Acknowledgment of the Ramapough Mountain Indians, Inc.," n.d., http://www.doi.gov/bia/ramasum.html (accessed 15 January 1998); Earle, *Report to the Governor*.

30. *Procedures*, 25 C.F.R. Part 83 (1997). Although the section stating that groups must live in a community viewed as Indian was extracted from the 1994 revised regulations, petitioners still must possess a distinct, Indian-identified community to secure acknowledgment.

31. House Committee on Interior, Subcommittee on Native American Affairs, *Federal Recognition*, 22 July 1994, 164; "Frequently Asked Questions, Acknowledgment Guide-lines," n.d., http://www.doi.gov/bar/arguide.html (accessed 6 April 2000); 25 C.F.R. Part 83 (1997); Senate Select Committee, *Federal Acknowledgment Administrative*, part 2, 5 May 1989, "Testimony of Jack Campisi," 78.

32. Senate Select Committee, *Indian Federal Recognition*, 22 October 1991, 143–44; House Committee on Interior, Subcommittee on Native American Affairs, *Federal Recognition*, 22 July 1994, "Statement of the Tulalip Tribes," 137–50; "Frequently Asked Questions, Acknowledgment Guidelines," n.d., " http://www.doi.gov/bar/arguide.html (accessed 6 April 2000). For a telling example of the BAR's methodology in determining "community" see "Summary under the Criteria and Evidence for Proposed Finding against Federal Acknowledgment of the Chinook Indian Tribe, Inc.," 11 August 1997, http://www.doi.gov/bia/bar/chinsum.html (accessed 15 January 1998).

33. Senate Select Committee, *Indian Federal Recognition*, 22 October 1991, 175–76.

34. Felix S. Cohen, *Handbook of Federal Indian Law*, 271–72; Quinn interview; Austin interviews; "Proposed Finding against Acknowledgment of the Chinook Indian Tribe, Inc.," 11 August 1997, http://www.doi.gov/bia/bar/chinsum.html (accessed 15 January 1998); "Proposed Finding against Acknowledgment of the Duwamish Tribal Organization," n.d., http://www.doi.gov/bia/bar/duwamsum.html (accessed 15 January 1998).

35. Senate Select Committee, *Federal Acknowledgment Administrative*, part 2, 5 May 1989, 52; *Procedures*, 25 C.F.R. Part 83 (1997).

36. Roth interview; Robin D. G. Kelley, *Race Rebels*, 36; Barth, *Ethnic Groups and Boundaries*, 9–17; Wilkins, "U.S. Supreme Court's Explication," 350.

37. "Final Determination for Federal Acknowledgment of the Wampanoag Tribal Council of Gay Head, Inc.," *Federal Register* 52 (10 February 1987): 4193, http://www.lexis-nexis.com/congcom (accessed 4 March 1998); "Proposed Finding, Matchebenashshe-wish Band of Pottawatomi Indians of Michigan," n.d., http://www.doi.gov/bia/bar/matchsum.html (accessed 16 July 1998); "Summary Status of Acknowledgment Cases," 29 October 1999, http://www.doi.gov/bia/bar/indexq.htm (accessed 6 April 2000).

38. *Procedures*, 25 C.F.R. Part 83 (1997); Richard Stoffle, interview by author; Austin interviews; "Reconsideration of the Final Determination, Golden Hill," 24 May 1999, GHP, BAR; Senate Select Committee, *Federal Acknowledgment Process: Oversight*, 26 May 1988, testimony of Joseph G. Jorgensen, 245.

39. House Committee on Interior, *Federal Acknowledgment*, 8 July 1992, 104–5.

40. Senate Select Committee, *Federal Recognition of the* MOWA, 26 June 1991, 173; Jim Wolfe, "Supreme Court Doesn't Clear Air," *Muscogee Nation News*, March 1991, 2.

41. Quinn interview; "Summary under the Criteria and Evidence for Final Determination against Federal Acknowledgment of the Ramapough Mountain Indians, Inc.," n.d., http://www.doi.gov/bia/ramasum/html (accessed 15 January 1998); Austin interviews.

42. Senate Select Committee, *Indian Federal Recognition*, 22 October 1991, 132.

43. House Committee on Interior, Subcommittee on Indian Affairs, *Federal Recognition*, 10 August 1978, 45.

44. Austin interviews; Senate Select Committee, *Federal Acknowledgment Administrative*, part 2, 5 May 1989, 41.

45. Senate Select Committee, *Oversight*, 21 July 1983, "Statement of John Shapard," 11; Quinn interview; Yvonne Hajda, "Creating Tribes," *Anthropology Newsletter* 28 (October 1987), 2; Russel L. Barsh and Yvonne Hajda, "Appearance of Unfairness?" *Anthropology Newsletter* 29 (March 1988), 2; George Roth, "Acknowledgment Process—Not Inconsistent," *Anthropology Newsletter* 29 (January 1988), 2; George Roth, "Not So!" *Anthropology Newsletter* 29 (March 1988), 2; Quinn interview; Austin interviews; Russel L. Barsh, personal correspondence with author, 17 February 2002; *Greene v. Babbitt*, 64 F.3d 1266 (9th Cir. 1995).

46. House Committee on Interior, *Federal Acknowledgment*, 8 July 1992, 495.

47. House Committee on Interior, Subcommittee on Native American Affairs, *Federal Recognition*, 22 July 1994, 166.

48. Quinn interview; Roth interview; Marie Mauzé, introduction to Mauzé, *Present Is Past*, 5; McIlwraith, "Problem of Imported Culture," 41–70; Jonathan Friedman, "Past in the Future," 837–59.

49. House Committee on Interior, *California Tribal Status*, 10 October 1991, 182.

50. House Committee on Interior and Affairs, *Federal Acknowledgment*, 8 July 1992, 92–93; "Resource People for Federal Acknowledgment Research," in Porter, *Nonrecognized American Indian Tribes*; confidential personal interviews; Senate Select Committee, *Federal Acknowledgment Administrative*, part 1, 28 April 1989, 279; "Summary Status of Acknowledgment Cases," 2 March 1999, http://www.doi.gov/bia/0302stat.htm (accessed 20 April 1999); "Index to Federal Acknowledgment Petitioners by State," 29 October 1999, http://www.doi.gov/bia/bar/indexz.htm (accessed 6 April 2000).

51. Linda Anisman, interview by author.

52. Senate Select Committee, *Federal Acknowledgment Administrative*, part 2, 5 May 1989, 73; Senate Select Committee, *Federal Acknowledgment Process: Oversight*, 26 May 1988, 7; Austin interviews.

53. Senate, Select Committee, *Federal Acknowledgment Administrative*, part 2, 5 May 1989, Orbis Associates, Final Report, 366–457; NCAI, transcript, National Conference on Tribal Recognition, 1978, HF, BAR; Cindy Darcy, interview by author,; Bud Shapard, "Status Report," n.d., HF, BAR; Anisman interview; Gregory interview; Rosamund Spicer, interview by author.

54. House Committee on Interior, *Federal Acknowledgment*, 8 July 1992, J. Matte testimony, 428; Barsh and Hajda, "Appearance of Unfairness?" 2; Barsh, "Are Anthropologists Hazardous," 18; James A. Clifton, introduction, and John A. Price, "Ethical Advocacy versus Propaganda: Canada's Indian Support Groups," in Clifton, *Invented Indian*.

55. James Greenberg, interview by author; Gregory interview.

56. Senate Select Committee, *Oversight*, 21 July 1983, 8; Senate Select Committee, *Federal Acknowledgment Administrative*, part 2, 5 May 1989, statement of John McCain, 36; Quinn, " 'Public Ethnohistory'?" 302; BAR, "Acknowledgment Guidelines," http://www.doi.gov/bia/bar/arguide.html (accessed 6 April 2000); *Miami Nation of Indians v. U.S. Department of the Interior*, 255 F.3d 342 (7th Cir. 2001).

57. Austin interviews; House Committee on Interior, *Indian Federal Acknowledgment*, 15 September 1992, 44–46.

58. "Reconsideration of the Final Report of the Golden Hill Paugussett," 24 May 1999, GHP, BAR.

59. Austin interviews.

60. Senate Select Committee, *Federal Acknowledgment Administrative*, part 2, 5 May 1989, 35; Senate Select Committee, *Indian Federal Recognition*, 22 October 1991, 31.

61. Senate Select Committee, *Federal Acknowledgment Administrative*, part 2, 5 May 1989, 85.

62. Senate Select Committee, *Federal Acknowledgment Process: Oversight*, 26 May 1988, 42.

63. House Committee on Interior, Subcommittee on Native American Affairs, *Federal Recognition*, 22 July 1994, 109; Quinn interview; "Acknowledgment Guidelines," n.d., http://www.doi.gov/bia/bar/arguide.html (accessed 6 April 2000); Austin interviews.

64. Senate Select Committee, *Federal Acknowledgment Administrative*, part 1, 28 April 1989, 49–50.

65. For example, Senate Select Committee, *Federal Acknowledgment Administrative*, part 2, 5 May 1989, 62; "Trip Report—Western Washington Area," n.d., HF, BAR.

66. House Committee on Interior, *California Tribal Status*, 10 October 1991, 69–70.

67. BAR, memorandum on Mashantucket Pequot bill, n.d., HF, BAR; NCAI, transcript, National Conference on Tribal Recognition, 1978, HF, BAR; AIPRC, *Meetings*, 203.

68. Dirk Johnson, "Census Finds Many Claiming New Identity: Indian," *New York Times*, 5 March 1991, sec. A, p. 1; Quinn, "Southeast Syndrome," 147–54; Stan Steiner, "The White Indians," *Akwesasne Notes*, early spring 1976, 38; Paredes, "Paradoxes of Modernism," 341–59; Rayna Green, "Tribe Called Wannabee," 30–55; Hagan, "Full Blood, Mixed Blood," 309–26. The rise in individuals self-identifying as Native American in the U.S. census continues unabated. "Census Bureau Facts and Figures," 26 October 1998, http://www.census.gov/population/estimates/nation/intfile3–1.txt (accessed 12 May 2003).

69. AIPRC, *Meetings*, 170–71.

70. Senate Select Committee, *Oversight*, 21 July 1983, 40; Gregory interview.

71. Senate Select Committee, *Oversight*, 21 July 1983, 8.

72. Senate Select Committee, *Federal Recognition of the Lumbee*, 12 August 1988, 9; Roth interview; David E. Wilkins, personal correspondence with author, 1999.

73. House Committee on Interior, Subcommittee on Native American Affairs, *Federal Recognition*, 22 July 1994, 133.

74. Senate Committee on Indian Affairs, *Federal Recognition*, 13 July 1995, R. Lee Fleming, registrar, Cherokee Nation, report, "The Cherokee Name and Sovereignty Are in Danger," 1995, 217–41; "Summary Status of Acknowledgment Cases," 29 October 1999, http://www.doi.gov/bia/bar/indexq.htm (accessed 6 April 2000); "Federal Activity in the State of Georgia," 9 February 1979, HF, BAR.

75. Senate Select Committee, *Federal Recognition of the Lumbee*, 12 August 1988, 36; Senate Select Committee, *Indian Federal Recognition*, 22 October 1991, 105; Chad Smith, principal chief, Cherokee Nation, correspondence with author, Sequoyah Research Center Symposium, Little Rock AR, 17 November 2001.

76. Senate Committee on Indian Affairs, *Federal Recognition*, 13 July 1995, 211–16; AIPRC, *Final Report*, vol. 2, Claude A. Cox, principal chief, Creek Nation, to Ernest L. Stevens, 25 April 1977; Senate Select Committee, *Federal Acknowledgment Administrative*, part 2, 5 May 1989, "Statement of Philip Martin, Chief, Mississippi Band of Choctaw

Indians, 268–71; Theodore Krenzke to Robert Trepp, 31 January 1979, HF, BAR; Joyce Bear, cultural preservation officer, Muscogee Nation, correspondence with author, 17 November 2001.

77. "Notice of Final Determination That the San Juan Southern Paiute Tribe Exists as an Indian Tribe," *Federal Register* 54 (15 December 1989): 51,502, http://web.lexis-nexis.com/congcom (accessed 4 March 1998); Austin interviews; Quinn interview; William Quinn Jr., "Comprehensive Ethnohistory, Report on Canoncito and Alamo Bands," Southwest Center, University of New Mexico, Albuquerque NM.

78. Senate Select Committee, *Federal Acknowledgment Administrative*, part 2, 5 May 1989, 58; "New Ways to Recognize Tribes Split Indians," *New York Times*, 4 August 1991, sec. L, p. 33.

79. Senate Committee on Indian Affairs, *Federal Recognition*, 13 July 1995, 2. The titles of these articles and others speak volumes as to linkages between acknowledgment and gaming: George Judson, "Land Claim by Indians Is a Tactic in Casino Bid," *New York Times*, 21 June 1993, sec. L, p. B1; Sam Libby, "Another Tribal Nation? Another Casino?" *New York Times*, 18 February 1996, sec. XIII-CN, p. 6.

80. Prucha, *Indian Policy*, 44–45; Spicer, *Short History*, 4, 123; Berkhofer, "White Conceptions of Indians," 522–29; Willie Clark to Cecil D. Andrus, 20 February 1977, box 116, fd. 5, Domenici Papers; Dan Noys, "Indian Backlash Group Seeking Contributions Illegally," *Akwesasne Notes*, summer 1978, 25; John Lewis, "Reaganomics and American Indians," *Indian Affairs*, December 1982.

81. Senate Select Committee, *Federal Recognition of the Lumbee*, 12 August 1988, 9.

82. "President Reagan Meets with Indian Groups," *New York Times*, 20 August 1988, sec. I, p. 8; "Watt Lies behind These Remarks?" *Akwesasne Notes*, late winter 1983, 24; Austin interviews.

83. National Wildlife Federation to John Cadwalader, 26 June 1975, box 33, RG 220, NACP; opposition gleaned from various letters and testimony in congressional hearings previously cited.

84. Senate Select Committee, *Federal Acknowledgment Administrative*, parts 1 and 2, 28 April 1989 and 5 May 1989. Various other reform bills have been cited elsewhere. Also see Senate Committee on Indian Affairs, *Federal Recognition Administrative Procedures Act of 1995*, 13 July 1995, and House Committee on Resources, *Indian Federal Recognition Administrative Procedures Act of 1997*, 20 March 1997.

85. Senate Select Committee, *Federal Acknowledgment Administrative*, part 2, 5 May 1989, 38–41.

86. Peters interview.

87. *Procedures*, 25 C.F.R. Part 83 (1997); BAR, "Acknowledgment Guidelines," http://www.doi.gov/bia/bar/arguide.html (accessed 6 April 2000); House Committee on Interior, Subcommittee on Native American Affairs, *Federal Recognition*, 22 July 1994, 114. For an example of the BAR methods under the revised regulations see "Summary under the Criteria and Evidence for Proposed Finding, Cowlitz Tribe of Indians,"

http://www.doi.gov/bia/bar/cowsum.html (accessed 21 January 1998). Even with the choice, some groups have requested consideration under the old rules because groups with unambiguous acknowledgment prior to 1900 would have to prove all criteria to that earlier date, including the identity criterion that requires proof only after 1900.

88. U.S. General Accounting Office (GAO), "Indian Issues: Improvements Needed," table 3.

89. BAR, "Summary Status of Acknowledgment Cases," 29 October 1999, http://www.doi.gov/bia/bar/indexq.htm (accessed 6 April 2000); GAO Report, "Indian Issues: Improvements Needed," 26.

90. Gover, quoted in "Congress Considers New Process for Tribal Recognition," *Indian Country Today*, 31 May 2000, http://www.indiancountry.com/?821 (accessed 26 December 2000).

91. "Wolf Calls for GAO Investigation," press release, Congressman Frank R. Wolf, (R-VA), 21 September 2000, http://www.house.gov/wolf/2000921GAOTribal.htm (accessed 8 February 2000); Connecticut Attorney General's Office, press release, "Attorney General's letter to the Senate Indian Affairs Committee asking for a moratorium on tribal recognition legislation," 7 June 2000, http://www.cslib.org/attygenl/press/2000/Indian/Campbell.htm (accessed 26 December 2001); "Clinton Aid Granted Status to Tribe after Leaving Office," 3 March 2002, http://www.nytimes.com (accessed 3 March 2002).

92. GAO Report, "Indian Issues: Improvements Needed," 14, 41–47.

93. BIA, "Changes in the Internal Processing of Federal Acknowledgment Petitions," *Federal Register* 65, no. 29 (11 February 2000): 7,052–53, http://www.gpoaccess.gov/fr/search.html (accessed 27 February 2002).

94. House Committee on Interior, Subcommittee on Native American Affairs, *Federal Recognition*, 22 July 1994, 127; Roth interview; Quinn interview; Paredes interview.

95. Philip Baker-Shenk, interview by author.

96. Senate Select Committee, *Federal Recognition of the Lumbee*, 12 August 1988, 33; Chuck Striplen, "A Journey East," 25 August 1998, http://www.indiancanyon.org/nosonpage.html#east (accessed 12 May 2003).

97. Senate Select Committee, *Federal Recognition of the Lumbee*, 12 August 1988, 98, 24–27, 89–99, 85–88.

98. Senate, Select Committee, *Indian Federal Recognition*, 22 October 1991, "Testimony of Henry J. Sockbeson," 196–210, and testimony of Alogan Slagle, 211–45; Senate Committee on Indian Affairs, *Federal Recognition*, 13 July 1995, "Testimony of Arlinda Locklear," 131–41.

99. Holly Reckord, quoted in Cynthia Brown, "The Vanishing Native Americans," *The Nation*, 11 October 1993, 384–89. Quinn perhaps best sums up the view of the BIA on the matter, arguing: "the unresolved ethnological debate in academia over the definition of tribes has been and appears to be interminable, with all of its attendant model-building and theoretical abstractions—the United States was forced to adopt a

practical definition [and process that] is the best procedure available in a fallible and imperfect world." Quinn, "Southeastern Indians," 37.

3. BYPASSING THE BUREAU

1. Anselmo Valencia, interview by author; "Task Force #10, Hearing—New Pascua Yaqui Village, Tucson, Arizona," 22–23 May 1976, box 47, RG 220, NACP. For an earlier version of this chapter's major points see Miller, "Yaquis Become 'American' Indians."

2. President Jimmy Carter to Secretary Cecil Andrus, 18 September 1978, HF, BAR; McCulloch and Wilkins, "'Constructing' Nations within States," 361–67; Castile, "Commodification of Indian Identity," 747; Jaimes, "Federal Indian Identification Policy," 126–37.

3. Spicer, "Highlights in Yaqui History," 2–6; Hu-Dehart, Missionaries, Miners and Indians, 23–39; Spicer, Yaquis, 2–15, 22, 54.

4. Spicer, Potam, 25–27; Spicer, Yaquis, 4–16, 22–23, 30–54; Spicer, Pascua, xiii, 10, 69–82.

5. Spicer, "Highlights in Yaqui History," 7; Dabdoub, Historia de el Valle, 115–55; Figueroa, Los que hablan Fuerte, 88–90; Jane Holden Kelley, Yaqui Women, 133–36; Edward Spicer to Paul Fannin, 9 January 1976, box 94, fd. 9/7, Fannin Papers; Spicer, Yaquis, 158–59; McGuire, Politics and Ethnicity, i, 21.

6. John H. Provinse to Sells Indian Agency, 5 April 1935, Provinse Papers; Edward H. Spicer to Paul J. Fannin, 9 January 1976, box 94, fd. 9/7, Fannin Papers; Bronislaw Malinowski, notes on Yaquis, SGISIFI, Painter Papers.

7. Spicer, Pascua, 4–5, 28–58; Spicer, Yaquis, 235–42; Tom Moore to Herbert H. Kaiser Jr., 12 April 1976, box 10, fd. 26, "I" series, Goldwater Papers; Spicer interview; Felipe S. Molina, personal correspondence, 17 March 1998; Valencia interview.

8. Spicer, Yaquis, 18–22, 59–60; Gruzinski, Conquest of Mexico; Lockhart, Nahuas after Conquest.

9. Spicer, Yaquis, 70–86; Molina and Evers, Yaqui Deer Songs, 39–40; Molina, personal correspondence.

10. Painter, With Good Heart, 17–19, 119; Molina and Evers, Yaqui Deer Songs, 7, 73, 77; Spicer, Yaquis, 73, 86–90, 99–105, 112; Molina, personal correspondence.

11. John Province to Sells Agency, 5 April 1935, Provinse Papers; "Rehabilitation Plan," Provinse Papers; Spicer, Yaquis, 238–39, 247–49.

12. "Rehabilitation Plan," Provinse Papers; Bogan, Yaqui Indian Dances; Spicer, Yaquis, 244; Malinowski, "notes," SG4S3F, Painter Papers; "A Project for the Study of a Group of Yaqui Indians in Arizona," 1935, and John Provinse to Sells Agency, 5 April 1935, Provinse Papers; Spicer, Pascua, 31.

13. "Rehabilitation Plan," Provinse Papers; Beinart, "Lost Tribes," 32–41; Sánchez, Becoming Mexican American, 209–26; "Chronological History of the Pascua Yaqui Indians," box 606, fd. 606/16, Udall Papers; "Hunt Assures Yaqui Safety," (Tucson) Arizona Daily

Star, 23 September 1931; John Provinse, letter to Sells Agency, 5 April 1935, Provinse Papers.

14. "Proposal to Rehabilitate Certain Yaqui Indians," 5 April 1935, Provinse Papers; H. L. Shantz to Isabella Greenway, 24 March 1934, Provinse Papers; Thamar Richey to Isabella Greenway, 5 March 1934, box 27, fd. 330, Greenway Papers.

15. Robert Redfield to John Provinse, 26 February 1936, Provinse Papers; "A Project for the Study of a Group of Yaqui Indians," Provinse Papers; John Provinse to R. M. Tisinger, 16 February 1935, Provinse Papers; John Provinse to Robert Redfield, 26 March 1936, Provinse Papers; Babcock, *Daughters of the Desert*, 77; Castile and Kushner, *Persistent Peoples*.

16. John Collier to Isabella Greenway, 14 May 1934, box 27, fd. 330, Greenway Papers; "A Project for the Study of a Group of Yaqui Indians," Provinse Papers.

17. R. M. Tisinger to John Provinse, 26 March 1935, Provinse Papers; Ruth Underhill, Associate Director, Indian Education, "Report on a Visit to Indian Groups in Louisiana, Oct. 15–25, 1938," CCF, General Services, 800–1931-10859 through 800–1931-71145, fd. 68776–31-800 pt. 2, NAB.

18. John Collier to Isabella Greenway, 28 June 1934, box 27, fd. 330, Greenway Papers; John Collier to Jasper Elliot, 28 June 1934, box 27, fd. 330, Greenway Papers; Isabella Greenway to Thamar Richey, 18 April 1935, box 27, fd. 330, Greenway Papers; John Collier, letter to all superintendents, 17 June 1935, Provinse Papers. Congress also failed to appropriate funds for reservations in Michigan at the same time, leaving several bands there without clear federal status or aid. Senate Committee on Indian Affairs, *Pokagon Band*, 10 February 1994, "Supplemental Testimony of Michigan Indian Legal Services," 402–6.

19. Valencia, quoted in "Cover Story on Yaqui Indians," *(Phoenix) Arizona Republic*, 2 September 1979 (copy in Spicer Papers, fd. "1976–81"); Valencia interview; Muriel Thayer Painter, "Project Diary, 1949–1969" (Painter Diary), SG4S3F1–15, Painter Papers.

20. Valencia interview; Spicer interview; Babcock, *Daughters of the Desert*, 82–83.

21. Spicer interview; Spicer, *Pascua*, 117–72; C. Edgar Goyette, Tucson Chamber of Commerce, to Muriel Painter, 5 July 1949, SG4S3F1, Painter Papers; Muriel Painter to Anselmo Valencia, 4 April 1962, SG4S1F6, Painter Papers.

22. Valencia, quoted in "Anselmo Valencia Is Part of Two Distinct Cultures," *Tucson Citizen*, 23 July 1955; Painter Diary, 8 February 1955 and 7 July 1955, SG4S3F2, 5 August 1961 and 5 March 1962, SG1S1F43, Painter Papers.

23. Painter Diary, 3 May 1947, 17 May 1949, 22 September 1949, and 15 March 1950, SG4S3F1, Painter Papers.

24. Painter Diary, 27 April 1949, 6 July 1949, 22 July 1949, and 26 July 1949, SG4S3F1, Painter Papers; Spicer, *Yaquis*, 244–56.

25. Painter Diary, 15 January 1949, 1 August 1949, 22 September 1949, 31 May 1950, SG4S3F1, Painter Papers; B. M. Thompson to E. S. Borquist, 15 March 1950, SG4S3F1, Painter Papers; Muriel Painter, memo, 9 May 1950, SG4S3F1, Painter Papers; Painter

Diary, 30 September 1953, SG4S3F1, Painter Papers; "Board Delays Yaqui Village Zoning Action," *(Tucson) Arizona Daily Star*, 21 November 1953, 1.

26. Theodore Heyl to Morris K. Udall, 29 January 1963, box 165, fd. 165/13, Udall Papers; Valencia interview; Muriel Painter to Morris K. Udall, 1 January 1963, box 165, fd. 165/14, Udall Papers; Gertrude Mason to Morris Udall, 15 May 1964, box 165, fd. 165/13, Udall Papers.

27. Valencia interview.

28. Spicer interview; Valencia interview; minutes, meeting of Committee for Pascua Community Housing, 19 September 1962 and 21 November 1962, SG4S3F6, Painter Papers.

29. Ray Johnson to Morris Udall, 1 February 1963, box 165, fd. 165/13, Udall Papers; Painter Diary, 24 October 1962, 5 February 1962, SG4S3F8, Painter Papers; Udall, *Too Funny to Be President*, xv, 29, 95; Spicer interview; Valencia interview.

30. Painter Diary, 17 June 1962, 24 October 1962, and 5 February 1963, SG4S3F8, Painter Papers; minutes, meeting of Committee for Pascua Community Housing, 23 July 1962, SG4S3F6, Painter Papers.

31. Wilma Klem to Morris Udall, 11 October 1962, box 520, fd. 520/19, Udall Papers; Janet Reylock to Morris Udall, 8 April 1973, box 573, fd. 573/20, Udall Papers; Matusow, *Unraveling of America*.

32. Morris Udall to Minerva Ortiz, 5 October 1970, box 114, fd. 114/13, Udall Papers.

33. Valencia interview; Painter Diary, 5 November 1962, 10 December 1962, SG4S3F8, Painter Papers; Willard, "Community Development Worker," 43; minutes, meeting of Committee for Pascua Community Housing, 31 October 1962, 21 November 1962, SG4S3F6, Painter Papers.

34. Valencia, quoted in Painter Diary, 16 October 1962, SG4S3F3, Painter Papers; Painter Diary, 6 January 1963 and 24 June 1963, SG4S3F8, Painter Papers; Spicer interview.

35. Painter Diary, 8 October 1962, 24 October 1962, 29 October 1962, and 3 November 1962, SG4S3F8, Painter Papers; minutes, meeting of Pima County Planning Commission, 21 November 1962, SG4S3F8, Painter Papers.

36. Richard Olson to Muriel Painter, 12 February 1963, box 165, fd. 165/14, Udall Papers; Theodore Heyl to Anselmo Valencia, 4 December 1962, SG4S3F7, Painter Papers; Valencia interview.

37. Valencia, quoted in Painter Diary, 18 February 1963, SG4S3F8, Painter Papers; Painter Diary, 28 June 1963 and 27 October 1963, SG4S3F8, Painter Papers; Morris Udall to S. Leonard Scheff, 14 March 1964, box 165, fd. 165/14, Udall Papers.

38. Articles of Incorporation, box 165, fd. 165/14, Udall Papers.

39. Anselmo Valencia to Morris Udall, 21 December 1962, in "Petition for Land for the Relocation of Residents of Pascua Village of Tucson, Arizona," 1 January 1963, box 1, fd. 7, Spicer Papers (also box 165, fd. 165/14, Udall Papers); Painter Diary, 2 December 1962, SG4S3F8, Painter Papers.

40. Painter, *Faith, Flowers and Fiestas*; Pascua Yaqui Association (PYA), "Petition," 14 January 1963, box 165, fd. 165/14, Udall Papers, and box 1, fd. 7, Spicer Papers.

41. Painter Diary, 1963, SG4S3F8, Painter Papers; Morris Udall to Anselmo Valencia, 31 January 1963, box 165, fd. 165/14, Udall Papers.

42. Morris Udall to S. Leonard Scheff, 14 August 1964, box 165, fd. 165/14, Udall Papers; PYA, "Petition," 1 January 1963, box 165, fd. 165/14, Udall Papers.

43. Cocio, quoted in Painter Diary, 26 March 1963, SG4S3F8, Painter Papers; Valencia interview.

44. Willard, "Community Development Worker," 109; John Provinse to Sells Agency, 4 April 1935, Provinse Papers.

45. A. Turney Smith to Morris Udall, 11 August 1964, box 165, fd. 165/13, Udall Papers (emphasis added).

46. Vivian Arnold to Morris Udall, 17 August 1964, box 165, fd. 165/13, Udall Papers.

47. Monte Seymour to Morris Udall, 10 August 1964, box 165, fd. 165/13, Udall Papers.

48. Morgan Maxwell Sr., letter to editor, *(Tucson) Arizona Daily Star*, attached to Joseph Cesare to Honorable Henry Jackson, 14 September 1964, box 165, fd. 165/14, Udall Papers; Joseph Cesare to Henry Jackson, 12 September 1964, box 165, fd. 165/14, Udall Papers.

49. John Swank to Morris Udall, 8 August 1964, box 165, fd. 165/14, Udall Papers.

50. John Swank, I. J. Gleason, and Bruce Garrison to Stewart Udall, 20 February 1964, box 165, fd. 165/14, Udall Papers.

51. S. Leonard Scheff to Richard Olson, 4 April 1964, box 165, fd. 165/14, Udall Papers; Morris Udall to Carl Hayden, 6 August 1964, box 165, fd. 165/14, Udall Papers; James E. Officer to John Swank, 6 March 1964, box 165, fd. 165/14, Udall Papers.

52. House Committee on Interior, *Bill to Provide for the Conveyance*, 14 August 1964 (also in box 165, fd. 165/13, Udall Papers).

53. Valencia, quoted in Don Robinson, "Yaqui Indians Promised New Village," *(Tucson) Arizona Daily Star*, 20 February 1963.

54. James Officer, interview by author; (anonymous), memo regarding Yaqui bill, n.d., box 165, fd. 165/13, Udall Papers; Morris Udall to Muriel Painter, 19 January 1963, box 165, fd. 165/13, Udall Papers; "Report to accompany H.R. 6233," 88th Cong., 2d sess., 8 August 1964, box 165, fd. 165/14, Udall Papers; Edward Spicer to Teno Roncalio, 1 March 1978, box 1, fd. 6, Spicer Papers; *An Act to Grant 81 Acres of Public Domain to the Cocopah Indians of Arizona*, Public Law 87–150, 87th Cong., 17 August 1961, box 94, fd. 94/12, Udall Papers; interoffice memo on Cocopah bill, box 94, fd. 94/12, Udall Papers; Muriel Painter to Roy Helmendollar, Bureau of Land Management, 29 January 1963, box 165, fd. 165/13, Udall Papers.

55. Carl Hayden to Florence Albaugh, 26 August 1964, SG4S3F8, Painter Papers; Morris Udall to Don Vosberg, 31 May 1963, box 165, fd. 165/14, Udall Papers.

56. Theodore Heyl to Anselmo Valencia, 4 December 1962, box 165, fd. 165/14, Udall Papers; Painter Diary, 25 February 1964, SG4S3F3, Painter Papers.

57. House, Congressman Morris Udall of Arizona speaking for the bill for the Conveyance of Certain Lands of the United States to the Pascua Yaqui Association, Inc., H.R. 6233, 88th Cong., 2d. sess., *Congressional Record*, 29 September 1964, 22,380, in box 165, fd. 165/14, Udall Papers; "Report to Accompany H.R. 6233," 88th Cong., 2d sess., 8 August 1964, in box 165, fd. 165/14, Udall Papers; Morris Udall to Wayne Aspinal, 14 May 1963, box 165, fd. 165/14, Udall Papers.

58. Senate, *Senate Calendar No. 1469, Providing for the Conveyance of Certain Lands to the Pascua Yaqui Association, Inc., Report to Accompany H.R. 6233*, 88th Cong., 2d sess., 8 September 1964, S. Rept. 1530, in box 165, fd. 165/13, Udall Papers; *An Act Relating to the Lumbee Indians of North Carolina*, 70 Stat. 254 (7 June 1956).

59. Morris Udall to Francis J. Green, 8 January 1963, box 165, fd. 165/13; House Committee on Interior, *Bill to Provide for the Conveyance*, 14 August 1964, in box 165, fd. 165/14, Udall Papers.

60. Robert Roessel Jr. to Morris Udall, 10 October 1962, box 165, fd. 165/14, Udall Papers.

61. House Committee on Interior, *Bill to Provide for the Conveyance*, 14 August 1964, in box 165, fd. 165/14, Udall Papers; *Senate Calendar No. 1469*, 88th Cong., 2d sess., 8 September 1964, box 165, fd. 165/13, Udall Papers; and Morris Udall to Carl Hayden, 16 September 1964, box 165, fd. 165/13, Udall Papers.

62. *An Act to Provide for the Conveyance of Certain Lands of the United States to the Pascua Yaqui Association, Inc.*, Public Law 88–350 (8 October 1964), 78 Stat. 1197; Painter Diary, 31 October 1964, SG4S3F8, Painter Papers.

63. Spicer interview; Matusow, *Unraveling of America*, 125, 237–43; Berman, *America's Right Turn*, 5–6; "A Summary of the Economic Opportunity Act of 1964," box 523, fd. 523/15, Udall Papers; Edward Spicer, letter to editor, *Tucson Weekly News*, 12 November 1980.

64. Roz Spicer, "What Would You Do?" in "Application for Community Action Program," 16 April 1965, box 537, fd. 537/13, Udall Papers.

65. Matusow, *Unraveling of America*, 243–44; Willard, "Community Development Worker," vii, 14; Margaret Kuehlthau, "Yaquis Receive Federal Grant," *Tucson Daily Citizen*, 15 September 1966; PYA, "A Chronological History of the Pascua Yaqui," box 64, RG 220, NACP; "OEO—Application for Community Action Program," 16 April 1965, box 536, fd. 537/13, Udall Papers.

66. Willard, "Community Development Worker," 2–19, 64, 95; Edward Spicer, letter to editor, *Tucson Weekly News*, 12 November 1980; Painter Diary, 13 August 1965 and 16 August 1965, SG4S3F4, Painter Papers; "OEO—Application for Community Action Program," 16 April 1965, box 537, fd. 537/13, Udall Papers; Painter Diary, 27 May 1967 and 23 September 1966, SG4S3F9, Painter Papers; Roz Spicer, "What Would You Do?" 16 April 1965, box 537, fd. 537/13, Udall Papers.

67. "Proposal to the Ford Foundation," 29 January 1968, box 537, fd. 537/13, Udall Papers; Tom Turner, "Yaqui Mystery: Where Has All the Money Gone?" *(Tucson) Arizona Daily Star*, 6 March 1970; "A Chronological History of the Pascua Yaqui," box 64, RG 220, NACP; George Blue Spruce Jr. to Governor Raul Castro, 22 January 1975, box 118, RG 220, NACP; Painter Diary, 6 January 1965, SG4S3F4, Painter Papers.

68. Painter Diary, 13 January 1965, 4 January 1965, 13 January 1965, 31 January 1965, 27 January 1965, 6 April 1965, SG4S3F4, Painter Papers; Edward Spicer to Melvin Moguloff, 23 October 1965, box 536, fd. 537/13, Udall Papers; Morris Udall to Sister Antonimus Hubatch, San Xavier Mission, 8 January 1969, box 541, fd. 541/11, Udall Papers.

69. Valencia interview; "OEO—Application for Community Action Program," box 537, fd. 537/13, Udall Papers; Painter Diary, 7 July 1966, SG4S3F4, Painter Papers; Edward Spicer, diary entry, 2 April 1970, no. 569, Spicer Papers; Margaret Kuehlthau, "New Petition Opposes Yaqui Resettlement," *Tucson Daily Citizen*, 2 November 1966; Margaret Kuehlthau, "Yaqui Move Called Voluntary," *Tucson Daily Citizen*, 21 September 1966; Margaret Kuehlthau, "Protestant Yaquis Charge Discrimination," *Tucson Daily Citizen*, 27 September 1966; Margaret Kuehlthau, "Yaqui Village Termed Museum with Indians as Pawns," *Tucson Daily Citizen*, 30 September 1966.

70. "Yaqui Indians Build toward a New Miracle,"*Tucson American*, 23 November 1966; Margaret Kuehlthau, "New Petition Opposes Yaqui Resettlement," *Tucson Daily Citizen*, 2 November 1966; Reverend John Swank to Barry Goldwater, 8 August 1964, box 10, fd. 27, Goldwater Papers; Valencia interview.

71. Morgan Maxwell, letter to editor, *Tucson Daily Citizen*, 20 September 1966; "Survey of Pascua Village," April–May 1965, 1 July 1967, box 537, fd. 537/13, Udall Papers; Margaret Kuehlthau, "Yaqui Move Called Voluntary," *Tucson Daily Citizen*, 21 September 1966; Margaret Kuehlthau, "Protestant Yaquis Charge Discrimination," *Tucson Daily Citizen*, 27 September 1966; "Yaqui Indians Build toward a New Miracle," *Tucson American*, 23 November 1966.

72. Dick Frontain, "Church of San Ignacio Returns to Dust," *(Tucson) Arizona Daily Star*, 3 October 1967; Edward Spicer, letter to editor, *Tucson Weekly News*, 12 November 1980; Valencia interview; Willard, "Community Development Worker," 38, 60, 64–66; Painter Diary, 2 April 1965, 12 August 1966, SG4S3F4, Painter Papers.

73. "Some Facts Concerning the Relocation of People in Pascua Village," 29 October 1966, box 537, fd. 537/13, Udall Papers; "A Proposal to the Ford Foundation," 29 January 1968, box 537, fd. 537/13, Udall Papers.

74. Willard, "Community Development Worker," 85–87; C. Lawrence Huerta, interview by author.

75. Spicer, *Yaquis*, 253–58; Pete Castillo, Governor of Yoem Pueblo, to Dan O'Neil, 11 June 1982, box 676, fd. 676/6, Udall Papers; Edward Spicer to Mayor Lewis C. Murphy, 17 September 1979, f.6, Spicer Papers; Edward Spicer diary entry, 2 April 1970, f.5, Spicer Papers; "Survey 1965," SG4S3F8, Painter Papers; Valencia interview; Antonio

Coronado, chairman, Guadalupe Yaqui Tribal Council, to Morris Udall, 10 June 1971, box 119, fd. 119/15, Udall Papers.

76. Edward Spicer to Morris Udall, 18 April 1967, box 165, fd. 165/11, Udall Papers; Raymond Ybarra to Senator James Abourezk, 29 March 1976, box 118, RG 220, NACP; Joaquina Garcia to Muriel Painter, 1967, Painter Papers.

77. Valencia, quoted in Tom Turner, "Yaqui Mystery: Where Has All the Money Gone?" (Tucson) Arizona Daily Star, 6 March 1970 and 10 March 1970 (6-part series); Edward Spicer to Dolores Baltazar, 31 May 1969, box 1, fd. 4, Spicer Papers; Edward Spicer to Dr. James Wilson, 11 May 1969, box 10, fd. 27, Goldwater Papers; Willard, "Community Development Worker," 123. The six-part series on the PYA, "Yaqui Mystery" by Tom Turner, ran starting 6 March 1970 in the (Tucson) Arizona Daily Star.

78. Edward Spicer to Morris Udall, 18 April 1967, box 541, fd. 541/11, Udall Papers; Edward Spicer, letter to editor, Tucson Weekly News, 12 November 1980; Spicer interview; "Economic Development of the Pascua Yaqui Association," 1975, box 64, RG 220, NACP.

79. Martinez, quoted in "Voice of the People," (Tucson) Arizona Daily Star, 18 February 1967; Valencia interview.

80. Transcript, "Task Force #10, Hearing—New Pascua Yaqui Village, Tucson, Arizona," 22–23 May 1976, box 47, RG 220, NACP; "Economic Development of the PYA," 1975, box 47, RG 220, NACP; Edward Spicer, "Letter to Friends of Pascua," 3 August 1970, box 557, fd. 557/25, Udall Papers.

81. Burnis G. Hicks to Morris Udall, 11 February 1976, box 592, fd. 592/8, Udall Papers; Earl J. Carnell to Morris Udall, 17 November 1976, box 592, fd. 592/8, Udall Papers; "Information on Interim OEO Procedures," February 1973, box 592, fd. 592/8, Udall Papers; Morris Udall to Robert Clark, 29 March 1973, box 570, fd. 570/8, Udall Papers.

82. Caspar Weinberger to Morris Udall, 17 April 1973, box 581, fd. 581/19, Udall Papers; transcript, "Task Force #10, Hearing—New Pascua Yaqui Village, Tucson, Arizona," 22–23 May 1976, box 47, RG 220, NACP.

83. K. S. Scharman, Pima County Board of Supervisors, to Raymond F. Ybarra, 25 March 1976, box 118, RG 220, NACP; Dan Huff, "Yaquis Ask Federal Help," Tucson Daily Citizen, 7 August 1976.

84. Raymond F. Ybarra to Pima County, 11 February 1976, box 203, fd. 203/3, Udall Papers; "Economic Development of the PYA," box 64, RG 220, NACP; "PYA: Appeal to other tribes," box 94, fd. 94: 9/7, Fannin Papers; Gary I. Thomas, Solicitor's Office, to Raymond F. Ybarra, PYA, 9 February 1976, Box 203, fd. 203/3, Udall Papers. A federal judge later determined that the Yaqui land was trust land not subject to local ordinances. "Pima Building Code Ruled Out for Yaquis," (Tucson) Arizona Daily Star, 19 October 1980.

85. Raymond F. Ybarra to James Abourezk, 29 March 1976, box 118, RG 220, NACP; "Economic Development of the PYA," box 64, RG 220, NACP; Wilmer D. Mizell, Department of Commerce, to Morris Udall, 31 March 1976, box 203, fd. 203/3, Udall Papers.

86. Transcript, Arizona Commission of Indian Affairs, 27 June 1975, box 203, fd. 203/3, Udall Papers; George Blue Spruce Jr. to Governor Raul Castro, 22 January 1975, box 64, RG 220, NACP; transcript, "Task Force #10, Hearing—New Pascua Yaqui Village," 22–23 May 1976, box 47, RG 220, NACP.

87. "Intertribal Council of Arizona Resolution #22–75" 17 March 1975, box 1, fd. 8, Spicer Papers; "Resolution: Colorado River Tribal Council," 14 June 1975, and "Resolution: Colorado River Tribal Council," 4 August 1975, box 94, fd. 94: 9/7, Fannin Papers.

88. Veronica Murdock, quoted in Richard La Course, American Indian Press Association release, 1975, box 94, fd. 94: 9/7, Fannin Papers.

89. Spicer interview.

90. Solorez, quoted in "Cover Story on Yaqui Indians," *(Phoenix) Arizona Republic*, 2 September 1979 (copy in Spicer Papers, fd. "1976–81").

91. Valencia, quoted in Elaine Nathanson, "Yaquis Request Status as Tribe," *(Tucson) Arizona Daily Star*, 23 May 1976.

92. Valencia, quoted in "Cover Story on Yaqui Indians," *(Phoenix) Arizona Republic*, 2 September 1979 (copy in Spicer Papers, fd. "1976–81"); Valencia interview.

93. Antonio Coronado to Barry Goldwater, 10 June 1971, box 10, fd. 25, "I" series, Goldwater Papers; draft, "A Bill," 1971, box 119, fd. 119/15, Udall Papers; interoffice memo, Udall Office, 21 June 1971, box 119, fd. 119/15, Udall Papers.

94. William L. Rogers to Barry Goldwater, 28 June 1971, box 10, fd. 25, "I" series, Goldwater Papers; Harris Loesch to Barry Goldwater, 1 October 1971, box 10, fd. 25, "I" series, Goldwater Papers.

95. Bernard L. Fontana to Beverly B. Ogden, 15 September 1975, box 94, fd. 94: 9/7, Fannin Papers; Spicer interview; Officer interview; Valencia interview.

96. Richard Olson, Udall Office, to Dale E. Biever, 7 December 1978, box 581, fd. 581/19, Udall Papers; Udall, *Addresses and Special Orders*, xi–xii.

97. Morris Udall to David Jansen, 11 March 1976, box 203, fd. 203/3, Udall Papers; Dan Huff, "Yaquis Put Try for Tribe Status on Back Burner," *Tucson Daily Citizen*, 8 January 1977; House Committee on Interior, *Bill to Provide for the Extension*, 8 July 1975, in box 203, fd. 203/3, Udall Papers; "Resolution: Colorado River Tribal Council, No. R-38–75," 4 August 1975, box 94, fd. 94: 9/7, Fannin Papers; Richard LaCourse, "bill rundown," 1975, box 94, fd. 94: 9/7, Fannin Papers; Paul Fannin, letter to *Arizona Daily Star*, 26 September 1975, box 94, fd. 94: 9/7, Fannin Papers.

98. John Arnold, Memo: "Yaquis vs. H.R. 8411," n.d., box 94, fd. 94: 9/7, Fannin Papers; Ramon Jarigue to Prior Pray, 30 December 1975, box 203, fd. 203/3, Udall Papers; Valencia interview.

99. Interoffice Memo, 13 October 1975, box 94, fd. 94:9/7, Fannin Papers; Ramon Jaurigue to Prior Pray, 30 December 1975, Box 203, fd. 203/3, Udall Papers; Valencia interview.

100. "Yaqui Elders Rebel at Becoming Wards," *Tucson Daily Citizen*, 19 November 1975; Valencia interview.

101. Valencia interview.

102. "Testimony of the Pascua Yaqui Indians," Task-Force #10, 22–23 May 1976, box 64, RG 220, NACP; Raymond Ybarra to James Abourezk, 29 March 1976, box 118, RG 220, NACP.

103. Transcript, "Task Force #10, Hearing—New Pascua Yaqui Village," 22–23 May 1976, box 47, RG 220, NACP; PYA, "Chronological History of the Pascua Yaqui Indians," box 94, fd. 94:9/7, Fannin Papers.

104. "A History of the Pascua Yaqui Indians," in AIPRC, *Report on Terminated and Nonfederally Recognized Indians*; Senate Select Committee, *Federal Acknowledgment Process*, 2 June 1980, testimony of National Indian Lutheran Board, 25; Porter, *Nonrecognized American Indian Tribes*, i.

105. Castaneda, *Teachings of Don Juan*; Rose, "Great Pretenders," 404–6; Nicholas P. Houser, interviews by author.

106. House Committee on Interior, H.R. 8411, 1977, box 203, fd. 203/3, Udall Papers; Roger Wolf, interview by author; Darcy interview; Edward Spicer to Bryan Michener, Friends Committee on National Legislation, 1 August 1975, box 5, fd. 317, Spicer Papers.

107. Paul Fannin to Arnold T. Butler, 14 August 1975, box 94, fd. 94: 9/7, Fannin Papers.

108. Bryan Michener to Edward Spicer, 1 August 1975, box 5, fd. 317, Spicer Papers; "Pascua Yaqui Association Membership Application," box 94, fd. 94:9/7, Fannin Papers; Sam Steiger to David Jensen, 25 February 1976, box 34, fd. 211, Steiger Papers.

109. Edward Spicer to Teno Roncalio, 1 March 1978, box 5, fd. 317, Spicer Papers; Edward Spicer to Morris Udall, 1 March 1978, box 5, fd. 317, Spicer Papers; Roger Wolf to Paul Fannin, 9 January 1976, box 5, fd. 317, Spicer Papers; Raymond F. Ybarra to Paul J. Fannin, 30 September 1975, box 94, fd. 94: 9/7, Fannin Papers.

110. Roger Wolf to Paul Fannin, 9 January 1976, box 5, fd. 317, Spicer Papers.

111. Raymond Ybarra to Paul Fannin, 30 September 1975, box 94, fd. 94: 9/7, Fannin Papers.

112. Senate Select Committee on Indian Affairs, *Trust Status*, 27 September 1977, "Prepared Statement of Senator Dennis DeConcini," 2; Senate Committee on Indian Affairs, *Pascua Yaqui*, 27 January 1994, "Testimony of Hon. Dennis DeConcini," 1; Valencia interview; interoffice memo, 12 August 1976, box 606, fd. 606/16, Udall Papers; Jon Kyl to Morris Udall, 16 August 1976, box 606, fd. 606/16, Udall Papers.

113. "Panel OKs Bill Giving Yaqui Tribal Status," *Tucson Daily Citizen*, 10 March 1978; *House Report No. 95–1021*, 30 March 1978, box 5, fd. 317, Spicer Papers.

114. Senate Select Committee, *Trust Status*, 27 September 1977, 5.

115. Senate Select Committee, *Trust Status*, 27 September 1977, 5; Edward Spicer to James Abourezk, 12 September 1977, box 94, fd. 94: 9/7, Fannin Papers; Edward Spicer to Paul J. Fannin, 9 January 1976, box 94, fd. 94: 9/7, Fannin Papers.

116. Senate Select Committee, *Trust Status*, 27 September 1977; *Procedures*, 25 C.F.R.

secs. 83.1–83.3 (1997); Edward Spicer to Paul Fannin, 9 January 1976, box 94, fd. 94: 9/7, Fannin Papers.

117. Senate Select Committee, *Trust Status*, 27 September 1977; Edward Spicer to Paul Fannin, 9 January 1976, box 94, fd. 94: 9/7, Fannin Papers.

118. Senate Select Committee, *Trust Status*, 27 September 1977, 2.

119. Valencia interview; Officer interview; Wolf interview; interoffice memo regarding Ak-Chin Tribe, 30 August 1978, box 601, fd. 601/14, Udall Papers; Forrest Gerard Jr. to Morris Udall, 20 March 1978, in *Report to Accompany H.R. 6612*, 95th Cong., 2d sess., 30 March 1978.

120. Raymond Cross to Edward Spicer, 19 October 1977, box 5, fd. 317, Spicer Papers; Forrest Gerard Jr. to Morris Udall, 20 March 1978, box 5, fd. 317, Spicer Papers.

121. Raymond Cross to Edward Spicer, 19 October 1977, box 5, fd. 317, Spicer Papers.

122. Bryan Michener to Edward Spicer, 1 August 1975, box 5, fd. 317, Spicer Papers; Raymond Cross to Edward Spicer, 19 October 1977, box 5, fd. 317, Spicer Papers; "Panel OK's Measure," *Tucson Daily Citizen*, 17 February 1978.

123. Bryan Michener to Edward Spicer, 1 August 1975, box 5, fd. 317, Spicer Papers.

124. House Committee on Interior, *Bill to Provide for the Extension*, 25 August 1977; Raymond Cross to David Ramirez, 28 April 1978, box 5, fd. 317, Spicer Papers.

125. Senate Select Committee on Indian Affairs, *Bill to Provide for the Extension*, 7 June 1977.

126. "No Veto Seen on Yaqui Bill," *Tucson Daily Citizen*, 24 June 1978; "New Law Makes Yaquis an Official Tribe," *(Tucson) Arizona Daily Star*, 19 September 1978.

127. House, Congressman Morris Udall speaking on "Conference Report on S. 1633," 95th Cong., 2d sess., *Congressional Record* 124 (16 August 1978): 789.

128. Anselmo Valencia to Edward Spicer, 22 August 1978, box 5, fd. 317, Spicer Papers; "No Veto Seen on Yaqui Bill," *Tucson Daily Citizen*, 24 June 1978; *Pascua Yaqui Indians, Ariz., Extension of Federal Benefits*, 25 U.S.C. sec. 1300f (1978); President Jimmy Carter to Cecil Andrus, 18 September 1978, HF, BAR.

129. Huerta interview; Valencia interview; Officer interview; Spicer interview; "No Veto Seen on Yaqui Bill," *Tucson Daily Citizen*, 24 June 1978.

130. Udall, quoted in "New Law Makes Yaquis an Official Tribe," *(Tucson) Arizona Daily Star*, 19 September 1978; *Procedures*, 25 C.F.R. sec. 83 (1997).

131. Senate Select Committee, *Indian Federal Recognition*, 22 October 1991, statement of John McCain, 1, 36; Senate Committee on Indian Affairs, *Mohegan Nation*, 1 August 1994, 21.

132. Valencia, quoted in "Cover Story on Yaqui Indians," *(Phoenix) Arizona Republic*, 2 September 1979 (copy in Spicer Papers, fd. "1976–81").

133. Stephanie Innes, "Yaqui Ballot Is Crowded," *(Tucson) Arizona Daily Star*, 1 June 2000; "Tucson through Time: Anselmo Valencia," *(Tucson) Arizona Daily Star*, 31 December 1999.

1. "Indian Village Housing Problem Discussion," 19 May 1966, DVTS, BAR; "Death Valley National Monument Annual Report 1938," CCF, RG 79, NACP; Senate Committee on Indian Affairs, *Federal Recognition Administrative*, 13 July 1995, "Task Force on Federal Recognition," 99; BAR, "Index to Federal Acknowledgment Petitioners by State," 29 October 1999, http://www.doi.gov/bia/bar/indexz.htm (accessed 6 April 2000); BAR, "Summary of Acknowledgment Cases," http://www.doi.gov/bia/0302stat.htm (accessed 28 April 1999).

2. Austin interviews; Death Valley Timbisha Shoshone Band (DVTS), "Petition for Federal Acknowledgment," 18 April 1979, DVNP.

3. President Herbert Hoover, "Death Valley National Monument—California, a Proclamation," 11 February 1933, CCF, RG 79, NACP; Tagg, *Timbi-Sha Survey*"; George M. Wright to Director, 24 April 1933, CCF, RG 79, NACP.

4. "Indian Village Housing Problem Discussion," 19 May 1966, DVTS, BAR; "Death Valley Indian Village Housing Policy," 9 May 1957, DVTS, BAR; John B. Wosky to Superintendent, Death Valley National Monument (DVNM), 14 August 1959, DVTS, BAR; Superintendent to Regional Director, 6 August 1959, DVTS, BAR; Deputy Regional Director to Superintendents, Death Valley, Grand Canyon, and Yosemite, 14 March 1978, DVTS, BAR; Keller and Turek, *American Indians*, 22, 139–40; Spence, *Dispossessing the Wilderness*.

5. Superintendent to Regional Director, 28 February 1963, DVTS, BAR; Catherine S. Fowler, "Residence without Reservation," unpublished manuscript, 48–49, and Theodoratus and LSA Associates, "Death Valley National Park," unpublished manuscript, 60–61, CF, DVNP; BAR, "Recommendation and Summary of Evidence for Proposed Finding," 9 February 1982, DVTS, BAR.

6. BAR, "Technical Reports regarding the Death Valley Timbi-Sha Shoshone Band," DVTS, BAR; Congress, House Committee on Interior, *Termination*, 15 February 1954, part 5, California, 358–98; "California Indians—Double Genocide," *Native American Rights Fund Announcement* 1, no. 4 (1972): 4.

7. BAR, "Technical Reports," DVTS, BAR.

8. Pauline Esteves, quoted in Catherine S. Fowler, "Residence without Reservation," 97; Area Director, Sacramento Area Office, to Fred Binnewies, 13 December 1956, DVTS, BAR; Superintendent to Regional Director, 28 February 1963, DVTS, BAR; Jackson Price to Regional Director, n.d., DVTS, BAR.

9. Frank J. Diaz de Leon, Inter-tribal Council of California, to Department of the Interior, 21 August 1972, DVTS, BAR; Daniel J. Tobin Jr. to Richard B. Collins Jr., California Indian Legal Services (CILS), 16 March 1970, DVTS, BAR; William D. Oliver, Acting Area Director, to John Babcock Jr., 23 February 1971, DVNP.

10. William D. Oliver to John Babcock Jr., 23 February 1971, DVNP; Stephen V. Quesenberry to Richard H. Burcell, n.d., DVTS, BAR.

11. Grapevine District Ranger to Chief Park Ranger, 10 June 1966, DVTS, BAR; "Indian Village Housing Problem Discussion," 19 May 1966, DVTS, BAR; Catherine S. Fowler, "Residence without Reservation," 48.

12. Richard L. Ditlevson to files, 22 October 1975, DVNP; National Park Service (NPS) to Richard B. Collins Jr., 16 March 1970, DVNP; William D. Oliver to John Babcock Jr., 23 February 1971, DVTS, BAR; Robert J. Murphy to Richard B. Collins Jr., 16 March 1970, DVTS, BAR; NARF memorandum, 18 October 1975, DVTS, BAR.

13. John McMunn, for Acting Field Solicitor, to Assistant Director, 22 February 1972, DVTS BAR; "Petition" for reservation, n.d. (late 1960s), DVTS, BAR; Frank Diaz de Leon to John E. Cook, 3 December 1973, DVTS, BAR; Robert J. Murphy to Director, Western Region, 21 December 1971, DVTS, BAR; John E. Cook and NPS to Frank J. Diaz de Leon, 12 September 1972, DVTS, BAR; Robert J. Murphy to Director, Western Region, 13 March 1972, DVNP.

14. Robert J. Murphy to Director, Western Region, 13 March 1972, DVNP; Staff Archeologist to Chief Archeologist, 16 February 1978, DVNP; George Von der Lippe to Nadeen Naylor, Native American Heritage Commission, 12 March 1980, DVNP.

15. Bruce R. Greene and Edward Forstenzer, NARF memorandum, 18 October 1975, DVNP; Stephen V. Quesenberry to Richard H. Burcell, 29 April 1977, DVNP; James A. Joseph to Stephen V. Quesenberry, 27 July 1977, DVNP; William E. Finale to Alice Eben, 24 August 1977, DVNP; Forest J. Gerard to Area Director, Sacramento, 18 November 1977, DVNP.

16. Timbi-sha Shoshone Band of Indians, "Petition of the Death Valley Timbi-sha Shoshone Band of Indians," 9 February 1976, DVTS, BAR; William E. Finale to Commissioner of Indian Affairs, 4 March 1976, DVTS, BAR; "Memorandum of Agreement," NPS, Timbi-Sha Band, and Indian Health Service, 13 March 1978, DVTS, BAR; George Von der Lippe to Ms. Betsy Cline, 6 July 1979, DVTS, BAR; Stephen V. Quesenberry to Donald M. Spaulding, 19 January 1978, DVTS, BAR; memorandum on meeting with California Native American Heritage Commission, 27 October 1977, DVTS, BAR.

17. Director to All Regional Directors, n.d., DVNP; Ralph G. Mihan, Field Solicitor, to Regional Director, 14 April 1978, DVNP; Superintendent to Chief, Cultural Resources Management, 11 September 1979, DVNP; memorandum, "National Park Service Comments on the Timbi-Sha Shoshone Indians," n.d., DVNP; James B. Thompson to Regional Director, 29 October 1975, DVNP.

18. Susan Sorrells, "Out of Tourists' Sight, Death Valley Indians Battle for Their Homes," Los Angeles Times, 10 June 1979; Linda Anisman to S. I. Hayakawa, 26 April 1979, DVTS, BAR; S. I. Hayakawa to Department of the Interior, 22 June 1979, DVTS, BAR; Gary R. Catron to S. I. Hayakawa, 1 August 1979, DVTS, BAR.

19. Rick Lavis to Pauline Esteves, 30 May 1979, DVTS, BAR; DVTS, "Petition for Federal Acknowledgment," 18 April 1979, DVNP; Roth interview; Procedures, 25 C.F.R. Part 83 (1997).

20. John C. Herron, "Documents Constituting the Legislative and Administrative History of Relations between Death Valley National Monument and the Timbisha Band of Shoshone Indians," Denver Service Center, National Park Service, DVNP.

21. Coville, "Panamint Indians of California," 351–61; Nelson, "Panamint and Saline Valley Indians," 371–72; Dutcher, "Pinon Gathering," 377–80; Kroeber, *Handbook of the Indians*, 589–92; Steward, *Basin-Plateau Aboriginal Sociopolitical Groups*. Frederick Webb Hodge also accepted the earlier articles on the existence of the Panamint group in his work on Indians in North America. Hodge, *Handbook of American Indians*, 199.

22. Lisbeth Haas, *Conquests and Historical Identities*, 42–43, 106–30; Monroy, *Thrown among Strangers*, 8, 23–36, 237–44; Cook, "Historical Demography," 91; DVTS, "Petition," DVNP; "Technical Reports," DVTS, BAR.

23. Madsen, *Lemhi*, 11–25; Kroeber, *Handbook of the Indians*, 574–75; "The Timbisha Shoshone Tribal Homeland: A Draft Secretarial Report to Congress to Establish a Permanent Tribal Land Base and Related Cooperative Activities," n.d., http://www.nps.gov/deva/Timbisha_toc.html (accessed 17 February 2000), 17; DVTS, "Petition"; BAR, "Technical Reports," DVTS, BAR; Dayley, *Tümpisa (Panamint) Shoshone Dictionary*, xv–xxii.

24. Crum, *Road on Which We Came*, 3–6, 13; Steward, *Basin-Plateau Aboriginal Sociopolitical Groups*, 2, 8–9, 72, 32, 72, 34–40, 78, 44–45; Kroeber, *Handbook of the Indians*, 582–83.

25. DVTS, "Supplement to Petition for Federal Acknowledgment," September 1979, DVNP; BAR, "Technical Reports," DVTS, BAR; Steward, *Basin-Plateau Aboriginal Sociopolitical Groups*, 2–3, 70–92; Thomas, Pendleton, and Cappannari, "Western Shoshone," 276; Kroeber, "Elements of Culture," 27.

26. Lingenfelter, *Death Valley*, 19; BAR, "Technical Reports," DVTS, BAR.

27. Tagg, *Timbi-Sha Survey*, 28–29, Catherine S. Fowler, "Residence without Reservation," 52–55, 84; Alida C. Bowler to John Collier, 3 March 1936, DVTS, BAR; BAR, "Technical Reports," DVTS, BAR.

28. Chief, Branch of Tribal Programs, to Fred W. Binnewies, 18 February 1959, and transcript, *United States v. Louise B. Grantham*, United States District Court, Southern District of California, Northern Division, No. 56-ND, Civil, DVTS, BAR; A. E. Demaray to Superintendent, 21 December 1940, CCF, RG 79, NACP; BAR, "Technical Reports," DVTS, BAR.

29. Susan Sorrells, "Out of Tourists' Sight, Death Valley Indians Battle for Their Homes," *Los Angeles Times*, 13 June 1979; DVTS, "Petition," DVNP; BAR, "Technical Reports," DVTS, BAR.

30. E. E. East, Automobile Club of Southern California, to Horace M. Albright, 23 February 1932, CCF, RG 79, NACP.

31. BAR, "Technical Reports," DVTS, BAR.

32. John R. White to Oscar H. Lippe, 3 May 1933, CCF, RG 79, NACP; John R. White to the Director, 19 July 1934, CCF, RG 79, NACP; Alida C. Bowler to John Collier, 14 April 1936, DVTS, BAR.

33. John R. White to Oscar H. Lippe, 3 May 1933, CCF, RG 79, NACP.

34. John R. White to Director, 19 July 1934, CCF, RG 79, NACP; handwritten note, NPS, to Mr. Demaray, n.d., CCF, RG 79, NACP.

35. T. R. Goodwin to Dane Coolidge, 11 May 1936, DVTS, BAR; Alida C. Bowler to John Collier, 19 November 1938, box 2, fd. "Alida C. Bowler (misc) 1938-9," Collier Files, RG 75, NAB; Alida C. Bowler, "Report on Relief Situation," 8 January 1937, box 2, fd. "Alida C. Bowler (misc) 1938-9," Collier Files, RG 75, NAB; Alida C. Bowler to Commissioner of Indian Affairs, 9 January 1937, box 2, fd. "Alida C. Bowler (misc) 1938-9," Collier Files, RG 75, NAB.

36. T. R. Goodwin to Harold Bryant, 13 September 1936, DVTS, BAR; T. R. Goodwin to Dane Coolidge, 11 May 1936, DVTS, BAR; Alida C. Bowler to Vierling Kersey, 25 June 1936, DVTS, BAR; T. R. Goodwin to John R. White, 11 August 1936, DVTS, BAR.

37. Alida C. Bowler to Commissioner of Indian Affairs, 3 March 1936, DVTS, BAR; Alida C. Bowler to Commissioner, 23 March 1936, DVTS, BAR; George L. Collins to Mr. Demaray, 23 August 1936, DVTS, BAR.

38. Alida C. Bowler to Commissioner of Indian Affairs, 3 March 1936, DVTS, BAR; Alida C. Bowler to John R. White, 19 February 1937, DVTS, BAR; Alida C. Bowler to John R. White, 23 March 1936, DVTS, BAR; John R. White to the Director, 15 April 1936, DVTS, BAR.

39. "Memorandum of Understanding between the BIA and NPS," 23 May 1936, DVNP; "Trust Agreement for Rehabilitation Grant to Unorganized Tribe," 12 July 1938, DVNP.

40. John R. White to Alida C. Bowler, 2 April 1936, DVTS, BAR; Fred H. Daiker to Alida C. Bowler, 4 February 1938, DVTS, BAR; Alida C. Bowler to Commissioner, 29 December 1937, DVTS, BAR; "Death Valley Annual Report, 1938," CCF, RG 79, NACP.

41. T. R. Goodwin to the Director, 15 August 1939, CCF, RG 79, NACP; Fred H. Daiker to Alida C. Bowler, 27 June 1939, CCF, RG 79, NACP; Alida C. Bowler to Commissioner of Indian Affairs, 23 November 1938, DVTS, BAR; Alida C. Bowler to Commissioner of Indian Affairs, 9 January 1937, box 2, fd. "Alida C. Bowler," Collier Files, NAB.

42. Fred H. Daiker to Don C. Foster, 7 November 1939, DVTS, BAR; Commissioner of Indian Affairs to Don C. Foster, n.d., DVTS, BAR; W. Barton Greenwood to Don C. Foster, 27 July 1940, DVTS, BAR.

43. DVTS, "Petition for Federal Acknowledgment," 18 April 1979, DVNP; "Trust Agreement for Relief and Rehabilitation Grant to Unorganized Tribe," Commissioner of Indian Affairs and Death Valley Shoshone Tribe, 2 February 1940, DVTS, BAR; Xavier Vigeant, Director, Rehabilitation Division, to Don C. Foster, 16 March 1940, DVTS, BAR; BAR, "Technical Reports," DVTS, BAR.

44. Pauline Esteves, quoted in Catherine S. Fowler, "Residence without Reservation," 94-95; Jane M. Jones to T. R. Goodwin, 31 January 1940, DVTS, BAR; T. R. Goodwin to Edith V. A. Murphy, 28 December 1943, DVTS, BAR; Ernest C. Mueller to Commissioner, 26 September 1941, DVTS, BAR.

45. DVTS, "Petition for Federal Acknowledgment," DVNP; Susan Sorrells, "Out of Tourists' Sight, Death Valley Indians Battle for Their Homes," *Los Angeles Times*, 13 June 1979; BAR, "Technical Reports," DVTS, BAR; *U.S. v. Grantham* (1940), United States District Court, Southern District of California, Northern Division, No. 56-ND, Civil, DVTS, BAR; B. F. Manley to the Director, 13 February 1952, DVNP; Conrad W. Wirth to Regional Director, 16 October 1952, DVNP.

46. "Obvious Deficiency Letter" to Pauline Esteves, 26 July 1979, DVTS, BAR; Timbi-Sha Shoshone Band, "Supplement to Petition for Federal Acknowledgment," September 1979, DVNP.

47. Roth interview; Rick Lavis to Edmund G. Brown, 29 October 1979, DVTS, BAR; Herron, "Documents," DVNP.

48. *Procedures*, C.F.R. Part 83 (1997); Porter, *Nonrecognized American Indian Tribes*, 65. For criticism and discussions of the problems Indian groups face in having to rely on external identification see McCulloch and Wilkins, " 'Constructing' Nations within States," 361–90; Castile, "Commodification of Indian Identity," 743–49; Greenbaum, "What's in a Label?" 107–24; Grabowski, "Coiled Intent," 432–33.

49. DVTS, "Petition," 18 April 1979, DVNP; BAR, "Technical Reports," DVNP; Herron, "Documents," DVNP; John G. Herron to George Roth, BAR, 21 January 1979, DVTS, BAR.

50. BAR, "Technical Reports," DVTS, BAR; Timbi-Sha Band, "Supplement," DVNP. As was common in early settlers' accounts in all regions of the United States, observers often failed to note tribal names or cultural details in their memoirs. As a result modern scholars often have difficulty identifying specific tribal groups during early periods of contact. However, the FAP team and the band relied upon several early historical accounts for general references to generic Indians or to Shoshones in Death Valley, such as Manly, *Death Valley in '49*, 142–43; Chalfant, *Story of Inyo*, 355–57; Perkins, *White Heart*, 118; Wheat, "Pioneer Visitors," 195–216.

51. BAR, "Summary of the Evaluation," and "Technical Reports," DVTS, BAR.

52. "Procedures," *Federal Register* 43, no. 106 (June 1978): 23,745 (emphasis added in quote); *Procedures*, 25 C.F.R. Part 83 (1997).

53. DVTS, "Petition," DVNP.

54. DVTS, "Petition," DVNP; T. R. Goodwin to John R. White, 11 August 1936, DVTS, BAR; "Legal description of the Indian Village," 6 December 1937, DVTS, BAR; Hoxie, "From Prison to Homeland," 1–24.

55. DVTS, "Petition," DVNP.

56. DVTS, "Petition," DVNP. The BAR has declined to recognize several groups in part because it determined that a substantial degree of members failed to constitute a tribal community, particularly after World War II. For one of the most contentious cases see "Final Determination That the Miami Nation of Indians of the State of Indiana, Inc. Does Not Exist as an Indian Tribe," *Federal Register* 57 (18 June 1992): 27,312, http://web.lexis-nexis.com/congcom (accessed 4 March 1998).

57. DVTS, "Petition," DVNP; House Committee on Interior, Subcommittee on Indian Affairs, *Federal Recognition*, 10 August 1978, "H.R. 12996," Sec. 5, (a), (3), and "Statement of the National Tribal Chairmen's Association," 154; Paredes, "Paradoxes of Modernism," 345. Several other BAR final determinations looked favorably upon the retention of language as an indicator of tribal identity. See "Proposed Finding for Federal Acknowledgment of the Jena Band of Choctaw Indians," http://www.doi.gov/bia/jensum.html (accessed 5 December 1997), and "Proposed Finding, Matchebenashshewish Band of Pottawatomi Indians of Michigan," BAR, http://www.doi.gov/bia/bar/matchsum.html (accessed 21 January 1998).

58. BAR, "Technical Reports," DVTS, BAR. For complex findings on groups that the BIA determined lacked such a central core see BAR, "Proposed Finding against Federal Acknowledgment of the Snohomish Tribe of Indians," *Federal Register* 48, no. 70 (11 April 1983): 15,540; "Proposed Finding against Acknowledgment of the Duwamish Tribal Organization," http://www.doi.gov/bia/bar/duwamsum.html (accessed 15 January 1998); BAR, "Proposed Finding, Cowlitz Tribe of Indians," http://www.doi.gov/bia/bar/cowsum.html (21 January 1998); BAR; "Final Determination to Acknowledge the Snoqualmie Tribal Organization," n.d., BAR, *http://www.doi.gov/bia/snofedrg.htm* (accessed 21 January 1998).

59. BAR, "Technical Reports" and "Genealogical Reports," DVTS, BAR. The BAR has questioned the tribal identity, tribal interaction, and Indianness of other petitioning groups based on out-marriage rates to whites or African Americans. Grabowski, "Coiled Intent," 432–37.

60. Senate Select Committee, *Federal Acknowledgment Administrative*, part 1, 28 April 1989, "Statement of Roy Hall," 49; Roth interview; Senate Select Committee, *Federal Acknowledgment Process: Oversight*, 26 May 1988, Statement of Alogan Slagle, CILS, 39.

61. *Procedures*, 25 C.F.R. Part 83 (1997); "Procedures," *Federal Register*, 43, no. 106 (June 1978): 23,745; Porter, *Nonrecognized American Indian Tribes*.

62. DVTS, "Petition," DVNP. Other early petitioners such as the Tunica-Biloxis had longer narratives on political influence and much lengthier petitions overall. "Tunica-Biloxi Petition," TB, BAR; BAR, "Technical Reports," DVTS, BAR.

63. T. R. Goodwin to Alida C. Bowler, 1 November 1937, DVTS, BAR; BAR, "Technical Reports," DVTS, BAR; DVTS, "Petition," DVNP.

64. BAR, "Technical Reports," DVTS, BAR; Roth interview.

65. BAR, "Anthropological Report," DVTS, BAR.

66. BAR, "Technical Reports," DVTS, BAR.

67. Roth interview; "Recommendation," Deputy Assistant Secretary-Indian Affairs (operations) to Assistant Secretary Indian Affairs, 9 February 1982, DVTS, BAR; BAR, "Technical Reports," DVTS, BAR.

68. "Procedures," *Federal Register*, 43, no. 106 (June 1978): 23,745; *Procedures*, C.F.R. Part 83 (1997; emphasis added); Porter, *Nonrecognized American Indian Tribes*, 68–69.

69. DVTS, "Petition," DVNP; BAR, "Genealogical Report on the Death Valley Timbi-Sha Shoshone Band," DVTS, BAR.

70. Fred H. Daiker to Don C. Foster, BIA, 7 November 1937, DVTS, BAR; *Procedures*, 25 C.F.R. Part 83 (1997).

71. *Procedures*, 25 C.F.R. Part 83 (1997); Morrison, introduction to *American Indian Studies*, 9. For legal issues of burden of proof on ancestry and Indian identification issues see Rayna Green, "Tribe Called Wannabee," 30–55; Carrillo, *Readings in American Indian Law*; Campisi, *Mashpee Indians*, 152–58; Clifford, *Predicament of Culture*, 278–319; Jaimes, "American Indian Identification."

72. DVTS, "Supplement to Petition," Sally Boland, interview by Linda Anisman and Pauline Esteves, 16 August 1979, and Hank Patterson, interview by Linda Anisman and Pauline Esteves, 9 August 1979, DVNP.

73. BAR, "Technical Reports" and "Genealogical Report," DVTS, BAR.

74. BAR, "Anthropological Report," DVTS, BAR. Very few petitioners have failed criteria (d), (f), or (g). The United Lumbee Nation of North Carolina and America (no relation to the much larger Lumbees of Robeson County, North Carolina) did apparently fail criterion (d), which called for a governing document or statement describing the membership criteria. The FAP researchers determined that the group "Accepted as members individuals who do not meet the blood degree requirement." The Yuchi Tribal Organization of Oklahoma failed criterion (f) because the FAP team determined that 92 percent of the group's membership derived from the recognized Muskogee (Creek) Nation. The Tchinouk Indians of Oregon failed (g) in 1985 because the FAP report concluded that the group was "forbidden the Federal relationship by the Western Oregon Termination Act of 1954. Although not specifically named in the act, the act's broad language applied to them." The Lumbee Tribe of North Carolina and related groups were also prohibited from the federal relationship under a congressional act. "Final Determination That the United Lumbee Nation of North Carolina and America, Inc. Does Not Exist as an Indian Tribe," *Federal Register* 50 (2 May 1985): 18,746, http://web.lexis-nexis.com/congcom (accessed 4 March 1998); BAR, "Proposed Finding against Federal Acknowledgment of the Yuchi Tribal Organization," http://www.doi.gov/bia/bar/yuchi.html (accessed 15 January 1999); BAR, "Notice of Proposed Finding against Federal Acknowledgment of the Tchinouk Indians of Oregon," *Federal Register* 50 (12 June 1985): 24,709, http://web.lexis-nexis.com/congcom (26 March 1998); BAR, "Summary of Acknowledgment Cases," 2 March 1999, http://www.doi.gov/bia/0302stat.htm (accessed 20 April 1999).

75. Theodore C. Krenzke to Sacramento Area Office, 17 March 1983, DVTS, BAR; Rachel A. Bluestone to Commissioner of Indian Affairs, 7 January 1980, DVTS, BAR; BAR, "Summary of the Evaluation," DVTS, BAR; Theodore C. Krenzke to Charles W. Getz IV, 18 November 1982, DVTS, BAR.

76. Pauline Esteves, quoted in "Timbisha Shoshone Tribal Homeland," 1.

77. Barbara Durham, quoted in "Timbisha Shoshone Tribal Homeland";
"Report on the Current Death Valley Timbi-Sha Shoshone Band of Indians," DVTS,

BAR; "Timbisha Shoshone Tribe Land Restoration Project," pamphlet, Timbisha Shoshone Tribe, Furnace Creek CA.

78. *California Desert Protection Act of 1994*, Public Law 103–433, 16 U.S.C. sec. 410 (31 October 1994).

79. "Restoration Project," pamphlet, Timbisha Shoshone Tribe.

80. "Shoshone Indians Plan Nuke Protest," *Las Vegas Sun*, 9 October 1997, http://www.lasvegassun.com (accessed 12 April 1999); "Timbisha Shoshone Death Valley Land Restoration Project," n.d., http://www.dickshovel.com/timup.html (accessed 21 May 2003); "March for Justice: DV Shoshone Call for Help II," 17 April 1996, http://www.neutral.com/lip/polabuse/2109.html (accessed 12 April 1999); Greenpeace, "Greenpeace Supports Timbisha Shoshone in Tribe's Fight for Justice," flyer, n.d.; *Western Shoshone Defense Project Newsletter* 5, no. 1 (1997), 3, 11; "Learning to Compromise," 10–11.

81. Esteves and Boland, quoted in *Western Shoshone Defense Project Newsletter* 5, no. 1 (1997), 3.

82. Richard Boland, quoted in "Urgent Request for Support," Timbisha Shoshone Tribe, http://www.yvwiiusdinvnohii.net/news/timbisha.html (accessed 12 April 1999).

83. Barbara Durham, quoted in "Timbisha Shoshone Tribal Homeland," 9; "Urgent Request for Support," Timbisha Shoshone Tribe, http://www.yvwiiusdinvnohii.net/news/timbisha.html (accessed 12 April 1999).

84. Catherine S. Fowler, "Residence without Reservation," 2; "Timbisha Shoshone Tribal Homeland," 12.

85. "Timbisha Shoshone Tribal Homeland," 12; Eddie Foronda, "Timbisha Shoshone: Heated Battle in Death Valley," 1996, http://www.nosuits.com/shoshone.htm (accessed 12 April 1999).

86. "Timbisha Shoshone Death Valley Land Restoration Project," n.d., http://www.dickshovel.com/timup.html (accessed 21 May 2003); "Urgent Request for Support," n.d., http://www.yvwiiusdinvnohii.net/news/timbisha.html (accessed 12 April 1999). Other groups acknowledged through the BAR have established federal trust reservations more quickly. For example, see "Grand Traverse Band of Chippewa and Ottawa Indians Establishment of Reservation," *Federal Register* 49 (17 January 1984): 2025, http://web.lexis-nexis.com/congcom (accessed 15 July 1998). The FAP acknowledged this band in May of 1980.

87. CILSNews 7 (spring 2001), http://www.calindian.org/timbisha.htm (accessed 20 May 2003); "Timbisha Celebrate Victory," *Native News*, http://www.escribe.com/culture/native_news/m5689.html (accessed 20 May 2003).

88. House Committee on Interior, *California Tribal Status Act*, 10 October 1991, testimony of Alogan Slagle.

89. Quinn, "Southeastern Indians," 34–52; Paredes, "Paradoxes of Modernism," 341–60; Carrillo, *Readings in American Indian Law*, 45–46.

1. Kirby Verret, interview by author; *American State Papers*, 265; "Proposed Finding against Federal Acknowledgment of the United Houma Nation, Inc.," *Federal Register* 59, no. 245 (22 December 1994): 66,118.

2. Churchill, "Tragedy and the Travesty, 18–19.

3. Gulf South Research Institute, "American Indians of Louisiana," 20–24.

4. United Houma Nation (UHN), "Petition for Federal Acknowledgment," 1985, 4, UHN, BAR.

5. BAR, "Historical Report: United Houma Nation," UHN, BAR; UHN, "Petition for Federal Acknowledgment," 1985, 4, UHN, BAR; Swanton, *Indian Tribes*, 285–86.

6. LeMoyne, *Iberville's Gulf Journals*, 67–79; Pénicaut, *Fleur de Lys*, 25; Swanton, *Indian Tribes*, 288; UHN, "Petition for Federal Acknowledgment," 1985, 4–11, UHN, BAR. M. de Sauvolle's account places Houmas on the Mississippi River in 1701. Le Baron Marc de Villiers, "Documents concernant l'historie des Indiens de la région orientale de la Louisiane," *Journal de la Société des Américanistes de Paris* 14(1922): 129. Du Pratz places them on the Mississippi above New Orleans after 1781. Du Pratz, *History of Louisiana*, 297–300.

7. Du Pratz, *History of Louisiana*, 297; Swanton, *Indian Tribes*, 287–88.

8. Giraud, *History of French Louisiana*, vol. 1, 84–85, 204; UHN, "Petition for Federal Acknowledgment," 1985, 12–24, UHN, BAR; BAR, "Historical Report," 3–4. The process of Indian-European colonial accommodation occurred throughout the Mississippi Valley and Great Lakes. See White, *Middle Ground*, and Kniffen, Gregory, and Stokes, *Historic Indian Tribes*.

9. Swanton, *Indian Tribes*, 279, 284; UHN, "Petition," 13–14; BAR, "Historical Report," 4–8.

10. Judice, quoted in UHN, "Petition," 6, 16, 19–24; BAR, "Historical Report," 13.

11. UHN, "Rebuttal to BIA's Proposed Finding against Acknowledgment," 13 November 1996, 54, UHN Headquarters, Golden Meadow, Louisiana.

12. Du Pratz, *History of Louisiana*, map; BAR, "Historical Report," 14, and BAR, "Proposed Finding against Federal Acknowledgment of the United Houma Nation, Inc.," UHN, BAR; UHN, "Rebuttal," 57–59. Though noting the records were wanting, based on his reading of colonial sources Swanton concluded that a band of Houma migrated down Bayou Lafourche at this time. Swanton, *Indian Tribes*, 291.

13. UHN, "Petition," 27; BAR, "Anthropological Report," 3.

14. Claiborne, *Official Letter Books*, vol. 4, 377; Smith, *Brief History*, 1904), 70–81; Downs, "Struggle of the Louisiana Tunica Indians," 72; Carol Meyer, "Louisiana Purchase," 17.

15. Claiborne, *Official Letter Books*, vol. 3, 347, and vol. 5, 275, 323.

16. UHN, "Petition," 31–32; BAR, "Historical Report," 18.

17. Sibley, "Historical Sketches," 82–83.

18. Dunbar, *Life, Letters and Papers*, 209, 162–67; Brackenridge, *Views of Louisiana*, 83.

19. Sibley, "Historical Sketches"; BAR, "Historical Report," 17–18; UHN, "Petition," 33–34; Drechsel and Makuakane-Drechsel, "Ethnohistory of 19th Century Louisiana," 25–28, 78–80, 89; BAR, "Historical Indian Tribes in Louisiana," 6; Jonathan Friedman, "Past in the Future," 837–38; Morrison, introduction to *American Indian Studies*, 9.

20. *American State Papers*, 265.

21. BAR, "Historical Indian Tribes," 45; *American State Papers*, 265, 256, 94; UHN, "Rebuttal," 74–77.

22. LeBreton, "History of the Factory System," viii; Purser, "Administration of Indian Affairs"; UHN, "Petition," 32–33; *United States v. John*, 437 U.S. 634 (1978); "Ruling Endangers Choctaws," *Indian Affairs*, May 1975, 6; Roy and Leary, "Economic Survey," 12; Porter, "Non-recognized American Indian Tribes," 3–15.

23. Austin interviews; BAR, "Historical Tribes," 44; BAR, "Historical Report," 14–18; UHN, "Rebuttal," 69.

24. Bloch, *Historian's Craft*; Lévi-Strauss, *Structural Anthropology*, 107.

25. UHN, "Petition," 34–35; BAR, "Anthropological Report," 2–3; Kersey, *Assumption of Sovereignty*; Blu, *Lumbee Problem*, 67; Peterson, "Indians in the Old South," 127.

26. UHN, "Petition," 34–35; BAR, "Anthropological Report," 21; BAR, "Genealogical Reports," 19–21, 51–66; Austin interviews.

27. Swanton, *Indian Tribes*, 291; Drechsel and Makuakane-Drechsel, "Ethnohistory," 78, 89; Watkins, "History of Terrebonne Parish," 5–6.

28. BAR, "Genealogical Report," 34–62, and "Appendix A"; UHN, "Petition," 34–36; UHN, "Rebuttal," 77–104.

29. Paredes interview.

30. BAR, "Genealogical Report," 35; BAR, "Summary under the Criteria," 7–10.

31. BAR, "Summary under the Criteria," 7–10; BAR, "Genealogical Report," 26, 31–32; BAR, "Proposed Finding against Federal Acknowledgment," 22 December 1994. For other time periods the BAR reports acknowledged the prevalence of kinship migrations among group members. BAR, "Anthropological Report," 56, 67. For the overall prevalence of kinship-chain migrations see Conzen, "Saga of Families," 341; Faragher, *Sugar Creek*, 57.

32. BAR, "Historical Report," 59.

33. BAR, "Genealogical Report," 45–46 (emphasis added).

34. BAR, "Genealogical Report," 34–54. It must be noted that the BIA reports are designed to present only information that makes their case against acknowledging Indian groups. Therefore, by design the BAR conclusions present a one-sided story that omits the complexities of various issues. However, much of the public discourse available concerning declined groups comes primarily from the BIA reports and conclusions. Their conclusions thus carry much weight beyond the narrow confines of the BIA offices.

35. U.S. Bureau of the Census, *Census Schedules—Terrebonne Parish, Louisiana*, 1860, 1900.

36. Webre, "Problem of Indian Slavery," 118–20; Forbes, *Africans and Native Americans*, 90, 249; BAR, "Genealogical Report," 56–57; U.S. *Census Schedules—Terrebonne Parish*, 1900.

37. Root, "Within, between, and beyond Race," 3, 5; Wilson, "Blood Quantum," 111; Daniel, "Passers and Pluralists," 91; U.S. *Census Schedules—Terrebonne Parish*, 1860 and 1900; BAR, "Anthropological Report," 30; BAR, "Genealogical Report," 31.

38. BAR, "Summary under the Criteria," 2; UHN, "Rebuttal," 97; Forbes, *Africans and Native Americans*, 250; UHN, "Petition," 39, 42.

39. Ruth Underhill, "Report on a Visit to Indian Groups in Louisiana, Oct. 15–25, 1938," GS 68776–31-800 pt. 2, CCF, RG 75, NAB.

40. Virginia DeMarce, quoted in UHN, "Rebuttal," 120; Virginia DeMarce, interview by author. DeMarce would not comment on this case.

41. Bowman and Curry-Roper, *Houma People of Louisiana*, 27–28; BAR, "Proposed Finding against Acknowledgment;" UHN, "Petition," 36–39; BAR, "Historical Report," 55–56, 58.

42. BAR, "Summary under the Criteria," 14; UHN, "Petition," 54.

43. Quote from UHN, "Petition," 131, 41–42, 81–83.

44. UHN, "Petition," 48, 50–54, 81–87; BAR, "Summary under the Criteria," 8, 11; BAR, "Proposed Finding against Acknowledgment."

45. BAR, "Proposed Finding against Acknowledgment"; UHN, "Petition," 43; BAR, "Summary under the Criteria," 7.

46. Harrington, cited in BAR, "Historical Report," 64; Usner, *American Indians*, 3; BAR, "Summary under the Criteria," 5; UHN, "Rebuttal," 120–29; Swanton, *Aboriginal Culture*; Swanton, *Indian Tribes*, 285–92 and plates 13–15.

47. Evelyn Truxillo, "Weaving History," *Louisiana Life*, July 1990, 104; BAR, "Historical Report," 64, and "Anthropological Report," 46.

48. UHN, "Petition," 43–44; Swanton, *Indian Tribes*, 291.

49. Swanton, *Indian Tribes*, 292; UHN, "Rebuttal," 342–45; Virginia DeMarce, testimony in transcript, *In the Matter of Houma Recognition Case*, 27 January 1995, 14–15, UHN, BAR.

50. John Reed Swanton, handwritten field notes, Bureau of American Ethnology, in possession of author.

51. Swanton, *Indian Tribes*, 284.

52. Swanton, *Indian Tribes*, 292.

53. Swanton, *Indian Tribes*, 28–29; UHN, "Petition," 45; BAR, "Historical Report," 64.

54. Swanton, handwritten field notes; BAR, "Historical Report," 57; BAR, press release on United Houma, UHN, BAR; Swanton, *Indian Tribes*, 9, 28–29; 32; BAR, "Summary under the Criteria," 27; UHN, "Rebuttal," 125–31; Brown and Hardy, "What Is Houma?" 521–48; Cecil H. Brown, interview by author.

55. BAR, "Historical Report," 61; BAR, "Summary under the Criteria," 27. For salient discussions of this larger issue see Daniel, "Passers and Pluralists," 106; Blu, *Lumbee Problem*, 5, 32, 65.

56. Ruth Underhill, "Report on a Visit to Indian Groups in Louisiana," CCF, RG 75, NAB; UHN, "Petition," 54–55; BAR, "Historical Report," 66–67; A. J. Martin to May Steinhauer, 22 October 1940, GS 48363–1931-260, CCF, RG 75, NAB; "Open Church for Indians in Louisiana," n.d., fd. 1491, Dorman Collection. For a thorough discussion of the education battles of the United Houma Nation, see "The Houma Tribe's Struggle for Education," in Bowman and Curry-Roper, *Houma People of Louisiana*. Certain primary sources on this issue are published in Downs and Whitehead, "Houma Indians," 2–22.

57. Underhill, "Report," CCF, RG 75, NAB; Reggie Billiot, interview by author.

58. Underhill, "Report," CCF, RG 75, NAB; Parenton and Pellegrin, "'Sabines,'" 148; Billiot interview.

59. Gindrat interview; BAR, "Historical Report," 67.

60. Charles Billiot to Indian Affairs, 2 August 1931, GS 48363–1931-260, CCF, RG 75, NAB; Numa Montet to Charles J. Rhoades, 11 December 1931, GS 68776–31-800 pt. I, CCF, RG 75, NAB; David Billiot to F. G. Speck, 18 September 1938, GS 68776–31-800 pt. 2, CCF, RG 75, NAB.

61. Frank Speck to Dr. Beatty, 7 February 1939, GS 68776–31-800 pt. 2, CCF, RG 75, NAB; Oliver La Farge to John Collier, 12 June 1940, GS 48363–1931-260, CCF, RG 75, NAB; John Collier to Caroline Dorman, 6 September 1935, fd. 1435, Dorman Collection.

62. David Billiot to Frank Speck, 18 September 1938, GS 68776–31-800 pt. 2, CCF, RG 75, NAB. Background information on Frank Speck, several articles on the Houma, federal reports, and some of the Billiot correspondence are published in *American Indian Journal of the Institute for the Development of Indian Law* 2, no. 3 (1976) and no. 4 (1976).

63. Marice Billiot, quoted in Underhill, "Report," 11, CCF, RG 75, NAB.

64. Roy Nash, "The Indians of Louisiana in 1931," UHN, BAR.

65. C. J. Rhoades, Commissioner, to Alice M. Peters, 21 September 1932, GS 68776–31-800 pt. I, CCF, RG 75, NAB.

66. C. J. Rhoades, Commissioner, to Mr. Numa Montet, 4 January 1932, GS 68776–31-800 pt. I, CCF, RG 75, NAB.

67. W. Carson Ryan, memorandum on Indian groups in the southern states, 3 April 1934, UHN, BAR.

68. Felix S. Cohen to Commissioner, 8 April 1935, HF, BAR; *Maynor v. Morton*, 510 F.2d 1254 (1975), 1256.

69. Underhill, "Report," 2, 3, CCF, RG 75, NAB.

70. Gatschet, "Shetimasha Indians," I.

71. Underhill, "Report," 4–5, CCF, RG 75, NAB.

72. Willard W. Beatty to Mr. Zimmerman, 7 February 1939, GS 68776–31-800 pt. 2, CCF, RG 75, NAB.

73. Harvey Meyer to Commissioner of Indian Affairs, 20 February 1940, GS 48363–

1931-260, CCF, RG 75, NAB; John Collier to May Steinhauer, 9 December 1940, GS 48363–1931-260, CCF, RG 75, NAB.

74. Willard W. Beatty to H. L. Bourgeois, 1 January 1942, GS 48363–1931-260, CCF, RG 75, NAB; Allen Ellender to Harold L. Ickes, 25 June 1942, GS 4834–1942-800, CCF, RG 75, NAB; H. L. Bourgeois to Willard W. Beatty, 7 September 1942, GS 4834–1942-800, CCF, RG 75, NAB; Willard Beatty to Frank G. Speck, 3 April 1943, GS 4834–1942-800, CCF, RG 75, NAB; Willard Beatty to Mr. Zimmerman, 18 August 1948, GS 4834–1942-800, CCF, RG 75, NAB.

75. BAR, "Summary under the Criteria," 14–16; Austin interviews.

76. Fischer, "History and Current Status," 227; Speck, "Houma Indians in 1940," 8, 6.

77. Speck, "Houma Indians in 1940," 7–9. Writing in the 1970s, scholar Max Stanton also studied the Houmas. He noted that the collective sense of peoplehood was quite weak and that the group expressed no tribal unity. Stanton, "Southern Louisiana Indian Survivors," 105–6; Stanton, "Remnant Indian Community," 82–87.

78. Berry, Almost White; Blu, Lumbee Problem, ix, 25.

79. Hudson, Southeastern Indians, 478; Hagan, "Full Blood, Mixed Blood," 309–21.

80. Gregory interview; Daniel, "Passers and Pluralists," 98–102; Stopp, "On Mixed-Racial Isolates," 344; Griessman, "American Isolates," 693–95; Van Rheenen, "Can You Tell Me," 4, 19, 40; Sider, Lumbee Indian Histories, xvii; Parenton and Pellegrin, "'Sabines,'" 148–52. For a group that apparently desired to be identified as white see Posey, "Origin, Development and Maintenance," 177.

81. Brenda Dardar, interview by author; Verret interview; Gindrat interview; Speck, "Houma Indians in 1940," 11; Milton, "Houma Indians since 1940," 16; Duthu and Ojibway, "Future Light or Feu Follet?" 28.

82. Verret interview; UHN, "Petition," 77; Gindrat interview; BAR, "Anthropological Report," 68.

83. Verret interview; Billiot interview; John Beecher, "Louisiana's 'Sabines'—Segregated Because of Their Names," San Francisco Chronicle, 18 September 1964, 13; "Indians Resist Integration Plan in Triracial County in Carolina," New York Times, 13 September 1970; Samuel Hoskins, "Lumbee Indians in for School Showdown," Baltimore Afro-American, 5 April 1958, 9; UHN, "Petition," 126, 145; Fischer, "History and Current Status," 229–32; Fred Barry, "Houmas Indians Seeking to Regain Former Lands," n.d., New Orleans Times-Picayune, Dardar Files; BAR, "Anthropological Report," 78–79.

84. Gindrat interview.

85. Gindrat interview; "Declaration of Indian Purpose," June, 1961, 17–18, box 35, RG 220, NACP; Laura Billiot, "An Update from the Chair," Talking Bayou: United Houma Newsletter, February 1997; Richard Baudouin, "Prejudice Motivates Houmas Indian Leader," Houma (LA) Daily Courier, 20 December 1976.

86. Gindrat, interview; UHN, "Petition," 146.

87. Gindrat interview; UHN, "Petition," 146; Dardar interview.

88. BAR, "Anthropological Report," 80; UHN, "Petition," 146; "Houma Indians Unite in Merger Ceremony," *Houma* (LA) *Daily Courier*, 13 May 1979; "Dulac Indians Splinter for State Tribal Group," *Houma* (LA) *Daily Courier*, 25 April 1974.

89. Ed Cullen, "Tunicas Move toward Organization, Recognition," 12 August 1973, UHN, BAR; Tunica Indian Tribe, meeting minutes, 12 August 1973, UHN, BAR; CENA transcript, n.d., 3, HF, BAR.

90. CENA transcript, n.d., 3, HF, BAR; Gregory interview.

91. "State Indian Tribes Will Meet in Dulac," 1970, UHN, BAR; "Indian Tribes Schedule Pow-Wow in BR [Baton Rouge] Saturday," 28 July 1970, UHN, BAR; Gindrat interview; "Indians Enthusiastic about New Commission," *Baton Rouge State-Times*, 12 July 1972; Gregory interview; Verret interview; Elizabeth Roberts, "4 Louisiana Indian Tribes Hold Powwow," *Alexandria* (LA) *Daily Town Talk*, 14 February 1971.

92. CENA transcript, 4. HF, BAR; Also see Quinn, "Southeast Syndrome."

93. Howard Dion, statements in AIPRC transcript, Dulac, Louisiana, 67, RG 220, NACP; Gregory interview; Senate Select Committee, *Houma Recognition Act*, 7 August 1990, 56; *Neka-camôn: A Publication for and about Louisiana's Native Americans*, March 1990, 3, Louisiana State Library, Baton Rouge, Louisiana.

94. Coreen Paulk, quoted in AIPRC transcript, Dulac, Louisiana, 75, RG 220, NACP.

95. "The Elderly Indians of Louisiana and Their Needs: A Report from the Office of Indian Affairs" (Baton Rouge: Louisiana Health and Human Resources Administration, 1 December 1975), 9–20, Louisiana State Library; AIPRC transcript, Dulac, Louisiana, RG 220, NACP; "Houma and Tunica Face Tough Recognition Fight," n.d. (1970s), Dardar Files; UHN, "Petition," 129.

96. Senate Select Committee, *Federal Acknowledgment Administrative*, part 2, 5 May 1989, Orbis Associates, "Final Report Evaluation of Status Clarification Projects," 406; Gindrat interview; Gregory interview; BAR, "Anthropological Report," 85–94.

97. Roy and Leary, "Economic Survey," 14; David Snyder, "Houma Indian Tribe Nears Nation Status," n.d., Dardar Files; Verret interview; AIPRC transcript, Dulac, Louisiana, RG 220, NACP; "U.S. Officials Scrutinize Houma Indians," *New Orleans Times-Picayune*, 17 May 1993.

98. Verret interview.

99. Helen Gindrat, quoted in Annabelle Armstrong, "On the 'Warpath' for Her People," n.d., Dardar Files; Dardar interview.

100. Greg Bowman to George Roth, 19 December 1978, UHN, BAR; Theodore Krenzke to J. Bennett Johnston, 21 April 1976, UHN, BAR; Constitution of the United Houma Nation, Inc., 1979, UHN, BAR; Verret interview; UHN, "Petition," 147–48; Roxanne Kearns, "Merger of Houmas Means Progress," *Thibodaux* (LA) *Daily Comet*, 13 April 1979.

101. Kirby Verret, quoted in Tom Guarisco, "Houma Indians Continue Waiting," *Thibodaux* (LA) *Daily Comet*, 8 February 1993; Billiot interview.

102. UHN, "Petition," 127; BAR, "Index to Federal Acknowledgment Petitioners

by State," 29 October 1999, http://www.doi.gov/bia/bar/indexz.htm (accessed 6 April 2000); Austin interviews.

103. Henry, *Ethnicity in the Americas*, 2; Morland, conclusion to *Not So Solid South*, 131–32.

104. "Program Will Unite Students and Elders through Reading," *Lafourche* (LA) *Gazette*, 13 December 1992; "Houma Indians Sign Pact to Run Two State Parks," 17 June 1988, Dardar Files; Frances Johnson, "Claims about Indians Disputed," and Delores Dardar, "Houma Indian Blasts Articles," *Houma* (LA) *Courier*, 24 August 1993; Brenda Pitre, "Tribal Official: Stories One-sided," *Houma* (LA) *Daily Comet*, 31 August 1993; "CETA Summer Job Program Tab $600,000 in 3-Parishes," n.d., Dardar Files; BAR, "Anthropological Report," 84–88; Mark Tilden, interview by author.

105. Verret interview; Dardar interview; Hudson, *Southeastern Indians*, 496.

106. Kirby Verret, "Houma Tribe Seeks Recognition," *Houma* (LA) *Daily Comet*, 5 February 1990; Senate Select Committee, *Houma Recognition Act*, 7 August 1990, 31; Kenneth Weiss, "Lawmakers Support Indians," *Houma* (LA) *Daily Comet*, 7 February 1990; Kirby Verret to Senator Johnson, 29 April 1988, UHN, BAR; John D. Geary to Kirby Verret, 12 December 1986, UHN, BAR.

107. Tribal Government Services to Kirby Verret, 1990, UHN, BAR.

108. Jack Campisi to Ronal Eden, 28 August 1990, UHN, BAR; Senate Select Committee, *Houma Recognition Act*, 7 August 1990, testimony of Faith Roessel, 20.

109. Senate Select Committee, *Federal Acknowledgment Administrative*, part 2, 5 May 1989, statement of Helen Gindrat, 71.

110. Austin interviews.

111. Kirby Verret to J. Bennett Johnston, 16 February 1990, "Statement by Senator J. B. Johnston," 5 April 1990, Johnston Papers; A Bill, S. 1918, 17 November 1989, and copies of Terrebonne, Jefferson, and St. Mary Parish resolutions, Johnston Papers; "GOP Backs Houma," *Houma* (LA) *Daily Courier*, 13 March 1990.

112. "Proposed Finding," *Federal Register*, 59, no. 245 (22 December 1994): 66,118; BAR, "Summary under the Criteria," 7–9, UHN, BAR.

113. BAR, "Summary under the Criteria," 15–21; BAR, "Transcript in the Matter of: Houma Recognition," 27 January 1995, UHN, BAR; BAR, "Anthropological Report," 83–91; BAR, "Historical Report," 102–4.

114. Gregory interview.

115. Verret interview; Gregory interview; Austin interviews; NARF, "Petition for Recognition of the Tunica-Biloxi Indian Tribe in Compliance with 25 C.F.R. Part 54," 40, 49, 64, 69–73, TB, BAR; Commissioner of Indian Affairs, memorandum on Tunica-Biloxi Indian Tribe, 4 December 1980, TB, BAR; BAR, "Anthropological Report on the Tunica-Biloxi Tribe," n.d., 2, 23, TB, BAR.

116. Reggie Billiot, quoted in Jennifer Lawson, "Group Seeks Confederation of Tribes," *Houma* (LA) *Daily Courier*, 12 March 1995; Billiot interview.

117. Billiot interview; Michael L. Dardar to Holly Record, 15 September 1992, UHN,

BAR; Reggie Billiot to Holly Reckord, 14 November 1992, UHN, BAR; *Talking Stick: Newsletter for the Jefferson Parish Group of the United Houma Nation*, August 1992, UHN, BAR; BAR "Anthropological Report," 89–95.

118. BAR, "Anthropological Report," 93.

119. Billiot interview; Pat Arnould, interview by author.

120. Billiot interview; Chief, BAR, to Rosalie Billiot, UHN, BAR.

121. Isle Jean Charles Indian Community materials, BCCM, BAR; petition materials and Point au Chien Indian Tribe (PACIT) petition, PACIT, BAR; Billiot interview; Austin interviews.

122. Billiot interview.

123. Dardar interview; Arnould interview; Verret interview; Billiot interview; T. Mayheart Dardar, "Hear Our Voice," *Talking Bayou: United Houma Newsletter* 3, no. 1 (March 1998); Brenda Dardar, "An Update from the Chair," *Talking Bayou: United Houma Newsletter* 2, no. 2 (July 1997); "Business Opportunity Sabotaged," *Talking Stick: Newsletter for the Jefferson Parish Group of the United Houma Nation*, August 1992; Michael L. Dardar to Holly Reckord, 15 September 1992, UHN, BAR.

124. Kirby Verret to Tribal Members, *Talking Bayou: United Houma Newsletter* 2, no. 3 (October 1997); McCulloch and Wilkins, " 'Constructing' Nations within States," 361–90; "The United Houma Nation: Anything but United," *Houma (LA) Courier*, 12 July 1993; BAR, "Anthropological Report," and "Historical Report."

125. "Complaint for Declaratory Judgment," in *Sidney Verdin vs. The Louisiana Land and Exploration Company*, n.d., office files, Louisiana Office of Indian Affairs, Baton Rouge, Louisiana; Charles D. Marshall Jr. to Bruce Babbitt, 27 October 1995, UHN, BAR; H. Leighton Steward, Louisiana Land and Exploration Company (LLE), to J. Bennett Johnston, 22 March 1994, Johnston Papers.

126. House Committee on Resources, Subcommittee on Native American Affairs, *Bill to Provide*, 18 June 1996, various testimony by BIA, BCCM, and PACIT; Jeff Lewis, interview by author.

127. Austin interviews; UHN, "Rebuttal," 70.

128. BAR, "Technical Reports regarding the Tunica-Biloxi Indian Tribe," TB, BAR; BAR, "Proposed Finding for Federal Acknowledgment of the Jena Band of Choctaw Indians," n.d., http://www.doi.gov/bia/jensum.html (accessed 5 December 1997); Sharon Sholars Brown, "Jena Choctaw," 180–93.

129. UHN, "Rebuttal," 303–4; BAR, "Louisiana Houma Tribe Denied BIA Recognition," press release, 14 December 1994, UHN, BAR.

130. Press release, 14 December 1994, UHN, BAR; UHN, "Rebuttal," 291–94; Dardar interview; Usner, *American Indians*, 2–3.

131. UHN, "Rebuttal," 141–54, 281–88; 25 C.F.R. Part 83 (1997).

132. Wax, "Social Structure," 205.

133. Chad Smith, personal communication to author, 17 November 2001.

134. Dardar interview; *Talking Bayou: United Houma Newsletter*, 1996–1999.

135. Verret interview.

136. Verret interview.

137. Gindrat interview; Dardar interview.

138. Ted Griggs, "Tribal Council the Key to Houmas," *Houma (LA) Courier*, 28 July 1993; Reggie Billiot to Ada E. Deer, 6 November 1996, UHN, BAR; Verret interview.

139. UHN, "Rebuttal," 389; Gregory interview; Verret interview.

6. FROM PLAYING INDIAN TO PLAYING SLOTS

1. "News Release," Bob Bullock, Comptroller of Public Accounts, 22 November 1985, box 1990/1–41, fd. 5, TIC; Anne Marie Kilday, "Texas Loses Political Legend," *San Antonio Express-News*, 19 June 1999, 1A; Don Miller, interview by author.

2. Raymond Ramirez to Bob Bullock, 6 January 1986, fd. 161, Diamond Papers.

3. Vine Deloria Jr., *Custer Died for Your Sins*, 243–47; Tom Diamond, interviews by author; *Tiwa Indians Act*, Public Law 90–287 (12 April 1968), 82 Stat. 93 (1973); *Lumbee Indians of North Carolina*, 70 Stat. 254 (7 June 1956).

4. Joe Sierra, interview by author,; Acts 1967, 60th Leg., R.S., ch. 276, p. 662 and codified as Art. 5421z, as amended, *Vernon's Texas Civil Statutes*; Acts 1967, 60th Leg., R.S. ch. 277, p. 666 and codified as Art. 542z-1, *Vernon's Texas Civil Statutes*; Diamond interviews; Raymond Apodaca, interview by author.

5. Although they were "lost" until the 1960s, there are several works on general tribal history, development, and photography; see Houser, "Tigua Pueblo," 336–42; Eickhoff, *Exiled*; Deborah Lee Martin, "Development at Ysleta Del Sur Pueblo"; Wright, *Tiguas*. For insightful works on other borderland tribes see Fontana, *Of Earth and Little Rain*; Latorre and Latorre, *Mexican Kickapoo Indians*; Nunley, "Mexican Kickapoo Indians."

6. Hodge, *Handbook of American Indians*, 622–24; Dozier, *Pueblo Indians*, 43; Parsons, "Isleta, New Mexico," 204; Ellis, "Isleta Pueblo," 351–355; Eggan, *Social Organization*, 18–19.

7. Hodge, *Handbook of American Indians*, 622; Gutierrez, *When Jesus Came*, xxiii–xxv, 46, 69–73, 90–91; Dozier, *Pueblo Indians*, 70, 75.

8. Dozier, *Pueblo Indians*, 67, 187, 167–68; Gutierrez, *When Jesus Came*, 157–58; Weber, *Spanish Frontier in North America*, 122–26; 133–34.

9. Weber, *Spanish Frontier in North America*, 134–36; Hackett, *Revolt of the Pueblo Indians*; Ellis, "Isleta Pueblo," 353–54; Eggan, *Social Organization*, 317; Parsons, "Isleta, New Mexico," 204; Houser, "Tigua Pueblo," 336–41.

10. Houser, "Tigua Pueblo," 339; Hodge, *Handbook of American Indians*, 624; Senate Select Committee, *Restoration*, 25 June 1986, 309.

11. Tom Diamond, "Legal Status of the Tiguas," fd. "Tigua-legislation," ITC; Alan H. Minter, "The Tigua Indians of the Pueblo de Ysleta del Sur, El Paso County, Texas," *West Texas Historical Association Year Book*, fd. 7, Diamond Papers; Newcomb, *Indians of Texas*, 346, 352, 358; La Vere, *Life among the Texas Indians*, 24–26, 37–40.

12. Griswold del Castillo, *Treaty of Guadalupe Hidalgo*, appendix 2, "The Treaty of Guadalupe Hidalgo, Article V," 183–99; "Plaintiff's Original Petition," and "Ysleta del Sur Indian Pueblo Recognized by US Indian Bureau," fd. 284, Diamond Papers; Keegan, *Pueblo People*, 49–50; Sando, *Pueblo Indians*, 89–93; Dozier, *Pueblo Indians*, 100–109; *United States v. Joseph* 94 U.S. 614 (1876); *United States v. Sandoval* 231 U.S. 28 (1913).

13. Rex Gerald, "History of the Tigua Indians of Ysleta del Sur, Texas," Indian Claims Commission materials, AA-16, Arizona State Museum, Tucson, Arizona.

14. Samuel Rosenberg, Principal, Albuquerque Indian School, to Nicholas P. Houser, 12 July 1966, fd. 70, Diamond Papers; "Plaintiff's Original Petition," n.d., fd. 284, Diamond Papers; Pueblo Indian Scout, Army Discharge Papers for Beiseslao Granillo, 22 March 1880, fd. 244, Diamond Papers.

15. United Bureau of Census, *Census Schedules*, Ysleta Precinct no. 2, censuses for 1870, 1880, 1890, fd. 261 and fd. 267, Diamond Papers; W. H. Timmons, "The Spanish Census of Ysleta in 1790—with a List of the Tiguas" (El Paso: Columbian Quincentenary, 1992); "Tiguas of Ysleta to Select Chief," *El Paso Herald*, 12 December 1890; "Indians to Have Xmas Dance," *El Paso Herald*, 22 December 1911; "The Indians Have Begun Their Dancing," *El Paso Herald Post*, 17 November 1910.

16. Bandelier, *Final Report*, 1: 316.

17. James Mooney Report (notes), Bureau of American Ethnology, Smithsonian Institution, December–January, 1897–98, fd. 266, Diamond Papers; Bandelier, *Final Report*, 248–49; Tom Diamond, "The Tigua Indians of El Paso," a monograph/petition published by the NCAI, 1966, box 1967, fd. "RCW and General Legislation," White Papers.

18. Fewkes, "Pueblo Settlements," 57–75; "Mooney Report," Diamond Papers; Nicholas P. Houser, "A Description and Analysis of the Tiwa Community of Ysleta, Texas," First Report to Project Bravo, 20 July 1966, 24, box 1967, fd. "RCW and General Legislation," White Papers.

19. Fewkes, "Pueblo Settlements," 62–64; Houser, "Description," 14–15, box 1967, fd. "RCW and General Legislation," White Papers; Procedures, 25 C.F.R. Part 83 (1997).

20. Fewkes, "Pueblo Settlements," 73–75; Dozier, *Pueblo Indians*, 106.

21. Calleros, *Tigua Indians*, 10–16; Tom Diamond to Bill Blackburn, 8 December 1967, WHC, fd. IN/T, LBJ; Joel W. Martin, "My Grandmother," 129–45; Nicholas P. Houser, interviews by author.

22. Sierra interview; Dozier, *Pueblo Indians*, 110–11.

23. Tom Diamond to T. W. Taylor, 4 April 1967, box 1967, fd. "RCW and General Legislation," White Papers; Louis Hofferbert, "Lost Indian Tribe Seeks Birthright," *Houston Chronicle*, 22 May 1966, sec. 1, p. 25.

24. Orren Beaty to Marvin Watson, 14 January 1966, WHC, IN/T, LBJ; Senate Select Committee, *Restoration*, 25 June 1986, 339; Tom Diamond, "Legal Status of the Tiguas," fd. "Tigua-legislation," ITC.

25. Bernard Fontana to Tom Diamond, 1966, box 1967, fd. "RCW and General

Legislation," White Papers; Edgar A. Hinton, "The Tigua Indians: A Sociological Study of a Minority Group," February 1966, fd. "Tigua-cultural background," ITC; Houser interviews.

26. Bernard Fontana, personal correspondence with author, 14 December 1999; Houser interview; Houser, "Description," 5, box 1967, fd. "RCW and General Legislation," White Papers; Sierra interview. For the greater phenomenon see Barth, *Ethnic Groups and Boundaries*, and Spicer and Thompson, *Plural Society in the Southwest*.

27. Houser, "Description," 8–9, 20–21, box 1967, fd. "RCW and General Legislation," White Papers; Houser interview; transcript, video recording, *People of the Sun: The Tiguas of Ysleta* by Leslie Burns and Dan Gelo, 18, fd. "Tigua-culture," ITC; Apodaca interview.

28. Brading, *First America*, 40; Sánchez, *Becoming Mexican American*, 30; Twinam, "Honor, Sexuality, and Illegitimacy," 118–55; Dozier, *Pueblo Indians*, 79–83; Tom Diamond to W. Marvin Watson, 21 January 1966, WHC, IN/T, LBJ; Apodaca interview; Houser interview.

29. Pedraza, quoted in Ed Curda, "Tiguas Struggled for Tribal Recognition," *El Paso Times*, 22 May 1978.

30. Sierra interview; Vicente Ordoñez, interview by author; Houser interviews; David Sheppard, "Tigua Elders Saved Tribe," *El Paso Times*, 13 June 1994; Houser, "Proposal for the Tigua Pueblo," 1966, fd. 225, Diamond Papers.

31. Apodaca interview.

32. "Forgotten People Seek Rights as Indians," *Southwest Catholic Register*, 28 January 1966; Houser, "A Description," 15, 17, 25, box 1967, fd. "RCW and General Legislation," White Papers; Bernard Fontana, various letters to Tom Diamond, 1966, box 1967, fd. "RCW and General Legislation," White Papers.

33. Houser, "A Description," 17, 25–26, box 1967, fd. "RCW and General Legislation," White Papers; Hinton, "Tigua Indians," ITC; Angelina Granillo Ortega and Joe Sierra, oral interviews by Francisco Hernandez, University of Texas at El Paso, Institute of Oral History, fd. 320, Diamond Papers.

34. Tom Diamond to W. Marvin Watson, 21 January 1966, WHC, IN/T, LBJ; Hinton, " Tigua Indians," ITC; Houser, "Description," 27, box 1967, fd. "RCW and General Legislation," White Papers.

35. Rayna Green, "Tribe Called Wannabee," 30–55; Philip Deloria, *Playing Indian*; Stan Steiner, "The White Indians," *Akwesasne Notes*, early spring 1976, 38–40.

36. Tom Diamond, interview by Nicholas P. Houser, 1967 fd. 161, Diamond Papers; Ed Curda, "Tiguas Struggled," *El Paso Times*, 22 May 1978; Ordoñez interview; Diamond interviews; Alex Candelaria to Enrique Paiz, 3 March 1995, fd. 297, Diamond Papers; Houser interviews.

37. Tom Diamond to Bernard Fontana, 17 November 1965, Diamond Papers; Tom Diamond, interview by Houser, 1967 fd. 161, Diamond Papers.

38. Houser interviews; Tom Diamond, interview by Houser, 1976, fd. 161, Dia-

mond Papers; Tom Diamond to Ralph Yarborough, 7 January 1968, fd. 161, Diamond Papers; Rosenthal, *Their Day in Court*, xi–xii; Tom Diamond to Richard C. White, 9 March 1967, box 1967, fd. "RCW and General Legislation," White Papers; Ed Curda, "Tiguas Struggled," *El Paso Times*, 22 May 1978; Diamond interview; Fontana, personal correspondence.

39. Bernard Fontana to Tom Diamond, 13 November 1965, WHC, IN/T, LBJ; Fontana, personal correspondence.

40. Bernard Fontana to Tom Diamond, 13 November 1965, WHC, IN/T, LBJ; Tom Bryan, "Anthropologist Finds Untapped Mine," *El Paso Times*, 19 September 1966; Fontana to Diamond, 18 December 1965, fd. 197, Diamond Papers; Fontana to Diamond, 27 July 1966, fd. 161, Diamond Papers.

41. Fontana, personal correspondence; Houser interviews; Tom Diamond to Fred Baldwin, 12 November 1965, fd. 225, Diamond Papers; Preston Clark to Tom Diamond, 19 October 1966, fd. 225, Diamond Papers; Diamond interviews.

42. Certificate of Tribal Membership, NCAI, Tigua Band of Isleta Pueblo, 2 August 1966, fd. 223, Diamond Papers; "23rd Annual Convention, Executive Director's Report," 1966, fd. 223, Diamond Papers; Josephy, Nagel, and Johnson, *Red Power*.

43. Vine Deloria Jr., *Custer Died for Your Sins*, 245; Tom Diamond to Vine Deloria Jr., 14 March 1967, fd. 223, Diamond Papers.

44. Oswald C. George to Richard C. White, 5 June 1967, box 1967, fd. "RCW and General Legislation," White Papers; Diamond interviews; Tom Diamond to Vine Deloria Jr., 14 March 1967, fd. 223, Diamond Papers.

45. Sierra interview.

46. Diamond interviews; Tom Diamond to Frank J. Berry, 26 July 1966, WHC, IN/T, LBJ; Orren Beaty to Marvin Watson, 14 January 1966, WHC, IN/T, LBJ; Tom Diamond to Crawford C. Martin, 19 November 1965, fd. 161, Diamond Papers; Tom Diamond to Richard C. White, 31 August 1964, box 1967, fd. "RCW and General Legislation," White Papers; "Tigua Bill to Get Hearing," *El Paso Times*, 1 August 1967.

47. House Committee on Interior, *Bill Relating to the Tiwa Indians*, 19 September 1966; House Committee on Interior, *Bill Relating to the Tiwa Indians*, 6 June 1967; Richard C. White to Tom Diamond, 6 September 1966, box 1967, fd. "RCW and General Legislation," White Papers; Theodore W. Taylor to Tom Diamond, 30 March 1967 WHC, IN/T, LBJ; Diamond interviews. The Tiguas did in fact later pursue an Indian land claim case, an action still pending in 2003.

48. Tom Diamond, interview by Nicholas Houser, 1967, Diamond Papers; Tom Diamond to Vine Deloria Jr., 23 January 1967, fd. 223, Diamond Papers; Georgeann Robinson, testimony for NCAI on Texas Bill, fd. 223, Diamond Papers; Fontana, personal correspondence; Diamond interviews.

49. Fontana, personal correspondence; Houser interviews; Nicholas Houser to Alton Griffin, 7 October 1969, fd. 16, Diamond Papers.

50. Fontana, personal correspondence; "Tiguas Become Texans: Connally Made

Cacique," *El Paso Herald-Post*, 23 May 1967; Houser interviews; Frank X. Tolbert, "Tiguas Required to Prove That They're Really Indians," *Dallas Morning News*, 14 April 1967.

51. Tom Diamond, interview by Houser, 1967, Diamond Papers.

52. Nancy Kowert, "Tiguas Give Connally Honorary Chief Title," *Dallas Morning News*, 24 May 1967; photograph, Cacique Jose Granillo applying paint to Governor John Connally, fd. 162, Diamond Papers; Diamond interview by Houser, 1967, Diamond Papers; "Tigua Indians Sing for Texas Legislators," *El Paso Herald-Post*, 13 April 1967; Fontana, personal correspondence; Diamond interviews.

53. Tom Diamond to Marvin Watson, 29 December 1966, WHC, IN/T, LBJ; Marvin Watson to Tom Diamond, 14 January 1966, WHC, IN/T, LBJ; Diamond interview; Houser interviews; Alfred Gagne, League of Nations Pan-Am. Indians, to Richard White, 7 June 1967, box 1967, fd. "RCW and General Legislation," White Papers; Bill Osceola, chair, Seminole Tribe of Florida, to Richard White, 2 June 1967, box 1967, fd. "RCW and General Legislation," White Papers; Bernard Fontana to Tom Diamond, 14 June 1966, Diamond Papers; statement of Vine Deloria Jr. for NCAI on H.R. 10599, 1967, fd. 223, Diamond Papers.

54. House Committee on Interior, *Bill Relating to the Tiwa Indians*, 6 June 1967; Tom Diamond to Marvin Watson, 30 November 1967, WHC, IN/T, LBJ; Vine Deloria Jr. to Tom Diamond, 24 March 1967, fd. 223, Diamond Papers; Stanley Cain to Wayne N. Aspinall, 28 July 1967, fd. 161, Diamond Papers; James Officer to Tom Diamond, 19 May 1967, box 1967, fd. "RCW and General Legislation," White Papers; Richard C. White to Tom Diamond, 7 June 1967, box 1967, fd. "RCW and General Legislation," White Papers.

55. Houser interviews; Tom Diamond, "The Tigua Indians of El Paso" 1966, box 1967, fd. "RCW and General Legislation," White Papers; Sarah McClendon, "Committee Approves Tiguas Bill," *El Paso Times*, 2 August 1967; Diamond interviews; *An Act Relating to the Tiwa Indians of Texas*, Public Law 90–287 (12 April 1968), 82 Stat. 93 (1968).

56. Robert Bennett to W. Marvin Watson, 25 January 1967, WHC, IN/T, LBJ; "Proposals for the Tigua Pueblo of San Antonio de Ysleta," WHC, IN/T, LBJ.

57. Tiwa Act, *Vernon's Texas Civil Statutes*, Art. 5421z; Bernard Fontana to Tom Diamond, 27 July 1966, fd. 161, Diamond Papers; "Tigua Indians Sing for Texas Legislators," *El Paso Times*, 13 April 1967; Taylor, *States and Their Indian Citizens*, 25–28, 34–35; Philp, *Termination Revisited*, xii, 166; Lerch, "State Recognized Indians," 44–71.

58. Mike Ward, "Sunset Panel Vote Sets Advocacy Role for Indian Board," *Austin American Statesman*, 26 January 1989; Taylor, *States and Their Indian Citizens*, 89, 209; *North Carolina Commission of Indian Affairs: Annual Report, 1998–1999*, Raleigh NC: North Carolina Commission of Indian Affairs; Cornell, *Return of the Native*, 132–33.

59. "The Texas Indian Commission and American Indians in Texas," 1986, Center for American History, University of Texas at Austin; Taylor, *States and Their Indian Citizens*, 98; Sierra interview.

60. Buffy St. Marie, quoted in *Village Voice*, 31 July 1969, reprinted in *Akwesasne Notes*

1 (July 1969); Philip Deloria, *Playing Indian*, 128–30, 137–43; W. M. Levre to Lyndon B. Johnson, 17 June 1964, WHC, IN/O, LBJ; Hine, *Community on the American Frontier*, 232–37; Richman, "Return of the Red Man," 52–77.

61. "Proposals for the Tigua Pueblo," 1966, WHC, IN/T, LBJ; Sierra interview; Ed Curda, "Indians Struggling with Cultural Clash," *El Paso Times*, 25 May 1978; Miles, "Tigua Indians"; Tom Diamond to W. Marvin Watson, 21 January 1966, fd. 161, Diamond Papers; Nicholas P. Houser to Alton Griffin, 7 October 1969, fd. 161, Diamond Papers.

62. Arthur and Gifford, "Research Study: Tourism in the El Paso Area," Bureau of Business and Economic Research, University of Texas at El Paso, 1973, box 1990/1–34, fd. "Tigua-EDA Project," TIC; "The Forgotten Americans," LBJ Policy Statement, 6 March 1968, box 138, SLU Papers; Dozier, *Pueblo Indians*, 109, 115.

63. Dempsie Henley, Texas Commission on Indian Affairs, to Governor Dolph Briscoe, 11 July 1975, fd. "Tigua Housing/Misc.," box 1990/1–34, TIC; Ed Curda, "Projects Just Didn't Work Out," *El Paso Times*, 24 May 1978.

64. "El Paso's Tigua Indians Still Tribal," fd. 162, Diamond Papers.

65. Ordoñez interview; mailgram to Governor Dolph Briscoe, 30 October 1973, box 1990/1–34, fd. "Tigua-EDA Project," TIC; Sierra interview; Tom Diamond to Dempsey Henley, 3 September 1969, fd. 161, Diamond Papers; Houser interviews.

66. "Statements of the Tribal Council of the Tiguas," tribal minutes, 25 May 1971, fd. 16, Diamond Papers; Tom Diamond to Dempsy Henley, 8 October 1969, fd. 10, Diamond Papers.

67. Sierra interview; Apodaca interview; Deloria and Lytle, *Nations Within*, 6; Prucha, *Great Father*, 376–78.

68. Tom Diamond to Dempsie Henley, 8 October 1969, fd. 10, Diamond Papers.

69. Sierra interview; Apodaca interview.

70. Darlene Munoz, quoted in Ed Curda, "Indians Struggling with Cultural Clash," *El Paso Times*, 25 May 1978; Houser interviews; Hook, *Alabama-Coushatta Indians*, 9; Gary Clayton Anderson, *Indian Southwest*, 3–4, 216, 249.

71. Apodaca interview.

72. Ed Curda, "Indians Struggling with Cultural Clash," *El Paso Times*, 25 May 1978; "Embattled Tigua Indians Making a Comeback," *San Antonio Light*, 2 July 1972, 10-C; Apodaca interview; Tigua Reservation pamphlet, box 117, RG 220, NACP; "Indian Dance to Honor Patron Saint," *El Paso Times*, 10 June 1977; "Around the State," *Texas Monthly* 4, no. 6 (1976); Andy C. Padilla to Indian Community Action Project—All Indian Pueblo Council, 19 March 1975, box 1990/1–34, fd. "Tigua Housing/Misc.," TIC; "A Short History," n.d., box 1990/1–41, fd. 8, TIC.

73. Ed Curda, "Projects Just Didn't Work Out," *El Paso Times*, 24 May 1978; Sierra interview; Rhoads, "Tigua Indians; "The Tigua Indian Reservation," pamphlet, fd. "Tigua-cultural life," ITC; Geneson, "Return of the Tigua," 62; "Visit the Tigua Indians," pamphlet, box 117, RG 220, NACP; Sierra interview.

74. Rhoads, "Tigua Indians; Parvin, "Tigua Territory."

75. Geneson, "Return of the Tigua."

76. Parvin, "Tigua Territory."

77. Princess Diana, quoted in Virginia Turner, "Princess Diana Pleased to Meet Tigua Indian," El Paso Herald-Post, 18 March 1986.

78. Sandra Barniea, "Tigua Indians Move," El Paso Times, 22 August 1976; Sierra interview; Senate Select Committee, Restoration, 25 June 1986, "Tribal Land Base," 113, 121; Walter Broemer to Grover Colter, 19 July 1975, fd. "Housing/Tigua," box 1990/1–34, TIC; "Fact Sheet on Mutual Help Housing Project," October 1977, box 1990/1–34, TIC; Ed Curda, "Tiguas Building Up by Their Hands," El Paso Times, 23 May 1978.

79. Indian Manpower Program/CETA, box 117, RG 220, NACP; "Indian Tribe Joins Council," El Paso Times, 21 November 1976; Senate Select Committee, Restoration, 25 June 1986, 115–21; Taylor, States and Their Indian Citizens, 98; Ken Flynn, "Tigua Claim Worries Park's Rock Climbers," El Paso Herald-Post, 17 August 1991; Sierra interview; Dempsie Henley to Texas Commission on Indian Affairs, 11 February 1972, fd. 16, Diamond Papers.

80. Tigua Tribe, resolution in favor of claims case, 29 September 1969, fd. 5, Diamond Papers; Maggie Rivas, "High Profile: Ray Apodaca," Dallas Morning News, 16 June 1991, E-1; Thaddeus Herrick, "Western Film 'Shouting' Match," El Paso Herald-Post, 29 November 1986; "Tigua Leader Deplores Mascots," El Paso Herald-Post, 24 October 1991.

81. "Testimony of Manuel V. Silvas," on H.R. 1344, 17 October 1985, box 1990/141, fd. 3, TIC; Senate Select Committee, Restoration, 25 June 1986, 118–19; Geneson, "Return of the Tigua"; Eleanor Morris, "Tigua Indian Reservation," San Antonio Light, 16 September 1984; "Minutes," Tigua Tribe, 1978, box 1990/1–34, fd. "Tigua-EDA Project," TIC.

82. Ed Curda, "Indians Struggling with Cultural Clash," El Paso Times, 25 May 1978; Sierra interview; Apodaca interview.

83. Walter Broemer, quoted in Ed Curda, "Projects Just Didn't Work Out," El Paso Times, 24 May 1978; Nicholas Houser to Alton Griffin, 7 October 1969, fd. 16, Diamond Papers; Texas House, Interim Report, Sixty Sixth Legislative Session, The Committee on State Affairs, Final Report: Subcommittee on Indian Affairs, n.d., fd. 174, Diamond Papers.

84. Ed Fifer quoted in "Tigua Leader Picked for Indian Director," Austin American Statesman, 28 August 1982; Apodaca interview.

85. Sierra interview.

86. Walter Broemer, quoted in Ed Curda, "Tiguas Building Up by Their Hands," El Paso Times, 23 May 1978.

87. Dempsie Henley to Governor Preston Smith, 2 November 1971, fd. 16, Diamond Papers; Apodaca interview; Senate Select Committee, Restoration, 25 June 1986, 131; Ed Curda, "Tiguas Building Up by Their Hands," El Paso Times, 23 May 1978; Ed Curda, "Tiguas Confront Texas," El Paso Times, 21 May 1978.

88. Morris Bullock and Miguel Pedraza to Senator Bentsen, 21 January 1986, TIC; Diamond interviews.

89. Apodaca interview.

90. Ramona Parras Paiz, quoted in Elisa Rocha, "Tigua Grandma, 89, Recalls the Changes," El Paso Herald, 26 March 1990; Ed Curda, "Tiguas Confront Texas," El Paso Times, 21 May 1978; Senate Select Committee, Restoration, 25 June 1986, 126; Geneson, "Return of the Tigua."

91. Charles D. Travis to Jim Mattox, 22 March 1983, box 1990/1–41, fd. 5, TIC; Law Firm of Wilkinson, Cragun, and Barker, memorandum, 19 May 1967, fd., "Ysleta Grant Legal Brief," Diamond Papers; "HR 1344 and High Stakes Bingo," Comptroller's Office, 1986, box 1990/1–41, fd. 5, TIC; Morris Bullock and Miguel Pedraza to Lloyd Bentsen, 21 January 1986, fd. 3, TIC.

92. Raymond Apodaca, memo, 30 January 1986, box 1990/1–41, fd. 3, TIC; Jim Mattox to Charles D. Travis, 22 March 1983, box 1990/1–41, fd. 5, TIC; Morris Bullock and Miguel Pedraza to Lloyd Bentsen, 21 January 1986, box 1990/1–41, fd. 3, TIC.

93. Ray Apodaca, memorandum for testimony to U.S. Senate, 30 January 1986, box 1990/1–41, fd. 4, TIC; Don B. Miller to Missy Solove, 19 May 1986, box 1990/1–41, fd. 4, TIC; Bob Bullock to Jim Mattox, 2 May 1986, box 1990/1–41, fd. 4, TIC; Bob Bullock to Jim Mattox, 2 May 1986, fd. 161, Diamond Papers; Apodaca interview; Schaller, Reckoning with Reagan, 44–45; Ken Ortolon, "UTEP, Tiguas and Park Face Slash of Budget Ax," El Paso Herald-Post, 8 August 1986; Ken Ortolon, "Tiguas Lose $70,000 from 1986 Budget," El Paso Herald-Post, 9 March 1985.

94. Miller interview; House, House Committee on Interior, Bill to Provide for the Restoration, 3 October 1984; House Committee on Interior, Bill to Provide for the Restoration, 28 February 1985.

95. Donna Peterson, memorandum to Don Miller, 2 July 1985, fd. 177, Diamond Papers; Miller interview; Apodaca interview; Burt, Tribalism in Crisis, 126–29; Peroff, Menominee Drums. The BIA established restoration criteria that were similar to its acknowledgment criteria, although less detailed. Senate Select Committee, Restoration, 25 June 1986, "Administration's Criteria for Restoration," 56.

96. Miller interview.

97. House Committee on Interior, Bill to Provide for the Restoration, 17 October 1985.

98. Tom Diamond to Don Hagans, 23 April 1986, box 1990/1–41, fd. 4, TIC; Tom Diamond to Charles W. Simpson, 22 April 1986, box 1990/1–41, fd. 4, TIC.

99. Miller interview; Apodaca interview.

100. Miller interview; Tom Diamond to El Paso Convention and Visitors Bureau, 2 June 1985, fd. 7, TIC; Senate Select Committee, Restoration, 25 June 1986, El Paso Convention and Visitors Bureau Resolution, 30 June 1985, 41.

101. Verna Williamson, quoted in transcript of People of the Sun: The Tiguas of Ysleta, video recording, Leslie Burns and Daniel Gelo, 2–3, fd. "Tigua-culture," ITC; Sierra interview; Miller interview.

102. Apodaca interview.

103. Apodaca interview.

104. Apodaca interview; Sierra interview; Miller interview.

105. Apodaca interview; "Testimony of Governor Gilbert Sanchez, on Behalf of the All Indian Pueblo Council on H.R. 1344," 17 October 1985, box 1990/1–41, fd. 7, TIC; Resolution of the NCAI Executive Committee, 18 May 1984, box 1990/1–41, fd. 7, TIC; Miller interview; Senate Select Committee, *Restoration*, 25 June 1986, 66, 437, 445.

106. *Seminole Tribe of Florida v. Butterworth*, 658 F.2d 310 (1981); "Interior Secretary Concerned That Golden Goose Not Be Killed," *Indian News Notes* (BIA), 2 August 1985, 1.

107. *Seminole Tribe of Florida v. Butterworth*, 658 F.2d 310 (1981); Kersey, *Assumption of Sovereignty*, xiii, 16–17, 109–33.

108. *Barona Group of Capitan Grande Band, Etc. v. Duffy*, 694 F.2d 1185 (9th Cir. 1982); *Lac du Flambeau Band of Lake Superior Chippewa Indians v. Williquette*, 629 F.Supp. 689 (W.D. Wis. 1986); *Mashantucket Pequot Tribe v. McGuigan*, 626 F.Supp. 245 (D. Conn. 1986); *Oneida Tribe v. Wisconsin*, 518 F.Supp. 712 (W.D. Wis. 1981), all cases cited in Mazurek, *American Indian Law Deskbook*, 343; Anders, "Indian Gaming," 98–108; "Indian Gaming: Law and Legislation," NARF *Legal Review*, fall 1985, 1.

109. Shayhyu'hati', "Bingo-Gaming-Gambling: Does Economic Development Equal Assimilation?" *Akwesasne Notes*, early winter 1985; Miller interview; Senate Select Committee on Indian Affairs, *Gaming Activities*, 18 June 1987, 267; "Indian Gaming: Law and Legislation," NARF *Legal Review*, fall 1985, 1; House Committee on Interior, *Indian Gaming Regulatory Act*, 25 June 1987, 325, 376.

110. House Committee on Interior, *Indian Gambling Control Act*, 25 June 1985, 305; Senate Select Committee, *Gaming Activities*, 18 June 1987, 436, 179–81, 268.

111. House Committee on Interior Affairs, *Indian Gaming Regulatory Act*, 25 June 1987, statement of Morris K. Udall, 109.

112. *California v. Cabazon Band of Mission Indians*, 480 U.S. 202 (1987); *Indian Gaming Regulatory Act of 1988*, Public Law 100–497 (1988), 102 Stat. 2467 (1988), codified at 18 U.S.C. sec. 1168 and 25 U.S.C. secs. 2701–21(1988); Mazurek, *American Indian Law Deskbook*, 338, 353–57; Anders, "Indian Gaming," 98–108; Christiansen, "Gambling and the American Economy," 45. On positive aspects of gaming see Lane, *Return of the Buffalo*; Tisdale, "Cocopah Identity and Cultural Survival."

113. "The Bitter Fruits of Indian Gambling," press release, fall 1985, Comptroller of Public Accounts, box 1990/1–41, fd. 5, TIC; Miller interview; Diamond interview; Darcy interview; "Direct Telegram to U.S. Congress," Price Daniel and Ralph Yarborough, December 9, 1985, box 1990/1–41, fd. 7, TIC.

114. "News Release," Bob Bullock, 22 November 1985, box 1990/1–41, fd. 2, TIC.

115. Bob Bullock, quoted in Eduardo Paz-Martinez, "Indians Say Comptroller out of Control," *Houston Post*, 19 January 1986, D-1; "Resolution No. 85-1," Conference of Western Attorneys General, 7 June 1985, fd. 2, TIC.

116. "Bitter Fruits," press release, fall 1985, TIC; and "News Release," Bob Bullock, 22 November 1985, box 1990/1–41, fd. 5, TIC.

117. Bob Bullock, quoted in Eduardo Paz-Martinez, "Indians Say Comptroller out of Control," *Houston Post*, 19 January 1986, D-1; "HR 1344 and High Stakes Bingo," memorandum, Comptroller of Public Accounts, n.d., box 1990/1–41, fd. 5, TIC; "News Release," Bob Bullock, Comptroller of Public Accounts, 25 November 1985, box 1990/1–41, fd. 2, TIC; Bob Bullock to Ray Apodaca, 8 January 1986, box 1990/1–41, fd. 2, TIC.

118. "News Release," Comptroller of Public Accounts, 25 November 1985, box 1990/1–41, fd. 2, TIC.

119. "Court Rules Indian Lands out of Bounds," *Dallas Morning News*, 19 December 1985, D-13; "New Ways to Recognize Tribes Split Indians," *New York Times*, 4 August 1991, sec. L, p. 33; Austin interviews.

120. "Press Release," Alabama-Coushatta Reservation, 1986, box 1990/1–41, fd. 2, TIC; Miller interview.

121. Raymond Ramirez to Bob Bullock, 6 January 1986, fd. 161, Diamond Papers; Eduardo Paz-Martinez, "Indians Say Comptroller out of Control," *Houston Post*, 19 January 1986, D-1.

122. "Direct Telegram," Price Daniel and Ralph Yarborough, 9 December 1985, TIC; Apodaca interview.

123. Diamond interviews.

124. Miller interview; "Bills, Budgets, and Bureaucratic Policies," *Akwesasne Notes*, summer 1986; Schaller, *Reckoning with Reagan*, 47.

125. Senate Select Committee, *Restoration*, 25 June 1986, "Prepared Statement of Ross O. Swimmer," 48–50; Hazel E. Elbert to Raymond D. Apodaca, 8 January 1986, box 1990/1–41, fd. 4, TIC.

126. Bob Bullock, quoted in Eduardo Paz-Martinez, "Indians Say Comptroller out of Control," *Houston Post*, 19 January 1986, D-1; David Anderson, memorandum to John Moore, 19 November 1985, box 1990/1–41, fd. 5, TIC; "Proposed Amendment," box 1990/1–41, fd. 5, TIC; House, *House Report 99–440: Providing for the Restoration of Federal Recognition to the Ysleta del Sur Pueblo*, report to accompany H.R. 1344, 99th Cong., 1st sess., 16 December 1985.

127. "Ysleta del Sur Pueblo Council Resolution Number TC-02–86," 12 March 1986, box 1990/1–41, fd. 7, TIC; "Alabama-Coushatta Tribal Council AC ITC Resolution #86–07," box 1990/1–41, fd. 7, TIC.

128. Senate Select Committee, *Restoration*, 25 June 1986, statement of Ross Swimmer, 24, 51; Jake Henshaw, "House Gets Tigua Benefit Bill," *El Paso Times*, 26 September 1986; Ralph Reeser to Legislative Counsel, 25 September 1986, box 1990/1–41, fd. 7, TIC; Don Miller to Senator Daniel Inouye, 16 April 1987, box 1990/1–41, fd. 5, TIC; Miller interview.

129. "Texas Senator Gramm Kills Tribes' Restoration Legislation," *NCAI News*, December 1986; Karen MacPherson, "Senators Hold on Tigua Bill," *El Paso Herald-Post*, 9 October 1986; Miller interview; Jake Henshaw, "Tribe Blames Gramm for Delay," *El Paso Times*, 17 October 1986; Cindy Darcy to Senator Phil Gramm, 30 September 1986,

box 1990/1–41, fd. 7, TIC; Gilbert Pena, chairman, All Indian Pueblo Council, to Senator Pete Domenici, 19 September 1986, box 1990/1–41, fd. 7, TIC.

130. Don B. Miller to Honorable Daniel Inouye, 16 April 1987, box 1990/1–41, fd. 5, TIC.

131. Miguel Pedraza, cited in Raul Hernandez, "Reagan Signs Tigua Bill," El Paso Herald-Post, 20 August 1987; Joyce Barrett, "Tiguas Seeking Survival," El Paso Herald-Post, 20 May 1987; Diamond interviews; Miller interview; Ysleta del Sur Pueblo and Alabama and Coushatta Indian Tribes of Texas Restoration Act, Public Law 100–89 (18 August 1987), 101 Stat. 666 (1987); Ysleta del Sur Pueblo: Restoration of Federal Supervision, 25 C.F.R. sec. 1300g (1997).

132. Donald Trump, quoted in Kirk Johnson, "Tribal Rights: Refining the Law of Recognition," New York Times, 17 October 1993, E-6.

133. Diamond interview. For examples of the linkage between gaming and acknowledgment see George Judson, "Second Tribe Recognized as a Nation: Mohegans May Build State's 2d Casino," New York Times, 8 March 1994, B-6; George Judson, "Indian Chief and Waterbury's Mayor Announce Plan for Casino," New York Times, 4 March 1994, B-1; Sam Libby, "Another Tribal Nation? And Another Casino?" New York Times, 18 February 1996, sec. XIII-CN, p. 6.

134. Ronald Red Bone Van Dunk, quoted in Andy Newman, "Laying Claim to a Tribe's History," New York Times, 26 November 1995, sec. XIII-NJ, p. 4.

135. Senate Committee on Indian Affairs, Mohegan Nation, 1 August 1994, statement of Senator John McCain, 21; Austin interviews.

136. John MacCormack, "Odds against Tribal Casino," San Antonio Express-News, 14 October 2001, B-1.

137. Miguel Pedraza, quoted in "Tigua Leader Vows to Reopen Casino," Houston Chronicle.com, 13 February 2002, www.chron.com/cs/CDA/story.hts/metropolitan/1252676 (accessed 14 February 2002); John MacCormack, "Odds against Tribal Casino," San Antonio Express-News, 14 October 2001, B-1.

CONCLUSION

1. Robert Gehrke, "Peyote 'Priest' Could Loose His Freedom," (Tucson) Arizona Daily Star, 7 January 2001.

2. Anisman interview.

3. Clara LeCompte, quoted in Stephen Magagnini, "California's Lost Tribes: Why Must We Prove We're Indians?" 1 July 1997, Sacramento Bee, http://www.sacbee.com/news (accessed 1 November 1999).

BIBLIOGRAPHY

ARCHIVAL MATERIALS

Branch of Acknowledgment and Research, Bureau of Indian Affairs, Department of the Interior, Washington DC
  Biloxi, Chitimacha Confederation of Muskogees Files
  Death Valley Timbisha Shoshone Files
  Golden Hill Paugussett Files
  History Files
  Jamestown Clallam (S'Klallam) Files
  Point au Chien Indian Tribe Files
  Tunica-Biloxi Files
  United Houma Nation Files
Brenda Dardar Personal Files, Raceland, Louisiana
Death Valley National Park, Central Files, Furnace Creek, California
Tom Diamond Personal Papers, Law Offices of Diamond, Rash, Gordon, and Jackson, El Paso, Texas
Peter Domenici Papers, Center for Southwest Research, University of New Mexico
Caroline Dorman Collection, Cammie G. Henry Research Center, Watson Memorial Library, Northwestern State University, Natchitoches, Louisiana
Paul J. Fannin Papers, Arizona Historical Foundation, Hayden Library, Arizona State University, Tempe, Arizona
Barry Goldwater Papers, Arizona Historical Foundation, Hayden Library, Arizona State University, Tempe, Arizona
Isabella Greenway Papers, Arizona Historical Society, Tucson, Arizona
Lyndon Baines Johnson Papers, Lyndon Baines Johnson Presidential Library, Austin, Texas
  Indian Affairs Files
  White House Central Files
J. Bennett Johnston Papers, Special Collections, Louisiana State University, Baton Rouge, Louisiana
Louisiana Indian Files, Louisiana State Library, Baton Rouge, Louisiana
National Archives, Washington DC
  Record Group 75, Records of the Bureau of Indian Affairs
    John C. Collier Files
    Central Classified Files, 1907–1939
National Archives, College Park, Maryland

Record Group 48, Records of the Office of the Solicitor
    Chronological Correspondence and Memorandum Files, 1930–1938
    General Correspondence and other Records, 1937–1958
Record Group 79, Records of the National Park Service
    Central Classified Files, 1907–1949
Record Group 220, Records of Special Commissions, Records of the American
    Indian Policy Review Commission
North Carolina Commission on Indian Affairs, Raleigh, North Carolina
Muriel Thayer Painter Papers, Arizona State Museum, Tucson, Arizona
John Provinse Papers, Arizona State Museum, Tucson, Arizona
Edward Holland Spicer Papers, Arizona State Museum, Tucson, Arizona
State of Louisiana, Office of Indian Affairs, Office Files, Baton Rouge, Louisiana
Sam Steiger Papers, Department of Archives and Manuscripts, Cline Library, Northern
    Arizona University, Flagstaff, Arizona
Texas Indian Commission Records, Texas State Archives, Austin, Texas
Texas Indian Commission Vertical File, Center for American History, University of Texas
    at Austin, Austin, Texas
Tigua Vertical File, University of Texas Institute of Texan Cultures, San Antonio, Texas
Morris King Udall Papers, Special Collections, Main Library, University of Arizona,
    Tucson, Arizona
Stewart L. Udall, Oral History Collection, Lyndon Baines Johnson Presidential Library,
    Austin, Texas
Stewart Lee Udall Papers, Special Collections, Main Library, University of Arizona,
    Tucson, Arizona
Richard C. White Papers, Sonnichsen Special Collections, University of Texas–El Paso,
    El Paso, Texas

INTERVIEWS

Anisman, Linda, former California Indian Legal Services attorney. Interview by author
    by telephone, 10 July 2000.
Apodaca, Raymond, former executive director of the Texas Indian Commission. Inter-
    view by author by telephone, 25 February 2000.
Arnould, Pat, United Houma member and deputy director of the Governor's Office of
    Indian Affairs. Interview by author, 11 January 1999, Baton Rouge, Louisiana.
Austin, Steve, Branch of Acknowledgment and Research. Interviews by author, May
    1999, Washington. Interviews by author by telephone, 20, 30 October 1998 and 1
    April 1999.
Baker-Shenk, Philip, former general counsel for John McCain, Senate Committee on
    Indian Affairs. Interview by author by telephone, 16 February 1999.

Billiot, Reggie, former chief of the Biloxi, Chitimacha Confederation of Muskogees. Interview by author, Houma, Louisiana, 14 January 1999.

Brown, Cecil, Department of Anthropology, Northern Illinois University. Interview by author by telephone, 28 February 2002.

Darcy, Cindy, former Native American affairs advocate, American Friends Service Committee. Interview by author by telephone, 24 May 1999.

Dardar, Brenda, United Houma Nation chairperson. Interview by author, 13 January 1999, Raceland, Louisiana.

DeMarce, Virginia, Branch of Acknowledgment and Research. Interview by author by telephone, 21 February 2002.

Diamond, Tom, attorney. Interviews by author, December 1998 and June 1999, El Paso, Texas.

Gindrat, Helen, former United Houma Nation chairperson. Interview by author by telephone, 28 January 1999.

Greenberg, James, Bureau of Applied Anthropology, University of Arizona. Interview by author, 25 March 1998, Tucson, Arizona.

Gregory, Hiram (Pete), Anthropology Department, Northwestern State University. Interview by author, 11 January 1999, Natchitoches, Louisiana.

Houser, Nicholas P., anthropologist for Tigua Tribe. Interviews by author, August 1999, El Paso, Texas.

Huerta, C. Lawrence, Yaqui. Interview by author, 5 February 1998, Tucson, Arizona.

Lewis, Jeff, Native American affairs officer for Senator John Breaux. Interview by author by telephone, 8 January 1999.

McClurken, James, anthropologist for Grand River Ottawa and Nipmuc. Interview by author by telephone, 21 February 2002.

Miller, Don, Native American Rights Fund attorney. Interview by author by telephone, 11 January 2000.

Officer, James, anthropologist and former BIA official. Interview by author, 29 March 1993, Tucson, Arizona.

Ordoñez, Vicente, Ysleta resident. Interview by author, 11 January 1998, El Paso, Texas.

Paredes, J. Anthony, former Poarch Creek anthropologist. Interview by author by telephone, 14 March 2002.

Peters, Jill, Indian Affairs Committee staff, Senator John McCain's office. Interview by author by telephone, 16 February 1999.

Quinn, William, Jr., former ethnohistorian, Branch of Acknowledgment and Research. Interview by author, 5 November 1998, Phoenix, Arizona.

Reckord, Holly, Branch of Acknowledgment and Research. Interview by author by telephone, 1 December 2000.

Roth, George, Branch of Acknowledgment and Research. Interview by author, 27 May 1999, Washington.

Sierra, Joe, former Tigua tribal governor. Interview by author by telephone, 21 December 1999.

Spicer, Rosamund, anthropologist. Interview by author, 26 March 1993, Tucson, Arizona.

Stoffle, Richard, Bureau of Applied Research in Anthropology, University of Arizona. Interview by author, 10 April 1998, Tucson, Arizona.

Tilden, Mark, Native American Rights Fund attorney. Interview by author by telephone, 21 February 2002.

Valencia, Anselmo, Yaqui leader. Interview by author, 6 May 1993, Tucson, Arizona.

Verret, Kirby, former United Houma Nation chairman. Interview by author, 13 January 1999, Houma, Louisiana.

Wolf, Roger, attorney. Interview by author, 30 March 1993, Tucson, Arizona.

SOURCES CONSULTED

An Act Relating to the Lumbee Indians of North Carolina, 70 Stat. 254–55 (7 June 1956).

An Act to Authorize the Acquisition of a Village Site for the Payson Band of Yavapai-Apache Indians, Public Law 92–470 (6 October 1972), 86 Stat. 783.

An Act to Provide for the Conveyance of Certain Lands of the United States to the Pascua Yaqui Association, Inc., Public Law 88–350 (8 October 1964), 78 Stat. 1197.

An Act to Provide for the Extension of Certain Federal Benefits, Services, and Assistance to the Pascua Yaqui of Arizona, Public Law 95–375 (18 September 1978), 92 Stat. 712.

An Act to Settle Certain Claims of the Mashantucket Pequot Indians, Public Law 98–134 (18 October 1983), 97 Stat. 851.

Albers, Patricia C., and William R. James. "On the Dialectics of Ethnicity: To Be or Not to Be Santee (Sioux)." Journal of Ethnic Studies 14 (spring 1986): 1–21.

Alexie, Sherman. "Recognition of Distance." Journal of Ethnic Studies 16, no. 2 (1988): 49.

American Indian Policy Review Commission (AIPRC). Final Report. Vol. 1 and vol. 2, Appendices and Index. Washington DC: U.S. Government Printing Office, 1977.

————. Meetings of the American Indian Policy Review Commission. Vol. 4. Washington DC: U.S. Government Printing Office, 1976.

————. Report on Terminated and Nonfederally Recognized Indians: Task Force Ten Final Report to the American Indian Policy Review Commission. Washington DC: U.S. Government Printing Office, 1976.

American State Papers: Class VIII, Public Lands. Washington DC: Gales and Seaton, 1934.

Amey, Arthur Lanthrop, Jr. "Indian Affairs and the Great Society." M.A. thesis, Southwest Texas State University, 1980.

Anders, Gary C. "Indian Gaming: Financial and Regulatory Issues." Annals of the Academy of Political and Social Science 556 (March 1998): 98–108.

Anderson, Gary Clayton. The Indian Southwest, 1580–1830: Ethnogenesis and Reinvention. Norman: University of Oklahoma Press, 1999.

Anderson, Karen. *Changing Woman: A History of Racial Ethnic Women in Modern America.* New York: Oxford University Press, 1996.

Anderson, Terry. "Federal Recognition: The Vicious Myth." *American Indian Journal of the Institute for the Development of Indian Law* 4, no. 5 (1978): 7–19.

Aronson, Dan R. "Ethnicity as a Cultural System." In *Ethnicity in the Americas,* ed. Frances Henry, 9–19. The Hague: Mouton, 1976.

Asher, Brad. *Beyond the Reservation: Indians, Settlers, and the Law in Washington Territory, 1853–1889.* Norman: University of Oklahoma Press, 1999.

Atkinson, Ronald R. "The Evolution of Ethnicity among the Alcholi of Uganda: The Precolonial Phase." *Ethnohistory* 36, no. 1 (1989): 19–43.

Axtell, James. *The Indians' New South: Cultural Change in the Colonial Southeast.* Baton Rouge: Louisiana State University Press, 1997.

Babcock, Barbara. *Daughters of the Desert: Women Anthropologists and the Native American Southwest, 1880–1980.* Albuquerque: University of New Mexico Press, 1988.

Bandelier, A. F. *Final Report of Investigations among the Indians of the Southwestern United States, Carried on Mainly in the Years from 1880 to 1885.* Cambridge: John Wilson & Sons, 1890.

Barona Group of Capitan Grande Band, Etc. v. Duffy, 694 F.2d 1185 (1982).

Barsh, Russel L., and Yvonne Hajda. "Appearance of Unfairness?" *Anthropology Newsletter* 29 (March 1988), 2.

Barsh, Russel Lawrence. "Are Anthropologists Hazardous to Indians' Health?" *Journal of Ethnic Studies* 15, no. 4 (1988): 1–38.

————. "Indian Policy at the Beginning of the 1990s: The Trivialization of Struggle." In *American Indian Policy: Self-Governance and Economic Development,* ed. Lyman H. Legters and Fremont J. Lyden, 55–70. Westport CT: Greenview Press, 1994.

Barth, Fredrik, ed. *Ethnic Groups and Boundaries: The Social Organization of Cultural Difference.* London: Allen & Unwin, 1969.

Beinart, Peter. "Lost Tribes." *Lingua Franca,* May/June 1999, 32–41.

Benedict, Jeff. *Without Reservation: The Making of America's Most Powerful Indian Tribe and Foxwoods, the World's Largest Casino.* New York: HarperCollins, 2000.

Berkhofer, Robert. "White Conceptions of Indians." In *Handbook of North American Indians.* Vol. 4, *History of Indian-White Relations,* ed. William C. Sturtevant. Washington DC: Smithsonian Institution, 1988.

————. *The White Man's Indian: Images of the American Indian from Columbus to the Present.* New York: Knopf, 1978.

Berman, William C. *America's Right Turn: From Nixon to Bush.* Baltimore: Johns Hopkins University Press, 1994.

Berry, Brewton. *Almost White.* New York: Collier-Macmillan, 1963.

Biolsi, Thomas. *Organizing the Lakota: The Political Economy of the New Deal on the Pine Ridge and Rosebud Reservations.* Tucson: University of Arizona Press, 1992.

Bishop, Kathleen L., and Kenneth Hansen. "The Landless Tribes of Western Washington." *American Indian Journal of the Institute for the Development of Indian Law* 4, no. 5 (1978): 20–30.

Bloch, Marc. *The Historian's Craft*. New York: Random House, 1953.

Blu, Karen. *The Lumbee Problem: The Making of an American Indian People*. Lincoln: University of Nebraska Press, 2001.

———. "Region and Recognition: Southern Indians, Anthropologists, and Presumed Biology." In *Anthropologists and Indians in the New South*, ed. J. Anthony Paredes and Rachel A. Bonney, 71–85. Tuscaloosa: University of Alabama Press, 2001.

Bogan, Phoebe M. *Yaqui Indian Dances of Tucson, Arizona*. Tucson: Archaeological Society, 1925.

Bowman, Greg, and Janel Curry-Roper. *The Houma People of Louisiana: A Story of Indian Survival*. Houma LA: United Houma Nation, 1982.

Brackenridge, Henry Marie. *Views of Louisiana: Together with a Journal of a Voyage up the Mississippi River, in 1811*. Chicago: Quadrangle Books, 1962.

Brading, D. A. *The First America: The Spanish Monarchy, Creole Patriots, and the Liberal State, 1492–1867*. Cambridge: Cambridge University Press, 1991.

Brown, Cecil H., and Heather K. Hardy. "What Is Houma?" *International Journal of American Linguistics* 66, no. 4 (2000): 521–48.

Brown, Cynthia. "The Vanishing Native Americans." *Nation* (11 October 1993): 384–89.

Brown, Sharon Sholars. "The Jena Choctaw: A Case Study in the Documentation of Indian Tribal Identity." *National Genealogical Society Quarterly* 75, no. 3 (1987): 180–93.

Bunte, Pamela Ann, and Robert J. Franklin. *From the Sands to the Mountain: Change and Persistence in a Southern Paiute Community*. Lincoln: University of Nebraska Press, 1987.

Burt, Larry. *Tribalism in Crisis: Federal Indian Policy, 1953–1961*. Albuquerque: University of New Mexico Press, 1982.

California v. Cabazon Band of Mission Indians, 480 U.S. 202 (1987).

Calleros, Cleofas. *The Tigua Indians: Oldest Permanent Settlers in Texas*. El Paso: American Printing, 1955.

Calloway, Collin G. "Introduction: Surviving the Dark Ages." In *After King Philip's War: Presence and Persistence in Indian New England*, 8–14. Hanover NH: University Press of New England, 1997.

Campisi, Jack. "The Iroquois and the Euro-American Concept of Tribe." *New York History* 78, no. 4 (1997): 455–72.

———. *The Mashpee Indians: Tribe on Trial*. Syracuse: Syracuse University Press, 1991.

———. "The New England Tribes and Their Quest for Justice." In *The Pequots in Southern New England: The Fall and Rise of an Indian Nation*, ed. Laurence M. Hauptman and James D. Wherry, 179–93. Norman: University of Oklahoma Press, 1990.

Campisi, Jack, and William A. Starna. "Why Does It Take So Long? Federal Recognition and the American Indian Tribes of New England." *Northeast Anthropology* 57 (spring 1999): 1–17.

Carrillo, Jo. "Identity as Idiom: Mashpee Reconsidered." In *Readings in American Indian Law: Recalling the Rhythm of Survival*, ed. Jo Carrillo. Philadelphia: Temple University Press, 1998.

Castaneda, Carlos. *The Teachings of Don Juan: A Yaqui Way of Knowledge*. Berkeley: University of California Press, 1968.

Castile, George Pierre. "The Commodification of Indian Identity." *American Anthropologist* 98, no. 4 (1996): 743–49.

Castile, George Pierre, and Gilbert Kushner, eds. *Persistent Peoples: Cultural Enclaves in Perspective*. Tucson: University of Arizona Press, 1981.

Chalfant, W. A. *The Story of Inyo*. Chicago: Hammond Press, 1922.

Cherokee Nation of Oklahoma v. Babbitt, 117 F.3d 1489 (DC Cir 1997).

Christiansen, Eugene M. "Gambling and the American Economy." *Annals of the Academy of Political and Social Science* 556 (March 1998): 36–52.

Churchill, Ward. "The Tragedy and the Travesty: The Subversion of Indigenous Sovereignty in North America." In *Contemporary Native American Political Issues*, ed. Troy R. Johnson, 17–72. Walnut Creek CA: Altamira Press, 1999.

Claiborne, W. C. C. *Official Letter Books of W. C. C. Claiborne, 1801–1816*. Ed. Dunbar Rowland. New York: AMS Press, 1917.

Clark, Barret H., ed. *Favorite Plays of the Nineteenth Century*. Princeton: Princeton University Press, 1943.

Clifford, James. *The Predicament of Culture: Twentieth-Century Ethnography, Literature, and Art*. Cambridge: Harvard University Press, 1988.

Clifton, James A. "Avocation Medicine Men, Inventive 'Traditions' and New Age Religiosity in a Western Great Lakes Akgonkian Population." In *Present Is Past: Some Uses of Tradition in Native Societies*, ed. Marie Mauzé, 145–57. Lanham MD: University Press of America, 1997.

————, ed. *The Invented Indian: Cultural Fictions and Government Policies*. Brunswick NJ: Transaction, 1990.

Cohen, Anthony P. *The Symbolic Construction of Community*. New York: Tavistock, 1985.

Cohen, Felix S. *Handbook of Federal Indian Law*. Albuquerque: University of New Mexico Press, 1970.

Congressional Record. 1963–64, 1967–68, 1985–87. Washington DC.

Connor, Walker. *Ethnonationalism: The Quest for Understanding*. Princeton: Princeton University Press, 1994.

"Constitution and By-laws of the Confederated Tribes of the Umatilla Reservation in Oregon." Washington DC: U.S. Government Printing Office, 1957.

"Constitution and By-laws of the Gila River Pima-Maricopa Indian Community." Washington DC: U.S. Government Printing Office, 1936.

Conzen, Kathleen Neils. "A Saga of Families." In *The Oxford History of the American West*, ed. Clyde A. Milner, Carol A. O'Connor, and Martha A. Sandweiss, 315–58. New York: Oxford University Press, 1994.

Cook, Sherburne F. "Historical Demography." In *Handbook of North American Indians*, vol. 8, *California*, ed. Robert T. Heizer, 91–98. Washington DC: Smithsonian Institution, 1978.

Cornell, Stephen. *The Return of the Native: American Indian Political Resurgence*. New York: Oxford University Press, 1988.

Coville, Frederick V. "The Panamint Indians of California." *American Anthropologist* 5, no. 1 (1892): 351–61.

Cow Creek Band of Umpqua Tribe of Indians Recognition Act, Public Law 97–391 (29 December 1982), 96 Stat. 1960.

Crum, Steven. *The Road on Which We Came: A History of the Western Shoshone*. Salt Lake City: University of Utah Press, 1994.

Dabdoub, Claudio. *Historia de el Valle del Yaqui*. Mexico, D.F.: Libreria M. Porrua, 1964.

Daniel, G. Reginald. "Passers and Pluralists: Subverting the Racial Divide." In *Racially Mixed People in America*, ed. Maria P. P. Root, 91–107. London: Sage, 1992.

Dayley, Jon P. *Tumpisa (Panamint) Shoshone Dictionary*. University of California Publications in Linguistics, vol. 116. Berkeley: University of California Press, 1989.

Deloria, Philip. *Playing Indian*. New Haven: Yale University Press, 1998.

Deloria, Vine, Jr. *Custer Died for Your Sins: An Indian Manifesto*. New York: Avon Books, 1969.

Deloria, Vine, Jr., and Clifford M. Lytle. *American Indians, American Justice*. Austin: University of Texas Press, 1983.

———. *The Nations Within: The Past and Future of American Indian Sovereignty*. New York: Pantheon Books, 1984.

Deloria, Vine, Jr., and David E. Wilkins. *Tribes, Treaties, and Constitutional Tribulations*. Austin: University of Texas Press, 1999.

Dole, Gertrude E. "Tribes as the Autonomous Unit." In *Essays on the Problem of Tribe*, ed. June Helm, 83–86. Seattle: University of Washington Press, 1968.

Downs, Ernest C. "A National Conference on Tribal Recognition." *American Indian Journal of the Institute for the Development of Indian Law* 4, no. 5 (1978): 2.

———. "The Struggle of the Louisiana Tunica Indians for Recognition." In *Southeastern Indians since the Removal Era*, ed. Walter Williams, 72–89. Athens: University of Georgia Press, 1979.

Downs, Ernest C., and Jenna Whitehead, eds. "The Houma Indians: Two Decades in a History of Struggle." *American Indian Journal of the Institute for the Development of Indian Law* 2, no. 3 (1976): 2–22.

Dozier, Edward P. *The Pueblo Indians of North America*. New York: Holt, Rinehart & Winston, 1970.

Drechsel, Emanuel J., and Teresa Haunani Makuakane-Drechsel. "An Ethnohistory of 19th Century Louisiana Indians: A Report Prepared for the National Park Service." Norman: Department of Anthropology, University of Oklahoma, 1982.

Dunbar, William. *Life, Letters and Papers of William Dunbar*. Ed. Eron Rowland. Jackson: Press of the Mississippi Historical Society, 1930.

Du Pratz, M. Le Page. *The History of Louisiana or of the Western Parts of Virginia and Carolina*. Baton Rouge: Claitor's, 1972.

Dutcher, B. H. "Pinon Gathering among the Panamint Indians." *American Anthropologist* 6, no. 1 (1893): 377–80.

Duthu, Bruce, and Hilde Ojibway. "Future Light or Feu Follet? Louisiana Indians and Federal Recognition." *Southern Exposure* 13, no. 6 (1985): 24–32.

Earle, John Milton. *Report to the Governor and Council Concerning the Indians of the Commonwealth*. Senate Report. 96. Boston: William White, Printer to the Senate, 1861.

Education Amendments Act of 1972, Public Law 92–318 (1972), 86 Stat. 345 (1972).

Eggan, Fred. *Social Organization of the Western Pueblos*. Chicago: University of Chicago Press, 1950.

Eickhoff, Randy Lee. *Exiled: The Tigua Indians of Ysleta del Sur*. Plano: Republic of Texas Press, 1996.

Eisler, Kim Isaac. *Revenge of the Pequots: How a Small Native American Tribe Created the World's Most Profitable Casino*. New York: Simon and Schuster, 2001.

Ellis, Florence Hawley. "Isleta Pueblo." In *Handbook of North American Indians: Southwest*, vol. 9, ed. Alfonso Ortiz, 351–55. Washington DC: Smithsonian Institution, 1979.

Fabila, Alfonso. *Las Tribus Yaquis de Sonora: Su cultura y anhelada autodeterminacion*. Mexico, D.F.: Instituto Nacional Indigenista, 1978.

Faragher, John Mack. *Sugar Creek: Life on the Illinois Prairie*. New Haven: Yale University Press, 1986.

Fewkes, J. Walter. "The Pueblo Settlements Near El Paso, Texas." *American Anthropologist* 4 (1902): 57–75.

Field, Les W. "Complicities and Collaborations: Anthropologists and the 'Unacknowledged Tribes' of California." *Current Anthropology* 40, no. 2 (1999): 193–209.

Fields, Barbara Jeanne. "Slavery, Race and Ideology in the United States of America." *New Left Review* 181 (May/June 1990): 95–118.

Figueroa, Alejandro. *Los que hablan fuerte: Desarollo del la sociedad Yaqui*. Hermosillo: Publicaciones del Centro Regional el Noroeste, 1985.

Fischer, Ann. "History and Current Status of the Houma Indians." In *The American Indian Today*, ed. Stuart Levine and Nancy Oestreich Lurie, 212–35. Baltimore: Penguin Books, 1972.

Fixico, Donald L. *Termination and Relocation: Federal Indian Policy, 1945–1960*. Albuquerque: University of New Mexico Press, 1986.

Fontana, Bernard L. *Of Earth and Little Rain: The Papago Indians*. Tucson: University of Arizona Press, 1989.

Forbes, Jack D. *Africans and Native Americans: The Language of Race and the Evolution of Red-Black Peoples*. Urbana: University of Illinois Press, 1993.

Foster, Morris W. *Being Comanche: A Social History of an American Indian Community*. Tucson: University of Arizona Press, 1991.

Fowler, Catherine S. "Residence without Reservation: Ethnographic Overview and

Traditional Land Use Study; Timbisha Shoshone." Unpublished manuscript. 15 August 1995.

Fowler, Loretta. *Shared Symbols, Contested Meanings: Gros Ventre Culture and History, 1778–1984.* Ithaca: Cornell University Press, 1987.

Fried, Morton. "The Myth of Tribe." *Natural History,* April 1975, 12–20.

———. *The Notion of Tribe.* Menlo Park CA: Cummings, 1975.

———. "On the Concept of 'Tribe' and 'Tribal Society.'" In *Essays on the Problem of Tribe,* ed. June Helm, 1–11. Seattle: University of Washington Press, 1968.

Friedman, Jonathan. "The Past in the Future: History and the Politics of Identity." *American Anthropologist* 94, no. 4 (1992): 837–59.

Friedman, Lawrence M. *The Horizontal Society.* New Haven: Yale University Press, 1999.

Gamino, John. "Bureau of Indian Affairs: Should Indians Be Preferentially Employed?" *American Indian Law Review* 2, no. 2 (1973–74): 111.

Gatschet, Albert S. "The Shetimasha Indians of St. Mary's Parish, Southern Louisiana." *Transactions of the Anthropological Society of Washington* 2 (1882–83): 148.

Geneson, Paul. "The Return of the Tigua." *Southwest Airlines Magazine* 14, no. 5 (1984): 57–62.

Getches, David H., Charles F. Wilkinson, and Robert A. Williams, eds. *Federal Indian Law: Cases and Materials.* 3d ed. St. Paul MN: West, 1993.

Giraud, Marcel. *A History of French Louisiana.* Vol. 1, *The Reign of Louis XIV, 1698–1715.* Vol. 5, *The Company of the Indies, 1723–1731.* Baton Rouge: Louisiana State University Press, 1974.

Gitlin, Todd. *The Sixties: Years of Hope, Days of Rage.* New York: Bantam Books, 1987.

Grabowski, Christine Tracey. "Coiled Intent: Federal Acknowledgment Policy and the Gay Head Wampanoags." Ph.D. diss., City University of New York, 1994.

Green, Michael K. "Cultural Identities: Categories for the Twenty-first Century." In Michael K. Green, ed., *Issues in Native American Identity.* New York: Peter Lang, 1995.

Green, Rayna. "The Tribe Called Wannabee: Playing Indian in America and Europe." *Folklore* 99, no. 1 (1988): 30–55.

Greenbaum, Susan. "In Search of Lost Tribes: Anthropology and the Federal Acknowledgment Process." *Human Organization* 44, no. 4 (1985): 361–67.

———. "What's in a Label? Identity Problems of Southern Indian Tribes." *Journal of Ethnic Studies* 19, no. 2 (1991): 107–24.

Greenberg, Adolph M., and James Morrison. "Group Identities in the Boreal Forest: The Origin of the Northern Ojibwa." *Ethnohistory* 29, no. 2 (1982): 75–102.

Greene v. Babbitt, 64 F.3d 1266 (9th Cir. 1995).

Greissman, B. Eugene. "The American Isolates." *American Anthropologist* 74, no. 5 (1972): 693–95.

Griswold del Castillo, Richard. *The Treaty of Guadalupe Hidalgo: A Legacy of Conflict.* Norman: University of Oklahoma Press, 1990.

Gruzinski, Serge. *The Conquest of Mexico: The Incorporation of Indian Societies into the Western World, 16th–18th Centuries*. Cambridge: Polity Press, 1993.

Gulf South Research Institute. "American Indians of Louisiana: An Assessment of Needs." Baton Rouge: U.S. Department of Commerce, 1973.

Gutierrez, Ramon A. *When Jesus Came, the Corn Mothers Went Away: Marriage, Sexuality, and Power in New Mexico, 1500–1846*. Stanford: Stanford University Press, 1991.

Haas, Lisbeth. *Conquests and Historical Identities in California, 1769–1936*. Berkeley: University of California Press, 1995.

Hackett, Charles W. *Revolt of the Pueblo Indians of New Mexico and Otermin's Attempted Reconquest, 1680–1682*. Albuquerque: University of New Mexico Press, 1942.

Hagan, William T. "Full Blood, Mixed Blood, Generic, and Ersatz: The Problem of Indian Identity." *Arizona and the West* 27 (winter 1985): 309–26.

Hajda, Yvonne. "Creating Tribes." *Anthropology Newsletter* 28 (October 1987).

Harmon, Alexandra. *Indians in the Making: Ethnic Relations and Indian Identities around Puget Sound*. Berkeley: University of California Press, 1998.

———. "Tribal Enrollment Councils: Lessons on Law and Indian Identity." *Western Historical Quarterly* 32 (summer 2001): 175–200.

Hauptman, Laurence M. *Tribes and Tribulations: Misconceptions about American Indians and Their Histories*. Albuquerque: University of New Mexico Press, 1995.

Helm, June, ed. *Essays on the Problem of Tribe: Proceedings of the 1967 Annual Spring Meeting of the American Ethnological Society*. Seattle: University of Washington Press, 1968.

Henry, Frances, ed. *Ethnicity in the Americas*. The Hague: Mouton, 1976.

Hine, Robert V. *Community on the American Frontier: Separate but Not Alone*. Norman: University of Oklahoma Press, 1980.

Hobsbawn, Eric, and Terrence Ranger, eds. *The Invention of Tradition*. London: Cambridge University Press, 1983.

Hodge, Frederick Webb. *Handbook of American Indians, North of Mexico*. Vol. 2. Smithsonian Institution, Bureau of American Ethnology Bulletin 30. Washington DC: U.S. Government Printing Office, 1912.

Hook, Jonathan B. *The Alabama-Coushatta Indians*. College Station: Texas A&M University Press, 1997.

Houser, Nicholas P. "Tigua Pueblo." In *Handbook of North American Indians: Southwest*, vol. 9, ed. Alfonso Ortiz, 336–42. Washington DC: Smithsonian Institution, 1979.

Hoxie, Frederick E. *A Final Promise: The Campaign to Assimilate the Indians, 1880–1920*. Lincoln: University of Nebraska Press, 1984.

———. "From Prison to Homeland: The Cheyenne River Indian Reservation before World War I." *South Dakota History* 10 (winter 1979): 1–24.

———. *Parading through History: The Making of the Crow Nation in America, 1885–1935*. Cambridge: Cambridge University Press, 1995.

Hu-Dehart, Evelyn. *Missionaries, Miners and Indians: Spanish Contact with the Yaqui Nation of Northwestern New Spain, 1533–1820*. Tucson: University of Arizona Press, 1981.

Hudson, Charles. *The Catawba Nation*. Athens: University of Georgia Press, 1970.
————. *The Southeastern Indians*. Knoxville: University of Tennessee Press, 1976.
Indian Education Act, 86 Stat. 345 (23 June 1972).
Indian Gaming Regulatory Act of 1988, Public Law 100–497 (1988), 102 Stat. 2467 (1988).
Indian Reorganization Act of 1934, Act of June 18, 1934, 48 Stat. 984 (1934).
Indian Self-Determination and Education Assistance Act of 1975, Public Law 93–638 (1975), 88 Stat. 2203 (1975).
Jackson, Deborah. "Card-Carrying Indians: The Significance of Tribal Enrollment in an Urban Indian Community." Paper presented at the 96th Annual Meeting of the American Anthropological Association, Washington DC, 19 November 1997.
Jaimes, Marie Annette. "American Indian Identification/Eligibility Policy in Federal Education Service Programs." Ph.D. diss., Arizona State University, 1990.
————. "Federal Indian Identification Policy: A Usurpation of Indigenous Sovereignty in North America." In *The State of Native America: Genocide, Colonization and Resistance*, ed. M. Annette Jaimes, 123–38. Boston: South End Press, 1992.
Josephy, Alvin M., Jr., Joane Nagel, and Troy Johnson, eds. *Red Power: The American Indians' Fight for Freedom*. Lincoln: University of Nebraska Press, 1999.
Keegan, Marcia. *Pueblo People: Ancient Traditions, Modern Lives*. Santa Fe: Clear Light, 1999.
Keller, Robert H., and Michael F. Turek. *American Indians and National Parks*. Tucson: University of Arizona Press, 1998.
Kelley, Jane Holden. *Yaqui Women: Contemporary Life Histories*. Lincoln: University of Nebraska Press, 1978.
Kelley, Robin D. G. *Race Rebels: Culture, Politics, and the Black Working Class*. New York: Free Press, 1994.
Kelly, Lawrence C. *The Assault on Assimilation: John Collier and the Origins of Indian Policy Reform*. Albuquerque: University of New Mexico Press, 1983.
Kersey, Harry A., Jr. *An Assumption of Sovereignty: Social and Political Transformation among the Florida Seminoles, 1953–1979*. Lincoln: University of Nebraska Press, 1996.
Kickingbird, Kirke, and Karen Duchenaux. *One Hundred Million Acres*. New York: Macmillan, 1973.
Kicza, John E., ed. *The Indian in Latin American History: Resistance, Resilience, and Acculturation*. Wilmington DE: Scholarly Resources, 1993.
Klein, Kerwin Lee. *Frontiers of Historical Imagination: Narrating the European Conquest of North America, 1890–1990*. Berkeley: University of California Press, 1997.
Kniffen, Fred B., Hiram F. Gregory, and George A. Stokes. *The Historic Indian Tribes of Louisiana: From 1542 to the Present*. Baton Rouge: Louisiana State University Press, 1987.
Kroeber, A. L. "Elements of Culture in Native American Culture." In *The California Indians: A Sourcebook*, ed. R. F. Heizer and M. A. Whipple, 3–67. Berkeley: University of California Press, 1951.
————. *Handbook of the Indians of California*. Berkeley: California Book, 1953. Reprint of

Bureau of American Ethnology Bulletin 78 (Washington DC: Smithsonian Institution, 1925).

———. "Nature of the Land-Holding Group." Ethnohistory 2, no. 4 (1955): 302–14.

Lane, Ambrose I., Sr. Return of the Buffalo: The Story behind America's Gaming Explosion. Westport CT: Bergin & Garvey, 1995.

Latorre, Felipe A., and Dolores L. Latorre. The Mexican Kickapoo Indians. Austin: University of Texas Press, 1976.

La Vere, David. Life among the Texas Indians: The WPA Narratives. College Station: Texas A&M University Press, 1998.

LeBreton, Marietta Marie. "A History of the Factory System Serving the Louisiana Indians, 1805–1825." M.A. thesis, Louisiana State University, 1961.

"Learning to Compromise: Tribes and the Park Service Struggle for Power and Solutions." American Indian Report 14 (August 1998): 10–11.

Le Moyne d'Iberville, Pierre. Iberville's Gulf Journals. Trans. and ed. Richebourg Gaillard McWilliams. Tuscaloosa: University of Alabama Press, 1981.

Lerch, Patricia Barker. "State Recognized Indians of North Carolina, Including a History of the Waccamaw Sioux." In Indians of the Southeastern United States in the Late Twentieth Century, ed. J. Anthony Paredes, 44–71. Tuscaloosa: University of Alabama Press, 1992.

Lévi-Strauss, Claude. Structural Anthropology. New York: Basic Books, 1963.

Levine, Frances. Our Prayers Are in This Place: Pecos Pueblo Identity over the Centuries. Albuquerque: University of New Mexico Press, 1999.

Lewis, David Rich. Neither Wolf Nor Dog: American Indians, Environment, and Agrarian Change. New York: Oxford University Press, 1994.

Liebow, Edward B. "Category or Community? Measuring Urban Indian Social Cohesion with Network Sampling." Journal of Ethnic Studies 16, no. 4 (1989): 67–97.

Lingenfelter, Richard E. Death Valley and the Amargosa: A Land of Illusion. Berkeley: University of California Press, 1986.

Lockhart, James. The Nahuas after Conquest: A Social and Cultural History of the Indians of Central Mexico, Sixteenth through Eighteenth Centuries. Stanford: Stanford University Press, 1992.

Lurie, Nancy Oestreich. "Problems, Opportunities, and Recommendations." Ethnohistory 2 (fall 1955): 357–75.

———. "Relations between Indians and Anthropologists." In Handbook of North American Indians, vol. 4, History of Indian-White Relations, ed. Wilcomb E. Washburn, 548–55. Washington DC: Smithsonian Institution, 1988.

———. "Report on the American Indian Chicago Conference." Current Anthropology 2, no. 5 (1961): 478–500.

Madsen, Brigham D. The Lemhi: Sacajawea's People. Caldwell ID: Caxton Printers, 1979.

Manly, William L. Death Valley in '49. New York: Wallace Hebberd, 1894.

Martin, Deborah Lee. "Development at Ysleta del Sur Pueblo, Texas: The Influence of

Culture on the Development Process within an American Indian Community."
Ph.D. diss., University of Wisconsin–Madison, 1994.

Martin, Joel W. "My Grandmother Was a Cherokee Princess: Representations of Indians in Southern History." In *Dressing in Feathers: The Construction of the Indian in American Popular Culture*, ed. Elizabeth S. Bird, 129–45. Boulder: Westview Press, 1996.

Masayesva v. Zah, 792 F.Supp 1165 (D. Ariz. 1992).

Mashpee Tribe v. New Seabury Corp., 592 F.2d 575 (1979).

Matusow, Allen J. *The Unraveling of America: A History of Liberalism in the 1960s.* New York: Harper Torchbooks, 1984.

Mauzé, Marie, ed. *Present Is Past: Some Uses of Tradition in Native Societies.* Lanham MD: University Press of America, 1997.

Maynor v. Morton, 510 F.2d 1254 (1975).

Mazurek, Joseph P., ed. *American Indian Law Deskbook.* Niwot CO: University Press of Colorado, 1998.

McCall, George J., and J. L. Simmons. *Identities and Interactions: An Examination of Human Associations in Everyday Life.* New York: Free Press, 1978.

McCulloch, Anne Merline, and David E. Wilkins. " 'Constructing' Nations within States: The Quest for Federal Recognition by the Catawba and Lumbee Tribes." *American Indian Quarterly* 19, no. 3 (1995): 361–90.

McGuire, Thomas. *Politics and Ethnicity on the Rio Yaqui: Potam Revisited.* Tucson: University of Arizona Press, 1986.

McIlwraith, Thomas. "The Problem of Imported Culture: The Construction of Contemporary Sto:lo Identity." *American Indian Culture and Research Journal* 20, no. 4 (1996): 41–70.

Merrell, James H. *The Indians' New World: The Catawbas and Their Neighbors from European Contact through the Era of Removal.* Chapel Hill: University of North Carolina Press, 1989.

Meyer, Carol. "The Louisiana Purchase and Indian Rights." *American Indian Journal of the Institute for the Development of Indian Law* 2, no. 10 (1976): 17.

Miami Nation of Indians v. U.S. Department of the Interior, 255 F.3d 342 (7th Cir. 2001).

Miller, Bruce. "After the F.A.P.: Tribal Reorganization after Federal Recognition." *Journal of Ethnic Studies* 17, no. 2 (1989): 89–100.

Miller, Mark E. "The Yaquis Become 'American' Indians: The Process of Federal Tribal Recognition." *Journal of Arizona History* 35, no. 2 (1994): 183–204.

Miles, Robert W. "The Tigua Indians—Can They Prove Who They Are?" *True West*, January/February 1967.

Milton, Spiller. "The Houma Indians since 1940." *American Indian Journal of the Institute for the Development of Indian Law* 2, no. 4 (1976): 16–17.

Moermon, Michael. "Being Lue: Uses and Abuses of Ethnic Identification." In *Essays on the Problem of Tribe*, ed. June Helm, 153–67. Seattle: University of Washington Press, 1968.

Molina, Felipe S., and Larry Evers. *Yaqui Deer Songs: Maso Bwikam, A Native American Poetry*. Tucson: Sun Tracks and the University of Arizona Press, 1987.

Monroy, Douglas. *Thrown among Strangers: The Making of Mexican Culture in Frontier California*. Berkeley: University of California Press, 1990.

Montoya v. United States, 180 U.S. 261 (1901).

Morland, J. Kenneth. Conclusion to *The Not So Solid South: Anthropological Studies in a Regional Subculture*, ed. J. Kenneth Morland, 82–90. Athens GA: Southern Anthropological Society, 1971.

Morrissey, Katherine G. *Mental Territories: Mapping the Inland Empire*. Ithaca: Cornell University Press, 1997.

Morrison, Dane, ed. *American Indian Studies: An Interdisciplinary Approach to Contemporary Issues*. New York: Peter Lang, 1997.

Nagel, Joane. *American Indian Ethnic Renewal: Red Power and the Resurgence of Identity and Culture*. New York: Oxford University Press, 1996.

Native American Graves Protection and Repatriation Act, Public Law 101–601 (16 November 1990), 104 Stat. 3048.

Nelson, E. W. "The Panamint and Saline Valley Indians." *American Anthropologist* 4 (October 1891): 371–72.

Newcomb, William W. *The Indians of Texas from Prehistoric to Modern Times*. Austin: University of Texas Press, 1961.

Nichols, Roger L. "Indians in the Post-termination Era." *Storia Nordamericana* 5, no. 1 (1988): 84.

———. *Indians in the United States and Canada: A Comparative History*. Lincoln: University of Nebraska Press, 1998.

Novick, Peter. *That Noble Dream: The 'Objectivity Question' and the American Historical Profession*. New York: Cambridge University Press, 1988.

Nunley, Mary C. "The Mexican Kickapoo Indians: Avoidance of Acculturation through a Migratory Adaptation." Ph.D. diss., Southern Methodist University, 1986.

Painter, Muriel Thayer. *Faith, Flowers, and Fiestas: The Yaqui Indian Year*. Tucson: University of Arizona Press, 1962.

———. *With Good Heart: Yaqui Beliefs and Ceremonies in Pascua Village*. Tucson: University of Arizona Press, 1986.

Paredes, J. Anthony. "Federal Recognition and the Poarch Creek Indians." In *Indians of the Southeastern United States in the late Twentieth Century*, ed. J. Anthony Paredes. Tuscaloosa: University of Alabama Press, 1992.

———. "In Defense of the BIA and the NPS: Federal Acknowledgment, Native American Consultation, and Some Issues in the Implementation of the Native American Graves Protection and Repatriation Act in the Southeastern United States." *St. Thomas Law Review* 10, no. 35 (1997), http://web.lexis-nexis.com/universe/printdoc (accessed 3 June 2002).

———. "Kinship and Descent in the Ethnic Reassertion of the Eastern Creek Indians."

In *The Versatility of Kinship*, ed. Linda S. Cordell and Stephen J. Beckerman, 166–73. New York: Academic Press, 1980.

———. "Paradoxes of Modernism and Indianness in the Southeast." *American Indian Quarterly* 19, no. 3 (1995): 341–60.

———. " 'Practical History' and the Poarch Creeks: A Meeting Ground for Anthropology and Tribal Leaders." In *Anthropological Research: Process and Application*, ed. John J. Poggie Jr., Billie DeWalt, and William W. Dressler, 209–26. Albany: State University of New York Press, 1992.

———, ed. *Indians of the Southeastern United States in the Late Twentieth Century*. Tuscaloosa: University of Alabama Press, 1992.

Parenton, Vernon J., and Roland J. Pellegrin. "The 'Sabines': A Study of Racial Hybrids in a Louisiana Coastal Parish." *Social Forces* 29, no. 1 (1950): 148–54.

Parsons, Elsie Clews. "Isleta, New Mexico." In *Forty-seventh Annual Report of the Bureau of American Ethnology, 1929–1930*. Washington DC: Smithsonian Institution, 1932.

Parvin, Bob. "Tigua Territory." *Texas Highways* 24, no. 8 (August 1977): 4–9.

Paschal, Rachael. "The Imprimatur of Recognition: American Indian Tribes and the Federal Acknowledgment Process." *Washington Law Review* 66 (1991): 209–28.

Pascoe, Peggy. "Miscegenation Law, Court Cases, and Ideologies of 'Race' in Twentieth Century America." In *Interracialism: Black-White Intermarriage in American Histories, Literature, and Law*, ed. Werner Sollers, 202–4. New York: Oxford University Press, 2000.

Passamaquoddy v. Morton, 528 F.2d 370 (1975).

Pénicaut, André. *Fleur de Lys and Calumet: Being the Pénicaut Narrative of French Adventure in Louisiana*. Trans. and ed. Richebourg Gaillard McWilliams. Baton Rouge: Louisiana State University Press, 1953. Reprint, Tuscaloosa: University of Alabama Press, 1988.

Perkins, Edna Brush. *The White Heart of the Mojave: An Adventure with the Outdoors of the Desert*. New York: Boni & Liveright, 1922.

Peroff, Nicholas C. *Menominee Drums: Tribal Termination and Restoration, 1954–1974*. Norman: University of Oklahoma Press, 1982.

Peterson, John H., Jr. "The Indians in the Old South." In *Red, White, and Black: Symposium on Indians in the Old South*, ed. Charles M. Hudson, 116–33. Athens: University of Georgia Press, 1970.

Philp, Kenneth R. *Termination Revisited: American Indians on the Trail to Self-Determination, 1933–1953*. Lincoln: University of Nebraska Press, 1999.

Porter, Frank W., III. "In Search of Recognition: Federal Indian Policy and the Landless Tribes of Western Washington." *American Indian Quarterly* 14, no. 2 (1990): 113–32.

———. *Nonrecognized American Indian Tribes: An Historical and Legal Perspective*. Chicago: Newberry Library, 1983.

———. "Non-recognized American Indian Tribes in the Eastern United States: An

Historical Overview." In *Strategies for Survival: American Indians in the Eastern United States*, ed. Frank W. Porter III. Westport CT: Greenwood Press, 1986.

Posey, Darrell A. "Origin, Development and Maintenance of a Louisiana Mixed-Blood Community: The Ethnohistory of the Freejacks of the First Ward Settlement." *Ethnohistory* 26, no. 2 (1979): 177–92.

Preference in Employment, 25 C.F.R. Part 1.2 (1997).

"Procedures for Establishing That an American Indian Group Exists as an Indian Tribe." *Federal Register* 43, no. 106 (June 1978): 23,743.

Procedures for Establishing That an American Indian Group Exists as an Indian Tribe. 25 C.F.R. Part 83.1–13 (1997).

Prucha, Francis Paul. *The Great Father: The United States Government and the American Indian.* Abridged ed. Lincoln: University of Nebraska Press, 1986.

————. *Indian Policy in the United States: Historical Essays.* Lincoln: University of Nebraska Press, 1981.

————. *The Indians in American Society.* Berkeley: University of California Press, 1985.

Purser, Mary Joyce. "The Administration of Indian Affairs in Louisiana, 1803–1820." M.A. thesis, Louisiana State University, 1961.

Quinn, William W., Jr. "Federal Acknowledgment of American Indian Tribes: Authority, Judicial Interposition, and 25 C.F.R. § 83." *American Indian Law Review* 17, no. 1 (1992): 37–69.

————. "Federal Acknowledgment of American Indian Tribes: The Historical Development of a Legal Concept." *American Journal of Legal History* (October 1990): 331–64.

————. " 'Public Ethnohistory'? or, Writing Tribal Histories at the Bureau of Indian Affairs." *Public Historian* 10, no. 2 (1988): 71–76.

————. "Southeastern Indians: The Quest for Federal Acknowledgment and a New Legal Status." *Ethnic Forum: Journal of Ethnic Studies and Ethnic Bibliography* 13, no. 1 (1993): 34–52.

————. "The Southeast Syndrome: Notes on Indian Descendent Recruitment Organizations and Their Perceptions of Native American Culture." *American Indian Quarterly* 14, no. 2 (1990): 147–54.

Rafert, Stewart. *The Miami Indians of Indiana: A Persistent People, 1654–1994.* Indianapolis: Indiana Historical Society, 1996.

Rhoads, Kathy. "The Tigua Indians: A Part of Texas History." *Texas Motorist* 21, no. 11 (1975).

Richman, Robin. "Return of the Red Man." Special issue. *Life*, 1 December 1967, 52–71.

Root, Maria P. P. "Within, between, and beyond Race." In *Racially Mixed People in America*, ed. Maria P. P. Root, 1. London: Sage, 1992.

Rose, Wendy. "The Great Pretenders: Further Reflections on White Shamanism." In *The State of Native America: Genocide, Colonization, and Resistance*, ed. M. Annette Jaimes, 404–15. Boston: South End Press, 1992.

Rosenthal, H. D. *Their Day in Court: A History of the Indian Claims Commission.* New York: Garland, 1990.

Roth, George. "Acknowledgment Process—Not Inconsistent." *Anthropology Newsletter* 29 (January 1988).

———. "Not So!" *Anthropology Newsletter* 29 (March 1988).

———. "Overview of Southeastern Indian Tribes Today." In *Indians of the Southeastern United States in the Late Twentieth Century,* ed. J. Anthony Paredes, 183–201. Tuscaloosa: University of Alabama Press, 1992.

Roy, Ewell P., and Don Leary. "Economic Survey of American Indians in Louisiana." *American Indian Journal of the Institute for the Development of Indian Law* 3, no. 1 (1977): 11–16.

Royce, Anya Peterson. *Ethnic Identity: Strategies of Diversity.* Bloomington: Indiana University Press, 1982.

Sánchez, George J. *Becoming Mexican American: Ethnicity, Culture and Identity in Chicano Los Angeles, 1900–1945.* New York: Oxford University Press, 1993.

Sando, Joe S. *The Pueblo Indians.* San Francisco: Indian Historian Press, 1976.

Schaller, Michael. *Reckoning with Reagan: America and Its President in the 1980s.* New York: Oxford University Press, 1992.

Seminole Tribe of Florida v. Butterworth, 658 F.2d 310 (1981).

Sibley, John. "Historical Sketches of the Several Tribes in Louisiana South of the Arkansas River and Between the Mississippi and the River Grand." In *Report to the President: Travels in the interior parts of America communicating discoveries made in exploring the Missouri, Red River and Washita by Captains Lewis and Clark, Doctor Sibley, and Mr. Dunbar.* London: J. G. Barnard, 1807.

Sider, Gerald M. *Lumbee Indian Histories: Race, Ethnicity, and Indian Identity in the Southern United States.* Cambridge: Cambridge University Press, 1993.

Slagle, Alogan. "Unfinished Justice: Completing the Restoration and Acknowledgment of California Indian Tribes. " *American Indian Quarterly* 13, no. 4 (1989): 325–45.

Smith, Walter Robinson. *A Brief History of the Louisiana Territory.* St. Louis: St. Louis News, 1904.

Snipp, C. Mathew. *American Indians: The First of This Land.* New York: Russell Sage Foundation, 1989.

Snyder Act, 25 U.S.C.A. Part 13 (1921).

Special Issue on Tribal Recognition. *American Indian Journal of the Institute for the Development of Indian Law* 4, no. 5 (1978).

Speck, Frank G. "The Houma Indians in 1940." *American Indian Journal of the Institute for the Development of Indian Law* 2, no. 1 (1976): 3–15.

Spence, Mark David. *Dispossessing the Wilderness: Indian Removal and the Making of the National Parks.* New York: Oxford University Press, 1999.

Spicer, Edward H. "Highlights in Yaqui History." *Indian Historian* 7, no. 2 (1974): 2–9.

———. *Pascua: A Yaqui Village in Arizona.* Chicago: University of Chicago Press, 1940.

————. *Potam: A Yaqui Village in Sonora*. Menasha WI: American Anthropological Association, 1954.

————. *A Short History of the Indians of the United States*. New York: Van Nostrand Reinhold, 1969.

————. *The Yaquis: A Cultural History*. Tucson: University of Arizona Press, 1980.

Spicer, Edward H., and Raymond H. Thompson, eds. *Plural Society in the Southwest*. New York: Interbook, 1972.

Stanton, Max E. "A Remnant Indian Community: The Houma of Southern Louisiana." In *The Not So Solid South: Anthropological Studies in a Regional Subculture*, ed. J. Kenneth Morland, 82–90. Athens GA: Southern Anthropological Society, 1971.

————. "Southern Louisiana Survivors: The Houma Indians." In *Southeastern Indians since the Removal Period*, ed. Walter L. Williams, 90–109. Athens: University of Georgia Press, 1979.

Starna, William A. " 'Public Ethnohistory' and Native-American Communities: History or Administrative Genocide?" *Radical History Review* 53 (spring 1992): 126–39.

————. "The Southeast Syndrome: The Prior Restraint of a Non-Event." *American Indian Quarterly* 15, no. 4 (1991): 493–502.

————. "We'll All Be Together Again: The Federal Acknowledgment of the Wampanoag Tribe of Gay Head." *Northeast Anthropology* 51 (spring 1996): 3–12.

Steiner, Stan. *The New Indians*. New York: Dell, 1968.

Steward, Julian H. *Basin-Plateau Aboriginal Sociopolitical Groups*. Smithsonian Institution, Bureau of Ethnology Bulletin 120. Washington DC: U.S. Government Printing Office, 1938.

Stillaguamish Tribe of Indians v. Kleppe, et al., no. 75–1718 (D. DC, 24 September 1976).

Stone, John Augustus. *Metamora; or, The Last of the Wampanoags; An Indian Tragedy in Five Acts*. In *Favorite Plays of the Nineteenth Century*, ed. Barret H. Clark. Princeton: Princeton University Press, 1943. x–32.

Stopp, G. Harry, Jr. "On Mixed-Racial Isolates." *American Anthropologist* 76 (1974): 343–44.

Suttles, Gerald D. *The Social Construction of Communities*. Chicago: University of Chicago Press, 1972.

Swanton, John Reed. *Aboriginal Culture of the Southeast*. Smithsonian Institution, Bureau of American Ethnology, Forty-second Annual Report, 1924–25. Washington DC: U.S. Government Printing Office, 1928.

————. *Indian Tribes of the Lower Mississippi Valley and Adjacent Coast of the Gulf of Mexico*. Smithsonian Institution, Bureau of American Ethnology Bulletin no. 43. Washington DC: U.S. Government Printing Office, 1911.

————. Unpublished field notes on Houma Indians, Bureau of American Ethnology.

Tagg, Martyn D. *The Timbi-Sha Survey and Boundary Fencing Project*. Publications in Anthropology no. 27. Tucson: Western Archeological and Conservation Center, National Park Service, 1984.

Taylor, Theodore W. *The States and Their Indian Citizens.* Washington DC: Department of the Interior, 1972.

Theodoratus, Dorothea, and LSA Associates. "Death Valley National Park: Cultural Affiliation Study." Unpublished manuscript. Irvine: 1998.

Thomas, David Hurst, Lorann S. A. Pendleton, and Stephen C. Cappannari. "Western Shoshone." In *Handbook of North American Indians: Great Basin,* vol. 11, ed. Warren L. D'Azevedo, 262–83. Washington DC: Smithsonian Institution, 1986.

Thompson, Mark. "Nurturing the Forked Tree: Conception and Formation of the American Indian Policy Review Commission." In *New Directions in Federal Indian Policy: A Review of the American Indian Policy Review Commission,* ed. Anthony D. Brown. Los Angeles: University of California, 1979.

"The Timbisha Shoshone Tribal Homeland: A Draft Secretarial Report to Congress to Establish a Permanent Tribal Land Base and Related Cooperative Activities." N.d., http://www.nps.gov/deva/Timbisha_toc.html (accessed 17 February 2000).

Tisdale, Shelby. "Cocopah Identity and Cultural Survival: Indian Gaming and the Political Ecology of the Lower Colorado River Delta, 1850–1996." Ph.D. diss., University of Arizona, 1997.

Tiwa Indians Act, Public Law 90–287 (12 April 1968), 82 Stat. 93.

Travers, Milton A. *The Wampanoag Indian Federation of the Algonquin Nation.* Boston: Christopher, 1957.

Tureen, Thomas N. "Federal Recognition and the *Passamaquoddy* Decision." RG 220, NACP.

Twinam, Ann. "Honor, Sexuality, and Illegitimacy in Colonial Latin America." In *Sexuality and Marriage in Colonial Latin America,* ed. Asuncion Lavrin, 118–55. Lincoln: University of Nebraska Press, 1992.

Udall, Morris K. *Addresses and Special Orders.* Washington DC: U.S. Government Printing Office, 1993.

United States v. Candelaria, 271 U.S. 432 (1926).

United States v. John, 437 U.S. 634 (1978).

United States v. Joseph, 94 U.S. 614 (1876).

United States v. Kagama, 118 U.S. 375 (1886).

United States v. Sandoval, 231 U.S. 28 (1913).

United States v. Washington, 520 F.2d 676 (1975).

U.S. Congress. House Committee on Interior and Insular Affairs. *A Bill: Native Americans Equal Opportunity Act (Hearing on H.R. 9054).* 95th Cong., 1st sess., 12 September 1977.

———. *A Bill Relating to the Tiwa Indians of Texas: H.R. 17819.* 89th Cong., 2d sess., 19 September 1966.

———. *A Bill Relating to the Tiwa Indians of Texas: H.R. 10599.* 90th Cong., 1st sess., 6 June 1967.

————. *A Bill to Amend the Act relating to the Lumbee Indians of North Carolina: Hearing on* H.R. 12216. 93rd Cong., 2d sess., 22 January 1974.

————. *A Bill to Provide for the Conveyance of Certain Lands of the United States to the Pascua Yaqui Association, Inc.: H.R. 6233.* 88th Cong., 2d sess., 14 August 1964. H. Rept. 1805.

————. *A Bill to Provide for the Extension of Certain Federal Benefits, Services, and Assistance to the Pascua Yaqui Indians of Arizona, and for Other Purposes: H.R. 8411.* 94th Cong., 1st sess., 8 July 1975.

————. *A Bill to Provide for the Extension of Certain Federal Benefits, Services, and Assistance to the Pascua Yaqui Indians of Arizona, and for Other Purposes: H.R. 6612.* 95th Cong., 1st sess., 25 August 1977.

————. *A Bill to Provide for the Restoration of Federal Recognition to the Ysleta del Sur Pueblo:* H.R. 6391. 98th Cong., 2d sess., 3 October 1984.

————. *A Bill to Provide for the Restoration of Federal Recognition to the Ysleta del Sur Pueblo:* H.R. 1344. 99th Cong., 1st sess., 28 February 1985.

————. *A Bill to Provide for the Restoration of Federal Recognition to the Ysleta del Sur Pueblo and the Alabama and Coushatta Indian Tribes: H.R. 1344.* 99th Cong., 1st sess., 17 October 1985.

————. *California Indian Oversight Hearings.* 93rd Cong., 1st sess., 27 August 1973.

————. *California Tribal Status Act of 1991: Hearing on H.R. 2144.* 102 Cong., 1st sess., 10 October 1991.

————. *Federal Acknowledgment of Various Indian Groups: Hearing on H.R. 3958, H.R. 1475,* H.R. 2349, H.R. 5562, H.R. 3607. 102nd Cong., 2d sess., 8 July 1992.

————. *Indian Federal Acknowledgment Process: Hearing on H.R. 3430.* 102 Cong., 2d sess., 15 September 1992.

————. *Indian Gambling Control Act: Hearing on H.R. 1920 and H.R. 2404.* 99th Cong., 1st sess., 25 June 1985.

————. *Indian Gaming Regulatory Act: Hearing on H.R. 964 and H.R. 2507.* 100th Cong., 1st sess., 25 June 1987.

————. *Termination of Federal Supervision over Certain Tribes of Indians: Joint Hearing before the Subcommittees of the Committees on Interior and Insular Affairs.* 83rd Cong., 2d sess., 15 February 1954.

U.S. Congress. House Committee on Interior and Insular Affairs. Subcommittee on Indian Affairs and Public Lands. *Federal Recognition of Indian Tribes: Hearing on H.R. 13773 and Similar Bills.* 95th Cong., 2d sess., 10 August 1978.

U.S. Congress. House Committee on Natural Resources. Subcommittee on Native American Affairs. *Auburn Restoration and MOWA Band Recognition: Hearing on H.R. 4228 and S. 282.* 103rd Cong., 2d sess., 17 May 1994.

————. *A Bill to Provide for the Recognition of the United Houma Nation: Hearing on H.R. 3671.* 104th Cong., 2d sess., 18 June 1996.

————. *Federal Recognition of Indian Tribes: Hearing on H.R. 2549, H.R. 4462, H.R. 4709.* 103rd Cong., 2d sess., 22 July 1994.

————. *Indian Federal Recognition Administrative Procedures Act of 1997: H.R. 1154.* 105th Cong., 1st sess., 20 March 1997.

U.S. Congress. Senate Committee on Indian Affairs. *Federal Recognition Administrative Procedures Act of 1995: Hearing on S. 479.* 104th Cong., 1st sess., 13 July 1995.

————. *Federal Recognition Administrative Procedures Act of 1997.* 20 March 1997.

————. *Mohegan Nation of Connecticut Land Claims Settlement Act: Hearing on S. 2329.* 103rd Cong., 2d sess., 1 August 1994.

————. *Pascua Yaqui Extension of Benefits: Hearing on H.R. 734.* 103rd Cong., 2d sess., 27 January 1994.

————. *Pokagon Band of Potawatomi Indians Act and the Little Traverse Bay Bands of Odawa Indians and the Little River Band of Ottawa Indians Act: Hearing on S. 1066 and S. 1357.* 103rd Cong., 2d sess., 10 February 1994.

U.S. Congress. Senate Committee on Interior and Insular Affairs. Subcommittee on Indian Affairs. *California Indian Oversight Hearings.* 93rd Cong., 1st sess., 27 August 1973.

————. *Establishment of the American Indian Policy Review Commission: Hearings on S.J. Res. 133.* 93rd Cong., 1st sess., 19 July 1973.

U.S. Congress. Senate Select Committee on Indian Affairs. *A Bill to Establish an Administrative Procedure and Guidelines.* 95th Cong., 1st sess., 15 December 1977.

————. *A Bill to Provide for the Extension of Certain Federal Benefits, Services, and Assistance to the Pascua Yaqui Indians of Arizona, and for Other Purposes: S.R. 1633.* 95th Cong., 1st sess., 7 June 1977.

————. *Federal Acknowledgment Administrative Procedures Act of 1989: Hearing on S. 611. Part 1.* 101st Cong., 1st sess., 28 April 1989.

————. *Federal Acknowledgment Administrative Procedures Act of 1989: Hearing on S. 611. Part 2.* 101st Cong., 1st sess., 5 May 1989.

————. *Federal Acknowledgment Process: Hearing before the Select Committee on Indian Affairs.* 96th Cong., 2d sess., 2 June 1980.

————. *Federal Acknowledgment Process: Oversight Hearing.* 100th Cong., 2d sess., 26 May 1988.

————. *Federal Recognition of Certain Indian Tribes: Hearing on S. 611.* 95th Cong., 1st sess., 27 September 1977.

————. *Federal Recognition of the Lumbee Indian Tribe of North Carolina: Hearing on S. 2672.* 100th Cong., 2d sess., 12 August 1988.

————. *Federal Recognition of the MOWA Band of Choctaw Indians: Hearing on S. 362.* 102 Cong., 1st sess., 26 June 1991.

————. *Gaming Activities on Indian Reservations and Lands: Hearing on S. 555 and S. 1303.* 100th Cong., 1st sess., 18 June 1987.

————. *Houma Recognition Act: Hearing on S. 2423.* 101st Cong., 2d sess., 7 August 1990.

———. *Indian Federal Recognition Administrative Procedures Act of 1991: Hearing on S. 1315.* 102d Cong., 1st sess., 22 October 1991.

———. *Indian Land Claims in the Town of Gay Head MA: Hearing on S. 1452.* 99th Cong., 2d sess., 9 April 1986.

———. *Issues of Concern to Southern California Tribes: Hearing before the Select Committee on Indian Affairs.* 101st Cong., 1st sess., 27 April 1989.

———. *Issues of Concern to Central and Northern California Tribes: Hearing before the Senate Select Committee on Indian Affairs.* 101st Cong., 1st sess., 28 April 1989.

———. *Oversight of the Federal Acknowledgment Process: Hearing before the Select Committee on Indian Affairs.* 98th Cong., 1st sess., 21 July 1983.

———. *Recognition of Certain Indian Tribes: Hearing on S. 2375.* 95th Cong., 2d sess., 18 April 1978.

———. *Recognition of MOWA Band of Choctaw Indians; Aroostook Band of Micmacs Settlement Act; Ponca Restoration Act; and Jena Band of Choctaw Recognition Act: Hearing on S. 381, S. 1413, S. 1747, S. 1918.* 101st Cong., 2d sess., 28 March 1990.

———. *Restoration of Federal Recognition to the Ysleta del Sur Pueblo and the Alabama and Coushatta Indian Tribes of Texas: Hearing on H.R. 1344.* 99th Cong., 2d sess., 25 June 1986.

———. *Trust Status for the Pascua Yaqui Indians: Hearing on S. 1633.* 95th Cong., 1st sess., 27 September 1977.

U.S. Department of the Interior. *Opinions of the Solicitor of the Department of the Interior Relating to Indian Affairs, 1917–1974.* Washington DC: U.S. Government Printing Office, 1974.

U.S. General Accounting Office. *Indian Issues: Improvements Needed in Tribal Recognition Process.* GAO-02-49. U.S. General Accounting Office, 2001.

Upper Chehalis Tribe v. United States, 155 F.Supp. 226, 140 Ct. Cl. 192 (1957).

Usner, Daniel H., Jr. *American Indians in the Lower Mississippi Valley: Social and Economic Histories.* Lincoln: University of Nebraska Press, 1998.

Van Rheenen, Mary B. "Can You Tell Me Who My People Are? Ethnic Identity among the Hispanic-Indian People in Sabine Parish, Louisiana." M.A. thesis, Louisiana State University, 1987.

Watkins, Marguerite E. "History of Terrebonne Parish to 1861." M.A. thesis, Louisiana Normal College, 1933.

Wax, Murray L. "Social Structure and Child Rearing Practices of Native American Indians." In *Nutrition, Growth, and Development of North American Indian Children,* ed. William M. Moore, Marjorie M. Silverberg, and Merrill S. Read, 205. HEW Publication no. (NIH)72-26. Washington DC: U.S. Government Printing Office, 1972.

Weatherhead, L. R. "What Is an 'Indian Tribe'? The Question of Tribal Existence." *American Indian Law Review* 8, no. 1 (1980): 1–47.

Weber, David J. *The Spanish Frontier in North America.* New Haven: Yale University Press, 1992.

Webre, Stephen. "The Problem of Indian Slavery in Spanish Louisiana, 1769–1803." *Louisiana History* 24, no. 2 (1983): 117–35.

Weibel-Orlando, Joan. *Indian Country, L.A.: Maintaining Ethnic Community in Complex Society.* Urbana: University of Illinois Press, 1991.

Wheat, Carl I. "Pioneer Visitors to Death Valley after the Forty-niners." *California Historical Quarterly* 18, no. 3 (1939): 195–216.

White, Richard. *The Middle Ground: Indians, Empires, and Republics in the Great Lakes Region, 1650–1815.* New York: Cambridge University Press, 1991.

———. *The Roots of Dependency: Subsistence, Environment, and Social Change among the Choctaws, Pawnees, and Navajos.* Lincoln: University of Nebraska Press, 1983.

Wilkins, David E. *American Indian Politics and the American Political System.* Lanham MD: Rowman & Littlefield, 2002.

———. "Breaking into the Intergovernmental Matrix: The Lumbee Tribe's Efforts to Secure Federal Acknowledgment." *Publius: The Journal of Federalism* 23, no. 4 (1993): 123–42.

———. "The U.S. Supreme Court's Explication of 'Federal Plenary Power': An Analysis of Case Law Affecting Tribal Sovereignty, 1886–1914." *American Indian Quarterly* 18, no. 3 (1994): 349–68.

Willard, William. "The Community Development Worker in an Arizona Yaqui Project." Ph.D. diss., University of Arizona, 1970.

Williams, Robert A. "Encounters on the Frontiers of International Human Rights Law: Redefining the Terms of 'Indigenous Peoples' Survival in the World." *Duke Law Journal* 660, no. 4 (1990): 660.

Wilson, Terry P. "Blood Quantum: Native American Mixed Bloods." In *Racially Mixed People in America,* ed. Maria P. P. Root, 108–25. London: Sage, 1992.

Wolf, Eric R. *Europe and the People without History.* Berkeley: University of California Press, 1982.

Woodward, C. Vann. *The Strange Career of Jim Crow.* New York: Oxford University Press, 1974.

Wright, Bill. *The Tiguas: Pueblo Indians of Texas.* El Paso: Texas Western Press, 1993.

Ysleta del Sur Pueblo and Alabama and Coushatta Indian Tribes of Texas Restoration Act, Public Law 100–89 (18 August 1987), 101 Stat. 666.

INDEX

Abieta, Andy, 224–25, 229
aboriginal sovereignty, 16
Abourezk, James, 39–40, 79, 114–15
acknowledgment: bills for individual groups, 279n18; congressional, 53; forms of, 3–4; judicial, 37; sovereignty issues and, 2
Acolapissa Indians, 159, 176–77
Administration for Native Americans, 158, 191, 193, 205
Alabama and Coushatta Indians, 209–10, 214, 228, 231–33, 238, 241–42, 246, 250–52
Alexie, Sherman, 22
Alliance to Protect Native Rights in National Parks, 151
American Anthropological Association, 55, 203
American Friends Service Committee, 65; Tigua Indians and, 247; Yaqui Indians and, 113
American Indian Chicago Conference, 33, 188
American Indian Movement, 33
American Indian Policy Review Commission, 38–39, 41; acknowledgment bills of, 39–40; Task Force on Terminated and Nonfederally Recognized Indians, 38–39; Yaqui Indians and, 112–13, 117; United Houma Nation and, 190–91
Americans for Indian Opportunity, 55, 65
Anderson, Clinton, 230
Andrews, Mark, 66
Anisman, Linda, 130, 139, 148
anthropologists (applied), 226
Apache Indians, 215, 222
Apodaca, Raymond, 221, 232, 235, 238–41, 244, 249
Articles of Confederation, 27

Aspinall, Wayne, 230
assistant secretary of the interior for Indian Affairs, role of, 50
Association on American Indian Affairs, 65, 181, 187
Attakapa Indians, 167, 176
Austin, Steve, 47, 50, 54, 62, 66, 67, 184

Babbitt, Bruce, 150
Baltazar, Virginia, 100
Bandelier, A. F., 215
Barsh, Russel Lawrence, 65
Barth, Fredrik, 12–13
Baton Rouge (LA), 159
Bayogoula Indians, 159
Bennett, Robert, 231
Bentsen, Lloyd, 250
Berkhofer, Robert, 6, 14
Billiot, Jean, 161–66
Billiot, Reggie, 198–99, 206
Biloxi, Chitimacha Confederation of Muskogees (BCCM), 199
Biloxi Indians, 166, 176–77, 199. See also Tunica-Biloxi Indians
blood quantum, 11, 41, 91–92, 147–48, 233, 251
Bourke, J., 215
Bowler, Alida, 136–37
Brackenridge, Henry, 163
Branch of Acknowledgment and Research (BAR). See Federal Acknowledgment Process
Breaux, John, 195, 201
Bullock, Bob, 209–10, 247–48
Bureau of Indian Affairs. See specific chapters on tribes and their relations with the BIA
Bureau of Land Management (BLM), 96, 153

Hueco Tanks (TX), 238, 244
Hunt, Jo Jo, 38, 112
hunting rights, 6, 241

Indian activism (1960s), 31–35, 188–91
Indian Angels, 190
Indian Claims Commission, 9, 31, 225, 238; See also land claims
Indian Education Act, 41
Indian Gaming Regulatory Act of 1988, 247
Indian Health Service, 3, 98, 107, 119, 129
Indian New Deal. See New Deal
Indian Nonintercourse Act (1790), 24, 36, 201, 238
Indian Non-Trade and Intercourse Acts. See Indian Trade and Intercourse Acts
Indian preference provisions, 43
Indian Reorganization Act of 1934, 27–28, 39, 74, 218; and Timbisha Shoshones, 128–29, 137–38; and United Houma Nation, 182
Indians. See Native Americans
Indian Self-determination Act, 109, 150
Indian Trade and Intercourse Acts, 24, 26, 36, 201, 238
Inouye, Daniel, 22, 55, 74, 251
Interior Board of Indian Appeals, 66
Inter-tribal Council of California, 128
Isle, Jean Charles, 175, 188, 200
Isleta Pueblo, 211, 213–14, 224–25, 227, 229, 236, 245

Jamestown S'kallam Indians, 51
Jena Choctaw Indians, 203
Jesuits, 82, 159
Johnson, Lyndon Baines, 32, 98, 189, 219, 224, 229–30
Johnston, J. Bennett, 195
judicial acknowledgment, 37. See also acknowledgment

Kawaissu Indians, 132
Kaweah Indian Nation, 52
Keep, Scott, 40
Kennedy, John F., 189, 219, 224

Kiowa Indians, 244–45
Koso Indians. See Timbisha Shoshone Indians
Kroeber, A. L., 9, 131
Ku Klux Klan, 34

LaFarge, Oliver, 181
Lafourche, Bayou, 160–63, 174
Lakota Indians, 29
land claims, 1, 9, 23–25, 36–37, 225, 228
La Salle, René-Robert, 158
Latin American Indians, 41–42
Lavis, Rick, 40
legislative acknowledgment, 16–17; and bills for individual groups, 279n18
Le Sauvage, Louis, 161–62, 166–68
Lincoln, Abraham, 214
Locklear, Arlinda, 50, 78
Loesch, Harris, 109
Louisiana Purchase, 162
Lumbee Indians, 34, 52, 70, 73, 97, 109, 111, 182, 186, 193, 210, 230–31
Lurie, Nancy O., 9

Mankiller, Wilma, 71–72
Manso Indians, 217, 220
Marshall, John, 26
Mashantucket Pequot Indians, 1–2, 53
Mashpee Wampanoag Indians, 37, 43
Matchebenashshewish Band of Pottawatomi Indians, 60
Mattaponi Indians, 34
McCain, John, 55, 66–67, 72, 74, 122, 253
McCaleb, Neal, 76
McCulloch, Anne, 11, 80
McGhee, Calvin, 52
Means, Russell, 33
Meeds, Lloyd, 69
Mennonites, 192
Menominee Indians, 242
Mescalero Apache Indians, 28
Metlakatla (Tsimshian) Indians, 85, 96
Mexican American War, 214
Mexican government, 80–81
Mexican Revolution, 81, 217

Miami Indians of Indiana, 53, 64, 66–67
Miccosukee Indians, 151
Miller, Don, 242, 249
Minnesota Chippewa Indians, 72
missionaries. *See specific tribal groups*
Mississippi Band of Choctaw Indians, 72, 164
Mohawk Indians, 211
Mohegan Indians, 66, 204
Montegut (LA), 161, 164–66, 173–74, 180, 204
Montoya v. United States, 28
Moony, James, 215
Mormons, 87
Mountain Maidu Indians, 266
MOWA Choctaws, 111, 248
Munsee-Thames River Delawares, 52
Murdock, Veronica, 42, 84, 107–8
Muskogee (Creek) Nation, 52, 72

Nagle, Joane, 12, 15
Narragansett Indians, 51, 62, 70
National Conference on Recognition (1978), 41–44
National Congress of American Indians, 22, 31, 33–34, 38, 40–43, 77; Tigua Indians and, 210, 226–29, 245, 247, 252; Yaqui Indians and, 108
National Forest Service, 151
National Indian Lutheran Board, 65
National Indian Youth Council, 31, 33
National Park Service (NPS). *See* Timbisha Shoshone Indians: National Park Service, relations with
National Tribal Chairmen's Association, 38–41, 245, 258
Native American Church, 256
Native American Equal Opportunity Act, 41
Native American Graves Protection and Repatriation Act, 153
Native American Rights Fund, 32, 33, 40, 54, 75, 77; Tigua Indians and, 247, 249–50, 252; Timbisha Shoshones and, 128; Yaquis and, 113, 115, 118–19; United

Houma Nation and, 189, 194–95, 198, 200, 202
Native Americans: definitions of, 7; racial identity issues, 1–2; rise in number of, 69; stereotypes of, 6–8. *See also* unacknowledged Indian groups
Native Hawaiians. *See* Hawaiians
Navajo Indians, 66, 246
Navajo Nation, 53, 72
Navarro, Linda Hall, 64
New Deal, 27–31. *See also specific tribal groups*
New Mexico Territory, 214
Nixon, Richard, 106, 242
nonreservation Indians. *See* relocation; termination policy; unacknowledged Indian groups
Northwest Ordinance, 26

objectivity (in FAP), 63, 65
Office of Economic Opportunity (OEO), 32; Tigua Indians and, 226, 236; United Houma Nation and, 191; Yaqui Indians and, 98, 105
Onassis, Jacqueline Kennedy, 23, 46
organized crime, 248
Otermín, Antonio de, 213
Owens Valley Paiute-Shoshone Tribe, 141

Painter, Muriel Thayer, 86, 88, 91, 93, 99
Paiutes, Southern, 132. *See also* San Juan Southern Paiute Indians
Panamint Indians. *See* Timbisha Shoshone Indians
Parsons, Elsie Clews, 229
Pascua Yaquis. *See* Yaqui Indians
Passamaquoddy Indians, 35–36, 38
Pedraza, Miguel, 220, 225, 228, 232, 240
Pénicaut, André, 159
Penobscot Indians, 35–36, 38
Pequot Indians. *See* Mashantucket Pequot Indians
Pequots, Eastern, 76
peyote, 256
Piro Indians, 213, 217, 220

Poarch Creek Indians, 42, 48, 51–52, 70–71, 77, 178, 203, 248
Point aux Chenes (LA), 175, 180
Point aux Chien Indian Tribe, 188, 199, 201
Poosepatuck Indians, 30
Public Law 280, 245
Pueblo Indians, 211–14, 216, 218–19, 230, 244–46, 250. See also Tigua Indians
Pueblo Revolt of 1680, 212, 225, 245
Pueblo of Ysleta del Sur. See Tigua Indians

Quesenberry, Stephen, 128
Quinault Indians, 43
Quinn, William, 62, 77

race. See unacknowledged Indian groups
Ramapoughs of New Jersey, 53, 62, 253
Ramirez, David, 114–15, 117
Rancheria Act, 126
rancherias, 125–26, 149
Reagan, Ronald, 73, 242, 252
Reckord, Holly, 49, 53, 78, 198
recognized tribes. See unacknowledged Indian groups
Red Power activists, 31, 33, 190, 227
relocation, 32–33
representations of Indians. See specific tribal groups' identity issues
reservations: state forms of, 213–14, 227–28, 230–35, 236–38
restoration of tribal status, 242
Rhoades, C. J., 182
Robinson, Georgeann, 228
Rocky Boys Band, 96, 114, 211
Roosevelt, Franklin D., 218
Ross, Esther, 37
Roth, George, 49, 54, 60, 63, 130, 140–41, 144, 146–47

Samish Indians, 63
San Carlos Apaches, 117
San Juan Southern Paiute Indians, 53, 72
Seminole Indians, 164, 245
Seminole Tribe v. Butterworth (1981), 245
Senecu Pueblo, 213

Shapard, John "Bud," 40, 48–49, 58, 63, 67, 140
Shasta Nation, 68, 145
Shinnecock Indians, 30
Sibley, John, 163
Sierra, Joe, 211, 219, 235, 239–40
Slagle, Alogan, 55, 78, 154
Small Tribes Organization of Western Washington, 38
Smith, Chad, 205
Smithsonian Institution, Bureau of American Ethnology, 175, 203, 215
Snipp, C. Mathew, 11
Snohomish Indians, 59, 62
Snoqualmie Indians, 53, 68
Snyder Act of 1921, 26
Socorro Pueblo, 213
Solicitor's Office. See U.S. Department of the Interior
Southeastern Cherokee Confederacy, 52
sovereignty issues, 10, 25, 27. See also specific tribal groups
Speck, Frank, 181, 185
Spicer, Edward Holland, 12, 84–85, 88, 91, 99, 109–10, 114–15
Spicer, Rosamund, 85, 99, 104
Starna, William, 194
state Indian commissions, 231–32
Stevens, John, 38
Steward, Julian, 10, 131–32, 141–42, 149
Stillaguamish Indians, 35, 37–38
Strickland, W. J., 33, 189
Sturtevant, William, 9, 56–57
Suma Indians, 217, 220
Swanton, John Reed, 167, 175–78, 198, 200, 203
Swimmer, Ross, 70, 73, 250

Tauzin, W. J., 195, 202
Taylor, Jonathan, 43, 71
Tax, Sol, 33
Tchinouk Indians, 34
termination policy, 31–33
Texas Parks and Wildlife Department, 241

Thomas, Craig, 53

Tigua Indians: academic studies on, 215–16, 226; ancestry of, 211, 215, 220, 234–35, 244–45; BIA, relations with, 220, 227–28, 242–43, 250–52; community characteristics of, 211, 214–16, 219–21, 223, 233, 240; discrimination against, 222; economic activities of, 211, 214–15, 219, 222, 232, 235–36, 238, 240, 247; evidentiary issues and, 215–16, 226–29, 243, 250; gaming issues and, 209–10, 245–55; governmental relations with, local/city, 219, 233, 243, —, state, 210–14, 227–28, 230–32, 242–55; —, Spanish, 213; —, U.S., 214–15, 220, 224, 238; Great Depression and, 218–19; hunting and fishing issues, 241; identity issues, 210, 215–21, 224–30, 235–39, 244–45; and inter-ethnic relations, 212–14, 216–17, 220–22, 224, 229–30, 237; and intertribal relations, 210, 214, 216, 222, 225–27, 229–30, 235–36, 238, 244–45, 250; and intra-group relations, 217–18, 220–21; land claims issues, 213–14, 223, 225, 227, 237–38; language, 211, 216, 218, 220, 225; leadership of, 217–18, 220, 222–23, 225, 232, 234, 238–39, 242, 248–49; legislation, 209–11, 228–31, 245–52; membership, 220–21, 233–35, 251–52; missionaries and, 212–13, 216; political organization of, 212–13, 215–18, 222–23, 233; politicians and, 209–10, 225, 229, 242–43, 250–55; origins of, 211–13, 217, 224–25, 244–45; religious practices of, 212, 215–16, 219, 221, 223, 226, 228, 234, 246, 248–49; sovereignty issues of, 210–11, 232, 234–35, 239, 251–55; tourism-related activities of, 232–38; and tribalism issues, 211, 215–16, 222–23, 226–27; termination era and, 210, 219, 227–28, 230–31; War on Poverty programs, 219, 226, 236, 238

Timbisha Shoshone Indians, 2, 51–52; academic studies on, 131–32, 141, 149; ances-

try of, 130, 137–40, 147–49; BIA, relations with, 125–26, 128–30, 133–38, 146–49; community characteristics of, 126–27, 130, 132–34, 137, 140–45, 150–51; economic activities of, 126, 133, 135–38, 150–53; evidentiary issues and, 131, 140–49; gaming issues and, 152–53; governmental relations with, 129–30, 135–37, 150–55; identity issues of, 131, 140–42, 147–49, 152, 154–55; Indian Health Service and, 129; and inter-ethnic relations, 127, 132–33, 140, 144–45, 147, 152; and intertribal relations, 141, 144–45, 147, 150–51; and intra-group relations, 128, 143–47; language, 131–32, 144, 155; land issues of, 123–27, 129, 133–37, 150–55; leadership of, 125, 143, 145–47; membership, 128–29; National Park Service, relations with, 123, 125–29, 134, 143, 146, 150–55; and New Deal activities, 128–29, 136–38, 146, 148; political organization of, 128, 132, 134, 136–38, 145–47; politicians and, 130; origins of, 130, 139–42, 147–49; religion/spirituality of, 125, 150; sovereignty of, 129; tourism-related activities of, 136, 138; and tribalism issues, 133–34, 136–38, 143–47, 149, 150; termination era and, 125–26, 128, 138–39, 147, 149

Timbisha Shoshone Homeland Act, 154

Tiwa Indians, 213. See also Tigua Indians

Tohono O'odham Indians, 72, 95, 98, 211

Tompiro Indians, 213

Tonti, Chevalier de, 158

Tortugas Indians, 225

trade and intercourse laws. See Indian Non-intercourse Act; Indian Trade and Inter-course Acts

treaties, 26–27

tribes: definitional issues, 7–11, 26–30, 44, 55–56; extinction of, 29; government repression of, 59; stereotypes of, 7; voluntary abandonment of, 29, 59–60. See also unacknowledged Indian groups; specific tribal groups

"tri-racial isolates," 185–86
Trump, Donald, 253
Tulalip tribes, 45, 53, 55, 68
Tunica-Biloxi Indians, 51–52, 178, 182, 190, 197–98, 202–4
Tureen, Tom, 24, 36, 38, 40

Udall, Morris, 89, 95, 97, 108–10, 114–15, 119–20, 246, 250
Udall, Stewart, 89, 95
Umatilla, Cayuse, and Walla Walla Indians, 29
unacknowledged Indian groups: acknowledged via FAP, 51–52; assimilation and, 27, 31–32; in California, 123–24; declined via FAP, 52; demands of, 2–3, 23–25; eligibility for federal programs (non-BIA), 273n27; ethnic identity issues of, 12–13; evidentiary issues of, 42; FAP, opinions on, 64; financial issues and, 33–34; and fishing rights, 35; geographic distribution of, 19–20; government repression of, 59; identity issues of, 8–11, 13–15, 19–20, 24–25, 27–32, 34–35, 41, 72–73; land claims of, 23–25, 36–37; motivations of, 14–15; problems of, 34; public perceptions of, 72–73; recognized tribes and, 33–34, 38–39, 56; scholarship and, 8–9; sovereignty issues of, 25, 27; state hegemony and, 15–16
Underhill, Ruth, 182–83, 198
United Houma Nation, 68, 70, 145; academic studies on, 163, 175–78, 185–86, 203–4; ancestry/origins of, 156, 158–61, 166–67, 169–72, 175–76, 183, 199; BIA, relations with, 156, 158, 181–84, 194, 198–200, 203–5, 207; community characteristics of, 156, 160–62, 165–66, 168–69, 172–75, 179–80, 184, 186–87, 191–92, 202–5, 208; discrimination against, 158, 178–79, 181, 183, 186–88, 190–91; economic activities of, 158–59, 168, 174–76, 180–81, 184, 190–91; governmental relations with, French and Spanish, 160, 162,

165; —, local/state, 180, 183–84, 190–93; —, U.S., 162–64; historical sources on, 159; identity issues, 156–65, 168–69, 174–75; and inter-ethnic relations, 159–63, 166–73, 180–81, 183, 186–87; and intertribal relations, 157, 168, 176–77, 188–90, 193, 205; and intra-group relations, 160, 166–69, 171–75, 184–88, 190–92, 196–200, 205–6; language, 159, 177–78; land claims issues, 164, 179, 188, 197, 201; leadership of, 159–60, 162–63, 166–67, 172–75, 184–93, 196–98, 205; legislation of, 184, 195, 201; membership, 192–93; missionaries and, 159, 180, 192; and New Deal activities, 181–84; political organization of, 156, 160, 165, 172–73, 184–86, 192, 196–97, 199–203; politicians and, 195, 201–2; racial issues, 169–72, 178–79, 181–83, 185–86, 190–91, 194, 199, 201, 207; religious practices of, 168, 172, 174; sovereignty of, 175; tribalism, issues of, 157, 165–68, 170, 175–76, 182–86, 189–93, 196, 200–205; War on Poverty programs of, 188–89, 191
United Lumbee Nation of North Carolina, 52
United Southeastern Tribes, 42
U.S. Congress, 26. See also specific tribal group's governmental relations
U.S. Constitution, 26
USDA Forest Service, 151
U.S. Department of Health, Education, and Welfare, 32, 191
U.S. Department of Housing and Urban Development, 237
U.S. Department of the Interior, 36–37, 50, 250; Solicitors Office of, 67; Tigua Indians and, 230; Timbisha Shoshones and, 130, 137, 153; United Houma Nation and, 183; Yaqui Indians and, 97, 115, 117
U.S. Department of the Treasury, 230
U.S. General Accounting Office, 76
U.S. Office of Management and Budget, 243
United States v. Washington, 35, 37

Upper Skagit Indians, 35
urban Indians, 32–33

Valencia, Anselmo, 79, 86–87, 89–90, 93, 95–96, 99–104, 108, 111–14, 117, 122
Verdin, Alexander, 161, 166
Verret, Kirby, 156, 188, 190, 192–94, 200, 206
Victorio, 28

War on Poverty, 32; Yaqui Indians and, 98
Washa Indians, 177
Watts, James, 73
Western Shoshone Defense Fund, 151
White, Richard C., 225
Wilkins, David, 11, 60, 80
Wilson, Charles, 242
World War II: and unacknowledged communities, 86, 138, 184

Yakima Indians, 41, 43
Yaqui Indians, 230, 248; academic studies on, 85, 112–13, 115; and American Indian Policy Review Commission, 112–13; ancestry of, 91–22, 114–15, 117; BIA, relations with, 84–86, 97–98, 106–8, 114, 117–18; community characteristics of, 81–82, 87–89, 91, 99–101, 103–4, 115; community of Guadalupe, 103, 108, 110–11; community of Marana, 103; community of New Pascua, 98–102, 108–11; community of Pascua, 79, 83–84, 88–89, 101–3, 110–

11; discrimination against, 86, 94, 105–6; economic activities of, 81–82, 86–87, 100–101, 103; evidentiary issues and, 97, 112–13, 115, 118; and FAP, 117–18, 121; gaming activities and, 122; governmental relations with, 80–81, 93, 97–98, 106–7, 114; and identity issues, 80–81, 85–86, 92–94, 97–98, 101–2, 104, 108–9, 111–15, 117; and inter-ethnic relations, 83–84, 88, 102; and intertribal relations, 104, 107–8, 110–11, 113–14, 117; and intragroup relations, 90, 94, 101–2, 110–11; land issues, 88–89, 95–96, 98, 110, 119; language, 80, 115; leadership of, 80, 86–89, 100, 103–5, 110, 112, 114–15, 117; legal precedents and, 96–97, 114–15, 118; legislation regarding, 79–80, 89–98, 109–15, 118–20; membership, 91–92, 103, 113–14, 118; missionaries and, 82, 87, 95, 111; New Deal and, 84–86; OEO programs, 98–107; ONAP programs, 99, 103–6; political organization of, 80–81, 91–92, 115; politicians and, 88–89, 96–98, 113–15; origins of, 80–81, 109, 112–13, 115, 117, 120; religious practices of, 80, 82–83, 86–87, 101–2, 115; sovereignty, 118–19; termination era and, 97; tourism-related activities, 86–87, 101; and tribalism issues, 80, 111–12, 115, 117, 118
Yarbrough, Ralph, 228, 230, 247
Ybarra, Raymond, 106–7, 112–14
Yosemite National Park, 125